# MACMILLAN
## PROFILES

# *Women in Science*

**Macmillan Reference USA**

*an imprint of the Gale Group*

*Detroit • New York • San Francisco • London • Boston • Woodbridge, CT*

Copyright © 2001 by Macmillan Reference USA, an imprint of the Gale Group.

Macmillan Reference USA
1633 Broadway
New York, New York 10019

Gale Group
27500 Drake Rd.
Farmington Hills, MI 48331-3535

Library of Congress Catalog Card Number: 00-108560

ISBN 0-02-865502-8
Printed in Canada
10 9 8 7 6 5 4 3 2 1

Cover design by Berrian Design

Front cover, clockwise from top: Jane Goodall, Barbara McClintock, Chien-Shiung Wu, Virginia Apgar. Jane Goodall photo reproduced by permission of Corbis. All others, permission of Corbis-Bettmann.

# Contents

# Preface

**M**acmillan Profiles: *Women in Science* is a unique reference work featuring 129 profiles of female scientists. The biographies of these extraordinary women, who excel in the fields of chemistry, physics, medicine, astronomy, biology, mathematics, and more, provide a starting point for student research in social studies, world cultures, and history. The articles describe the struggles, triumphs, and perseverance of some of the most important scientists of our time while providing information about their early years and personal development.

Science is an integral part of American and world culture and history, and Macmillan Reference USA recognizes the need for reliable, accurate, and accessible biographies of notable figures within that framework. In *Women in Science*, the vast majority of the biographies are new and were commissioned to supplement entries from original sources, which include Macmillan's award-winning reference materials for libraries across the world. In fact, it is likely that several of the encyclopedias on the shelves in this library were published by Macmillan Reference or Charles Scribner's Sons.

The goal of *Women in Science* is to present an exciting introduction to the life and times of female scientists from American and world history who have, through hard work and talent, become the best in their field. Students will be drawn to the focused, determined nature of these characters and, along the way, learn a great deal about history. Carefully researched and prepared by well-respected scholarly writers, these biographies are uplifting and informative. The article list was based on the following criteria: relevance to the curriculum, importance to history, and representation of as broad a cultural range as possible.

As we made the article selections for this volume, we were forced to make some difficult choices, but we feel that these biographies represent a broad cross-section of international women scientists. The article list was refined and expanded in response to advice from a lively and generous team of librarians from school and public libraries across the United States.

## FEATURES

*Women in Science* is the sixteenth volume in the **Profiles Series.** To add visual appeal and enhance the usefulness of the volume, the page format was designed to include the following helpful features:

- Time Lines: Found throughout the text in the margins and also compiled in a master time line in the appendices, time lines provide a quick reference source for dates and important events in the life and times of these athletes

- Notable Quotations: Found throughout the text in the margins, these thought-provoking quotations are drawn from interviews, speeches, and writings of the person covered in the article. Such quotations give readers a special insight into the distinctive personalities of these great men and women.

- Definitions and Glossary: Brief definitions of important terms in the main text can be found in the margin. A glossary at the end of the book provides students with an even broader list of definitions.

- Sidebars: Appearing in shaded boxes throughout the volume, these provocative asides relate to and amplify topics.

- Pull Quotes: Found throughout the text in the margin, pull quotes highlight essential facts.

- Suggested Reading: An extensive list of books and articles about the athletes covered in the volume will help students who want to do further research.

- Index: A thorough index provides thousands of additional points of entry into the work.

## ACKNOWLEDGMENTS

This work would not have been possible without the hard work and creativity of our staff in New York and in Farmington Hills. We offer our sincere thanks to all who helped create this marvelous work.

Macmillan Library Reference

# Anastasi, Anne

DECEMBER 19, 1908– ● PSYCHOLOGIST

Throughout modern society, tests are administered in schools, businesses, government, hospitals, and the military. Students, employees, and others are tested on personality, intelligence, achievement, aptitudes, or interests. Anne Anastasi became a leader in the field of such mental testing, called *psychometrics*. The development, administration, and interpretation of mental tests is the work of those in psychometrics. Anastasi's lifelong research and practice in this area elevated her among psychologists as a highly influential thinker, writer, and teacher on questions concerning the nature, formation, and measurement of psychological traits of the individual.

Anne Anastasi was born on December 19, 1908, in New York City. Her father, Anthony Anastasi, died when she was only a year old. Her mother, Theresa Gaudiosi Anastasi, raised Anastasi with help from the girl's grandmother and her uncle. Until the age of nine, Anastasi's grandmother educated her at home. When Anastasi did attend school, she excelled. Barnard College in New York City accepted her at the amazingly young age of 15, in 1924. Anastasi had intended to study mathematics, but became interested in statistics used in psychology. She received a bachelor's degree in psychology in 1928, then went on to earn her Ph.D. from Columbia University in 1930, while still remarkably young.

At Columbia, Anastasi studied under Harry Hollingworth, a professor of psychology who was known for his work on methods

**psychometrics:** a field of mental testing of intelligence, aptitude, and interest.

1

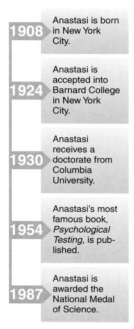

of measuring human traits and aptitude. He worked on matching people with vocations based on their personal traits, aptitudes, and attitudes. Anastasi was also influenced by English psychologist Charles Spearman, whose theory of intelligence became a major contribution to intelligence testing. In addition, Anastasi admired the work of Otto Klineberg, a renowned social psychologist who pioneered studies on intelligence and used psychology to interpret and influence national events as well as cross-cultural and international relations.

While at Columbia, Anastasi met a fellow Ph.D. candidate, John Porter Foley, Jr., who became her husband in 1933. Sadly, one year later, Anastasi was diagnosed with and treated for cancer, which left her unable to have children. She became an instructor of psychology at Barnard, where she stayed until 1939. Meanwhile, her husband had to move to Washington, D.C., to work. When he later took a job at the Psychological Corporation in New York City, he returned and the couple remained there.

In 1939, Anastasi became assistant professor and chair of the new department of psychology at Queens College of the City University of New York. Around 1950, Anastasi began teaching at Fordham University, where she ultimately became a professor and remained until her retirement in 1979. Several universities also awarded honorary doctorates to Anastasi.

Throughout her academic career, Anastasi wrote several books that became very important for psychologists and students of psychology in the United States and abroad. Her most famous work, *Psychological Testing*, was first published in 1954 and was revised six times by the end of the century. The book is known for its clear and understandable style. In addition to providing a thorough overview of the principles of psychological testing, it covers intelligence, aptitude, and personality tests in detail. In each update of the book, Anastasi addressed new trends in testing. Two of Anastasi's other books are also considered classics: *Differential Psychology* (1937), concerning the branch of psychology that deals with individual and group differences in behavior, and *Fields of Applied Psychology* (1964), which relates to the use of scientific psychology to solve practical problems.

Testing people can be very controversial, and Anastasi examined many of these difficult themes. One major problem in intelligence testing is how to design a test that contains questions on subjects to which everyone has been equally exposed.

For example, a child growing up in a family that reads and travels a great deal may score higher on an intelligence test than a child who did not have that broad range of experience. So, a test may not determine which child actually has more natural intelligence. Some psychologists and others have tried to create tests that are called "culture fair" or "culture free." These tests may include only symbols or words that are recognized by people of all backgrounds.

Anastasi also investigated such issues as language development in African American and Puerto Rican children. Her research also addressed such issues as family size and gender differences in relation to psychological traits.

Anastasi was a longtime fellow of the American Psychological Association (APA), a major professional organization for educational psychologists in the United States. She served as the APA's third female president, in 1971 and 1972. She won the APA Distinguished Scientific Award for the Application of Psychology in 1981 and the American Psychological Foundation Gold Medal in 1984. In 1987, she received the prestigious National Medal of Science, which is awarded by the National Science Foundation. ◆

# Anning, Mary

MAY 21, 1799–MARCH 9, 1847 ● PALEONTOLOGIST

Just an amateur fossil collector, Mary Anning made discoveries that still draw admiration from **paleontologists** (scientists who study the earth's history through fossils and rocks). In spite of her famous work, Mary remained a simple self-educated collector who never left her hometown. Although the details of her life are not well known, her fame became magnified with a mythical aura. The people of her village told the legend that a bolt of lightening struck Anning's baby carriage when she was an infant, killing her nurse and giving Anning a supernatural gift for finding rare fossils. Whether her gift was supernatural or not, Anning still ranks among the first serious fossil collectors. Many in the field also consider her the first woman paleontologist.

Mary Anning was born May 21, 1799, to Richard and Mary Anning in a small town called Lyme Regis on the southern

**paleontologist:** a scientist who studies fossils and rocks to help determine the earth's physical history and the geological time periods in which dinosaurs and other animals roamed the earth.

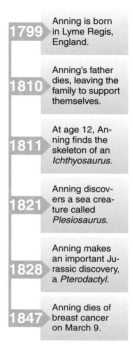

**1799**  Anning is born in Lyme Regis, England.

**1810**  Anning's father dies, leaving the family to support themselves.

**1811**  At age 12, Anning finds the skeleton of an *Ichthyosaurus*.

**1821**  Anning discovers a sea creature called *Plesiosaurus*.

**1828**  Anning makes an important Jurassic discovery, a *Pterodactyl*.

**1847**  Anning dies of breast cancer on March 9.

**Jurassic Period:** a period identified by paleontologists which began roughly 205 million years ago; the period of the Mesozoic era between the Cretaceous and the Triassic periods, and distinguished by the presence of dinosaurs and the first appearance of birds.

shores of England. Among the many children born to the Annings, only Mary and her brother Richard survived to adulthood. Richard Anning worked as a carpenter and a vendor of fossils. Cliffs at Lyme Regis, which were formed by layers of ancient rock, were rich in fossils. As the waters of the English Channel washed against the cliffs, fossil shells became exposed. Amateur collectors from Lyme Regis gathered those shells and other fossils, calling them "curiosities." When tourists came to Lyme Regis to enjoy the sea air, they often bought fossils from local vendors.

The pretty fossil shells with coiled inner chambers, called ammonites by scientists, came from the ancient seas of the **Jurassic period**. Beginning 205 million years ago, the Jurassic occurred during what is called the Age of Dinosaurs. The Lyme Regis fossils have become key to scientific understanding of the Jurassic period.

But Richard surely knew nothing of the Jurassic when he took his children fossil hunting. They would climb the cliffs with hammers and chisels to gather their curiosities. The Annings built a modest business as fossil hunters, but sadly, Richard died in 1810 at age 44, leaving his family with no money. However, Mary used the fossil hunting skills her father taught her and carried on the family business. After a time, Joseph began working in another business, and by the mid 1820s, Mary alone hunted fossils.

In the early 1820s, a well-to-do fossil collector, Lieutenant-Colonel Thomas Birch, came to know the Annings and helped them financially. He raised money for the family by selling one of his own fossil collections. Birch also helped the family by giving them credit for major discoveries in the area, which was not a common occurrence at that time. Many fossils that Anning and her family found went to well-to-do Europeans who were fond of building private collections of fossils and other "curiosities." Although many of these items eventually made their way into museums, those institutions usually credited the people who donated the fossils, not the people who found them. For that reason, it is difficult for historians to trace many of Anning's contributions.

However, Anning is clearly credited with a number of very important finds. In 1811, at the mere age of 12, Anning found the skeleton of an *ichthyosaurus* ("fish lizard"), a giant sea reptile of the Jurassic. This animal looked much like a porpoise. Anning's specimen later became the first ichthyosaurus acknowledged by the Geological Society in London, and it now resides in the Natural History Museum in London.

A few years later, in 1821, Anning made an even more important discovery—the first nearly complete example of a sea creature called *plesiosaurus* ("nearer to a lizard"). This was perhaps her most important find, from a scientific point of view. These long-necked, marine reptiles have been found as fossils in rocks of the Late Triassic through the Late Jurassic periods. The plesiosaurus measured about 15 feet long, with a broad, flat body and short tail. Its long, flexible neck and long, sharp teeth are thought to have allowed it to eat by swinging its head from side to side through schools of fish. When the famous French anatomist and paleontologist, Georges Cuvier, verified Anning's plesiosaurus as a genuine find, Anning earned some respect in the eyes of the scientific community.

In 1828, Anning made a third Jurassic discovery when she found a jumble of bones resembling the shape of a bird. In 1829, the eccentric Oxford professor and fossil sleuth, William Buckland, identified Anning's bones as that of a *pterodactyl* ("wing finger"). These extinct flying reptiles of the Late Jurassic fit the same ecological role as birds do today.

Anning's social status and gender may have caused the scientific community and historians to disregard her as a serious scientist. In addition, since she was not affiliated with any academic institution, scientists paid little attention to her special skills. However, some observers noted that she possessed considerable skill in her field. Lady Harriet Sivester, widow of a London official, visited Anning in 1824 and wrote in her diary that Anning impressed her as a self-taught scholar. Anning, she noted, carefully categorized the bones she found, made detailed drawings, and mounted and framed her skeletons.

Anning became a legend in her own time, drawing even more tourists to Lyme Regis and finally winning the respect of contemporary scientists. In the last decade of her life, she received an allowance from the British Association for the Advancement of Science. The Geological Society of London, the most important organization for geologists and paleontologists in the early 19th century, collected money for Anning. This was remarkable since the society did not admit women, even as guests. Anning was also named the first Honorary Member of the new Dorset County Museum in 1846. When Anning died of breast cancer March 9, 1847, the *Quarterly Journal of the Geological Society* featured her obituary.

Anning became a legend in her own time, drawing even more tourists to Lyme Regis and finally winning the respect of contemporary scientists.

A famous tongue twister "She Sells Seashells by the Seashore" is often said to have been inspired by the story of Mary Anning. Paleontologists today admire the spirit of the young woman who ventured out in the cliffs and beaches of England's shore to search for clues to our planet's history. Some of science's greatest discoveries have been made by such amateurs, and paleontology especially needs more Mary Annings to help uncover mankind's ancient beginnings. ◆

# Apgar, Virginia

JUNE 7, 1909–AUGUST 7, 1974 ● PHYSICIAN

Virginia Apgar was born in Westfield, New Jersey, the daughter of Charles Emory Apgar, a businessman and automobile salesman, and Helen May. Her family, which included a brother, shared musical interests. Apgar studied violin from the age of six and joined in family concerts. She was a member of the Amateur Chamber Music Players and performed with the Teaneck New Jersey Symphony. She also belonged to the Catgut Acoustical Society, where she learned the craft of building her own stringed instruments.

As early as high school Apgar set her sights on a medical career. Following graduation from Westfield High School in 1925, she enrolled in Mount Holyoke College, where she undertook a rigorous premedical curriculum. Apgar worked as a librarian and a waitress, earned letters in athletics, was a violinist in the orchestra, and a reporter for the college newspaper. She majored in zoology and graduated in 1929.

In 1933, Apgar was awarded a degree in medicine from Columbia University College of Physicians and Surgeons in New York City, and she became a surgical intern at

Virginia Apgar

Presbyterian Hospital, the fifth woman to be awarded that internship. After the two-year internship she was dissuaded by the professor of surgery from pursuing a specialty in surgery because of the obstacles posed to women in that field. She reluctantly switched to **anesthesiology**, a relatively new field in medicine. In 1937, she became the 50th physician to be certified as an anesthesiologist in the United States.

For the next 20 years, Apgar remained at Columbia Presbyterian Medical Center, where she was clinical director of the department of anesthesiology. Under her direction the department gained a national reputation for excellence. In 1949, she was appointed a full professor at the College of Physicians and Surgeons, where she remained until 1959. The delivery room held a particular fascination for Apgar. During her tenure at the hospital she assisted in the delivery of thousands of babies as attending anesthesiologist.

Apgar's work as an anesthesiologist in the delivery room ultimately prompted the development of the Apgar Score System. She noticed that newborn infants were largely ignored while medical attention focused on the mother's well-being. Infants were usually examined later in the nursery. This was hazardous for infants with medical problems because there were sometimes serious complications that needed prompt attention. Apgar believed that some type of health test that could alert medical staff to the infants' general condition at the time of delivery was needed. Her careful observations of the signs of newborn infants led to the publication of the Apgar Score System in 1952.

The Apgar Score System is designed to rate an infant on a scale of 0 to 2 on five infant signs, one minute and five minutes after birth. The five functions are heart rate, respiration, reflex irritability, muscle tone, and color. On each item a score of 0 shows no response, a 1 is marginal functioning, and a 2 represents the best response. Thus a baby's total score may range from 10 for best functioning to 0 for a baby in extreme jeopardy. Generally, Apgar scores of 7 and above indicate no risk for survival, while scores of 4 and below alert physicians to possible risk factors. The assessment is easy and quick to administer and has been adopted worldwide as a useful screening examination for neonates.

After 30 years at Columbia, teaching, mentoring, and assisting in delivering more than 15,000 babies. Apgar surprised her colleagues and friends by leaving her post to enter the

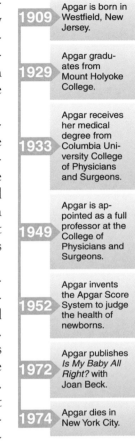

1909 Apgar is born in Westfield, New Jersey.

1929 Apgar graduates from Mount Holyoke College.

1933 Apgar receives her medical degree from Columbia University College of Physicians and Surgeons.

1949 Apgar is appointed as a full professor at the College of Physicians and Surgeons.

1952 Apgar invents the Apgar Score System to judge the health of newborns.

1972 Apgar publishes *Is My Baby All Right?* with Joan Beck.

1974 Apgar dies in New York City.

**anesthesiology:** the branch of medical science relating to substances used in surgical procedures to render the patient temporarily unconscious.

Johns Hopkins University School of Hygiene and Public Health in Baltimore. There, while pursuing a master's degree in public health, she was offered the directorship of the division of clinical malformations in the March of Dimes Foundation.

The foundation was embarking on a program of research on birth defects. Apgar was not convinced that she knew enough about birth defects to lead the program. She expressed her reservations publicly, but the directors of the March of Dimes had complete confidence in her and assured her that she would learn about birth defects while she led the program. She obtained her master's in 1959 and was appointed to the March of Dimes Foundation the same year.

At the foundation in New York City, Apgar's work centered on birth defects and prenatal care. Her responsibilities as director included distributing more than $5 million annually in research grants. She remained with the foundation until her death. In 1967 she became vice-president and director of basic research, and in 1973 she became senior vice-president in charge of medical affairs. Her research and lectures focused on the dangers of drugs and radiation for the developing fetus. She was an outspoken advocate of early prenatal care. She published numerous articles and in 1972, with Joan Beck, the book *Is My Baby All Right?*

Throughout her career, Apgar, who never married, received national international honors. She was a sought-after medical consultant, and her addresses to medical meetings were enthusiastically received. Nevertheless, she remained modest and unassuming, and has been described as compassionate and warm. Apgar died in New York City. ◆

> "They ... were looking for someone ... who likes to travel and talk. I love to see new places and I certainly can chatter, and I definitely did not want to retire ... but I had to tell ... the truth. I knew very little about birth defects. They insisted I could learn."
>
> Virginia Apgar, in the *New York World-Telegram and Sun,* 1959

# Avery, Mary Ellen

MAY 6, 1927– ● PEDIATRICIAN

When Mary Ellen Avery was born in 1927, women's roles in caring for infants remained largely confined to the home. Avery's early interest in medicine, though, led her to the greater responsibility of caring for infants in hospitals, offices, and classrooms. Avery became a pediatrician, a doctor who receives special training in health care for children. She became more than an average pediatrician, though, as her discoveries helped save the lives of thousands of newborn infants.

Avery added significantly to the field of neonatology, a field that began and grew during her lifetime. Neonatology is a branch of medicine that addresses the concerns of infants within the first 28 days of life. This neonatal period is when the highest rate of death occurs. Much of the work of neonatologists is aimed at babies born prematurely. While a normal pregnancy ranges from 37 to 42 weeks, premature births are those that take place between 20 and 37 weeks. These infants once had a very poor chance of survival, but each year more is being done to save them.

Avery was born May 6, 1927, in Camden, New Jersey. Her father, William C. Avery, was a businessman, and her mother, Mary (Miller) Avery, was a teacher. Avery earned a B.A. degree from Wheaton College, in Norton, Massachusetts, in 1948. She earned her M.D. from Johns Hopkins University School of Medicine in Baltimore in 1952. The school, established in 1893, is famous for research, teaching, and patient care and is among the best medical schools in the world.

Also in 1952, while in her mid-20's, Avery's life changed when she spent a year recovering from **tuberculosis**. This personal encounter with lung disease contributed to her later interest in pulmonary (lung-related) medicine in babies. From 1954 through 1957, Avery completed her internship and residency in pediatrics at Johns Hopkins. She then became a research fellow at the school, later advancing to assistant and then associate professor between 1960 and 1965.

In 1969, Avery accepted the prestigious position of Professor and Chairman of the Department of Pediatrics at McGill University, in Montreal, Quebec, Canada. At McGill, Avery helped staff the department of pediatrics at the University of Nairobi, Kenya, and also became interested in Eskimo health. Her interest in international health issues began here but it continued throughout her life and included work with the United Nations Children's Fund (UNICEF), which aids children in over 100 countries by providing help with medical care, nutrition, and other health concerns.

Early in her work as a pediatrician, Avery became concerned with a serious lung problem that she often saw among premature babies. Called respiratory distress syndrome (RDS), or hyaline membrane disease, it still ranks as a major cause of death among premature infants. The underdevelopment of

1927 Avery is born in Camden, New Jersey.

1952 Avery earns her M.D. from the Johns Hopkins University School of Medicine in Baltimore.

1960 Avery becomes a research fellow at Johns Hopkins.

1962 Avery publishes her findings on pulmonary surfactant in premature infants.

1969 Avery becomes Chairman of the Department of Pediatrics at McGill University in Montreal, Canada.

1971 Avery is chosen as a fellow of the American Academy of Arts and Sciences.

1974 Avery becomes physician-in-chief of the Children's Hospital of Harvard.

1990 Avery begins a term as president of the American Pediatric Society.

**tuberculosis:** a disease highly communicable in man and other vertebrates which is characterized by toxic symptoms or allergic reactions primarily impacting the lungs.

"Neonatologists must be pioneers by definition, because we are now looking after infants who would not have survived before."

Mary Ellen Avery on the role of the neonatologist

**hyaline membrane disease:** a respitory disease suffered by some newborn babies, characterized by the inability of the baby's pulmonary air sacs to properly collapse.

these infants causes the air sacs of the lungs to collapse, causing rapid, difficult breathing and, in many cases, death by suffocation. Upon autopsy, doctors find a clear, glassy membrane in the lungs of these babies, which they call the hyaline membrane. Physicians now believe that these membranes occur as a reaction to lung damage caused by the strain of breathing air in an immature lung.

As a young doctor, Avery watched these babies die and saw the typical appearance of their lungs. Although doctors knew that the **hyaline membrane** formed because the babies were premature, they did not know why. Avery delved deeply into the subject of lungs and the normal fluids of the lungs. She learned about a substance called pulmonary surfactant that helps keep lungs inflated, preventing the air sacs from collapsing. She theorized that the premature infants lacked this substance. Her research soon showed her to be correct: the underdeveloped lungs lacked pulmonary surfactant.

Avery published her findings in a 1962 issue of the medical journal *Pediatrics*. Her article is now recognized as especially advanced because she wrote it before much was known about hyaline membrane disease and surfactant. Although Avery pointed out a number of unknowns in her article, others soon explored and extended her findings. Doctors soon discovered answers that pointed the way to successful therapies for RDS.

Soon many hospital intensive care units included respirators and high-humidity incubators for treating hyaline membrane disease victims. Such treatment keeps many babies alive long enough for their lungs to develop to the point of producing pulmonary surfactant. This takes four to five days in most cases, but it may require several weeks. Most infants who recover have no permanent aftereffects. Scientists have also developed artificial surfactants that can be given to infants soon after birth to prevent the disease.

In the early 1970's, doctors discovered how to determine if an unborn baby's lungs lacked pulmonary surfactant before it was even born. They could then try to delay the premature birth until the lungs developed sufficiently. If the premature birth is not delayed, the mother can be given a hormone to speed the lung development of the fetus. These advances all resulted from Avery's work.

In 1971, Avery was chosen as a fellow of the American Academy of Arts and Sciences, one of the oldest academic societies in the United States. Members are selected for their achievements in the arts, scientific professions, or public affairs.

The year 1974 brought many important changes in Avery's life. She became the Thomas Morgan Rotch Professor of Pediatrics at Harvard Medical School and then became physician-in-chief of the Children's Hospital in Boston, another part of the Harvard Medical School. Avery remained at Children's Hospital for the next 25 years, continuing her great achievements.

Also in 1974, Avery formed the Joint Program in Neonatology (JPN), later called the Division of Newborn Medicine (DNM) at the Children's Hospital. The DNM provides intensive medical, surgical, and nursing care for newborns.

From 1990 to 1991, Avery served as the president of the American Pediatric Society. In 1991, she won the Virginia Apgar Award from the American Pediatric Society and also the National Medal of Science. In 1994, Avery was elected to the National Academy of Sciences, an organization that advises the United States government and consists of scientists who have been selected for their achievements in research.

Throughout her career, Avery faced the same obstacles that all women in medicine face. In 1979, the average salary for female doctors was $28,000 compared to $48,000 for men. At a special two-day conference for female physicians that year, participants debated the value of women's role in medicine. Avery argued that women doctors offer a unique viewpoint to medicine. "Some of the traditionally feminine attributes, whether present by nature or nurture, are exactly what modern medicine should have," she said.

During her long career, Avery wrote and co-wrote many important pediatric papers and textbooks. ◆

# Bascom, Florence

JULY 14, 1862–JUNE 18, 1945 ● GEOLOGIST

A geologist's workplace can range from a classroom, to a desk, to a mountain range best climbed on horseback, to any other extreme outdoor location. None of these locales was a typical domain for a woman when Florence Bascom joined the field of geology at the end of the 19th century. However, she broke the gender barrier as a student, as an educator, and as a geological scientist, earning the designation of America's first woman geologist.

Bascom came from a high achieving and close-knit family. She was born July 14, 1862, in Williamstown, Massachusetts, the youngest of several children. Her mother, Emma (Curtiss) Bascom, was a schoolteacher and a **suffragist** (supporter of women's right to vote). Her father, John, was a professor of speech who also supported women's suffrage and advocated educating women along with men.

In 1874, her father made a move that would greatly influence Florence's life—he became president of the University of Wisconsin (UW) in Madison. The university first admitted women in the early 1870s, and Florence enrolled in 1877. Women students had limited access to the library and gymnasium, and if a class became full, women had to quit the class to make room for men. Clearly, though, the restrictions on women did not inhibit Bascom's achievement, as she earned three bachelor's degrees from UW—one in Arts and one in Letters, both in 1882, and then one in Science, in 1884. She then taught at the newly

Bascom became an expert on the crystalline rocks of the Piedmont Region, as well as an expert in crystallography (the scientific study of crystals).

**suffragist:** an individual in support of the full enjoyment of the right to vote, usually associated with the struggle for a woman's right to vote.

**hydrology:** the science dealing with the distribution, properties, and circulation of water on the earth's surface and atmosphere.

founded school for freed slaves and for American Indians from 1884 to 1885; the school is now known as Hampton University.

Bascom developed an interest in geology during her college career, allegedly from a trip she took with her father and his friend, who was a geology professor. She enrolled at UW again and earned a master's degree in geology in 1887. She went on to teach for two years at Rockford College in Illinois.

In 1889, Johns Hopkins University in Baltimore, Maryland, permitted Bascom to attend graduate school classes while sitting behind a screen so she would not "disrupt" male students. Although another woman earned the first Ph.D. from Johns Hopkins, the school's trustees did not grant it to her until 1926. Therefore, in 1893, Bascom became the first woman to receive a Ph.D. from Johns Hopkins. Her dissertation became one of her earliest contributions to the field of geology, showing that rocks previously considered sediments were actually from lava flows. Upon graduating, Bascom moved on to teach at Ohio State University for two years, from 1893 to 1895.

Next came Bascom's major career move, as she joined the faculty of Bryn Mawr College, near Philadelphia. One of the first American colleges for women, Bryn Mawr had been established just a decade earlier. At Bryn Mawr, Bascom founded the school's department of geology, and under her direction, the department gained a national reputation, especially for training some of the most accomplished female geologists of the early 1900s. Beginning in 1896, Bascom served as the associate editor of the journal *American Geologist*, a job she held until 1908.

Also in 1896, Bascom made another important career move when she became an assistant geologist with the United States Geological Survey (USGS)—the first woman ever to receive that appointment. Established in 1879, the USGS is the largest single employer of geologists in the nation. The agency conducts research in geology, **hydrology** (study of water), mapmaking, and related sciences and publishes thousands of reports and maps each year.

At the time the USGS hired Bascom, the agency was involved in making geological maps of all of the various areas throughout the United States, primarily to locate oil and mineral deposits as well as to learn about how mountains and other land formations were created. Bascom was sent to the Piedmont Region, a hilly land area that stretches from the Appalachian Mountains down to the area known as the Atlantic Coastal Plain. The Piedmont begins roughly in Georgia, where it is more than 125 miles wide, and ends north near Virginia and Maryland, where it tapers to about 50 miles wide. It is sometimes called the Piedmont Plateau and was named after the Piedmont region in Italy.

Bascom traveled into remote wooded areas of the Piedmont hills, sometimes riding on horseback in long skirts, studying and collecting rocks. During and after her work in the Piedmont Region, Bascom published more than 40 scientific articles, many of them in USGS publications. It is this series of articles for which she is perhaps best known in the geology community.

Bascom became an expert on the crystalline rocks of the Piedmont Region, as well as an expert in **crystallography** (the scientific study of crystals). She also became expert in **mineralogy**, which is the study of minerals, and **petrography**, which is the systematic classification of rocks. Bascom also studied under leading scientists in the field of **metamorphism**, the processes by which rocks change in form. These areas of geology were still being formed as academic disciplines during Bascom's career.

Although Bascom has been known as "the first woman geologist," she was the second woman to earn a Ph.D. in geology in the United States. However, she did accomplish a number of true firsts. She became the first woman to present a paper before the Geological Society of Washington, in 1901; the first woman elected to the Council of the Geological Society of America (GSA), in 1924; the first woman to be made a fellow of the Geological Society of America; and the first woman officer of the GSA (vice president in 1930). Bascom also became a four-star geologist in the first edition of *American Men and Women of Science* (1906), signifying that her colleagues selected her as one of the country's 100 leading geologists.

Bascom semiretired from her professorship in 1928 and left the USGS in 1936. She died June 18, 1945, in Northhampton, Massachusetts. ◆

**crystallography:** the study of crystal formations and their structure.

**mineralogy:** the study of crystallography, physical, and chemical properties of minerals; the classification of minerals and methods of distinguishing them.

**petrography:** the system of describing and classifying rocks.

**metamorphism:** the physical constitutional change in rocks effected by pressure, heat, and water; a rock which changes condition into a more crystalline form.

# Bender, Lauretta

AUGUST 9, 1897–JANUARY 4, 1987 ● CHILD NEUROPSYCHIATRIST

Lauretta Bender was the daughter of John Oscar Bender, an attorney, and Katherine Parr (Irvine) Bender. She attended Leland Stanford University for two years (1916 to 1918), then transferred to the University of Chicago, from

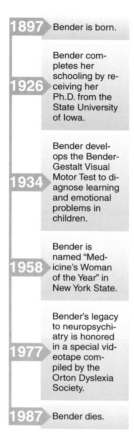

1926  Bender completes her schooling by receiving her Ph.D. from the State University of Iowa.

1934  Bender develops the Bender-Gestalt Visual Motor Test to diagnose learning and emotional problems in children.

1958  Bender is named "Medicine's Woman of the Year" in New York State.

1977  Bender's legacy to neuropsychiatry is honored in a special videotape compiled by the Orton Dyslexia Society.

1987  Bender dies.

**neuropathology:** the pathology of the nervous system.

**neurology:** the study of the nervous system.

**electroconvulsive therapy:** treatment of mental disorders through the use of an electric current which induces a coma on the patient.

which she earned a B.S. degree in 1922 and an M.A. degree in **neuropathology** in 1923. In 1926 she received a Ph.D. from the State University of Iowa.

Bender did her residency in **neurology** at Billings Hospital at the University of Chicago (1928) and her psychiatric residency at Boston Psychopathic Hospital (1928–1929). She spent 1929 to 1930 as a research associate at the Phipps Clinic at Johns Hopkins Hospital in Baltimore.

The majority of Bender's professional career was spent at Bellevue Hospital in New York City, where she worked as a senior psychiatrist from 1930 to 1956 and was in charge of children's services from 1934 to 1956. While at Bellevue, she fostered the development of the Bellevue School for inpatients, as well as the provision of tutoring services for children with language disabilities in the clinic, services that were innovative at the time. She also used **electroconvulsive therapy** (ECT) in treating 100 children at Bellevue. Patients showed no improvement or got worse, and Bender abandoned this controversial method in the 1950s.

Early in her career, working with children from foster homes, Bender noticed that the institutional environment led to emotional problems. In 1934 she developed the Bender-Gestalt Visual Motor Test, which became a widely used diagnostic instrument for children with learning difficulties. The test consists of nine geometric patterns comprising dots, lines, angles, and curves. The designs are presented singly in a specific order to the subject, who is asked to copy each of them. The patterns were borrowed from Max Wertheimer's classic study on the theory of Gestalt psychology.

Bender originally conceptualized the test as a maturational measure for use with children and as a device for exploring regression or retardation and detecting possible brain damage. Later, it was used predominantly for detection of organic cerebral damage. The test's name derived from Bender's advocacy of Gestalt psychology and her use of Gestalt principles in the construction of the test. In 1938 Bender published the monograph *A Visual Motor Gestalt Test and Its Clinical Use.* The test was later abandoned when positive results proved to be fleeting.

In 1936 Bender married Paul Ferdinand Schilder, a prominent Viennese neurologist and psychoanalyst; they had three children. In December 1940 Schilder had just visited his wife in the maternity ward when he was struck and killed by a truck as he crossed the street outside of the hospital. Bender later married Henry B. Parkes in 1967.

Bender taught from 1930 to 1958 at New York University, where for seven years (1951 to 1958) she was a professor of clinical psychiatry. She taught as a professor of clinical psychiatry at Columbia College of Physicians and Surgeons from 1959 to 1962 and, after moving to Maryland, at the University of Maryland School of Medicine from 1974 to 1987. In clinical practice, after leaving Bellevue, Bender served as the director of research in child psychiatry at Creedmoor State Hospital from 1959 to 1967 and attending psychiatrist at New York State Psychiatric Institute from 1969 to 1974. During this time she also worked (from 1969 to 1973) as an attending psychiatrist at the New Jersey State Neuropsychiatric Institute. She continued to teach, consult, lecture, and write until her death.

In addition to her clinical work, Bender belonged to numerous professional organizations. She was a consultant for various state, federal, and academic programs in the field of psychiatrics and mental health from the 1940s to the end of her career. In 1955 she became New York State's principal research psychiatrist, and in 1958 New York State named her "Medicine's Woman of the Year." She edited *Bellevue Studies in Child Psychiatry* (1952–1955), and throughout her life she served on the child-welfare committees of various civic organizations. She received numerous honors for her wide-ranging contributions in psychiatry and the understanding of human development and learning. Most notably, she was the first recipient of the Samuel Torrey Orton Award (named for the neuropsychiatrist who pioneered the study of dyslexia).

Near her 80th birthday, the Orton Dyslexia Society produced a videotape about Bender's work in which her colleagues describe her legacy. Bender's colleague Ralph D. Rabinovitch noted in the tribute that "for so many of us, perhaps especially her students, she was concerned, giving, loyal, and a wonderful friend."

Bender's earliest professional studies were laboratory studies in basic biology. This approach continued to influence her later work. Her highly respected research focused on the causes of childhood **schizophrenia** and other children's psychiatric illness; she published numerous books and articles on the topic of child suicides and violence. A pioneer in identifying learning disabilities in preschool children, she used the concept of the plasticity of the human organism to describe the ability to adapt to change, and she contributed to the understanding of

"Dr. Bender's approach demonstrated for generations of clinicians the richness of developmental, longitudinal, motility, and graphic techniques in understanding the problems of children and youth."
Neuropsychiatrist Rosa A. Hagin in a videotape tribute to Dr. Bender, 1977

**schizophrenia:** a mental disorder characterized by a identifiable decrease in an individual's ability to function in everyday life; the presence of differing qualities or antagonistic parts.

**dyslexia:** an inability to sometimes properly see letters as they appear in sequence.

developmental lag. Bender was herself **dyslexic**, a fact that contributed to her longtime interest in language disorders. Her writings, whether focused on brain-behavior relationships or the emotional components of language impairment, consistently focused on the whole child. ◆

# Benedict, Ruth Fulton

JUNE 5, 1887–SEPTEMBER 17, 1948 ● ANTHROPOLOGIST

**ethnology:** a science which classifies mankind into origin and race, relations, and characteristics.

Ruth Fulton Benedict

Ruth Fulton Benedict became a leading American anthropologist; her theories greatly influenced cultural anthropology, which is the study of human culture. Cultural anthropologists study the art, housing, tools, and other products of a culture. They also research a culture's nonphysical creations, such as its music, religion, symbols, and values. Benedict became a recognized authority on the **ethnology** of Native Americans. Ethnology is a part of anthropology that deals with the racial aspects of cultures and their origins and distribution.

Ruth Fulton was born June 5, 1887, in New York City. She spent much of her early years on Shattuck Farm, her maternal grandparents' home near Norwich, New York, which was to serve as a home base throughout her life. Fulton's father, Frederick, was a successful surgeon, but he died at age 32 of an obscure illness, leaving Ruth, only 18 months old, and her baby sister, Margery, only three months old. Fulton's mother, Bertrice Shattuck Fulton, a long-grieving young widow, began teaching and moved the girls to St. Joseph, Missouri, and Owatonna, Minnesota, before settling into a librarian job in Buffalo, New York, when Fulton was 11.

Fulton studied English literature at Vassar, a women's college in Poughkeepsie, New York. After graduating with honors in 1909, she traveled to Europe with several friends. She worked as a social worker for a year, then spent three years teaching. Benedict struggled with the conflict of being a working woman whose real purpose in life was to have "a great love, a quiet home, and children." But, she wrote, "A great love is given to very few. Perhaps this make-shift time filler of a job *is* our life work after all." In 1914, feeling she had found her great love, Fulton married Stanley Benedict, a biochemistry professor at Cornell Medical College, in New York City.

As a young wife, Benedict waited hopefully for children, but finally learned she would be unable to bear a child without a risky operation, which her husband would not agree to. During her years of waiting, Benedict filled her time with different activities, one of which was attending lectures at the New School for Social Research, where the renowned cultural anthropologist, Elsie Clews Parsons, aroused Benedict's interest in anthropology. At age 34, in 1921, Benedict began taking courses at Columbia University in New York City, studying under Franz Boas, the most influential United States anthropologist of the early and mid-1900s. She received her Ph.D. in 1922. Her doctoral thesis on North American Indians was published as *The Concept of the Guardian Spirit in North America* (1923).

Benedict began teaching at Columbia in 1923, remaining there throughout her career. Late in her life, in 1948, she became the first woman to achieve the status of full professor in the Faculty of Political Science at Columbia. From 1925 until 1940, Benedict served as editor of the *Journal of American Folk-Lore*.

Benedict's work in the field comprised trips to Native American reservations during the years 1922 to 1939. She studied the Serrano Indians of California, the Blackfoot in the Northwest, and the Zuñi, Cochiti, Mescalero Apache, and Pima in the Southwest. Her research resulted in the books *Zuni Mythology* (1935) and *Tales of the Cochiti Indians* (1931). Benedict's field work fueled her classic work, *Patterns of Culture* (1934), which became a best-selling book that was translated into 14 languages. In the book, Benedict contrasted three cultures—the Pueblos of New Mexico, the natives of Dobu in Melanesia, and Native American tribes of the Northwest. She also elaborated on the thesis she is most known for, which is that each culture has a unique character, "a personality," in her words. She asserted that each culture displays a unique range of human behavior. She did not believe that a model could be constructed that all cultures should fit into, but rather that

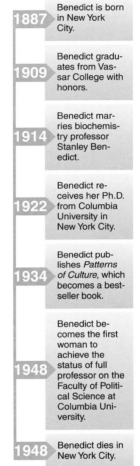

**1887** Benedict is born in New York City.

**1909** Benedict graduates from Vassar College with honors.

**1914** Benedict marries biochemistry professor Stanley Benedict.

**1922** Benedict receives her Ph.D. from Columbia University in New York City.

**1934** Benedict publishes *Patterns of Culture*, which becomes a best-seller book.

**1948** Benedict becomes the first woman to achieve the status of full professor on the Faculty of Political Science at Columbia University.

**1948** Benedict dies in New York City.

each culture, besides being unique, is also continually changing and developing. Her colleague, anthropologist Margaret Mead, wrote, "She was committed to a picture of developing human cultures for which no limit could be set because the possible combinations were so many and so varied as to be inexhaustible."

This theory contributed to a concept known as cultural relativism, which holds that no culture should be judged by the standards of another. That is because the unique patterns of behavior that work well for one group may not work well for another group. A cultural relativist would argue that the rules of all cultures deserve equal respect, even if those rules allow behaviors different from our own. Some may go so far as to say that no moral code can apply to all people. Those who argue against cultural relativism hold that certain fundamental values are held by all societies. Scholars such as Benedict recognized the dilemma that cultural relativism presents: If one set of values is as good as any other, how can we establish and hold firmly our own beliefs? Benedict's response to this was that all cultures should be free to develop in their own way unless what they do hurts others.

Benedict eventually drifted apart from her husband, and the two lived separately. After he died of a heart attack in 1936, she became more involved in social and political activities. In 1939, she reacted to the rise of Nazi racism by examining issues in her book, *Race: Science and Politics*. From 1943 to 1946, Columbia granted Benedict an extended leave, during which she advised the U.S. government on Japanese culture during World War II. She worked in Washington, D.C., with the Bureau of Overseas Intelligence of the Office of War Information using anthropological methods to study Japanese culture. Her experience led her to write *The Chrysanthemum and the Sword: Patterns of Japanese Culture* (1946). Her book became a bestseller and a classic work in the study of Japanese culture.

After Benedict's death, on September 17, 1948, in New York City, her professional and personal papers were sent to anthropologist Margaret Mead's office at the American Museum of Natural History. The bond between Mead and Benedict had spanned many years, beginning when they met at Barnard College in 1922. Mead was first Benedict's pupil then her friend and colleague. Using Benedict's vast writings, Mead wrote *An Anthropologist at Work: Writings of Ruth Benedict* (1959) and a biography, *Ruth Benedict*, published in 1974.

Benedict's papers, now at the Vassar libraries, also served as the basis for two biographies, *Ruth Benedict: Patterns of a Life* (1983), by Judith Schachter Modell, and *Ruth Benedict: Stranger in This Land* (1989), by Margaret M. Caffrey.

During her life, Benedict published many poems, mainly under the pen name of Anne Singleton. Many of Benedict's poetry manuscripts are located in the Vassar collection, along with stories she wrote as a child and young adult. ◆

# Blackwell, Elizabeth

FEBRUARY 3, 1821–MAY 31, 1910 ● PHYSICIAN

Elizabeth Blackwell became the first woman to receive a medical degree in the United States. Her long life of battling social injustice, caring for the needy, and opening doors for women has made her a beacon of inspiration for many generations of aspiring women doctors.

Blackwell was born February 3, 1821, in Bristol, England, the third of nine children of Samuel and Hannah Blackwell. The family lived comfortably on income from the successful sugar refinery Samuel Blackwell owned. Samuel and Hannah held progressive political and spiritual views that influenced how they raised Elizabeth and her sisters and brothers. They actively opposed slavery and child labor, and belonged to a religion closely related to Quakers. Most importantly for Blackwell, her parents believed that boys and girls should be educated equally. Their large house served as their school, where tutors and governesses gave them individual instruction.

After the family business experienced serious setbacks, the Blackwells immigrated by ship to New York City in 1832, where Samuel set up a new sugar business. For the six

Elizabeth Blackwell

**1821** Blackwell is born in Bristol, England.

**1832** Blackwell and her family immigrate to New York City.

**1849** Blackwell graduates from medical school, becoming the first American woman doctor.

**1853** Blackwell opens a small infirmary for poor women and children in New York City.

**1857** Blackwell and her sister Emily open the New York Infirmary for Women and Children.

**1868** Blackwell opens the Women's Medical College of the New York Infirmary.

**1874** Blackwell helps found the London School of Medicine for Women.

**1895** Blackwell's autobiography, *Pioneer Work in Opening the Medical Profession to Women*, is published.

**1910** Blackwell dies at age 89.

years the family lived in New York and New Jersey, they hosted many famous progressives of their era, particularly those opposed to slavery. One such guest was American journalist and reformer William Lloyd Garrison. In 1838, the family relocated to Cincinnati, Ohio, where Samuel hoped to expand the business.

Sadly, Samuel died shortly after their arrival in Ohio, leaving his large family to support themselves. The boys quickly found work, and 17-year-old Elizabeth and her sisters helped their mother establish a boarding school for girls. The family "became acquainted with the very intelligent circle of New England society settled in Cincinnati," according to Blackwell's later writing. These family friends included admirers of transcendentalism, a philosophy and social movement whose leading writer was Ralph Waldo Emerson. Blackwell and her sisters also became acquainted with the ideals of the women's rights movement. Their brother, Henry Blackwell, later married women's rights leader Lucy Stone, and became active in the cause for women's suffrage (voting rights).

As the brothers became financially secure, the family closed the boarding school. Elizabeth accepted a position as head of a girl's school in a Kentucky village, where she first saw slaves. She became frustrated and bored and returned home. In 1845, Blackwell's life changed when she attended to a friend dying of a "women's" disease. The friend said she had suffered doubly because there were only male doctors to treat her. She urged Elizabeth to become a doctor. Blackwell had not been interested in medicine, but she could not shake the woman's dying plea. She had also been thinking about her future, and decided that she would rather work than enter the restrictive state of marriage, even though she had fallen in love with several men in her life.

Blackwell sought advice from several doctors and some thought a woman doctor would be a good idea, but they advised her that it would be too difficult to try. Blackwell viewed the obstacles as a social injustice, which fueled her determination to fight. While holding teaching jobs, she began reading medical books and studying privately with several supportive male doctors. Soon Blackwell had saved enough money to go to medical school, and she applied to every one throughout the northeastern United States. They all turned her down until finally, in 1847, the Geneva Medical College (now Hobart & William Smith Colleges) in Geneva, New York, accepted Blackwell as a student.

On November 4, 1847, Blackwell arrived in Geneva filled with hope and enthusiasm. She did not know that her applica-

**Elizabeth Blackwell Award**

In honor of the life and achievements of Elizabeth Blackwell, the first American woman to receive the Doctor of Medicine degree, Hobart and William Smith Colleges occasionally confer the Elizabeth Blackwell Award to a woman "whose life exemplifies outstanding service to humanity." The first recipient of the award (1958) was Gwendolyn Grant Mellon, who with her husband Larry Mellon founded the Hôpital Albert Schweitzer in Deschapelles, Haiti, to bring improved basic health services to a region beset by malaria, tuberculosis, and malnutrition. In the decades to follow, the 31 recipients of the award would span various fields of endeavor, including politics (Barbara Jordan, Margaret Chase Smith, Frances Perkins, Sandra Day O'Connor), the arts (Agnes George de Mille, Antonia Brico, Marian Anderson), and education (Hanna Holborn Gray, Mina Rees, Barbara Aronstein Black). But in keeping with the legacy of Elizabeth Blackwell, the award has given pride of place to female leaders in medicine and public health. They include Catharine Macfarlane, physician; Marty Mann, founder and executive director of the National Council on Alcoholism; Fe del Mundo, physician and cofounder of the Children's Medical Center of the Philippines; and Mary S. Calderone, founder of the Sex Information and Education Council of the United States. The most recent recipient (1998) is women's tennis legend and rights pioneer Billie Jean King.

tion had been submitted to a vote by the student body, who accepted it as a joke. Although the students expected her to faint and fall apart in tears, they accepted her presence with some bewilderment and curiosity. The people of Geneva, where she lived in a boarding house, treated her coldly. Blackwell struggled with loneliness, but remained determined and worked hard, earning the respect and affection of her classmates and professors. A news report that annoyed her said she was "a pretty little specimen of the feminine gender," whose presence in class had a good effect on the men.

During a summer break, Blackwell practiced medicine for the first time at the large Blockley Almshouse in Philadelphia. In a **syphilis** ward for poor women, she observed terrible poverty and illness among unmarried women. In 1849, Blackwell graduated at the head of her class, becoming Dr. Blackwell.

Blackwell soon traveled to Europe in hopes of getting practical training she could not get in the United States. Her chances were not much better there, so she enrolled in a rigorous midwifery training program at the La Maternité hospital for women and babies in Paris. One day, as she syringed fluid from the eye of an infected baby, a drop hit her own eye, and

**syphilis:** a contagious venereal disease which can continue over many years if left untreated.

Blackwell contracted a serious eye infection. She became blind in one eye and had a glass eye inserted, crushing her dreams of becoming a surgeon. While continuing her studies at St. Bartholomew's Hospital, London, she established a social network, making friends with such people as Florence Nightingale, founder of modern nursing.

Returning to New York in 1851, Blackwell met with great prejudice, unable to practice medicine because no institution would hire her. Male doctors snubbed her, and city hospitals barred her from their wards. To keep occupied, Blackwell presented a series of lectures on the importance of hygiene, diet, and exercise, especially for women. This modern and daring information drew a "small but very intelligent audience of women," many of who also became patients of Dr. Blackwell. They referred more patients, and Blackwell's practice began to grow.

In 1853, Blackwell rented a small room in a poor area of town and formed a small dispensary for the care of poor women and children. She soon bought a nearby house and moved her practice there. During this lonely period, Blackwell adopted a seven-year-old Irish orphan, Katharine (Kitty) Barry, who became a great companion throughout her life. Blackwell soon gathered reinforcement when her sister Emily, a surgeon, and German doctor Marie Zakrzewska joined her in 1856. The women rented a house on Bleecker Street, a poor area that is now Greenwich Village, and in 1857 opened the New York Infirmary for Women and Children. They developed a nursing training program, and the hospital was staffed completely by women. The hospital created many new health care practices, such as emphasizing good hygiene and providing follow-up care.

During the American Civil War, Blackwell and her staff created a nursing service for sick and injured soldiers. The war delayed Blackwell's plans to open a women's medical college, but she realized that dream in 1868 with the opening of the Women's Medical College of the New York Infirmary. It was the first women's medical college, and Blackwell made sure it maintained even higher standards than other medical schools. The school became a leader in many areas of health care education.

After years of medical pioneering in the United States, Blackwell decided to return to England, where women were calling on her expertise. She had spent one year there in 1858, during which time she had become the first woman to be listed in the British Medical Register. She left the operation of the hospital and college to her sister and moved to England in

1869. There she helped establish England's National Health Society in 1871, with the motto of "Prevention is better than cure." She helped found the London School of Medicine for Women in 1874, and the next year became a professor of gynecology at that school.

Blackwell wrote several books and lectured widely. Her autobiography, *Pioneer Work in Opening the Medical Profession to Women*, was published in 1895. Blackwell lived in an English country house with Kitty for the last 30 years of her life, making one last visit to the United States in 1906. At age 81, Elizabeth fell down a flight of stairs and never fully recovered. She died of a stroke at age 89 on May 31, 1910. ◆

# Blackwell, Emily

OCTOBER 8, 1826–SEPTEMBER 7, 1910 ● PHYSICIAN

Emily Blackwell became one of the first female physicians in the United States, following in the footsteps of her famous sister, Elizabeth Blackwell, the first woman physician in the United States. Together, the sisters pioneered the idea that women could excel as doctors, a previously unheard of idea.

The family that produced two such outstanding women was a unique one. Emily was born in 1826, five years after her sister Elizabeth. She was one of nine children of Samuel and Hannah Blackwell. The sisters recalled their large childhood home in Bristol, England, as a happy one. Samuel owned a successful sugar refinery, and the family enjoyed material comforts. They belonged to a progressive religious group related to the Quakers, and often entertained well-educated and liberal-thinking people. Samuel applied his moral views by opposing such practices as child labor. Emily's parents also believed in educating girls as well as boys, so the children received their education at home under the guidance of tutors and governesses.

After the family experienced some financial losses, the Blackwells moved to the United States to start over, sailing for New York City in 1832. The Blackwell homes in New York and New Jersey became a stopping place for famous progressives of their era, particularly those opposed to slavery. Blackwell and her sisters became acquainted with the ideas of feminism, and their brother, Henry Blackwell, eventually married women's

**1826** Blackwell is born in Bristol, England.

**1832** Blackwell and her family immigrate to New York City.

**1854** Blackwell completes medical school at Case Western Reserve University.

**1856** Blackwell joins her sister, Elizabeth, at her infirmary in New York City.

**1857** Blackwell and her sister Elizabeth open the New York Infirmary for Women and Children.

**1868** Blackwell joins her sister Elizabeth in opening the Women's Medical College of the New York Infirmary.

**1910** Blackwell dies just a few months after her sister does.

rights leader Lucy Stone and worked for women's suffrage (voting rights). Another brother, Sam, later married Antoinette Brown, the first female minister ordained in the United States. The family moved to Cincinnati, Ohio, in 1838, where Samuel hoped to begin a new business. Sadly, he died of a fever shortly after their arrival, leaving his large family to fend for themselves. The boys found work and Emily and her sisters helped their mother establish a boarding school for girls.

In 1849, Elizabeth Blackwell became the first woman in the United States to receive a medical degree when she graduated from Geneva Medical College (now Hobart & William Smith Colleges) in Geneva, New York. Emily later applied for admission to study medicine at Geneva, but her application was denied. Even though Elizabeth had graduated at the top at her class, the school had at first accepted her purely as a joke and did not wish to accept more female students. Emily applied to and was turned down by many more medical colleges. Finally, after six years of trying, Rush Medical College in Chicago, Illinois, accepted her in 1852.

Things went well for one year. However, after she successfully completed the first year of medical school, Rush caved in to pressure from Illinois physicians and refused to accept Blackwell for a second year. Emily was able to complete her medical school training in 1854 at Case Western Reserve University in Cleveland, Ohio. After graduating with highest honors, Dr. Emily Blackwell traveled to Europe for two years to do postgraduate work in England, France, and Germany.

Meanwhile, Elizabeth, facing opposition to practicing her skills in New York, set up a small dispensary in 1853 for the care of poor women and children. In 1856, Emily and Marie Zakrzewska joined Elizabeth in New York City. Zakrzewska, born in Germany in 1829, had been trained in midwifery before immigrating to the United States in 1853. Elizabeth Blackwell helped her gain admission to Case Western Reserve. After completing a two-year course, Zakrzewska joined the Blackwells in New York. She helped the siblings by traveling to Philadelphia and Boston to seek funds for the hospital the women planned to start.

In 1857, the women rented a space on Bleecker Street in a poor area of Manhattan and opened a hospital, the New York Infirmary for Women and Children. They trained nurses and staffed the hospital entirely with women. Emily performed surgery, since Elizabeth could not because she had become blind in one eye from an infection she contracted while working in

Paris. Emily proved to be a very effective administrator and fundraiser. When Elizabeth went to Europe for a year in 1858, Emily took sole charge of the clinic. In 1859, Zakrzewska moved to Boston to teach at the newly created New England Female Medical College.

In 1868, Elizabeth and Emily opened the Women's Medical College of the New York Infirmary, and Emily accepted additional duties of teaching and educational administration. A year later, Elizabeth returned to England permanently, and Emily ran the hospital and medical college alone. Thanks to her exceptional organizational and managerial skills, the enterprise continued to expand. By the 1870's, Emily had moved the hospital and school into a converted mansion, where more than 7,000 patients received treatment annually. The medical college also expanded from a two-year program to four years, putting the school ahead of other medical schools, which still only required a two years of medical training.

For more than 30 years, Emily served as the institution's dean and professor of obstetrics and gynecology. Her high standards made the college one of the finest of its time for educating students in medicine. Before women were routinely admitted to medical schools with men, many women physicians graduated into medical practice under Blackwell's care and guidance. Many women were challenged and inspired by the example of both Emily and Elizabeth. Their medical college trained more than 350 physicians during its existence. It closed in 1899 when Cornell University began admitting women students to its medical program. The infirmary still exists today as Beth Israel Medical Center.

Emily Blackwell retired at the turn of the century and spent the next 10 years at her summer home in Maine. She died in 1910, a few months after Elizabeth's death in England. ◆

# Blodgett, Katherine Burr

JANUARY 10, 1898–OCTOBER 12, 1979 ● CHEMIST

Each time you peer through the lens of a camera, telescope, or microscope, you benefit from the creative and curious mind of physical chemist Katharine Burr Blodgett. She was the first female research scientist at General

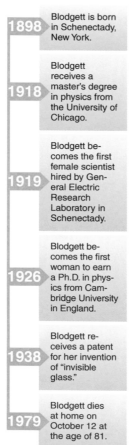

**1898**  Blodgett is born in Schenectady, New York.

**1918**  Blodgett receives a master's degree in physics from the University of Chicago.

**1919**  Blodgett becomes the first female scientist hired by General Electric Research Laboratory in Schenectady.

**1926**  Blodgett becomes the first woman to earn a Ph.D. in physics from Cambridge University in England.

**1938**  Blodgett receives a patent for her invention of "invisible glass."

**1979**  Blodgett dies at home on October 12 at the age of 81.

Electric Company (GE), one of the largest corporations in the United States. It was there that she invented the method for creating nonreflecting glass, nicknamed "invisible glass," for which she became famous. Invisible glass has coatings of a chemical film that cuts the normal loss of light by reflection. This allows more light to pass through the glass, making it clearer.

Katherine Burr Blodgett was born January 10, 1898, in Schenectady, New York. Her father, George Blodgett, a patent attorney, died before his daughter was born after he was shot by an intruder in the family home. Blodgett's widowed mother, Katharine Buchanan Burr Blodgett, raised her two small children in New York City. She moved the family to France for several years, exposing young Blodgett to French and German culture and language.

After winning a scholarship, in 1913 Blodgett entered Bryn Mawr College near Philadelphia, one of the first U.S. colleges for women. After receiving her degree from Bryn Mawr, Blodgett studied at the University of Chicago (UC), where she received a master's degree in physics in 1918. While such an achievement was advanced for a woman of her day, UC was one school that had committed to giving women equal educational and teaching opportunities.

While still a student, Blodgett visited the GE Research Laboratory in Schenectady, where her father had been head of the patent department before his untimely death. This sparked her interest in pursuing science studies. After graduation from UC at the early age of 19, Blodgett became the first female scientist hired by GE's lab when she began there in 1919. She would remain there for most of the next 44 years. Blodgett took a break from GE to study at world famous Cambridge University in England, where, in 1926, she became the first woman to earn a Ph.D. in physics. She then returned to Schenectady, the first female Ph.D. scientist at GE.

Many of Blodgett's years at GE were spent working with famous researcher Irving Langmuir, who won the 1932 Nobel Prize in chemistry for his discoveries concerning molecular films absorbed on surfaces. Langmuir conducted research at the GE lab from 1909 to 1950. Blodgett first assisted Langmuir in his work on monomolecular coatings—oily chemical compounds that cover the surface of water, metal, or glass in a film precisely one molecule thick. Langmuir had discovered these coatings during experiments in which he spread substances on water.

Langmuir's monomolecular coatings were scientifically interesting, but had no practical application until Blodgett found a way to add the molecule-thick layers to metal and glass one at a time. She found that, by dipping a plate through the film and then pulling it out again repeatedly, she could deposit single-molecule layers on solid surfaces. She then realized that, just as these films reduced glare on the surface of water, they could reduce the glare reflected off glass. She soon found that coating a sheet of glass with 44 layers of liquid soap molecules almost completely eliminated glare on the glass. Even the clearest glass reflects 8 to 10 percent of the light shining on it. Blodgett had discovered a way to allow more then 99 percent of the light to go through the glass. Eventually, Blodgett refined her discovery by finding a thickness of barium stearate film that could be coated on glass, resulting in the "invisible" glass.

Blodgett received a patent on March 16, 1938, for the "Film Structure and Method of Preparation" that created invisible glass. For the first time, eyeglasses, telescopes, microscopes, and camera and projector lenses could allow images to pass through without any distortion. Blodgett's glass helped during World War II in such items as periscopes, range finders, and aerial cameras. Blodgett also invented a thickness gauge that became a standard tool for measuring the number of layers contained on glass slides with an unknown number of films. This impressive gauge measured the thickness of films so thin that 35,000 layers were no thicker than a sheet of paper.

For the rest of the century, Blodgett's coatings found many different applications, including making airplane wings ice-resistant and even artificial rainmaking. Blodgett co-authored many scientific papers with Langmuir, but she also published many of her own. In 1935, she published "Films built by depositing successive monomolecular layers on a solid surface" in the *Journal of the American Chemical Society*. In that paper, Blodgett described the methods of adding two different types of films, x-films and y-films, to a glass slide.

Blodgett lived her whole life in the town she was born in, spending summer weekends at a favorite lake. Coworkers knew her as cheerful and hardworking. She enjoyed antique collecting, performing in amateur theater, astronomy, and playing bridge. She died at home on October 12, 1979, at the age of 81. ◆

# Bondar, Roberta

DECEMBER 4, 1945– ● PHYSICIAN

Canadian physician Roberta Bondar was a payload specialist in the crew of STSC42, the eight-day flight of the International Microgravity Laboratory in January 1992. The IML mission was devoted to space manufacturing and studies in life sciences. Ultimately over 50 experiments were performed. They had been developed by 200 scientists in 13 different countries, especially Canada, which contributed a suite of experiments in space physiology.

Bondar was born December 4, 1945, in Sault Ste. Marie, Ontario, where she attended primary and secondary schools. She earned several university degrees: a B.S. in zoology and agriculture from the University of Guelph (1968), M.S. in experimental pathology from the University of Western Ontariio (1971), Ph.D. in neurobiology form the University of Toronto (1974), and M.D. degree from McMaster University in 1977. She has been a Fellow of the Royal College of Physicians and Surgeons of Canada since 1981.

While still an undergraduate, Bondar began working for the Canadian Fisheries and Forestry Department, an association that lasted for six years. She also completed medical training at Toronto General Hospital and at Tufts New England Medical Center in Boston. Her specialization was neuro-opthalmology. In 1982 she became assistant professor of medicine at McMaster University while also serving as director of the Multiple

Roberta Bondar

Sclerosis Clinic for the Hamilton-Wentworth Region. After joining the Canadian space program she also served as a part-time lecturer at the University of Ottawa and taught at Ottawa General Hospital.

Bondar was one of the six astronauts of Space Team Canada selected in December 1983. In 1984 and 1985 she trained as a backup payload specialist to Robert Thirsk for a shuttle mission then scheduled for launch in 1987. She also headed the Life Sciences Subcommittee for Canada's participation in the NASA Freedom Space Station.

She was named an IML candidate payload specialist in 1989 and selected as one of the two prime PS in March 1990. In August 1992 she resigned from the Canadian astronaut program to return to full-time medical work at McMaster University, and lecturing on her experiences as an astronaut.

She is currently distinguished professor at the Centre for Advanced Technology Education (CATE), Ryerson Polytechnic University in Toronto and also serves as a visiting professor/scientist with the University of Western Ontario, the University of New Mexico, and the Universities Space Research Association at the NASA Johnson Space Center. ◆

# Brown, Dorothy

JANUARY 7, 1919– ● SURGEON AND EDUCATOR

Dorothy Lavinia Brown's life is a story of determination and will in the face of peculiar circumstances and difficult obstacles. Yet Brown has consistently demonstrated from the start that she is unable to shrink from the pursuit of her dreams, and in the process has served her fellow citizens with honor and competency.

Dorothy Brown was born on January 7, 1919 in Philadelphia, Pennsylvania, to a young, unmarried mother. Brown's mother, fearful of being unable to provide for her new baby, left Brown in an orphanage in the town of Troy, New York, when Brown was just an infant. Brown enjoyed the orphanage and considered it her permanent home. However, her mother was permitted to be reunited with her daughter when Brown was 13, and Brown moved in with her at that time. But by that time, she was accustomed to life at the orphanage, and she

Dorothy Brown

**1919** Brown is born in Philadelphia, Pennsylvania.

**1941** Brown receives her B.A. degree from Bennett College.

**1954** Brown completes her residency at Meharry Medical College.

**1957** Brown takes over as chief of surgery at Riverside Hospital in Nashville, Tennessee, a position she holds until 1983.

**1966** Brown is the first African-American woman elected to the Tennessee State Legislature.

missed her friends and the people who raised her. Five times she ran away from her mother's home and fled to the orphanage. Eventually, Brown was hired as a mother's helper in a private home in Albany, New York. With the blessing of her employer, Brown had the opportunity to move back to her beloved Troy with a foster family to pursue a high school diploma, which she received.

Brown's persistence impressed the Methodist Church in her community and the Women's Division of Christian Service nominated her for an academic scholarship to Bennett College in Greensboro, North Carolina. Brown won the scholarship and enrolled at Bennett. Brown had been fascinated by doctors and the practice of medicine since she had her tonsils removed as a young girl. At Bennett, she geared her undergraduate curriculum towards eventually enrolling in medical school. She received her bachelor's degree from Bennett in 1941, and then worked in a series of jobs for the United States Army Ordinance Department, with the goal of saving enough money to attend medical school. Her patience was rewarded in 1944 when she was accepted to the Meharry Medical College in Nashville, Tennessee.

Brown was determined to become a surgeon, despite the fact that female surgeons were rare, and those who expressed a desire to become surgeons were frowned upon. Brown graduated in the top third of her Meharry class and moved north to intern at Harlem Hospital in New York City. When she was denied a surgical residency there, Brown went back to Meharry and persuaded the chief of surgery to admit her to a surgical residency. Brown completed her Meharry residency in 1954, and was named an assistant professor of surgery the next year.

Brown practiced in Nashville at Riverside Hospital from 1957 until 1983, thereby becoming the first African American female surgeon in the American South. Brown also was the first black woman to be named to as a Fellow of the American College of Surgeons. Following her time at Riverside Hospital, Brown practiced as an attending surgeon at George W. Hubbard Hospital while also continuing to teach at Meharry.

*Rachel Fuller Brown*    **33**

Brown's extraordinary life extended well beyond the operating room and the classroom. At age 40, she became the first single woman in years to adopt a child in Tennessee, a girl she named in honor of her foster mother. In 1966, Brown decided to run for public office, and was elected to the Tennessee State Legislature as a representative, the first African American woman to be elected to that post. In 1968, Brown ran for a seat in the Tennessee Senate, but lost the race.

Brown continues to be active as a physician and teacher, and has also been invited to lecture around the nation and overseas. Brown has also been a tireless fundraiser for the Methodist Church and the 12 predominantly black colleges the church supports. ◆

# Brown, Rachel Fuller

## November 23, 1898–January 14, 1980 ● Biochemist

Infections caused by microscopic fungi are difficult to treat, because many fungi resist agents that can kill other microbes. American biochemist Rachel Fuller Brown struck a major blow in the war against disease when she and microbiologist Elizabeth Lee Hazen developed the fungicide nystatin. A fungicide kills fungi, and nystatin quickly became a key weapon to fight fungus infections of the skin, mucous membranes, and intestinal tract. It was the first antibiotic that worked safely in humans to treat such common fungal infections as ringworm and athlete's foot, as well as ones that are more serious. The long-distance collaboration between Hazen and Brown that gave rise to the world's first successful fungus-fighting antibiotic became one of medical science's famous historical tales.

Brown was born in Springfield, Massachusetts, in 1898. During her

Rachel Fuller Brown

**1898** Brown is born in Springfield, Massachusetts.

**1933** Brown receives her Ph.D. degree in organic chemistry and bacteriology from the University of Chicago.

**1948** Brown and Hazen work to develop a medicine to kill various forms of fungus.

**1950** Brown and Hazen present their discovery of nystatin to the National Academy of Sciences.

**1975** Brown becomes the first woman awarded the Pioneer Chemist Award of the American Institute of Chemists.

**1980** Brown dies.

**pneumococcus:** the bacteria which is the cause of pneumonia.

**actinomycetes:** rod-shaped bacteria found in the soil which produce antibiotics.

**nystatin:** an antibiotic which is used in the treatment of vaginal yeast infections, and other fungal diseases of the skin, mouth, throat, and intestinal tract.

childhood in Webster Groves, Missouri, Brown developed an interest in science by learning how to collect and mount insects. In her teens, she returned to Springfield, where she became interested in chemistry in high school. She then attended Mount Holyoke College in nearby South Hadley, majoring in history and chemistry and graduating in 1920 with a bachelor's degree. She then entered the University of Chicago (UC), in Illinois. In 1921, Brown received an M.A. degree in organic chemistry at UC and, in 1933, a Ph.D. degree in organic chemistry and bacteriology. Between degrees, Brown taught chemistry and physics at the Francis Shimer Preparatory School for Girls near Chicago.

Brown landed her first research job as an assistant chemist in the Division of Laboratories and Research at the New York State Department of Health. She ended up spending the next 42 years at the Department of Health, and her hard work resulted in regular promotions, first to assistant biochemist, then senior biochemist, associate biochemist, and research scientist. Early in her career, Brown studied ***pneumococcus***, the bacterium that causes pneumonia, and developed a vaccine that is still used today. "I was left pretty much to myself to make contributions to health-related problems at the times when they were currently important," Brown said of her work at the health department.

In 1948, Brown teamed up with Hazen, also an employee of the Department of Health and already a leading authority on fungi. Hazen, working in New York City, wanted to develop a medicine that could kill a fungus. Brown, in Albany, New York, used her expertise to provide Hazen with specific forms of bacteria on which to work. Brown had the skills to identify, characterize, and purify substances produced when she cultured bacteria found in hundreds of soil samples.

Researchers already knew that microorganisms called **actinomycetes** lived in soil, and that these organisms produced antibiotics. However, not all antibiotics could be used in humans. Hazen and Brown sought to isolate an antifungal antibiotic from soil samples and then test this substance for safety in humans. Hazen took a soil sample from a friend's dairy farm and identified a microorganism now known as *Streptomyces norsei*. Analyzing the organism, Brown discovered that it produced two antifungal substances. One was too poisonous for humans to use, but Brown and Hazen purified the other one into a safe antibiotic. They named it **nystatin**, for the New York State Department of Health.

In 1950, Brown and Hazen presented their findings to the National Academy of Sciences (NAS), an organization that encourages research in the sciences and serves as a scientific adviser to the United States government. The two women then received patents for nystatin, was first introduced in practical form in 1954 following Food and Drug Administration (FDA) approval. The drug manufacturing company E. R. Squibb and Sons received the license for the patent and began marketing the new antibiotic under the name Mycostatin. Doctors still prescribe Mycostatin today for vaginal yeast infections and other fungal diseases of the skin, mouth, throat, and intestinal tract. It can also be combined with antibacterial drugs. In other applications, scientists use nystatin to treat Dutch elm disease, a fungus that kills elm trees, to fight mold in the food industries, and even to kill mildew on fine artwork.

Brown and Hazen used the money they earned from nystatin's royalties, more than $13 million by the time the patent expired, to establish the nonprofit Brown-Hazen Fund for scientific research. Their generosity has provided for a great deal of further medical research, and their example has inspired many women to pursue a scientific career. Later in their careers, Brown and Hazen also discovered two other antibiotics, phalamycin and capacidin.

Brown became the first woman to be awarded the Pioneer Chemist Award of the American Institute of Chemists in 1975. In 1968, she received the Distinguished Service Award from the New York State Department of Health. Brown filled her personal life with hiking, swimming, golf, and gardening. She was also active in her church and in the American Association of University Women. She died in 1980. ◆

# Browne, Marjorie Lee

SEPTEMBER 9, 1914–OCTOBER 19, 1979 ● MATHEMATICIAN

Marjorie Lee Browne was reared in Memphis, Tennessee, by her father, Lawrence J. Lee, a railroad postal service worker, and by her stepmother, Lottie Taylor Lee, a schoolteacher. Her father was an avid reader who shared with her his excitement for travel, visualization, and

Marjorie Lee Browne

learning through the written word. Reading—first the classics, then mysteries—became an obsession with her and provided excellent preparation for the development of the analytic reasoning skills she would later employ in her mathematical studies. She was an excellent tennis player, and won many city of Memphis women's singles tennis championships. She was also a singer of some repute and a lover of music, as well as a gifted mathematics student.

Browne was a 1935 cum laude graduate of Howard University and received her master of science (1939) and Ph.D. (1949) degrees in mathematics from the University of Michigan. She was one of the first two African American women to receive a Ph.D. in mathematics (the other was Evelyn Boyd Granville from Yale). Her teaching career at North Carolina Central University in Durham spanned 30 years (1949 to 1979), and under her leadership as mathematics department chair (1951 to 1970), the university achieved many firsts.

For example, in 1961 she received a $60,000 IBM educational grant to establish the first academic computer center at the university; in 1969 she received the first of seven Shell Foundation scholarship grants for outstanding mathematics students. Browne directed the first National Science Foundation (NSF) Undergraduate Mathematics Research Participation Program (1964 and 1965), and was a principal investigator, coordinator of the mathematics section, and lecturer in 13 NSF Institutes for Secondary School Teachers of Science and Mathematics (1957 to 1971).

In 1974 the North Carolina Council of Teachers of Mathematics awarded Browne the first W. W. Rankin Memorial Award for Excellence in Mathematics Education in recognition of her efforts in improving the quality of the mathematics preparation of secondary school teachers in the state. She was one of six African American women included in the 1981 Smithsonian traveling exhibition "Black Women: Achievements Against the Odds."

Pursuing what she would later call "the life of an academic nomad," she completed four postdoctoral fellowship programs that included studies and research in combinatorial topology (her specialty), the applications of mathematics in the behavioral sciences, numerical analysis and computing, differential topology, Lie groups, and Lie algebra. These activities were undertaken at universities in the United States and abroad, including Cambridge University (1952–53), Stanford University (summer 1957), UCLA (1958–59), and Columbia University (1965–66).

Browne's published works include "A Note on the Classical Groups" (*Mathematical Monthly*, August 1955) and four manuscripts: "Sets, Logic and Mathematical Thought," 1957; "Introduction to Linear Algebra," 1959; "Algebraic Structures," 1964; and "Elementary Matrix Algebra," 1969. At the time of her death in 1979, she was pursuing a research project titled "A Postulational Approach to the Development of the Real Number System."

During the 1950s, Browne was an ardent advocate for the integration of the previously segregated professional organizations in which she held membership, including the North Carolina Teachers Association, the Mathematical Association of America, and the American Mathematical Society. She also held membership in Beta Kappa Chi, the Society of Sigma Xi, Pi Lambda Theta Honorary Societies, the Woman's Research Society, and Alpha Kappa Alpha sorority. She was a faculty consultant in mathematics with the Ford Foundation (1968–69) and served three terms as a member of the advisory panel to the NSF Undergraduate Scientific Equipment Program (1966, 1967, and 1973). In 1979, four of her former students established the Marjorie Lee Browne Trust Fund at North Carolina Central University to support the Marjorie Lee Browne Memorial Scholarship, awarded annually to a mathematics student who best exemplifies those traits that Browne sought to instill in young people.

Browne was a mathematical purist who, like many great mathematicians of the 19th century, viewed mathematics as an art form, as an intellectual quest, free from the limitations of the physical universe, in search simply for truth and beauty. ◆

**1914** Browne is born in Memphis, Tennessee.

**1949** Browne receives her Ph.D. in mathematics from the University of Michigan, one of the first two African American women to receive such a degree.

**1951** Browne takes over as chair of the department of mathematics at North Carolina Central University, a post she holds until 1970.

**1969** Browne receives the first of seven Shell Foundation grants for outstanding mathematics students.

**1979** Browne dies in Durham, North Carolina; four of her former students establish the Marjorie Lee Browne Trust Fund at North Carolina Central University.

# Burbidge, E. Margaret

AUGUST 12, 1919– ● ASTROPHYSICIST

**astrophysicist:** an astronomer who studies the solar system and the universe utilizing the principles of physics and astronomy.

*Burbidge became interested in stars as a small child looking through her father's binoculars, and her parents encouraged her interest in science.*

Following her childhood dream of measuring the distances of stars, E. Margaret Burbidge moved nimbly through a man's world to become one of the leading astrophysicists of the 20th century. An **astrophysicist** is an astronomer who studies our solar system and the rest of the universe by applying principles of physics to astronomy. Burbidge won recognition for her estimates of the weights of stars and for discoveries concerning quasars, which are star-like distant objects in the universe. Burbidge also played a major role in developing the Hubble Space Telescope, which was launched in 1990 and has sent back the most spectacular photos of space ever obtained.

Among the many firsts she achieved, Burbidge became the first woman appointed director of the Royal Greenwich Observatory, a global center of astronomy research. She also became the first woman astronomer elected to the National Academy of Sciences, an elected group of scientists that advises the United States government.

Burbidge was born Eleanor Margaret Peachey in Davenport, England, on August 12, 1919. Her father, Stanley John Peachey, taught chemistry at the Manchester School of Technology, where her mother, Marjorie (Stott) Peachey, studied chemistry. Margaret had one sister, Audrey. The Peacheys relocated to London when Burbidge was a toddler, and there her father set up a laboratory after receiving patents in rubber chemistry.

Burbidge became interested in stars as a small child looking through her father's binoculars, and her parents encouraged her interest in science. When she was only 12, she became fascinated with an astronomy book from her grandfather. When she read that the nearest star to Earth, besides the sun, was 26 trillion miles away, "I decided then and there that the occupation I most wanted to engage in 'when I was grown up' was to determine the distances of the stars," she wrote later.

She studied astronomy at the University College of London, earning a bachelor's degree in science in 1939. Burbidge then joined the university's observatory staff, and later received her Ph.D. there in 1943. She served as assistant director of the observatory from 1948 to 1950 and acting director from 1950 to 1951. In 1948, she married fellow graduate student, Geoffrey Burbidge. He became a theoretical physicist, and the couple began a lifelong professional relationship. They had one daughter, Sarah, born in 1956.

In 1951, the Burbidges moved to the United States, where Geoffrey would study at Harvard University and Margaret began working at the University of Chicago's Yerkes Observatory, at Williams Bay, Wisconsin. In 1953, she returned to work at the Cavendish Laboratory in Cambridge, England.

In 1955, Burbidge's husband obtained a prestigious Carnegie Fellowship for astronomical research at the Mount Wilson Observatory, near Pasadena, California. Ironically, Burbidge had applied for the same fellowship in 1947 but had been rejected because only men were allowed to work at the Wilson telescopes. When Geoffrey accepted the appointment, Burbidge had to accept a minor research post at the California Institute of Technology, Pasadena. She was still not allowed to use the Wilson telescopes, but the couple pretended she was Geoffrey's assistant so she could use the facilities.

Beginning in 1954, the Burbidges teamed up with English astronomer Fred Hoyle and American physicist William Fowler to study the content of stars. In 1957, the foursome published a major scientific paper that showed how the heavy chemical elements, such as carbon, oxygen, and iron, are produced by nuclear reactions inside stars. They called their theory the B2FH theory, using their own initials. The theory was groundbreaking in showing that the elements that make up our everyday world—even our bodies—once came from stars.

In 1957, Burbidge became associate professor of astronomy at the Yerkes Observatory. She later took a position as research astronomer at the University of California, San Diego, in 1962, and from 1964 she remained there as professor of astronomy.

In 1967, the Burbidges collaborated to publish *Quasi-Stellar Objects,* the first comprehensive work on quasars, which are celestial objects that resemble stars. From 1972 to 1973, Burbidge took a leave of absence from UC-San Diego, returning to England to serve in the prestigious position of director of the Royal Greenwich Observatory. Until 1971, the director of that observatory had held the title of Astronomer Royal. Her husband also took a position there, but the couple returned to San Diego after disputes that occurred at Greenwich.

During her career, Burbidge earned many honors. In 1964, she was elected a fellow of the Royal Society of London, the

**1919** Burbidge is born in Davenport, England.

**1943** Burbidge earns her Ph.D. at the University College of London.

**1948** Burbidge marries fellow graduate student, Geoffrey Burbidge.

**1951** Burbidge moves to the United States.

**1957** Burbidge and her husband publish a major scientific paper that shows how the heavy chemical elements are produced by nuclear reactions inside stars.

**1964** Burbidge becomes professor of astronomy at the University of California.

**1972** Burbidge serves as director of the Royal Greenwich Observatory for 15 months.

**1990** Burbidge's work on the Hubble Space telescope is rewarded when the orbiting telescope is launched.

world's oldest continuously existing scientific organization. In 1976, she served as the first woman president of the American Astronomical Society, the most prominent U.S. astronomy association. In 1981, Burbidge served as the president of the American Association for Advancement of Science. In 1985, U.S. President Ronald Reagan awarded Burbidge the National Medal of Science in honor of her many scientific accomplishments.

In the year 2000, Burbidge continued at UC-San Diego as an active researcher. In the 1990s, she worked with the National Aeronautics and Space Administration (NASA) in planning and producing the Hubble Space Telescope. One of the devices on the telescope was a faint object spectrograph. A spectrograph is like a prism, creating a band of light called a spectrum. Viewing those colors, astronomers can determine the composition of stars and galaxies. When Burbidge first viewed these results from the space, she felt a thrill to "see the universe in a new color." ◆

# Burnell, Jocelyn Bell

JULY 15, 1943– ● ASTROPHYSICIST

*Burnell herself gave the signals the fanciful name LGMs, or "little green men."*

Susan Jocelyn Bell was born in Belfast, Northern Ireland. As members of the Society of Friends, or Quakers, her parents supported education for women and encouraged their daughter academically, but her scholastic career did not get off to a very promising start. When she was 11 years old, she failed the examination that would have qualified her to go to college under Great Britain's stringent educational system. Her failure prompted her parents to send her to a private boarding school in England to give her a second chance. While the school had little in the way of science equipment, it did have a physics teacher who inspired Bell. She improved her academic skills enough that she was able to enroll in Scotland's Glasgow University, where she earned a degree in physics in 1965.

Bell, who later took the name Burnell when she married, played a major role in an important discovery while she was studying for her Ph.D. in radio astronomy at England's Cambridge University. Under the supervision of Anthony Hewish, she began to work on an astronomy project designed to study the scintillation, or twinkling, of compact radio waves from other planets. At that time, radio astronomy was in its infancy. The chief obstacle to progress in the field was the lack of a suitable type of radio telescope. At Cambridge, Burnell was active in the development and construction of such a radio telescope, which consisted of thousands of poles with wires and cables that ran over four-and-a-half acres of ground. After the telescope became operational in 1967, it received radio signals that were recorded on paper printouts. Burnell's job—not a very glamorous one—was to analyze the printouts.

Jocelyn Bell Burnell

In November of that first year, Burnell began to notice unusual signals, which she referred to as "bits of scruff." At first, no one knew what these signals were. One possibility was that they came from quasars (celestial objects that resemble stars), but the signals were too fast and too regular for quasars. Other possible sources included radio wave interference, radar, French television signals, the moon, or orbiting satellites, but each of these possibilities assumed that the source was something within Earth's solar system.

Soon, though, it was apparent that these clearly distinguishable and regularly occurring signals were from outside the solar system, and excited scientists throughout the world began to speculate that they were evidence of extraterrestrial life. Burnell herself gave the signals the fanciful name LGMs, or "little green men." She began to observe, however, that similar signals came from different locations, and she concluded that it was unlikely that more than one extraterrestrial civilization would be trying to contact Earth on the same radio frequency. Further, Burnell saw that the sources of the radio waves changed their positions in the sky in much the same way that stars did. This proved that the signals were not made by intelligent life but were from some kind of planetary body.

After examining the evidence and scientific papers on the subject, Burnell and Hewish determined that the source of the

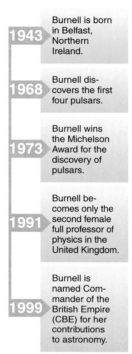

signals had to be a special category of neutron stars. A neutron star is a compact star core that remains when a massive star explodes; it is so compact that a teaspoon of its material weighs 100 million tons. These superdense, rotating cores emit, or "pulse," beams of radiation at regular intervals and hence came to be called pulsars. Over the next few months Burnell discovered three additional pulsars, and within weeks, other scientists embarked on similar projects leading to the discovery of still others. Burnell, though, had the distinction of discovering the first four pulsars, and her discovery opened up a whole new field of astrophysics.

In 1974 Hewish and Sir Martin Ryle, also from Cambridge, were awarded the Nobel Prize in physics for the discovery of pulsars—the first time the prize was given for work in astronomy. Burnell's exclusion from the prize created a great deal of controversy; many scientists felt that she should have received the prize, or at least have been a corecipient. Burnell remained modest about her accomplishment, though, stating publicly that much of it was the result of luck and that research students normally should not receive such a prestigious award. For her discovery, however, she did share the Michelson Award with Hewish in 1973.

After her marriage in 1968, Burnell worked in an assortment of positions because her husband, a government employee, was frequently required to move. From 1968 to 1970, she held a Science Research Council fellowship, in the meantime completing her Ph.D. in 1969. From 1970 to 1973, she was at the University of Southampton, where she developed a gamma-ray telescope. From 1974 to 1982, she worked as a researcher at the Mullard Space Science Laboratory at University College in London, where she studied X-ray astronomy and worked on an X-ray satellite called Ariel 5.

In 1982 Burnell was appointed senior research fellow at the Royal Observatory in Edinburgh, Scotland, where she studied infrared astronomy and was head of the James Clerk Maxwell Telescope section, part of a telescope project based in Hawaii used by astronomers throughout the world. In 1991 she joined the physics department at England's Open University, a 150,000-student university designed for nontraditional students and others who, like Burnell, need a second chance at higher education. With her appointment, the number of full professors of physics in the United Kingdom who were women doubled from one to two.

In 1969 Burnell was elected a fellow of the Royal Astronomical Society in England, and from 1995 to 1997 she served as the society's vice president. In 1987 she received the Beatrice M. Tinsley Prize from the American Astronomical Society, and in 1989 she received the Herschel Medal from the Royal Astronomical Society. In 1999 she was named Commander of the British Empire (CBE) "for her services to astronomy." In addition to her professional interests, she gardens, sews, swims, knits, and listens to choral music. She is also an active Quaker. ◆

# Cannon, Annie Jump

DECEMBER 11, 1863–APRIL 13, 1941 ● ASTRONOMER

Throughout her life Annie Jump Cannon suffered a severe hearing problem, but she overcame obstacle and became one of the early 20th century's most accomplished astronomers. She was born in Dover, Delaware, the oldest of three children. Her father, Wilson Cannon, was a prosperous shipbuilder, a state senator, and a prominent member of Dover society. Her mother, Mary Jump, owned a collection of astronomy books and encouraged her daughter's interest in studying the stars.

As a child, Cannon loved to read these books by candlelight in the attic of the family's house. She also enjoyed climbing out a trap door in the attic to the roof outside, where she would spend hours gazing at the stars. Two other early interests later played an important role in Cannon's scientific career. One was rainbows; she was fascinated by the ribbons of color cast by light passing through a glass candle holder in the family living room. The other was the emerging field of photography. In 1892 Cannon traveled through Europe taking pictures, and when she returned, she compiled a booklet of photos entitled *In the Footsteps of Columbus* that was used as a souvenir at the 1893 Chicago World Fair.

As Cannon grew up, her family and wide circle of friends expected that she would become a society lady in Dover. Her teachers, though, recognized her intellectual gifts and urged her to continue her education. Her father sent her to Wellesley

Annie Jump Cannon

College in Massachusetts, where she studied under Sarah F. Whiting, a professor of physics and astronomy. She graduated in 1884, then returned to Dover, where for 10 years she lived the society life she had been expected to lead. But when her mother died in 1894, Cannon found solace for her grief in the stars. Looking for a purpose in her life, she decided to return to Wellesley to continue her studies and work as a junior instructor. Additionally, she enrolled as a "special student" in astronomy at nearby Radcliffe College, and she later completed a master's degree at Wellesley in 1907.

In the meantime, a turning point in Cannon's career occurred in 1896 when she took a position as an assistant at the Harvard University Observatory, at that time one of the best places in the world to study the stars. There, her job was to study the stars' spectra, the "rainbows" they made when their light passed through a prism—much like the candle holder in her childhood living room. Referring to the spectrum, she once said, "It is not just a streak of light, but a gateway to a wonderful new world." By looking at the color pattern created by a star's light, a technique called **spectroscopy**, astronomers can determine the star's size, temperature, age, and the speed at which it is spinning.

In the late 19th and earlier 20th centuries, Harvard had the world's largest collection of star photographs, but no one had ever come up with a system for putting the photos and the stars they depicted in order. Over nearly three decades, Cannon would change that, relying on her interest not only in the stars but in light and photography. She worked tirelessly to develop a system of star classification. She identified several major classes of stars and divided each class into subclasses, using a system of letters and numbers to name them. This system was later adopted by the International Astronomical Union and is still in use today. Her incredible visual memory enabled her to hold pictures in her mind and almost instantly classify the stars in them.

In 1911 Dr. Charles Edward Pickering, director of the Harvard Observatory, appointed Cannon curator of the entire collection of photographs. She held this position until 1938, although she completed the bulk of her work on the photos between 1911 and 1924. Early on she was able to classify and name up to 5,000 stars per month, but that number increased as the years went by. In 1918 she began publishing the *Henry Draper Catalogue* (named in honor of the man whose widow funded the project). By 1924 the catalogue—still used today—had grown to nine volumes and classified, catalogued, and named more than 250,000 stars. Cannon was not done, though; the *Henry Draper Extension*, published between 1925 and 1949, expanded the catalogue to a total of 350,000 stars. Additionally, Cannon discovered five new novas, or exploding stars, and 300 variable stars—stars that grow bright, then dim, then bright again.

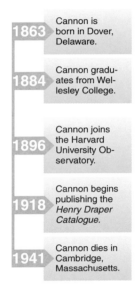

**1863** Cannon is born in Dover, Delaware.

**1884** Cannon graduates from Wellesley College.

**1896** Cannon joins the Harvard University Observatory.

**1918** Cannon begins publishing the *Henry Draper Catalogue*.

**1941** Cannon dies in Cambridge, Massachusetts.

**spectroscopy:** a branch of physics related to the theories and interpretations of interactions between matter and radiation.

> **"In our troubled days it is good to have something outside our planet, something fine and distant for comfort."**
>
> Annie Jump Cannon

During her career Cannon received many honors. In 1914 the Royal Astronomical Society in England named her an honorary member. In 1925 she became the first woman to receive an honorary doctorate from England's Oxford University, and that year she also became one of the few female members of the American Philosophical Society. In 1938 she was appointed professor by Harvard University. She was also awarded a medal by the National Academy of Sciences, and the American Association of University Women annually presents the Annie Jump Cannon Award to women launching careers in astronomy.

Cannon was not just a distinguished astronomer. She was an avid bridge player and an accomplished pianist. She was an advocate for women's suffrage and a member of the National Women's party. Her first love, though, was always the heavens. ◆

# Carr, Emma Perry

JULY 23, 1880–JANUARY 7, 1972 ● CHEMIST

Emma Perry Carr, a prominent American chemist in the early 20th century, was born in 1880 in Holmesville, a small town 60 miles south of Cleveland, Ohio, the third of five children. She was the descendant of 17th-century English settlers, and both her father and grandfather were distinguished physicians. Her mother was a homemaker and was active in the Methodist church and in the community. A younger brother died at an early age, but her three remaining siblings went on to distinguish themselves in medicine and community service.

Shortly after Carr's birth, the family moved to Coshocton, Ohio, where Carr attended high school. Then, in 1898, she enrolled as one of the few female students at Ohio State University. After her freshman year, she transferred to Mount Holyoke College in South Hadley, Massachusetts for her sophomore and junior years. By this time she had developed a strong interest in chemistry, and rather than completing her degree, she worked as an assistant in the Mount Holyoke chemistry department for three years. She took a leave of absence to complete her bachelor's degree in chemistry at the

University of Chicago in 1905. She returned to Mount Holyoke to teach for two years, then returned to the University of Chicago for graduate studies. In 1910 she became only the seventh woman ever to receive a doctorate in chemistry from the University of Chicago. While working on her doctoral thesis, she showed distinction by winning both the Mary E. Woolley and Lowenthal Fellowships.

Carr's travels between Chicago and Massachusetts finally ended when she returned to Mount Holyoke in 1910 to accept an appointment as full professor of chemistry. In 1913, she was appointed head of the Department of Chemistry, and she remained at Mount Holyoke until her retirement in 1946. Throughout her career she made important contributions to the emerging field of spectroscopy, which is the analysis of the dispersion of emissions (such as particles or radiation) according to a property such as mass or energy. In particular, she developed spectroscopic methods for examining the electronic configurations of organic molecules. In 1918 she published a first paper on the subject, entitled "The Absorption Spectra of Some Derivatives of Cyclopropane." Her paper was one of the first American contributions to the field of spectroscopy—a field that had been dominated by Europeans—and played a key role in establishing a research program at Mount Holyoke.

In 1919 Carr traveled to Queens University in Belfast, Ireland, to study current theories and methods in ultraviolet absorption spectroscopy. She then began to conduct research on the ultraviolet spectrum, with emphasis on the relationship between ultraviolet spectra and the heats of combustion of hydrocarbons. She pioneered a vacuum spectrograph project—a joint student-faculty effort—that developed a set of purified hydrocarbons and examined the ultraviolet absorption spectra in the hydrocarbons' liquid and vapor forms.

That project was important because it changed the way scientists understood the carbon-carbon double bond, and thus it was of interest to the petroleum industry. She first presented her findings on this subject in a convention paper (1929), then in several papers to scientists interested in petroleum chemistry in the 1930s and early 1940s. In 1937, she was awarded the first Garvan Medal from the American Chemical Society; the medal is the most prestigious prize given to female chemists in the United States. In addition, she received honorary doctorates from Allegheny College (1939), Russell Sage College (1941), and Hood College (1947).

1880 &gt; Carr is born in Holmesville, Ohio.

1910 &gt; Carr earns a doctorate in chemistry from the University of Chicago.

1918 &gt; Carr publishes her first paper on spectroscopy.

1946 &gt; Carr retires from Mount Holyoke College.

1972 &gt; Carr dies in Evanston, Illinois.

Carr was a valued faculty member at Mount Holyoke not only as a researcher but as an administrator and popular teacher as well. For a time she was head of the residence hall on campus and ate at the dinner table with students, where she led conversations ranging from international politics to the respective advantages of being a monkey or a cow. Many students came to her for personal advice, and her home was later the center of the department's social life.

Carr's research laboratory was important both for its findings and for its role in inspiring numerous women to pursue careers in science. Throughout her career, Carr remained involved in political issues, particularly those connected with science. As researchers began to unlock the secrets of the atom, for example, she was concerned about the development of the atomic bomb and argued that nuclear fission should be explored as a potential source of energy rather than as a weapon of mass destruction. Additionally, she was a cellist and played the organ at the local Methodist church. After her retirement in 1946 she became a popular speaker at universities, sororities, and clubs, and even served as a member of the town council for South Hadley, Massachusetts.

When her health began to fail, Carr entered a Presbyterian nursing home in Evanston, Illinois, where she was looked after by her family. The president of Mount Holyoke College, who had never met Carr, donated funds in 1971 to help defray her medical expenses. She died of heart failure on January 7, 1972. ◆

# Carson, Rachel

May 27, 1907–April 14, 1964 ● Biologist and Environmentalist

Rachel Carson was a pioneer of the modern environmental movement in the United States. She was born in Springdale, Pennsylvania on May 27, 1907 and died in Silver Spring, Maryland on April 14, 1964. Carson made a career of her fascination with wildlife and concern for the environment, working for the U.S. Bureau of Fisheries and its successor, the U.S. Fish and Wildlife Service, from 1936 to 1952. Her best-known book, *Silent Spring* (1962), provided a catalyst that changed the way Americans thought about their surroundings and particularly the impact of modern chemicals on the landscape. Rachel Carson played a significant role in the ideological enlightenment that led policy makers to focus on the serious study of environmental issues. The first Earth Day on April 22, 1970 was one outcome of the new environmental awareness, and a second was the creation of the Environmental Protection Agency (EPA) the same year.

Rachel Carson

Carson attended public schools in Springdale and nearby Parnassus, Pennsylvania. Her mother taught her to enjoy the outdoors and fostered her daughter's interest in wildlife. Carson showed an early talent for writing, and on graduation from Parnassus High School enrolled in the Pennsylvania College for Women in Pittsburgh to study English, with the intention of becoming a writer.

Instead, a course in biology rekindled her interest in science and led to a change to a science major. Carson was awarded her bachelor of arts in 1929, and went on to postgraduate studies at Johns Hopkins University. Commencing in 1930, she taught at Johns Hopkins summer school for seven years. She joined the zoology staff of the University of Maryland in 1931, and obtained a master of arts from Johns Hopkins in 1932.

Carson developed a special interest in sea life and undertook further postgraduate work at the Woods Hole Marine Biological Laboratory in Massachusetts. In 1936 she accepted a position as an aquatic biologist with the U.S. Bureau of Fisheries in Washington, D.C. She became editor-in-chief at the U.S. Fish and Wildlife Service, the successor to the Bureau of Fisheries, in 1947.

During her years with the service, Carson practiced her writing skills by preparing many leaflets and informational brochures that publicized the central objective of the bureau, which was "to insure the conservation of the nation's wild birds, mammals, fishes, and other forms of wildlife, with a view to preventing the destruction or depletion of these natural

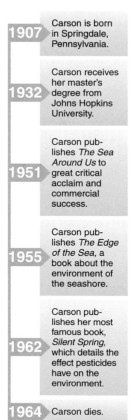

**1907** Carson is born in Springdale, Pennsylvania.

**1932** Carson receives her master's degree from Johns Hopkins University.

**1951** Carson publishes *The Sea Around Us* to great critical acclaim and commercial success.

**1955** Carson publishes *The Edge of the Sea*, a book about the environment of the seashore.

**1962** Carson publishes her most famous book, *Silent Spring*, which details the effect pesticides have on the environment.

**1964** Carson dies.

resources, and to promote the maximum present use and enjoyment of the wildlife resources that is compatible with their perpetuity."

Her first book *Under the Sea-Wind* appeared in 1941. The subtitle was "A Naturalist's Picture of Ocean Life" and the narrative told the life of the shore, the open sea, and the sea bottom. *Under the Sea-Wind* was well received both for the accuracy of its scientific content and its accessible style. Her second book, *The Sea Around Us* (1951), was delayed both by war work and a painstaking and prolonged period of research and writing. By her own admission. Carson was a slow writer who subjected her work to multiple revisions. As a general rule Carson declined offers from magazines to publish extracts from her books, fearing that serialization would detract from the coherence of her arguments. However, before its publication in book form, *The Sea Around Us* was excerpted in the *New Yorker* in the summer of 1951.

When *The Sea Around Us* appeared in book form in July 1951, it was an immediate success. The work was greeted with praise for its literary style, approachability, and informative content. In a *New York Herald Tribune Book Review*, Francesca La Monte described Carson's story of the sea as "one of the most beautiful books of our time." *The Sea Around Us* provides a layman's geological guide through time and tide. It begins with an account of the contemporary understanding of the origins of the Earth and Moon, and then proceeds through the geological timetable, mapping the evolution of the planet, the formation of mountains and islands and oceans.

The book then provides a description of the sea, commencing with the surface and its inhabitants, and descending through lower depths to the sea bottom. Carson reveals the fascination of the hidden world of the oceans to nonscientists, exploring the mystery of the sea, its history, and its treasures. The book went into nine printings and was at the top of the nonfiction best-seller lists nationwide. It was selected by the Book of the Month Club, condensed for *Reader's Digest*, and translated into 33 languages. The same year it was published, the book received the National Book Award for Non-Fiction.

The success of *The Sea Around Us* wrought major changes in Carson's life. In 1951 she accepted a Guggenheim fellowship that enabled her to take a year's leave of absence from her government job to start work on a third book. Her future secured by her success, she resigned her position at the U.S. Fish and

Wildlife Service in 1952 to devote herself full time to her writing. The result was *The Edge of the Sea*, published in 1955. Conceived as a popular guide to the seashore, studying the ecological relationship of the seashore to animals on the Atlantic Coast of the United States, this work complemented her previous book and evidenced Carson's growing interest in the interrelationship of Earth's systems and the holistic approach that would mark *Silent Spring*.

*Silent Spring* opens with a brief account of a fictional town in the American heartland "where all life seemed to live in harmony with its surroundings." Prosperous farms line roadsides alive with wildflowers and ferns. In winter, birds feed on colorful berries above the snowline. Then a blight spreads through the region. Sheep and cattle sicken and die. Chickens become ill. In the spring the hens brood but no chicks are hatched. The birds disappear. Crops fail. The hedgerows wither and die.

The cause of this "creeping death" is the widespread use of **pesticides**. In *Silent Spring*, Carson propounds an eloquent argument for the careful and thorough consideration of both the short- and long-term effects of the use of chemicals for a range of applications. The book documents the negative effects that result from the use of pesticides, chemical fertilizers, and an array of chemical treatments designed to enhance production or simplify the production process.

The information contained in *Silent Spring* was not new. All the issues she covered had been discussed in the scientific journals. Carson's contribution was her presentation of "the overall picture" in a highly readable style. Carson highlighted the fact that while individual chemical products might be viewed as safe because they achieved what they were designed to do, the combined effects of an assortment of chemical products could be deadly. As an example, Carson cited the streams that became chemical soups carrying the outpourings of chemical treatment plants and the run-off from fields treated with pesticides and chemical fertilizers, killing algae, plant life, fish, and animals.

Carson began to awaken the public to the need to think beyond short-term, quick chemical fixes and profit taking: "The central problem of our age has become the contamination of man's total environment with substances of incredible potential for harm—substances that accumulate in plants and animals and even penetrate the germ cells to shatter or alter the very material of heredity upon which the shape of the future

> "The chemical war is never won, and all life is caught in its violent crossfire."
> Rachel Carson, after the publication of *Silent Spring*

**pesticides:** chemical agents used to destroy plants.

Located in Springdale, in southwestern Pennsylvania, the Rachel Carson Homestead is the five-room farmhouse where Carson was born and spent her childhood. Now a museum, the buildings were restored by its governing body, the Rachel Carson Homestead Association (est. 1975); they currently house an array of educational programs designed to teach the public about Carson's views on human responsibility for the environment. Events and features of this museum include programs for use by schools, on-site classes in environmentalism geared for students of all ages, a nature trail, and a bookstore where visitors can buy Carson's classic work, *Silent Spring,* as well as a variety of other helpful books and resources that teach more about Carson and the environmentalist movement. These programs seek not only to give students more information, but also, in the spirit of Carson's essay "The Sense of Wonder," to awaken in children a sense of the majesty and beauty of the natural world.

Those who cannot visit the Homestead in person can use its Internet resources. The Association's Web site (http://www.rachelcarson.org/homestead/educate.html) provides links to a worldwide selection of web pages devoted to environmentalist issues. In addition, visitors to the site can order books and videos, including the educational video "Rachel Carson's Silent Spring."

depends." Carson used her considerable literary skills to bring these scientific concerns to the attention of the general public.

In detailed, well-documented accounts, *Silent Spring* revealed the vested interest of a chemical industry that marketed the effectiveness of a product designed to destroy pests without any reference to the irrevocable changes that would be wrought in the pest habitat. She emphasized that the ecology of the soil had essentially been ignored in the rush to apply chemical solutions to pest problems, as if the soil would remain unaffected by the poisons being poured onto it and channeled into it by affected insects. Carson also noted that it was well documented that some pests could and did develop resilience to the pesticides requiring ever more powerful pesticides resulting in an escalating toxic spiral.

On publication, *Silent Spring* received much adverse criticism. The chemical industry united against Carson accusing her of ignorance, sensationalism, and distortion. There was even an attempt to convince her publisher that the book should not be published. More balanced reviews appeared in the scientific press, including one in *Scientific American* that suggested that *Silent Spring* "may help us toward a much needed reappraisal of current policies and practices." Acceptance by the establishment was not long delayed. A 1963 report by the President's Science Advisory Committee was reviewed by the journal *Science* as "a fairly thorough-going vindication of Rachel Carson's *Silent Spring* thesis." ◆

# Châtelet, Marquise du

DECEMBER 17, 1706–SEPTEMBER 10, 1749 ● MATHEMATICIAN

The Marquise du Châtelet was born Gabrielle-Émilie Le Tonnelier de Breteuil in Paris, France. She was a member of a noble family at a time when a girl in her station in life was trained primarily in the art of attracting a suitable husband. During her childhood, though, she showed promise in academics and defied convention by persuading her father to provide her with an education. She mastered Latin and Italian by age 12 and later added English. She also studied such writers as Tasso, Virgil, and Milton. While she showed talent in languages, her first love was mathematics, a pursuit in which she was encouraged by Monsieur de Mezieres, a family friend who recognized her talent in that field.

Despite her interest in education—and despite her unusual height and physical awkwardness—Émilie had a passionate, romantic nature and never lacked for suitors. At age 19, she married the 34-year-old Marquis du Châtelet, the governor of Semur-en-Auxois, and she gave birth to three children. Her husband, though, pursued a military career and saw his wife only infrequently throughout the rest of her life. She filled the void he left by maintaining an active social life at court, including several affairs (she tried to commit suicide after the first ended), and by continuing her study of mathematics.

At various times she employed well-known tutors, including Pierre-Louis de Maupertuis, an important mathematician and astronomer, and Samuel Koenig. She was so stubborn and posed such difficult, unanswerable questions that she managed to drive her tutors away; a dispute with Koenig about the nature of the infinitely small was so intense that it actually ended their friendship.

In 1733, du Châtelet met and embarked on a long-standing affair with Voltaire, the author of *Candide* and perhaps the

**1706** du Châtelet is born in Paris, France.

**1733** du Châtelet begins a relationship with Voltaire.

**1740** du Châtelet publishes a commentary on the mathematics of Leibniz.

**1745** du Châtelet begins a translation of Newton's *Principia mathematica*.

**1749** du Châtelet dies in Lunéville, France.

**1756** du Châtelet's translation of Newton is published posthumously.

foremost writer and philosopher in France at that time. Voltaire was in the forefront of the intellectual winds sweeping across Europe that gave the era its name—the Enlightenment, or the Age of Reason. Like many thinkers of the day, Voltaire had a profound distrust of religion, believing that science and rational thought, not religious faith, held the key to human progress.

Voltaire's views, though, often placed him at odds with civil and religious authorities. After the publication of his radical book *Lettres philosophiques* in 1734, he faced an arrest warrant, so he fled Paris to northern France and du Châtelet's chateau in Cirey, accompanied by the marquise and her 200 pieces of luggage. There the couple, free from the distractions of Paris, pursued their scientific studies, often independently, often in a shared laboratory. In the meantime, the marquise used her influence to get Voltaire a reprieve.

At Cirey, the marquise was at first interested in the work of the German philosopher and mathematician Gottfried Wilhelm Leibniz, whose philosophical optimism Voltaire satirized in *Candide*. In 1740 she published an explanation of part of his mathematical system in a book entitled *Institutions de physique*. In 1738 she and Voltaire competed independently for a prize from the French Academy of Sciences for an essay on the nature of fire; she worked on her treatise in secret because her ideas were in opposition to those of Voltaire. Neither won the prize, but in 1744 her *Dissertation sur la nature et la propagation du feu* was published by the academy at its own expense. During this period she wrote several other scientific treatises. She studied intensely, yet still maintained her love of society; a servant who worked at her chateau remarked, "Mme du Châtelet passed the greater part of the morning with her writings, and did not like to be disturbed. When she stopped work, however, she did not seem to be the same woman. The serious air gave place to gaiety and she gave herself up with the greatest enthusiasm to the delights of the society." She often said that the only pleasures that remained for a woman when she is old are study, gambling, and greed.

The Marquise du Châtelet is best known for her French translation of Sir Isaac Newton's *Philosophiae naturalis principia mathematica* (usually shortened to *Principia mathematica*). Newton, who had died in 1727, was perhaps the most influential scientist of the 17th century. In the *Principia mathematica* he formulated the law of gravitation—conceived, legend has it, while he was sitting under an apple tree and watching an apple fall—and showed that it explained celestial motions, the tides, and celestial gravitation. He also developed calculus, invented the reflecting telescope, and, using prisms, discovered that white light is a combination of all colors. Du Châtelet had long been fascinated by his work, and starting in 1745 she devoted herself to bringing the *Principia* to French-speaking readers.

Although du Châtelet worked tirelessly on her translation of Newton, she still found time to begin an affair with the Marquis de Saint-Lambert, a courtier and minor poet. She carried on the affair while still living with Voltaire, who helped her conceal the relationship from her husband, even after she became pregnant with Saint-Lambert's child. In September of 1749 she gave birth to a girl while working at her writing desk at the home of the Duke of Lorraine. Voltaire reported that she set the infant on a geometry book while she gathered her papers before going to bed. She seemed healthy, but on September 10 she suddenly died; the baby died a few days later.

Her translation of the *Principia mathematica*, with a preface by Voltaire and her own "algebraical commentary," was published after her death (1756–59) under the direction of the French mathematician Alexis-Claude Clairaut, another of her tutors, and for many years was the only French translation of the work. ◆

> "She translated easily the mathematical terms; the numbers, the extravagances, nothing stopped her. Is not that really astonishing?"
>
> Mme. de Graffigny, describing the Marquise du Châtelet's oral reading of a Latin geometry book at Cirey

# Clark, Eugenie

MAY 4, 1922– ● ZOOLOGIST

Eugenie Clark, a zoologist specializing in ichthyology, or the study of fish, was the daughter of Charles Clark, a barber, and Yumico Mitomi. She was born on May 4, 1922 in New York City. Her father died when she was two. At times Clark's mother earned money as a swimming instructor, and as a young girl Clark admired her mother's graceful movement in the water.

Perhaps as a result of her time spent around the water, Clark became interested in fish at an early age. When Yumico obtained a job in lower Manhattan, she left her daughter off at the city's aquarium, which was then near the Battery at the island's southern tip. "I pressed my face as close as possible to the

glass and pretended I was walking on the bottom of the sea," she recalled later. Clark persuaded her mother to buy her an aquarium as a Christmas present, and soon she had quite a collection of fish; later she added an alligator and a snake to her animal collection.

Entering Hunter College in Manhattan in the late 1930s, Clark majored in zoology and graduated with a bachelor of arts degree in 1942. That year she married pilot Hideo Umaki, the first of her four husbands. From 1942 to 1946, Clark worked nights in a plastics factory in Newark, New Jersey, that was owned by the Celanese Corporation. During the day she did graduate studies at New York University, specializing in the puffing mechanism of the blowfish; she obtained her master of science degree there in 1946.

In 1947 Clark served as a research assistant at the Scripps Institute of Oceanography at the University of California at La Jolla. There, she began her career as a diver, starting with a helmet but then using a face mask to give herself more freedom. Subsequently, in her work she would use submersibles, or small underwater craft, and remote operated vehicles (ROVs). In 1948 and 1949 Clark was a research assistant at the American Museum of Natural History in New York City. Meanwhile, she was working toward a Ph.D. in zoology at New York University. Her doctoral project, backed by the New York Zoological Society, was a study of the reproductive behavior of platies (a type of fish) and swordtail fish and involved the first successful attempt in the United States to artificially inseminate fish. She was awarded her Ph.D. in 1950.

In 1949 Clark went to the South Seas on behalf of the U.S. Office of Naval Research to study poisonous fish. The visit included Guam, Saipan, the Palaus, Kwajalein, and other islands in the vicinity. With the help of indigenous fishermen, she learned underwater spear fishing and collected many types of poisonous fish. The following year, she obtained a Fulbright Scholarship to work at the Ghardaqa Biological Station in Egypt. Her mission, which was on behalf of a U.S. Navy research project at the School of Tropical Medicine at Loma Linda, California, was to gather specimens of puffers, or blowfish, a family of highly poisonous fish. She was stationed at the Red Sea, where she would do much of her research during the following decades.

In 1955 Clark became the first executive director of the new Cape Haze Marine Laboratory in Placida, Florida, which, thanks to her, became a highly regarded center for research on sharks. She herself became known as the "shark lady" because the study of that class of fish became one of her major interests. Her studies of sharks began when she tested their intelligence by training them to press a target to obtain food; Clark found them to be more intelligent than previously throught. Later, Clark studied their ability to distinguish visually among targets of various shapes and colors.

During the 1990s she used submersible vehicles to study shark behavior at depths from 1,000 to 12,000 feet. In addition, during that decade Clark studied the behavior, movement, and population density of various large deep-sea fish off Grand Cayman Island, Bermuda, the Bahamas, California, and Japan. In those years she also examined the reproductive behavior, territoriality, and ecology of tropical sand-dwelling fishes of Papua New Guinea, the Red Sea, and the Caribbean.

Clark has stated that "There is little point to traveling around the world and learning new things about fishes in far-off places, if you don't make your findings available for the possible use by others." She did just that, both for scientific audiences and the general public.

Leaving the Cape Haze Marine Laboratory, Clark became an associate professor of biology at the City University of New York in 1966 and 1967. Clark served as an associate professor of biology at the University of Maryland from 1968 to 1973 and as full professor from 1973 to 1992. By the year 2000 she had lectured to scientific and general audiences at over 70 colleges and universities in the United States, as well as in more than 20 foreign countries, including China, Israel, England, Mexico, India, and New Zealand.

In addition to scores of papers in professional journals, Clark wrote extensively for a general audience in magazines including *National Geographic* and *Natural History*. She also authored two popular book-length accounts of her research: *Lady with a Spear* (1953), which became a Book of the Month Club selection, and *The Lady and the Sharks* (1969). Clark was the narrator and or consultant for various film documentaries, including *The Sharks* (1982), a National Geographic special on public television; *Reefwatch, Live from the Red Sea* (1988); and *The Great Sharks* (1993), an IMAX film.

As of the end of the 20th century, Clark had been granted three fellowships and four scholarships. She had also won six medals, including the gold medal of the Society of Women

**"Whenever I swim in deep open water, I keep glancing around through my face mask with a mingled feeling of fear and hope. I don't want to miss seeing it if a large shark should be cruising nearby."**

Eugenie Clark, quoted in *Lady with a Spear*, 1953

Geographers and the President's Medal of the University of Maryland, plus more than 30 additional awards in marine biology. In addition, Clark had the honor of having four fishes named after her in the 1970s and 1980s.

In 1992 Clark became professor *emerita* at the University of America, but she remained there as a researcher and lecturer. In December 1999, however, she announced that she had given her last lecture there and that she would be doing research at the Mote Marine Laboratory in Sarasota, Florida; the lab was, in fact, the old Cape Haze Marine Laboratory in a new location and with a new name. In 1998 she said: "I plan to keep on diving and researching and conserving until I'm at least 90 years old." ◆

**emerita:** a female professor retired from professional work yet continuing to hold this rank as an honorary title.

# Clark, Mamie Phipps

OCTOBER 18, 1917–AUGUST 11, 1983 ● PSYCHOLOGIST

Mamie Clark was born Mamie Katherine Phipps, one of two children of Harold H. Phipps, a physician in Hot Springs, Arkansas, and Katie Smith Phipps, and grew up amid an extended family she would recall as warm and protective. She completed her secondary education at Langston High School in 1934, at the height of the Great Depression, but her prospects for attending college were slight, particularly in view of discrimination in admissions against African Americans by southern universities. With the assistance of a scholarship, however, she was able to travel to Washington, D.C., to attend Howard University, where she intended to major in mathematics.

At Howard she met Kenneth Bancroft Clark, a graduate student and her future husband. It was he who first raised the possibility that she might pursue a career in psychology at Howard, where, under the leadership of Francis Cecil Sumner, the Department of Psychology was the leading undergraduate program for black students in this field. Switching majors, Clark performed part-time work in the department and also engaged in research with Max Meenes. In 1938 she graduated with a B.A. degree in psychology, magna cum laude. On April 14th of that year, she married Kenneth Clark, who by this time

Additional research Clark conducted with her husband made it clear that African American children were aware of their racial identity at a very early age and were acquiring a negative self-image.

was at Columbia University, where he would earn a Ph.D. in psychology in 1940, the first African American ever to do so. The couple had two children.

Remaining at Howard to do her master's work, Clark became involved in discussions with Ruth and Eugene L. Hartley that led to her thesis, *The Development of Consciousness of Self in Negro Pre-School Children.* She was awarded her master's in psychology in 1939. Together with her husband, she developed a coloring test and a doll test of racial self-identification and submitted a proposal for funding to extend her master's research to the Julius Rosenwald Foundation, which was striving to encourage all-white colleges and universities to hire African Americans as professors.

The financial support she received from the Rosenwald Foundation enabled her to pursue her Ph.D. at Columbia, and in 1940 she became the only black student and one of only two women in the doctoral program in psychology. Her major adviser was Henry E. Garrett, a future president of the American Psychological Association who was a vigorous opponent of efforts to end the segregation of public schools. Nevertheless, under his supervision Clark completed her dissertation on the development of primary mental abilities in children, and in 1943 she became the second black person to earn a Ph.D. in psychology from Columbia.

In the mid-1940s, Clark began to conduct psychological testing at the Riverdale Home for Children, a private agency in New York City for black homeless girls, an experience that made her keenly aware of the lack of availability of psychological services for minority children in New York. To change this, in 1946 she and her husband established the Northside Center for Child Development, the first full-time child-guidance center offering psychological, psychiatric, and casework services for children and families in Harlem.

The Northside Center soon became involved in the psychological testing of minority and deprived children in the New York City public schools. Illegally, and often without parental permission, these children were being shifted into classes for the mentally retarded. Testing showed that many were above the intelligence level for such placement, and they were eventually returned to their normal classes. Thus the Northside Center quickly developed an activist and advocacy role in support of disadvantaged children. Psychological and psychiatric

**1917** Clark is born in Hot Springs, Arkansas.

**1938** Clark marries Kenneth Bancroft Clark.

**1943** Clark becomes the second African American to complete the Ph.D. program at Columbia University.

**1946** Clark and her husband found the Northside Center for Child Development.

**1954** Clark's work on racial identity and self-esteem play an important part in the landmark Supreme Court case, *Brown v. Board of Education of Topeka*, which ended desegregation in the schools.

**1980** Clark retires from her work as a psychologist.

**1983** Clark dies from cancer.

Clark's research
on racial identity
and self-esteem
in African
American chil-
dren played a
major role in the
Supreme Court's
1954 decision in
*Brown v. Board of
Education of
Topeka, Kansas.*

services were soon supplemented with a remedial reading and arithmetic program, a remarkable innovation for a mental health clinic in the 1940s.

Additional research she conducted with her husband made it clear that African American children were aware of their racial identity at a very early age and were acquiring a negative self-image. Her research on racial identity and self-esteem was described in "Racial Identification and Preference in Negro Children," in *Readings in Social Psychology* (1947), and in "Emotional Factors in Racial Identification and Preference in Negro Children," which appeared in the *Journal of Negro Education* in 1950. Both articles were cowritten with her husband. These research findings were cited in expert testimony in school desegregation cases in South Carolina, Delaware, and Virginia.

Clark's research on racial identity and self-esteem in African American children played a major role in the Supreme Court's 1954 decision in *Brown v. Board of Education of Topeka, Kansas,* which overturned legal segregation in U.S. public schools. Her research findings were part of a summary prepared by a group of prominent social scientists, including Gordon Allport, Kenneth Clark, and Otto Klineberg, of the negative effects upon children of racial segregation. This summary was submitted to the Supreme Court by Robert Carter, Thurgood Marshall, and other lawyers working with the National Association for the Advancement of Colored People, whose strategy was in part to demonstrate that segregation had detrimental effects on personality.

In the court's decision there was a summary description of Clark's 1947 and 1950 research findings: "To separate [children] from others of similar age and qualifications solely because of their race generates a feeling of inferiority as to their status in the community that may affect their hearts and minds in a way unlikely ever to be undone." The decision was noteworthy for being one of the first Supreme Court cases in which the decision was grounded in large part upon psychological arguments and evidence from psychological research.

In the years following the *Brown* decision, Clark became an influential voice in both academic and social policy circles. Between 1958 and 1960, she was a visiting professor of experimental methods and research design at Yeshiva University in New York City. As executive director of the Northside Center, she helped bring about construction in the 1960s of Schomburg Plaza in Harlem, which included housing for 600 families.

Clark also served as the first woman trustee of Union Dime Savings Bank; as a member of several advisory groups, including Harlem Youth Opportunities Unlimited and the National Headstart Planning Committee; and on the boards of Teachers College at Columbia University, the American Broadcasting Company, the New York Public Library, the Museum of Modern Art, the New York Mission Society, and the Phelps Stokes Fund. In 1957, Howard University presented Clark with its Alumni Achievement Award. In 1972, Williams College awarded her an honorary Doctor of Humane Letters degree. Clark was a member of Phi Beta Kappa, the American Psychological Association, and a fellow of the American Association of Orthopsychiatry. She retired in 1980 and died of cancer three years later.

During the course of her life, Clark was able to move from childhood in a small, segregated southern town to positions of visibility within the profession of psychology and of leadership within the New York metropolitan area. Living at a time of extraordinary changes in the status of women and minorities within American society, Clark both reflected those changes in her own life and, through her scholarship and social activism, did much to reinforce and accelerate those changes. ◆

# Clarke, Edith

FEBRUARY 10, 1883–OCTOBER 29, 1959 ● ELECTRICAL ENGINEER

Edith Clarke, one of the most prominent electrical engineers of the early 20th century, was late in coming to the field. She was born and raised on a farm in Howard County, Maryland, where she passed much of her time reading, playing tennis, swimming, and becoming a crack shot with a rifle. As a child she did not particularly enjoy school, and she described herself as lazy. She did, however, have a remarkable memory and showed an aptitude for mathematics—an aptitude that served her well in one of her lifelong passions, whist (a card game similar to bridge).

Using an inheritance to pay tuition, at age 18 Clarke enrolled at Vassar College in New York to study mathematics and astronomy. After graduating with honors and as a Phi Beta Kappa in 1908, she taught mathematics at a private girls'

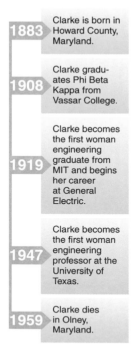

**1883** Clarke is born in Howard County, Maryland.

**1908** Clarke graduates Phi Beta Kappa from Vassar College.

**1919** Clarke becomes the first woman engineering graduate from MIT and begins her career at General Electric.

**1947** Clarke becomes the first woman engineering professor at the University of Texas.

**1959** Clarke dies in Olney, Maryland.

school in San Francisco, then at Marshall University in West Virginia. Teaching, however, did not satisfy her, so in 1911 she enrolled in civil engineering courses at the University of Wisconsin in Madison.

After her first year at Wisconsin, Clarke accepted a summer position with the American Telephone and Telegraph company (AT&T). At that time, people did not have calculators or computers, and skilled mathematicians—like Clarke—who were employed by companies like AT&T to do the time-consuming task of performing mathematical calculations were called "computers." Clarke found the work at least as interesting and as challenging as whist, so she stayed at AT&T for six years as a computer under Dr. George Campbell, a research engineer. She was so good at the job that she trained other computers, and in 1915 she was put in charge of calculations in the company's transmission and distribution department.

In the spring of 1918, Clarke enrolled in the master's degree program at the Massachusetts Institute of Technology (MIT). In 1919 she became the first woman to receive a degree in electrical engineering from that school, and eventually she became one of the few professional engineers licensed by the state of New York. Upon her graduation she accepted a position with General Electric (GE), where she remained for more than 20 years and made her most important contributions to the field of electrical engineering.

In the 1920s, power transmission systems were becoming more complex and power transmission lines were becoming longer as the nation's energy needs grew. Because the systems were carrying ever-increasing electrical loads, the chances for instability and failure were greater. Unfortunately, the mathematical models available at the time for running the systems were becoming outdated, for they applied to smaller systems.

In response to that deficiency, Clarke used a mathematical technique called the method of symmetrical components to model the way power systems should behave. Her work, as head of a group of computers in the turbine engineering department at GE, allowed her and other engineers to analyze systems and solve transmission line problems. In 1921 Clarke applied for a patent for a "graphical calculator" that would make this job easier. Clarke was thus a pioneer in the development of so-called electromechanical aids to aid in complex computing, an effort that eventually led to the development of modern, non-human computers.

In 1921 Clarke took a leave from GE and accepted a position as professor of physics at the U.S.-founded Constantinople Women's College in Turkey. When she returned to GE in 1922, she was officially designated an engineer and assigned to the company's central station engineering department. In 1923 she published her first paper, entitled "Transmission Line Calculator," and in 1926 she became the first woman to present a paper (called "Steady-State Stability in Transmission Systems") before the American Institute of Electrical Engineers.

In the years that followed she published many additional papers having to do with power distribution. All these papers shared a reliance on charts, graphs, and similar aids that would relieve other engineers from the laborious task of making calculations themselves. In 1932, her paper "Three-Phase Multiple-Conductor Circuits" was judged the best paper of the year in the American Institute of Electrical Engineers' northeastern district. In 1943 she published the first volume of a textbook, *Circuit Analysis of AC Power Systems, Symmetrical and Related Components*, which became a classic in the field and a standard textbook in engineering schools and colleges. The second volume was published in 1950.

In the meantime, Clarke retired from GE in 1945. She returned to farming in Maryland, but in 1947 she interrupted her retirement to became the first woman professor in the electrical engineering department at the University of Texas—and possibly in the United States. She taught there until her second retirement in 1956. In 1948 she was the first woman to be named a fellow of the American Institute of Electrical Engineers (later called the Institute of Electrical and Electronic Engineers), and in 1954 the Society of Women Engineers recognized her with its Achievement Award. After leaving the University of Texas, Clarke returned to her native Maryland, where she died in Olney in 1959.

In a 1985 paper on Clarke's life, Dr. James E. Brittain commented on the significance of her career: As a woman who worked in an environment traditionally dominated by men, she demonstrated effectively that women could perform at least as well as men if given the opportunity. Her outstanding achievements provided an inspiring example for the next generation of women with aspirations to become career engineers. ◆

"There is no demand for women engineers, as such, as there are for women doctors; but there's always a demand for anyone who can do a good piece of work." Edith Clarke, in an interview with *The Daily Texan*, March 15, 1948

# Cleveland, Emeline Horton

SEPTEMBER 22, 1829–DECEMBER 8, 1878 ● PHYSICIAN

Emeline Horton Cleveland, a physician and a medical educator and administrator, was born on September 22, 1829 in Ashford, Connecticut. She was the third of the nine children of Chauncy Horton and Amanda Chaffe. In 1831 the family moved to an isolated farm in Madison County, New York, where Cleveland and her siblings received their earliest formal education from private instructors who came to the farm. She subsequently went to local schools. Cleveland probably would have gone directly to college, but because of her father's death when she was 19, she had to work as a schoolteacher to earn money for her further education.

In 1850 Cleveland enrolled at Oberlin College in Ohio. She enjoyed studying the classics, but during her time at Oberlin she decided to become a medical missionary. She graduated from Oberlin in 1853 with a bachelor of arts degree. Later that year she entered the Female Medical College (after 1967, it switched "Female" to "Woman's") of Philadelphia, Pennsylvania, where she graduated in 1855 with a medical degree.

Meanwhile, in 1854, she married Giles Butler Cleveland, a Presbyterian minister. The couple had planned to become missionaries, but he suffered health problems that not only made that impossible, but also forced Dr. Cleveland to become the family's sole breadwinner from 1858 onward. Twice then, the death or illness of a male authority figure had forced her to depend on herself.

After graduating from the Female Medical College, Dr. Cleveland began a medical practice back in Madison County. In 1856 she obtained a teaching position as demonstrator of anatomy at her alma mater, the Female Medical College. To supplement her income, she opened up a new private practice in Philadelphia. In 1857 Dr. Cleveland became chair of anatomy and physiology at the college.

With the help of a group of Quaker women interested in establishing a hospital for women and children, Cleveland went abroad on her own in 1860 to do postgraduate work at the School of Obstetrics at the Maternité hospital in Paris. The following year she received a diploma along with five awards. Before returning to the United States, she visited hospital wards and medical colleges in Paris and London to improve her medical knowledge and administrative skills.

In the fall of 1861 Cleveland became chief resident at the new Woman's Hospital of Philadelphia, which was associated with the Female Medical College. She held that post for seven years. During that time she created an innovative program for training nurses' aides, one of the first of its kind. From 1862 Cleveland was also professor of obstetrics and diseases of women and children at the medical college, and in addition conducted a private practice. As if her work responsibilities were not enough, she gave birth to a boy in 1865. Cleveland was known to appear at the hospital or college with the baby on her shoulder, the two of them "beaming brightest smiles each upon the other," according to one observer.

Cleveland worked hard to open Pennsylvania's medical institutions to women. She managed to get hospitals to provide access to her students so they could get a complete medical education, not just in-class training. The Philadelphia County Medical Society ended its exclusion of women in 1869. She herself was admitted to several previously all-male medical societies. Two things explain her success. First, she was highly respected for her medical skills, to the extent that top male doctors consulted with her. Second, she had considerable feminine charm, so that the males in the medical professions felt less threatened than might otherwise have been by a female physician. Still, her efforts were not a total success. The Pennsylvania State Medical Society, for example, rejected her request to repeal its ban on women. Several negative votes blackballed her from the Philadelphia Obstetrical Society.

Cleveland was chosen as dean of the Woman's Medical College in 1872. During her two-year tenure, enrollment increased by 5 percent. Women planning to be surgeons were particularly drawn to the school. The students were encouraged to work as medical missionaries. Cleveland resigned her position in 1874 because of illness.

In 1875 Cleveland apparently became the first woman ever in recorded history to perform a major surgery when she successfully removed ovarian tumors. She went on to perform several more ovariotomies, as the procedure was called. In 1878 she became gynecologist to the department for the insane at Pennsylvania Hospital, one of the first times that a woman physician joined the staff of a public hospital. However, Cleveland's career

**1829** Cleveland is born in Ashford, Connecticut.

**1855** Cleveland graduates from the Female (later Woman's) Medical College of Pennsylvania.

**1861** Cleveland becomes the chief resident at the Women's Hospital of Philadelphia.

**1875** Cleveland apparently becomes the first woman ever in recorded history to perform a major surgery when she successfully removes ovarian tumors.

**1878** Cleveland becomes a gynecologist to the department for the insane at Pennsylvania Hospital, one of the first woman physicians to join the staff of a public hospital.

was cut short when she died of tuberculosis in Philadelphia on December 8, 1878. ◆

# Cobb, Jewell Plummer

JANUARY 17, 1934– ● BIOLOGIST

Jewell Plummer Cobb has spent her life pursuing the advancement of science and the inclusion of women and minorities in the study of science. Coming from an educated family which placed a premium on social consciousness, Cobb has made a significant contribution to science in particular and society in general.

Jewell Plummer Cobb was born on January 17, 1934, in Chicago, Illinois. She was the only child of Frank and Carriebel Plummer. Her father was a Cornell-educated physician who ran his own practice in Chicago. Her mother held a degree in physical education from Sargeants, a college affiliated with Harvard. Carriebel taught dance and physical education in the Chicago public schools, and earned another bachelor's degree from Roosevelt University in 1944. Cobb grew up in a household which stressed the importance of education, culture, and social awareness. Her parents made sure she had access to important books, magazines, and scientific journals, and that they attended cultural events such as the ballet and theater. The Plummers were also active members in the Episcopal Church.

Cobb's exposure to such a wide array of information and art helped her excel in school. Reading all of the scientific books and magazines her parents provided her, she developed a love for biology and enrolled in many college-preparatory courses in a range of sciences, such as zool-

Jewell Plummer Cobb

ogy, chemistry, and botany. Cobb graduated from high school with honors in 1941 and enrolled at the University of Michigan that fall, spending a year there before transferring to Talladega College in Alabama, where she enrolled in an accelerated program and graduated in 1944 with a degree in biology.

Following graduation, Cobb was accepted to a teaching fellowship at New York University, and began work which culminated in a Ph.D. dissertation on cell physiology, which she completed in 1950. That same year, Cobb was awarded a fellowship at the National Cancer Institute, and decided to focus her studies on biology theory, researching the growth of cancerous tumors in tissue cultures. She also studied the impact chemotherapy treatment had on cancer cells, and designed new experiments to study the effects of cells grown in cancer patients using cells that were originally grown in test tubes. In 1952, she took a teaching position with the University of Illinois Medical College and in 1954, she married Roy Cobb. They divorced in 1967, and have a son, Roy Jonathan Cobb, who is now a radiologist.

Cobb returned to New York University in 1955 and, as an assistant professor, did thorough work on cell pigmentation and **melanin**'s influence on skin color. In 1960, Cobb took a job with Sarah Lawrence College as a full professor of biology. She continued her experiments and studies regarding pigmentation and was eventually named dean of the school. Cobb also took on the positions of biology professor and dean at Connecticut College in 1969, where she established scholarship programs for women and minorities who wished to study medicine and dentistry. Cobb saw it as her role to be an advocate for an increased role in science in the elementary and secondary levels for girls, and through her example tried to destroy the assumption that women could not equal or better their male peers in the sciences.

Following a stint at Rutgers University (where today there is a dormitory named in her honor), Cobb accepted the presidency of the California State University at Fullerton in 1981. Cobb soon thrived in her new post, and she managed to work to open a privately funded **gerontology** center on campus. She also lobbied the state government for funds to aid the construction of new engineering and computer science buildings to expose her students to more modern tools. Cobb retired from CSU-Fullerton in 1990, yet continued to serve the school as president

**1924** Cobb is born in Chicago, Illinois.

**1950** Cobb earns her Ph.D. in cell physiology.

**1954** Cobb marries Roy R. Cobb.

**1955** Cobb establishes the Tissue Culture Research Laboratory at the New York University Bellevue Hospital Medical Center.

**1974** Cobb is named a member of the National Science Foundation's National Science Board.

**melanin:** dark brown or black pigmentation in animals and/or plants.

**gerontology:** a scientific branch dedicated to the study of aging and the problems of elderly people.

emeritus and trustee. Cobb's work in her field and tireless efforts to promote the study of science has left a lasting impact. ◆

# Cori, Gerty Radnitz

AUGUST 15, 1896–OCTOBER 26, 1957 ● BIOCHEMIST

> "Gerty Cori could cut you down to shreds if your mind wasn't working right, and her standards were pretty high. But I thought it was wonderful."
> Luis Glaser, a graduate student in the Coris' lab

**B**orn Gerty Theresa Radnitz in Prague, the capital of what is now the Czech Republic, Gerty Cori was the first American woman, and just the third woman worldwide, to win the Nobel Prize in science. She was born to a moderately wealthy Jewish family, and until the age of 10, she was tutored at home. She was then sent to a girls' finishing school, which equipped her with the social graces a woman of her station was expected to display at that time.

An uncle persuaded Cori to attend medical school, but her school did not teach Latin, mathematics, physics, or chemistry, which were required subjects for entry to the university. When she was 16, however, she met a high school teacher who offered to tutor her in Latin; over the summer she mastered three years of Latin, and by the end of the following year she was ready to take the university entrance examinations. She passed, and in 1914, at age 18, she entered the medical college of the University of Prague.

In her first year of medical school, Cori became enamored of both biochemistry and Carl Cori, one of her classmates. The two conducted a six-year-long courtship over their books, and they even published a jointly written paper, beginning a professional collaboration that would span four decades. The Coris completed their medical degrees in 1920, and that same year they were married.

Upon graduation, Cori accepted a position at the Karolinen Children's Hospital in Vienna, Austria, where she published several papers on congenital thyroid deficiency. Carl tried to conduct medical research at the nearby University of Graz, but Austria, like much of Europe after World War I, was in shambles, and he lacked even the most basic equipment and supplies. Further, the Coris were disturbed by the rising tide of anti-Semitism in Europe. They concluded that to ensure Gerty's safety and to conduct the kind of research that interested them, they had to emigrate to the United States.

Gerty Cori (left)
conducts an experiment
as her husband looks on.

In 1922 Carl set sail for the United States, where he had accepted a position at the New York State Institute for the Study of Malignant Diseases in Buffalo, New York. Gerty joined him six months later after Carl secured a position for her as an assistant pathologist. During this period, the Coris had to endure a great deal of bias against women. The University of Rochester had passed up the opportunity to hire the Coris, arguing to Carl that it was "un-American" to want to work with

**1896** Cori is born in Prague, Czechoslovakia.

**1920** Cori earns a medical degree from the University of Prague.

**1929** Cori publishes a basic explanation of the Cori cycle.

**1947** Cori wins the Nobel Prize.

**1957** Cori dies in St. Louis, Missouri.

**glycogen:** a tasteless amorphous white polysaccharide that is the principal form in which animal tissues store carbohydrates.

**glucose:** a sugar which is the usual form in which carbohydrates are assimilated by animals.

**enzymes:** numerous complex proteins produced by living cells which catalyze biochemical reactions at certain body temperatures.

his wife. The New York State Institute threatened to fire Gerty if she did not stay in her own lab and stop working with Carl.

The two quietly ignored the threat and published 50 joint papers, while Gerty published 11 under her own name. To make matters worse, both had to thwart efforts by the director of the institute to put his name on their research papers. Despite these annoyances, though, the Coris remained at the institute for nine years. In 1928 they became American citizens, and in 1931 they moved to Washington University in St. Louis, Missouri, where Carl was appointed professor of pharmacology and biochemistry. Gerty had to wait until 1947 to gain a professorship, but in the meantime the two were at least given freedom to work collaboratively.

The Coris' research, started in Buffalo and continued in St. Louis, had profound implications for biochemists' understanding of how the body converts food into energy and how it stores energy for later use. By studying blood glucose, a complex substance called glycogen, and the hormones that control them, they were finally able to explain these processes. They discovered that energy moves in a cycle from the muscles to the liver and back to the muscles.

When a runner, for example, begins to sprint, **glycogen** in the muscles is broken down into **glucose**, a source of energy. The muscles extract the energy, but they leave some of it behind in the form of lactic acid. The body then sends the lactic acid from the muscles to the liver. As the sprinter breathes heavily to take in more oxygen, the liver converts the lactic acid into sugar, which returns to the muscles, where it is converted back into glycogen for storage. The Coris called the process "the cycle of carbohydrates." The scientific community called it the Cori cycle, the name by which it is still known in standard textbooks.

The Coris published the broad outline of their discovery in 1929; they spent much of the rest of their career filling in the details. Specifically, they studied the enzymes that control the cycle, the hormones that influence it, and the diseases that can develop when one of the **enzymes** is damaged or absent. In 1936 they identified the "Cori ester," the substance that initiates the cycle. In 1943 they were able to synthesize glycogen in the lab.

Their work also had important implications for the study and treatment of diabetes. Although insulin had been discovered in 1921, no one was sure how it worked. The Cori cycle, though, helped scientists understand the relationship between exercise, food, and blood sugar. For their "discovery of how glycogen is catalytically converted," the Coris shared (with a third scientist) the 1947 Nobel Prize for Medicine or Physiology.

During the 1940s and 1950s, the Cori lab was an important center for biochemical research, and hardly a day went by without the lab producing some kind of useful information. One of its enduring legacies was the production of six other Nobel laureates. While Carl was relaxed and easygoing, the chain-smoking Gerty was driven and passionate about her work, and she ran the lab with all the fervor and precision of a general leading troops into battle. She was also admired, though, for her vivacity and sense of humor, and lunches with the Coris featured stimulating discussions not only about science but about books, art, and topics of the day.

In 1947, just weeks before traveling to Stockholm, Sweden, to accept the Nobel Prize, Gerty was diagnosed with a fatal type of anemia. She continued to work for the next 10 years, surviving on frequent blood transfusions and Carl's care. She died on October 26, 1957, at home, with Carl at her side. ◆

# Crosby, Elizabeth Caroline

OCTOBER 25, 1888–JULY 28, 1983 ● NEUROLOGIST

Elizabeth Caroline Crosby was born in Petersburg, Michigan. She enjoyed a normal childhood, with interests in reading, taking piano lessons, working on puzzles, and playing basketball—although some might find her enjoyment of geometry in school outside the norm.

Early on Crosby demonstrated a capacity for sheer hard work. As a high school graduation gift, her father gave her four years of college. She attended Adrian College in Michigan, but she completed her bachelor's degree in mathematics (1910) after just three years because she wanted to save the fourth year to continue her education. She enrolled at the University of Chicago and so impressed Professor C. Judson Herrick that he allowed her to take both his medical school anatomy course and his neuroanatomy course at the same time. Herrick later said that he worried about his hard-working student's health— throughout her life she was small and frail—and tried to lock her out of the lab. His efforts failed, however, for she took her books and slides home with her to continue her work.

*Early on Crosby demonstrated a capacity for sheer hard work.*

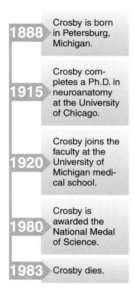

**1888** Crosby is born in Petersburg, Michigan.

**1915** Crosby completes a Ph.D. in neuroanatomy at the University of Chicago.

**1920** Crosby joins the faculty at the University of Michigan medical school.

**1980** Crosby is awarded the National Medal of Science.

**1983** Crosby dies.

**neuroanatomy:** the study of the makeup of the human brain.

After completing her Ph.D. in **neuroanatomy** in 1915, Crosby returned to Petersburg to care for her ailing mother and took a job as superintendent of the local high school. When her mother died in 1918, Crosby decided to apply for a position as a junior instructor at the University of Michigan medical school. She won the job in 1920, and she spent the rest of her distinguished career at Michigan with the exception of a one-year leave (1939–40) to help Marischal College at the University of Aberdeen in Scotland set up a teaching and research department in neuroanatomy.

Always humble about her accomplishments, she professed to be surprised when the university promoted her to assistant professor in 1926, associate professor in 1929, and, in 1936, professor of anatomy; she was the first woman professor in the medical school's history. In an interview she gave late in life, Crosby denied ever feeling discriminated against because she was a woman. She did acknowledge, though, that the men in her department were paid more.

Crosby's research centered on the nervous system of vertebrates. As a graduate student she wrote her thesis on the forebrain of the alligator. She also researched and wrote about the mammalian midbrain, and her work was noteworthy for its wide-ranging reference to many different types of organisms. In 1962 she was the co-author of a textbook on neuroanatomy for medical students and graduate students, and in her later years she collaborated on a reference work on comparative vertebrae neuroanatomy.

As an example of the practical implications of her work, Crosby wrote a paper examining the brain vasculature of an astronaut, discussing tests that could be used to uncover potentially dangerous brain problems in astronaut candidates. Her list of publications on neuroanatomy is seemingly endless. While many researchers were experts on a particular part of the brain or spinal cord, Crosby was known and respected by colleagues for her encyclopedic knowledge and understanding of the entire nervous system of the vertebrate phylum.

Crosby was also a dedicated teacher. During her career it is estimated that she taught neuroanatomy to some 8,500 medical students, and her students usually presented her with a ritual box of roses at the end of her courses. At Michigan she trained 39 students for the Ph.D. program and directed the research of at least 30 postgraduate students. Fifteen of her students went on to become department heads at the University of Michigan.

She earned a reputation as a warm and compassionate teacher who always had time for her students, even when they wanted to discuss personal issues. In 1946 she was the first woman recipient of the university's Henry Russell Lectureship, and from that point on she lectured all over the world—always without notes.

Upon her "retirement" from Michigan in 1958, though, Crosby did not stop working. In fact, she hated the notion of retirement, and at a party given in her honor, guests were urged not to mention the subject to her. She remained at Michigan as a consultant in neurosurgery and simultaneously accepted an appointment as a consultant to the Department of Anatomy at the University of Alabama in Birmingham, usually spending half of each month in each location.

Crosby's association with UAB lasted for nearly 20 years, and during that time she directed the research of a group of scientists studying comparative neurology. She also guided 16 students who earned Ph.D.'s in neuroanatomy. For her many accomplishments she was awarded nine honorary doctorates from such institutions as Marquette University, Smith College, Denison University, and Wayne State University. In 1981 she was the recipient of the National Medical Women's Association Award. Her highest honor came in 1980, when President Jimmy Carter awarded her the National Medal of Science for 1979.

Although she was totally devoted to her work, Crosby maintained an active personal life. She enjoyed detective stories, history, and poetry. She also liked to travel and attend plays. Though she never married, in 1940 she adopted an 11-year-old girl from Scotland, and in 1944 another young girl came to live with them. She provided both girls with an education. At the time of her death in 1983, Crosby was still living with her daughter, and she had five grandchildren and a great-granddaughter. ◆

> "In a world hungry for power, wealth, and status, Elizabeth Caroline Crosby was an anachronism of modesty and self-effacement."
>
> From a press release issued by the University of Alabama at Birmingham, 1987

# Curie, Marie

NOVEMBER 7, 1867–JULY 4, 1934 ● SCIENTIST

Marie Curie was born Marya Sklodowska in Warsaw, Poland, in 1867. At that time, Poland had lost its independence and been annexed to **czarist** Russia. Her father, Wladislaw Sklodowski, had been lucky and had studied

**czarist:** description of a nation or state under the rule of a czar, an autocratic leader or ruler.

Marie Curie

sciences in Russia and was successfully teaching physics and mathematics in Warsaw. Her mother, Bronislava Boguska, managed a boarding school for girls, and the Sklodowski family lived in the same building. Marya was the last of four children—three girls and one boy—and the incomes of her parents were modest. Zozia, the eldest daughter, died in 1876 from typhus, and Bronislava died two years later from tuberculosis.

Sklodowska began her studies in a public school in Warsaw and she succeeded brilliantly. She finished her secondary school in 1883 but, very tired, she spent the following year in the country, living with a peasant family. Back in Warsaw in 1884, she began to follow some lectures at a traveling university and was attracted by the positivist ideas of Auguste Comte in France. Her experiences changed her life, as she lost her mother's religious faith and brought her ideals to science.

Sklodowska lived in close relation with her sister Bronia, who was three years older and who earned her living by giving lessons to children. Bronia wanted to become a doctor and she wished to go to Paris to study. Sklodowska decided to help her sister by sending her money that she earned by becoming a private teacher. She worked first for a Warsaw family and, one year later, she left for the country to enter the service of a landowner's family. Three years later she returned to Warsaw and lived there with her father. Bronia, who was finally studying in Paris, announced her marriage in 1890 and insisted that her sister come to Paris to be with her. Bronia promised to assist with Marya's lodging.

Sklodowska hesitated for a while but finally decided to go to Paris to study physics at the Sorbonne, arriving and enrolling in classes in September 1891. She lived first with her sister and her brother-in-law, but she later found an independent room nearer the Sorbonne.

**Female Nobel Laureates**

The Nobel Prize, perhaps the best-known series of prizes in the world, were established according to the will of Alfred Nobel (1833–1896), the Swedish inventor of dynamite and dozens of other innovations. The prizes are awarded annually in six categories: peace, literature, physics, chemistry, physiology/medicine, and economics; the economics award was added in 1968. It is not known why Nobel excluded mathematics from his list, though as an inventor he may have regarded mathematics as too abstract and impractical. The gold-plated medals were designed by Erik Lindberg (the three science medals and the literature medal), Gustav Vigeland (the peace medal), and Gunvor Svensson-Lundqvist (the economics medal). Excellent photographs of the medals can be viewed at http://www .nobel.se/prize/medal.html. The prizes for economics, physics, and chemistry are awarded by the Royal Swedish Academy of Sciences; the Nobel Assembly at the Karolinska Institute in Stockholm administers physiology/medicine; the literature prize is awarded by the Swedish Academy in Stockholm; and the peace prize, which is perhaps the most famous of the awards, by a select committee.

Marie Curie was the first woman to win a Nobel Prize in one of the science categories, and the only woman to win two awards. There have been two women Nobel laureates in physics (Curie, 1903, and Maria Goeppert-Mayer, 1963) and three in chemistry (Curie, 1911, Irène Joliot-Curie, 1935, and Dorothy Crowfoot Hodgkin, 1964). Six women have won the prize for physiology and medicine, including: Gerty Radnitz Cori, 1947, for her study of the catalytic conversion of glycogen; Rosalyn Sussman Yalow, 1997, for the development of radioimmunoassays of peptide hormones; Barbara McClintock, 1983, for her discovery of mobile genetic elements; Rita Levi-Montalcini, 1986, for the discovery of growth factors; Gertrude Elion, 1988, for her work on principles for drug treatment; and Christiane Nüsslein-Volhard, 1995, for her study of the role of genes in early embryo development.

Despite some difficulties with the language, Sklodowska clung to her studies. **Obstinate** and clever, she succeeded in her enterprise by working hard, although she lived in relative poverty. In July 1893 she received a bachelor's degree in physics from the Sorbonne. In July 1894 she also received one in mathematics.

**obstinate:** stubborn, not easily dissuaded.

Marya, who was by then known as Marie, Sklodowska met Pierre Curie for the first time in 1894 at a friend's home. Seven years older than Marie, Curie was already well known in scientific circles. With his brother Jacques, he had discovered piezoelectricity around 1880. He had developed a piezoelectric quartz crystal, able to detect and measure very weak electric currents (~ $10^{-12}$ A). In 1882, before he was 25, he became a lecture demonstrator at the *Ecole de Physique et de Chimie Industrielle de Paris* (Paris School of Physics and Chemistry).

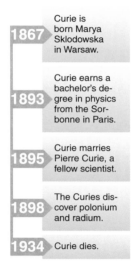

**1867** Curie is born Marya Sklodowska in Warsaw.

**1893** Curie earns a bachelor's degree in physics from the Sorbonne in Paris.

**1895** Curie marries Pierre Curie, a fellow scientist.

**1898** The Curies discover polonium and radium.

**1934** Curie dies.

Sklodowska and Pierre had the same passion for science and they were attracted to each other. They married in July 1895. From that marriage, three girls were born. Irène in 1897, a baby in 1903 who lived only a few hours, and Eve in 1904. Irène with her husband Frédéric Joliot discovered artificial radioactivity in 1934. Eve worked in journalism.

Upon completion of her academic studies, the new Mrs. Curie began to work on magnetism in the laboratory of Gabriel Lippman, her professor of physics. Her husband succeeded in obtaining for her the possibility of working at the *Ecole de Physique et de Chimie* (School of Physics and Chemistry), where he was now a professor. Marie Sklodowska Curie published her first paper at the end of 1897.

Meanwhile, at the beginning of 1896. Henri Becquerel had discovered the existence of new rays emitted by uranium salts that he named "uranic rays." This was the discovery of radioactivity. This completely new subject attracted Curie's attention, and she decided, on the advice of her husband, to study this new property of matter.

Curie decided to investigate salts and minerals she obtained from various laboratories. The powder to be examined was set on a metallic plate connected to an electric potential of 100 V. Facing this plate was another metallic plate, connected to an electrometer controlled by the piezoelectric quartz crystal invented by Pierre Curie. This apparatus played the role of an ionization chamber activated by rays emitted by the substance to be studied. She verified the radioactivity of uranium salts, and she discovered the same property for other substances, namely, for thorium compounds. In her publication of April 1898, she noted that thorium and uranium were the two elements having the biggest atomic masses known at that time. However, she also noted that two uranium minerals under examination were more active than uranium itself. This fact lead her to the belief that the minerals might contain an element that was more active than uranium.

From that time on, Pierre Curie joined his wife in trying to isolate this postulated new element. Their common work led to the discovery of two new radioactive substances. The first, which they named polonium in remembrance of Marie's native country, was brought to the attention of the Academy of Sciences on July 18, 1898; the second was called radium and was brought forward on December 26, 1898, in a note to the Academy of Sciences.

The technique the couple used consisted of submitting the compound to be studied to various chemical treatments so as to obtain a stronger radioactivity for the resulting product. The new elements were not isolated, but **polonium** was expected to have chemical properties similar to those of **bismuth**, and radium similar to those of **barium**.

Even though small, the quantity of radium present seemed to be greater than that of polonium, but more ore was necessary to isolate radium. After various researches, the Curies received, at the end of 1898, 100 kg of a residue of pitchblend from a factory in Czechoslovakia that extracted uranium from that ore. The residue seemed promising and the Curies arranged to buy about one ton of the ore at a low price.

The Curie's hard work had just begun. After four years of very hard work extracting the ore, in 1902 about 0.1 gram (g) of radium chloride was isolated with great purity after numerous operations, notably fractional crystallizations. By **dosimetry** of the radium chloride, Marie Curie determined an atomic mass of radium of 225, with a precision of about 1 unit. In 1907, radium was extracted by industrial means and Marie Curie obtained a sample of 0.4 g of pure radium chloride. She then published an atomic mass for radium of 226.2 " 0.5. Radium is now known as the element $_{88}Ra^{226}$.

The discovery of radium brought international fame to the Curies. In 1900 Marie Curie was appointed as lecturer at the *Ecole Normale Supérieure des jeunes filles de Sèvres* (a college of education for young women) near Paris. In May 1903, she defended her doctoral thesis in which she described her work in isolating radium. That same year, Marie and Pierre shared the Nobel Prize in Physics with Henri Becquerel for the discovery of radioactivity. In 1904, Pierre Curie was appointed full professor in the Faculty of Sciences of Paris, and a little later Marie was made responsible for students' practical work in physics for this chair.

After the discovery of radium, Pierre Curie took great interest in the study of its physiological effects. With two medical doctors, he participated in the first attempts to treat cancer by radium. Unfortunately, in April 1906 Pierre was struck down by the horses of a carriage and thrown under the wheels of the vehicle. Marie Curie suffered a severe shock. However, obstinate and determined as she was, she managed to face this adversity and decided to continue her research work. Until then,

The discovery of radium brought international fame to the Curies.

**polonium:** radioactive metallic element, emitting a helium nucleus to form an isotope of lead.

**bismuth:** a heavy, brittle metallic element that resembles arsenic chemically; used in pharmaceuticals and alloys.

**barium:** a metallic element of the alkaline-earth group; occurs only in a combination with other elements.

**dosimetry:** measurement of a dosage of radiation.

Marie Curie was the first scientist to obtain the Nobel Prize twice, an extraordinary honor.

honors seemed to have been reserved for her husband but, in May 1906, to replace her deceased husband, she was appointed as a physics lecturer in the Faculty of Sciences in Paris and she became full professor in 1908.

In August 1906 Lord Kelvin, at the age of 82, published an article in which he doubted the reality of radium. Even if this idea was not taken seriously by specialists, Marie Curie was offended by it and decided to isolate "her radium" as a pure metal. With André Debierne, a devoted chemist, she decided to proceed by electrolysis of radium chloride. She overcame numerous difficulties and succeeded in her enterprise, determining in particular the melting point of radium. In 1911 she was awarded the Nobel Prize in Chemistry for her work on radium. Marie Curie was the first scientist to obtain the Nobel Prize twice, an extraordinary honor.

After her husband's death, Curie experienced terrible times on two occasions. In 1911, she was encouraged to become a candidate for the Academy of Sciences, to which her husband had belonged. However, she lost the election by just one vote in January 1911 to radio receiver inventor Edouard Branly. While losing was bad enough, Curie also had to endure some harsh and unfair remarks made by members about her, which affected her deeply. She never ran for election again.

Also in 1911, some reporters learned that Curie was possibly seeing Paul Langevin, a renowned physicist and former student of Pierre Curie. This was probably true as Langevin had an unpleasant relationship with his wife. Reporters found or received some compromising letters written by Curie to Langevin, published them in newspapers, and the scandal burst out. It was maintained by the press: "Out foreigner!" was the cry in the street near her home. The rumors came to a stop when Langevin was divorced in late 1911 without any mention of Curie. Still, Curie broke off her relationship with Langevin and lived alone until her death.

Despite these events, Curie enjoyed a generally excellent reputation in France. Before receiving her 1911 Nobel Prize, she had obtained from the Sorbonne and the government funds for building a new Radium Institute containing a physics laboratory, directed by herself, and a biology laboratory to study the biological effects of radioactive substances.

The construction of the Radium Institute had just been finished when World War I began in August 1914; scientific research stopped in civilian laboratories. Curie decided to contribute to the war effort. Ten days after the declaration of war, the Ministry of Defense officially asked Curie to set up operator teams for x-ray radiology services. Her idea was to take care of wounded soldiers. She succeeded in buying cars and equipping them with radiological instruments. With a driver, a surgeon, and two assistants, she undertook a first test near Paris. One of her assistants was Irène Curie, age 17, who wanted to devote herself to this task. Wounded soldiers were examined with x-rays to detect the presence of bullets or shell splinters in the body. During the four years of war, Marie and Irène were occupied with that task. In 1916, Curie began to train new assistants at the Radium Institute, which was then empty. In all, some 200 cars were equipped and about one million soldiers were examined in different hospitals.

After the war, Curie returned to her new laboratory at the Radium Institute, equipped it and resumed research on radioactivity. She trained new research workers, among them her daughter Irène, who submitted her doctoral thesis in 1925. Curie was by now very well known. In 1920, near the Radium Institute, the construction of a hospital for cancer treatment was started. It was called "Fondation Curie." In 1920 Curie was visited by an American journalist, Marie (Missy) Meloney, who proposed to undertake a campaign in the United States to collect some $10,000, the sum necessary to buy 1 g of radium, to be offered to Curie. Meloney asked, in case she was successful, that Curie promise to go to the United States to receive this radium in person. Meloney herself would be in charge of the official reception.

Thus, in 1921, Curie boarded a ship for the United States with her two daughters, Irène and Eve. As soon as she landed in New York, she was received with great enthusiasm by journalists. She was rather terrified as she disliked public honors. However, she had to attend numerous official receptions, and she finally received front the hands of President Warren Harding the gift of radium. By temperament, Curie was suspicious. In her discussions with Meloney, she asked to receive an official document specifying that this radium was given to herself for the needs of her laboratory.

Since the heroic epoch of radium separation, Curie had had health problems from time to time owing to the toxic effects of radioactive substances. Nevertheless, she was an attentive director of her laboratory. She followed with great care the work of her assistants and nothing was decided without her

*After the war, Curie returned to her new laboratory at the Radium Institute, equipped it and resumed research on radioactivity.*

authorization. Concerning her personal work, she had become an experienced chemist and was devoted in particular to the preparation of various radioactive sources. Thus, at the time, her laboratory had the most intense sources of various radioactive substances in the world. A number of researchers began their work in her laboratory and some of them, such as Solomon Rosenblum and Frédéric Joliot, became renowned as scientists.

In 1932, Curie was obliged to take a rest after a fall, and in June 1934, she had to leave her laboratory and was hospitalized. Doctors believed that she suffered from tuberculosis and sent her to a sanatorium in the Alps. There, leukemia was detected, and Curie died on July 4. For succeeding generations, she was an eminent figure of science and a model personality. Starting from nothing, she had become a successful scientist, owing to her intelligence, her energy, and her tenacity. ◆

# Deutsch, Helene Rosenbach

OCTOBER 9, 1884–MARCH 29, 1982 ● PSYCHOANALYST

Raised in what was then the Polish part of the Austro-Hungarian Empire, Helene Deutsch was one of four children born to Wilhelm Rosenbach and Regina Fass. She was the favorite of her father, a prominent Jewish lawyer who often took her with him to court. In later years she would attribute her thriving professional life to her identification with her father. In contrast, Deutsch openly despised her mother, a homemaker who, she claimed, beat her and thwarted her scholarly aspirations. Although she grew up in relative luxury, Deutsch was often isolated and unhappy, deriving much of her companionship and support from her father and an older sister.

As a teenager Deutsch was active in the socialist movement, even attempting at one point to join the Polish Worker's Party. At 16 she met Herman Lieberman, a man who would become the center of her emotional life for many years. "Our love," she wrote in her autobiography, "was full of passion, happiness, and tragedy." Sixteen years her senior, Lieberman was a charismatic leader in the Social Democratic party; he had children and a wife who would not divorce him. Deutsch's affair enraged her mother, who plotted with Lieberman's wife to break up the relationship. In 1907 Deutsch left Poland to study medicine in Vienna. Lieberman, who was elected a delegate to Parliament that spring, would spend much of his political life in that same city.

**1884** Deutsch is born Helene Rosenbach in Poland.

**1907** Deutsch leaves Poland to enroll at the University of Vienna.

**1912** Deutsch marries Felix Deutsch.

**1913** Deutsch graduates from medical school.

**1914** Deutsch begins work at the Vagner Jauregg clinic.

**1924** Deutsch delivers her first essay on female psychology.

**1935** Deutsch flees for the United States to avoid the threat of the Nazis.

**1935** Deutsch takes a position with Massachusetts General Hospital.

**1982** Deutsch dies after a long and productive career.

One of a handful of women to enter medical school at the University of Vienna, Deutsch had originally planned to become a pediatrician but soon switched her focus to psychiatry. A lover of art and literature, she found that this latter study allowed her to indulge her creativity. She excelled at her work but suffered periodic emotional and physical disorders. Realizing that her relationship with Lieberman was stunting her mental and professional development, she broke off their affair in 1911. On April 14, 1912 she married Felix Deutsch, a brilliant physician who specialized in internal medicine. Although the relationship lacked the tempestuous passion of her affair with Lieberman, it provided the peace and emotional stability she needed.

After she passed her first exam with "excellent success," her mother recognized her potential and allowed her father to support her financially. Deutsch always received good grades, although they were never very important to her. Graduating from medical school in 1913, she prepared for the field of psychiatry through exhaustive and systematic reading, often up to eight hours a day. During this time she became fascinated by the work of Sigmund Freud and began to think about a career in psychoanalysis.

In 1914 Deutsch began working full-time at Wagner-Jauregg, the most prestigious psychiatric clinic in Vienna. The onslaught of World War I and the departure of other clinicians to the front brought new opportunities to Deutsch, and she rose to a prominence unprecedented for a woman in her post. She left the clinic in 1918 when she had the opportunity to undergo analysis with Freud. Her treatment ended abruptly after a year when Freud informed her that he needed her analytic hour to resume work with his former patient the "Wolf-Man." Deutsch always worried that her analysis bored Freud. Twice, she recalled, he fell asleep during her session. On January 29, 1917, Deutsch gave birth to her only child, Martin. Throughout her life she would be plagued by the difficulty of reconciling her professional life with her responsibilities as a mother.

The 1920s were Deutsch's most productive years. She emerged as a superb clinician, teacher, writer, and training analyst. In 1924 she garnered broad recognition after delivering her first essay on female psychology. That same year she was asked to head the newly established Vienna Training Institute. She remained director until the threat of Nazi occupation forced her to emigrate to America in 1935. Settling in Cambridge with her husband and son, Deutsch took a position at Massachusetts General Hospital. She served as president of the Boston Psychoanalytic Society and Institute from 1939 to 1941 and continued her clinical work as well as teaching and supervision until well into her 80s.

Although psychoanalysis remained her true passion, Deutsch continued her lifelong engagement in political activism, marching against the Vietnam War in the 1960s and 1970s. In 1973 she published her autobiography, *Confrontations with Myself*. She died in her home in Cambridge, Massachusetts, at the age of 97.

Helene Deutsch's most original clinical contribution was her notion of the "as if" personality. This concept referred to the patient who derived a sense of self only through identification with others. Although she used this concept to understand emotionally disaffected populations, she believed it could have more general applicability. In less theoretical circles Deutsch is best known for her two volumes on the psychology of women. At once her most substantial and most controversial contribution to the field, this project both derived and departed from Freudian notions of femininity and female sexuality.

Deutsch believed that women are characterized by three essential traits—narcissism, passivity, and masochism—and that the conjunction of or conflict among these elements contributes to the formation of more "feminine" or "masculine" personalities. While her supporters praise her originality, her contribution to Freudian thought, and her exhaustive data, her detractors criticize her equation of passivity with femininity. Throughout her life Deutsch maintained that her psychoanalytic notions about female development contributed to the cause of women's emancipation. ◆

# Dickens, Helen Octavia

FEBURARY 21, 1909– ● PHYSICIAN

Helen Octavia Dickens has dedicated her life to the practice, teaching, and social service of medicine. Dickens's life demonstrates how far African Americans have progressed in the United States.

**1909** ▶ Dickens is born in Ohio.

**1932** ▶ Dickens earns a bachelor of science degree from the University of Illinois.

**1934** ▶ Dickens graduates from medical school and takes a residency in Chicago.

**1943** ▶ Dickens marries Purvis Henderson.

**1950** ▶ Dickens becomes the first African American woman to be named as a fellow of the American College of Surgeons.

**1969** ▶ Dickens is named associate dean of the University of Pennsylvania medical school, her current position.

Dickens was born on February 21, 1909, the oldest of three children of Charles and Daisy Jane Green Dickens. Her father had been born into slavery in Tennessee and was just nine years old when the Civil War ended; he then moved to Ohio with a white family. He taught himself to read and write, and eventually met and married Daisy after attending Wilberforce University and Oberlin College.

Dickens, who was raised in Dayton, Ohio, was very much influenced at a young age by her parents' insistence that she take advantage of every educational opportunity available to her, and her father strongly encouraged her early interest in medicine. Unfortunately, Charles died from an infection when his daughter was only eight years old. However, his influence on her life and her goals would never perish.

Dickens devoted a good deal of her time to studying and enrolled in night school and summer school so that she could graduate from high school at the age of 17. Along with her late father, Dickens had been encouraged to act upon her interest in becoming a medical doctor by her family dentist, and by Blanche Arnold, a secretary at the local YWCA. Arnold had traveled to Africa on aid missions and brought back stories of how helpful the physicians were who went on the trip. Dickens was inspired by the difference she knew that doctors can make, and decided to make medicine her life's work.

Following high school, Dickens' superlative grades won her acceptance into Crane Junior College in Chicago, where she began a premedical curriculum. Once she finished at Crane, Dickens earned her bachelor of science degree at the University of Illinois in 1932, and then entered the university's college of medicine. Dickens was one of only five women in the 137-student class, and she graduated with her medical degree in 1934. Dickens moved back to Chicago to begin her internship and residency at Provident Hospital, located on the south side of the city. Dickens was somewhat frustrated because, although there was a great deal of poverty and tuberculosis in the area near the hospital, the interns and residents did not do much community practice.

Just before finishing her residency at Provident, Dickens heard of a position at a Philadelphia home practice run by Virginia Alexander, a Quaker doctor. Dickens was intrigued by the possibilities an alternative practice could give as opposed to a large hospital. Dickens took the position and began to practice. She took over the entire operation when Alexander left to attend Howard University Medical College for a year. In 1941, Dickens enrolled in the University of Pennsylvania's graduate school and earned a master's degree in medical science, specializing in obstetrics and gynecology.

The following year, Dickens returned to Provident for another residency, and it was there that she met Purvis Henderson. They married in 1943 and Dickens accepted a residency at Harlem Hospital in New York the same year, finishing in 1946 and becoming certified by the American Board of Obstetrics and Gynecology. Dickens returned to Philadelphia two years later as the director of Obstetrics and Gynecology at Mercy Douglass Hospital, one of the few integrated hospitals in the city. In 1950, Dickens became the first African-American woman to be named as a fellow of the American College of Surgeons, and was also honored as a Distinguished Daughter of Pennsylvania by the governor.

Dickens and her husband raised two children before he died in 1961. However devastating that loss was, it did not diminish her determination to practice and serve. In 1965, Dickens was appointed an instructor at the University of Pennsylvania School of Medicine, and moved quickly to assistant and then associate professor before being named professor of obstetrics and gynecology in 1966. Her career at Penn took on an administrative capacity when she was named associate dean of the medical school in 1969 and is still active there in 2000. She also established an Office of Minority Affairs at Penn, which assists in counseling minority students and in retention.

Dickens's research work focused on women's illnesses, and specifically the prevention of vaginal cancer. Dickens also dedicated a good portion of her work to the study of the treatment received by pregnant teenagers in clinics in and around Philadelphia, and she has published a wide array of papers and articles concerning the subject. For her work, Dickens has received numerous awards and honors from all over the nation, but especially in Chicago and Philadelphia, where her work has been immediately felt. ◆

Dickens returned to Philadelphia as the director of Obstetrics and Gynecology at Mercy Douglass Hospital, one of the few integrated hospitals in the city.

# Dresselhaus, Mildred S.

November 11, 1930– ● Physicist

Mildred Dresselhaus, whose birth name was Mildred Spiewak, was born in extreme poverty in New York City, but her distinguished career as a physicist emblemizes fulfillment of the American dream. Her parents were immigrants who had moved to the United States at the beginning of the Great Depression. Lacking money, the family lived in an immigrant ghetto, and often her parents did without food so that Mildred and her brother could eat. She once remarked that she knew "what it is like to have just one set of clothing to wear and one pair of shoes."

Throughout her childhood, Mildred took any job she could find, including the most menial ones. One of these jobs, which she took at age 11, was to teach a mentally retarded child to read and write. The job occupied her five days a week for three hours a day—all for 50 cents a week—but the work convinced her that she wanted to become an elementary school teacher. Additionally, she and her brother showed musical talent, and the two played for many community organizations.

Mildred S. Dresselhaus at an awards ceremony in 1998.

Toward the end of high school Dresselhaus took her first steps toward escaping the grinding poverty of her childhood. With a perfect score in mathematics, a subject in which she had always excelled, she passed the examination needed for admission to New York's Hunter College High School, an exclusive college preparatory school usually attended by middle- and upper-income students. Here she discovered an interest in science, an interest she had never displayed in earlier years. She continued to work after school, though, to help support her family and save tuition money for college.

As it happened, Dresselhaus did not need to use her savings for tuition. She attended Hunter College, where tuition was free, and she earned a scholarship that helped her with other expenses. At Hunter a physics instructor (Nobel Prize winner Rosalyn Sussman Yalow) noticed her aptitude for science and persuaded her to major in science rather than elementary education. After graduating with highest honors in 1951, she attended graduate school at Newnham College, the women's college at England's Cambridge University.

After a year at Newnham, Dresselhaus returned to the United States and completed her master's degree in physics at the women's graduate school at Radcliffe College in Massachusetts. She then pursued her doctorate in physics at the University of Chicago, perhaps the top physics program in the world. There she focused on solid-state physics, the branch of physics that studies matter in a condensed rather than a gaseous or liquid state, and composed her 1958 doctoral thesis, "Magnetic Field Dependence of High-Frequency Penetration into a Superconductor." She also met and married Gene Dresselhaus, also a solid-state physicist who specialized in semiconductors.

After completing their Ph.D.'s, Dresselhaus and her husband accepted positions at the Lincoln Laboratory at the Massachusetts Institute of Technology (MIT) in 1960. In 1964 they began work in the Francis Bitter National Magnet Laboratory, a research center that focused on the theory and application of magnetic fields. With her husband and with the help of students working on their Ph.D.'s, Dresselhaus conducted research on superconductivity, which is the disappearance of electrical resistance as a conducting substance's temperature approaches absolute zero. Their chief interest was studying the electronic structure of conducting materials.

In 1965 Bell Labs announced that it had found superconductivity in substances called graphite intercalation compounds. Dresselhaus and her associates began to study these compounds using a technique called **magnetoreflection**. They also began to research carbon fibers and the effects of ion implantation into polymers and carbon-based materials. This research enabled her to improve these materials so that they could withstand higher temperatures, allowing more current to flow through them. The main practical application of her discoveries was that they led to improvement in semiconductors and superconductors.

Dresselhaus was a distinguished member of the MIT faculty. In 1967 she was appointed to the Abby Rockefeller Mauze

1930   Dresselhaus is born in New York City.

1951   Dresselhaus graduates from Hunter College.

1960   Dresselhaus joins the faculty at the Massachusett's Institute of Technology (MIT).

1968   Dresselhaus is promoted to full professor at MIT.

1990   Dresselhaus receives the National Medal of Science.

chair as visiting professor in the electrical engineering department. A year later she was promoted to full professor. In 1972 and again in 1974 she was named associate chair of the electrical engineering department. She has also served as director of the university's program in materials science and engineering. She was a member of the executive committee of the Assembly of Mathematical and Physical Science of the National Academy of Sciences, and she was an adviser to the Division of Materials Research at the National Science Foundation. Beginning in 1975 she was a member of the Committee on the Education and Employment of women in science and engineering for the National Research Council. Various universities around the world have hosted her as a visiting professor.

In 1972 Dresselhaus was elected to the Hunter College Hall of Fame. In 1973 Radcliffe recognized her with its Alumnae Medal. In 1974 she became a member of the National Academy of Engineering and the American Academy of Arts and Sciences. In 1976 Brazil made her a member of the that nation's Academy of Science. Throughout her career Mildred Dresselhaus was an outspoken advocate for women in engineering, and at the turn of the century she was still teaching at MIT. Commenting on her life she said, "All the hardships I encountered provided me with the determination, capacity for hard work, efficiency, and a positive outlook on life that have been so helpful to me in realizing my professional career." ◆

# Dunbar, Bonnie Jean

MARCH 3, 1949– ● ASTRONAUT

Bonnie Dunbar has made five shuttle flights, including the first shuttle-Mir docking mission, STS-71. That June 1995 flight of the orbiter *Atlantis* carried two Russian cosmonauts—Anatoly Solovyov and Nikolai Budarin—in addition to its crew of five NASA astronauts. Solovyov and Budarin replaced the *Mir* crew of Yuri Dezhurov, Gennady Strekalov, and NASA astronaut Norman Thagard, who had been aboard Mir since that March. *Atlantis* returned to Earth with a crew of eight.

Dunbar trained for a year as Thagard's backup, undergoing Russian-language schooling and learning to serve as a Soyuz-

*Mir* crew member. She returned to *Mir* as a mission specialist in the crew of STS-89. This flight of the orbiter *Endeavour* delivered Andy Thomas, the seventh and last NASA-*Mir* crew member, to the Russian station, while returning David Wolf to Earth; STS-89 also delivered four tons of water, food, and other supplies to Mir.

Dunbar had previously flown as mission specialist aboard Shuttle Mission 61-A/Spacelab D1 in October and November 1985. During the week-long flight, Dunbar and seven other astronauts performed scientific experiments designed and controlled by the Federal German Aerospace Research Establishment (DFVLR) and the European Space Agency (ESA).

Dunbar was also a mission specialist aboard STS-32 in January 1990. On that flight she used the shuttle *Columbia's* remote manipulator arm to grapple the massive Long Duration Exposure Facility (LDEF), a scientific satellite that had been in orbit for nearly six years. LDEF was then photographed and latched into Columbia's payload bay for return to Earth. Data from LDEF is expected to assist scientists and engineers in the design of future space stations.

Dunbar's third flight was STS-50, launched June 25, 1992. This two-week mission carried the U.S. Microgravity Laboratory and a crew of seven, who performed experiments in space manufacturing.

Dunbar was born March 3, 1949, in Sunnyside, Washington. She graduated from Sunnyside High School in 1967 and attended the University of Washington, where she received a B.S. and M.S. in ceramic engineering in 1971 and 1975, respectively. She later earned her Ph.D. in biomedical engineering from the University of Houston in 1983.

After graduating from college in 1971, Dunbar worked for two years at Boeing as a computer systems analyst, then began researching her master's thesis. In 1975 she was invited to be a visiting scientist at Harwell Laboratories in Oxford, England, then became a senior research engineer at Rockwell International Space Division in Downey, California, where she worked on the development of the space shuttle thermal protection system. She became a payload officer and flight controller at NASA's Johnson Space Center in 1978, working as one of the guidance and navigation officers during the Skylab reentry in 1979.

Dunbar was selected as an astronaut candidate in May 1980, and in August 1981 she qualified as a shuttle mission specialist.

1949 Dunbar is born in Sunnyside, Washington.

1971 Dunbar earns a bachelor's degree in ceramic engineering from the University of Washington.

1978 Dunbar becomes a payload officer and flight controller at NASA.

1980 Dunbar is selected as an astronaut candidate, and qualifies as a shuttle mission specialist the next year.

1983 Dunbar is awarded a doctorate in biomedical engineering from the University of Houston.

1995 Dunbar is aboard STS-71, the first docking between the Russian spacecraft *Mir* and the space shuttle.

She worked in the Shuttle Avionics Integration Laboratory before being assigned to Spacelab D1 in 1983. In the hiatus caused by the *Challenger* accident, she participated in the astronaut office Science Support Group.

She is a private pilot with more than 200 hours of flying time and has also logged 700 hours as a T-38 jet copilot. In addition to her astronaut duties, she is an adjunct assistant professor of mechanical engineering at the University of Houston.

Following STS-50 Dunbar spent a year (1993) at NASA Headquarters in Washington as deputy associate administrator for materials science. She was assigned as Thagard's backup in February 1994, and named to the STS-71 crew that June. From October 1995 to November 1996 she was detailed to the Johnson Space Center's mission operations directorate as assistant director for International Space Station readiness and Russian-American cooperation. ◆

# Eastwood, Alice

JANUARY 19, 1859–OCTOBER 30, 1953 ● BOTANIST

Although she never attended college, Alice Eastwood became one of the foremost naturalists in North America in the late 19th and early 20th centuries. Through most of her 94 years, Eastwood had her keen eyes trained on the ground to learn everything she could about the flowers of the American West.

Eastwood was born in Toronto, Ontario, Canada, and in many respects had a difficult childhood. Her mother died when she was six, and her grief-stricken father sent her and her sister to live with an uncle in Highland Creek, Ontario. Two years later she rejoined her father, who had opened a grocery story in Whitby, but in 1867 the business failed and Alice was sent to a Catholic convent in the nearby town of Oshawa. In 1873 she again rejoined her father, this time in Denver, Colorado, where she later lived with him in the back of his store and was responsible for most of the household chores. Once again her father's business failed, and when he took a job as a school custodian, Alice lived with him in the school's basement, waking at four each morning to tend the furnace. As a teenager she also worked in a department store afternoons and on weekends to earn money for books and clothes.

Throughout Eastwood's childhood, though, the one constant was flowers. She was fascinated by the flowers that grew

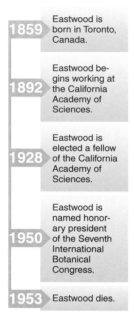

1859 — Eastwood is born in Toronto, Canada.

1892 — Eastwood begins working at the California Academy of Sciences.

1928 — Eastwood is elected a fellow of the California Academy of Sciences.

1950 — Eastwood is named honorary president of the Seventh International Botanical Congress.

1953 — Eastwood dies.

**herbarium:** a collection housing dried plant specimens which are arranged and mounted in a sytematic fashion.

in her uncle's lush garden, and he encouraged the budding naturalist under his care to call flowers by their Latin scientific names. At the convent, she trailed along behind the aging priest as he tended his garden and fruit orchards. Shortly after she arrived in Denver, she lived for a time with a wealthy cattle rancher who spent the summers in the Rocky Mountains. Eastwood used the time to explore the lush meadows filled with columbines, lilies, and other colorful wildflowers she had never seen back east.

Plants and flowers remained a constant throughout the rest of Eastwood's life. She graduated from high school at the top of her class in 1879 and became a schoolteacher in Kiowa, Colorado. There she was surrounded by fields and flowers, and by saving money from her meager earnings she could indulge what by then had become a passion—tramping through remote parts of Colorado to locate, identify, and name plants, often using botanical guidebooks her high school teacher had given her. She explored the Uncompahgre Canyon in western Colorado, climbed the 14,000-foot-high Gray's Peak with the famous English naturalist Henry Wallace, and ascended Pikes Peak outside Colorado Springs with a group of men who had come from the East Coast to climb mountains. She often traversed the state riding sidesaddle on a horse, but she also took advantage of free railroad passes given to her by a railroad builder who admired her Wild West independence. By the end of the 1880s she was a self-taught expert in the plants of the West, and botanists from around the world, eager to expand their knowledge, relied on her expertise.

Earlier, Eastwood and her father had bought property in downtown Denver. The two sold the property, and with the proceeds Eastwood bought rental houses whose income enabled her to retire from teaching in 1890. Thus, at the age of 31 she became a full-time botanist. That year she traveled to California, where she made herself an expert in the plants that grew along the California coast. In San Francisco she met Katherine Brandegee, who was curator of the **herbarium**, or plant collection, of the California Academy of Sciences. Brandegee was so impressed with Eastwood's work—especially her folders of pressed plant samples—that in 1891 she offered her a position as an assistant curator. Eastwood was uncertain whether to accept. She did not want to leave Denver, but she finally took the job, perhaps because of the death of the man she considered marrying, and moved to San Francisco in 1892. Just as she had in Colorado, though, she spent much of her time on solitary expeditions collecting and identifying plants throughout the state, and in 1901 she published the Pacific Coast edition of *Key and Flora.* ("Key" refers to the a sequential method of identifying a plant by its characteristics, a common practice in botany field guides before photographs were practical.)

In 1906—the same year Eastwood was listed in the *American Men of Science*—the San Francisco earthquake destroyed the Academy of Sciences building, so Eastwood spent most of the next five years traveling. She studied the plants of the American South, and for a while she worked at Harvard University. In 1911 she traveled to England, where she met the famous botanist Sir Joseph Hooker. In 1912 she returned to California to rebuild the academy's herbarium collection, and in 1916 the academy opened a new building, where she served as curator until her retirement. In the meantime, she spent the spring of 1914 exploring Alaska and the Yukon Territory.

During these years and the years that followed, Eastwood continued to write about plants. She published important articles not only about individual species but about plant communities. Further, she was one of the first botanists to discuss the beneficial effects of fires, which often improve growing conditions for some plants and allow others to take hold. She also became active in conservation efforts, including those to save the California redwood trees, and she spearheaded efforts to create state parks to protect the land from development.

Eastwood never slowed down. In 1926 she helped found the San Francisco Garden Club. In 1928 she was elected a fellow of the California Academy of Sciences. Her dream of starting an arboretum in Golden Gate Park came to fruition in 1938 when a wealthy family provided her with the funds she needed. In 1949, at the age of 90, she retired as curator of the California Academy of Sciences, and that year, Camp Alice Eastwood in Mount Tamalpais State Park outside San Francisco was dedicated. In 1950 she was named honorary president of the Seventh International Botanical Congress and traveled, alone, to Sweden to preside. Two years later the California Academy of Sciences announced that it was establishing the Alice Eastwood Hall of Botany. Then, after her death in 1953, the Alice Eastwood Grove, a redwood preserve, was established near California's Redwood National Park. ◆

Eastwood never slowed down. In 1926 she helped found the San Francisco Garden Club.

# Eigenmann, Rosa Smith

OCTOBER 7, 1858–JANUARY 12, 1947 ● ICHTHYOLOGIST

ichthyologist: a
zoologist specializing in
studying fish of all kinds.

" ... in science, as
everywhere in the
domain of
thought, women
should be judged
by the same stan-
dard as her
brother. Her work
must not be
simply well done
*for a woman.*"
Rosa Smith Eigen-
mann in the *Pro-
ceedings of the
National Science
Club,* 1895, as
quoted in *Notable
American Women,
1607–1950,* 1972

osa Smith Eigenmann holds the distinction of being one
of the first women to gain fame as an **ichthyologist**—a
zoologist who specializes in the study of fishes.

Rosa Smith was born in Monmouth, Illinois, the last of
nine children. Her mother, Lucretia Gray, was a poet of some
distinction, and her father, a printer by trade, founded the first
newspaper in the county. Because of her mother's health problems, the family in 1876 moved to the warmer climate of San
Diego, California, where her father became a member of the
school board. Smith attended Point Loma Seminary in San
Diego and later a business college in San Francisco, and she began her professional life as the first woman reporter for the *San
Diego Union,* a newspaper owned by her brother and brother-
in-law.

In the meantime, though, Rosa was growing interested in
natural history, in particular her collection of spiders and plants.
She also began studying the fishes of the San Diego area, and
her professional break came in 1880. That year, noted ichthyologist and Indiana University president David Starr Jordan traveled to San Diego to attend a meeting of the San Diego Society
of Natural History, of which Smith was the first woman
member. Jordan, who would later become the first president of
Stanford University and president of the California Academy of
Sciences, heard her deliver a paper—her first contribution to
the field—on a species of fish she had discovered, the Point
Loma blind fish. He was so impressed that he encouraged her to
join him on a fishery study he was conducting on the West
Coast. He then urged her to further her education at Indiana
University, where she studied from 1880 to 1882.

In the summer of 1881 Smith and 33 other students—who
dubbed themselves "Jordan's Tramps" —accompanied Jordan
to Europe to study natural history, most of the time traveling
on foot. Back in San Diego, in 1884 she was appointed curator
of ichthyology—the first known woman curator of an ichthyological collection—at the California Academy of Sciences, an
organization of which she was a life member. Through Jordan
she learned about one of his star zoology students, German native Carl H. Eigenmann, and the two carried on a formal corre-

spondence until they met in person; family papers contain copies of his published work with the note "To Miss Smith, with the compliments of CHE."

Smith and Eigenmann married in August 1887 and then spent 1887 to 88 at Harvard University, where they conducted joint research on the large collection of South American fishes housed at the university's Agassiz Museum. As a result of their research, the two co-wrote a paper on South American nematognathi, an order of scaleless fishes. During that year, Eigenmann was a special student in cryptogamic botany—which is the study of plants that reproduce through spores rather than flowers or seeds—under William G. Farlow.

In 1888 the Eigenmanns returned to San Diego, where Carl became a curator of the San Diego Society of Natural History and where he and Rosa conducted independent research in their own private zoological laboratory. By 1893 they had co-authored 15 papers on fish taxonomy, including monographs on the freshwater fishes of South America and the fishes of western North America, as well as topics involving embryology and evolution.

Under her maiden name (Smith), Eigenmann published 20 scientific papers, most of them about the fishes of the San Diego region, and with Joseph Swain she cowrote a monograph on the fishes of Johnson Island in the central Pacific. The Eigenmann's work, some of which was conducted for the Smithsonian Institution, had practical value on the West Coast, for it described the habits and spawning seasons of food fishes, precious information for the fishery industry. "Eigenmann and Eigenmann" were the most respected ichthyologists on the coast, and their names were known in professional circles throughout the country.

In the meantime, the Eigenmanns moved back to Indiana University 1891 after Jordan invited Carl to take a position as professor of zoology. Carl went on to a career as a respected teacher and researcher and, starting in 1908, dean of the graduate school. In 1893 Rosa discontinued her research to care for a large and growing family—a burden made heavier by the fact that the first of her five children was born mentally retarded and the third, her only son, became mentally ill. With her household in disarray, she took little part in university or community activities, though she continued to help her husband by editing his scholarly papers and she was the first woman president of the Indiana University chapter of Sigma Xi, a scientific

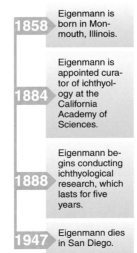

**1858** Eigenmann is born in Monmouth, Illinois.

**1884** Eigenmann is appointed curator of ichthyology at the California Academy of Sciences.

**1888** Eigenmann begins conducting ichthyological research, which lasts for five years.

**1947** Eigenmann dies in San Diego.

society whose membership was predominantly male. In 1926, with Carl in failing health, they returned to San Diego, and Carl died the following year. Eigenmann stayed in San Diego, where she underwent a series of unsuccessful operations on her eyes and died in 1947 of **chronic myocarditis**.

**chronic myocarditis:** repeated inflammation of the heart, especially the middle layer of the heart wall.

In an 1895 article published in the *Proceedings of the National Science Club*, Eigenmann reflected on the role of women in science. She pointed out that women often faced special challenges because the demands of family interrupted their scientific careers—and science demands years of uninterrupted work and observation. For this reason, she wrote, "... we often find that women popularize the results of students of science rather than add to a positive knowledge by studies and researches of their own." Yet she also noted that women have to be judged by the same standards as men, and she objected when, in her view, a woman scientist received more praise than was her due just because there were so few female scientists. ◆

# Elders, Jocelyn

AUGUST 13, 1933– ● PHYSICIAN

Born in Schaal, Arkansas, Joycelyn Jones was the eldest daughter of Haller and Curtis Jones. She attended Philander Smith College in Little Rock, Arkansas, where she received her B.A. in 1952. Wishing to become a doctor, she joined the U.S. Army and trained in physical therapy at the Brooke Army Medical Center at Fort Sam Houston, Texas. In 1956 she left the army and enrolled at the University of Arkansas Medical School, one of the first African Americans to attend, and received her M.D. degree in 1960, the same year she married Oliver Elders. Elders did an internship in pediatrics at the University of Minnesota, then returned to the University of Arkansas in 1961 for her residency period. Elders was ultimately named chief resident, and also received an M.S. in biochemistry in 1967. In 1971 Elders was hired by the University of Arkansas Medical School as an assistant professor in pediatrics, and five years later was named a full professor. Over the succeeding years, she published 138 articles, mostly on child growth problems and diabetes.

In 1987, Arkansas governor Bill Clinton named Elders as the Arkansas Health Commissioner. Elders's advocacy of making birth control information and condoms available in schools as ways of fighting teenage pregnancy and AIDS caused a storm of controversy. Conservative critics decried her supposedly permissive attitudes toward sex, and her implementation of a kindergarten-to-college health education program that included sex education as well as the usual information about hygiene, substance abuse, and other matters.

In 1993 Clinton, by then president of the United States, appointed Elders U.S. surgeon general. Despite conservative opposition in Congress over her advocacy of abortion rights and sex education, she was confirmed, and was sworn in on September 10, 1993. During Elders's first year as surgeon general, she faced continued opposition by conservatives to her advocacy of condom distribution and sex education in schools and stirred debate through several controversial stands, such as her support of the medical and compassionate use of marijuana, her warnings to parents against purchasing toy guns for children, and most notably her proposal that the question of legalizing drugs in order to "markedly reduce" the nationwide crime rate be studied. Her supporters claimed that Elders was simply being used as a target by opponents of the administration, and her courageous, forthright style made her a hero to thousands of African Americans and whites throughout the United States. In the wake of continuing controversy, however, President Clinton asked for her resignation; she left the surgeon general's office on December 30, 1994. Elders returned to the University of Arkansas Medical School to teach pediatrics. In 1996 she published an autobiography, *Joycelyn Elders, M.D.: From Sharecropper's Daughter to Surgeon General of the United States of America.* ◆

Joycelyn Elders

# Elion, Gertrude Belle

JANUARY 23, 1918–FEBRUARY 21, 1999 ● BIOCHEMIST

Gertrude Belle Elion was born in New York City to an immigrant family. Her father, who could trace his lineage back through a line of Jewish rabbis to the year 700, came to the United States from Lithuania at age 12, worked his way through the New York University School of Dentistry, and often took "Trudy" to performances of the New York Metropolitan Opera. Her mother, who immigrated from Poland at age 14, learned English in night school and worked as a seamstress. She encouraged her daughter to have a career so that she could have her own money and spend it as she pleased.

As a child, Elion was a bookworm and excelled at history, languages, and the sciences. She particularly enjoyed reading about the lives of scientists such as Louis Pasteur and Marie Curie—"people who discovered things." She graduated from high school at age 15, and it was a given that she would attend college. Her father, though, went bankrupt as a result of the stock market crash of 1929, limiting Elion's college choices. Although entrance requirements were high and the competition was fierce, she gained entrance to the woman's section of Hunter College in New York, where the tuition was free. Her father hoped that she would study medicine or dentistry; her teachers of English, French, and history tried to recruit her into their programs. Ironically, only her chemistry teacher seemed indifferent to her major.

Gertrude Elion

A turning point in Elion's life was the death of her beloved grandfather from stomach cancer. She later said, "It was as though the signal was there: 'This is the disease you're going to have to work against.' I never really stopped to think about anything else." She went on to declare a major in chemistry and graduated from Hunter College with highest honors in 1937.

The next seven years were difficult ones for Elion. She wanted to pursue a doctorate so that she could do research in biochemistry, but she was unable to secure a fellowship because she was a woman. She worked at any job she could find, and even attended secretarial school. At one job she had to endure daily anti-Semitic jokes from the company president. She also lost the man she loved to a bacterial disease. Working as a substitute teacher on the side, she scraped together enough money to take graduate chemistry classes at New York University and completed a master's degree in chemistry in 1941, the only woman in her class. She took a job testing food products for a grocery store chain in 1942. In 1944 she finally secured a lab job with Johnson & Johnson, but six months later the lab closed.

A second turning point in Elion's life came when her father received a drug sample from a company that he had never heard of, Burroughs Wellcome, and urged his daughter to call the company and ask about employment opportunities. She interviewed with researcher George Hitchings and got the job— over the objections of Hitchings's assistant, a woman who thought that Elion looked too "elegant" to do chemical research. From scrambling around to find a job, Elion went on to a four-decade-long career with Burroughs Wellcome (later Glaxo Wellcome). She published more than 225 research papers, received 45 patents, won a Nobel Prize, and developed drugs that have saved the lives of countless persons.

Unlike many drug researchers at the time, Elion was not content to develop drugs and let other people figure out how they work. She—and Hitchings—wanted to place drug research on a more rational footing, one based on an understanding of cell growth. She began her career investigating **nucleic acids**, needed by every cell to grow and reproduce. In particular, she investigated the purines, which include **adenine** and **guanine** and which are the building blocks of DNA and RNA.

A third turning point in Elion's life came in 1950. Based on her investigation of the purines, she synthesized two effective cancer treatments that year. One was a purine compound that blocked the formation of leukemia cells. The compound, called diaminopurine, was tested on acutely ill leukemia patients at the Sloan-Kettering Memorial Hospital in New York. The drug seemed to work, at least in the short run; the patients who took it experienced complete remission, although they later had relapses and died. They also suffered severe side effects. So Elion turned her attention to the biochemistry of the drug, believing that if she

**1918** ▶ Elion is born in New York City.

**1944** ▶ Elion joins the research department at Burroughs Wellcome.

**1950** ▶ Elion develops 6-MP, an effective cancer drug.

**1988** ▶ Elion wins the Nobel Prize.

**1999** ▶ Elion dies in Chapel Hill, North Carolina.

**nucleic acids:** various acids made up of a sugar or derivativ, phosphoric acid, and a base found in cell nuclei.

**adenine:** a purine base which codes hereditary information in DNA and RNA.

**guanine:** a purine base containing genetic information in DNA and RNA.

knew how it worked, she could modify it to make it work better. The result was 6-mercaptopurine, or 6-MP, a drug still used against leukemia. Over the next 18 years Elion worked on other drugs that, used in combination with 6-MP, have given leukemia patients a better-than-fighting chance against the disease.

At it turned out, her research on 6-MP had other implications. A relative of the compound called Imuran was an effective immune-system suppressant. This compound made organ transplants between unrelated people possible, and since 1961 tens of thousands of kidney transplant patients have not rejected their new kidneys because of Elion's drug. It was also discovered that 6-MP reduces the body's production of uric acid, leading to an effective treatment for gout. The drug and its cousins also proved to be effective against rheumatoid arthritis and several tropical diseases, including malaria. Elion's later research led to the development in 1974 of Acyclovir, used against shingles, the Epstein-Barr virus, and herpes encephalitis, an often fatal brain infection in children. She also played a key role in training scientists in the methods they needed to produce AZT, for years the only effective treatment against the AIDS virus.

On October 17, 1988, Elion received a phone call informing her that she had been selected as a corecipient (with Hitchings and a third researcher) of the Nobel Prize, a rarity for drug researchers. The prize committee noted, however, that she and her colleagues had "introduced a more rational approach based on the understanding of basic biochemical and physiological processes." In addition to the Nobel Prize, Elion was the recipient of numerous top awards and 25 honorary doctorates. She accomplished all this without the Ph.D. she had coveted as a young woman.

Elion retired from Burroughs Wellcome in 1983. She died of a brain hemorrhage in Chapel Hill, North Carolina, in 1999. ◆

# Esau, Katherine

APRIL 3, 1898–JUNE 4, 1997 ● BOTANIST

World-renowned botanist Katherine Esau was born in Yekaterinoslav, a Mennonite community in the Ukraine. Her father, a mechanical engineer, built the town's waterworks, a streetcar line, and numerous large buildings, including several schools, and eventually the town elected him mayor. As a child Esau learned to read and write at home, then attended a Mennonite primary school. At age 11 she entered the "gymnasium"—a college-preparatory secondary school—and graduated in 1916.

That fall Esau entered the Golitsin Women's Agricultural College in Moscow, where she studied the natural sciences, physics, chemistry, and geology. She wanted to focus on agriculture rather than botany because, she believed, botany at the time was more concerned with naming and classifying plants than with studying how they worked. After her first year, though, political and military turmoil interrupted her education. World War I was raging, and the German army had occupied the Ukraine. Further, after the Communists seized power in 1917, **Bolshevik** revolutionaries removed her father from office and placed the family under surveillance. When the war ended in 1918, the Esau family took the advice of occupying German officers and fled to Germany—leaving just one day before posters appeared in the town proclaiming Esau's father an "enemy of the country."

In Germany Esau was able to complete her education at the Agricultural College of Berlin. After further study she passed an examination in plant breeding given by the famous geneticist Erwin Baur. By that time the family had decided to settle in the United States, and in late 1922 they passed through Ellis Island in New York on their way to Reedley, California, a Mennonite town near Fresno. Esau achieved her initial goal of finding a job with a seed company when she joined a firm in Oxnard that wanted her to develop a new strain of sugarbeets. Although the company went bankrupt just a year later, the job gave Esau the experience she needed to take a similar job with the Spreckels Sugar Company near Salinas. There her job was to develop a sugarbeet strain resistant to curlytop, a viral disease spread by the leafhopper.

Esau's career took a new direction when the chair of the botany division at the University of California at Davis, W. W. Robbins, paid a visit to Spreckels to observe the research the company was conducting. Esau asked him about graduate studies at UC Davis, and Robbins offered her a graduate assistant position. At Davis she continued to study the effects of the curlytop virus on sugarbeets, but she refocused her research interests on pathological plant anatomy. When she completed her doctorate in 1931, Robbins invited her to join the university's

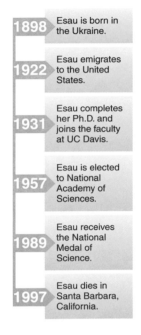

| | |
|---|---|
| **1898** | Esau is born in the Ukraine. |
| **1922** | Esau emigrates to the United States. |
| **1931** | Esau completes her Ph.D. and joins the faculty at UC Davis. |
| **1957** | Esau is elected to National Academy of Sciences. |
| **1989** | Esau receives the National Medal of Science. |
| **1997** | Esau dies in Santa Barbara, California. |

**Bolshevik:** an individual allied with the extreme Russian Social Democratic Party that came to power in Russia through armed insurrection in November, 1917; a Communist.

"I don't know
how I happened to
be elected. I have
no idea what im-
pressed them
about me."

Katherine Esau,
modestly reacting
to her National
Medal of Science,
1989

faculty. Esau accepted and remained at Davis for more than three decades.

One of Esau's earliest publications was based on her discovery that the curlytop virus spreads through a plant by way of the phloem, or food-conducting tissue, and phloem research dominated her career. She was interested not only in the effects of viruses on the structure and development of plants but on the anatomy of the phloem. In 1940 the John Simon Guggenheim Foundation recognized her work by giving her a one-year fellowship to further her research. She is perhaps best known, though, as the author of several standard textbooks in the field of botany. In the 1940s she began work on *Plant Anatomy*, and after the book was published in 1954, Dr. Ray Evert, who became chair of the botany department at the University of Wisconsin, said that it "had an enormous impact worldwide, literally bringing about a revivification of the discipline." She wrote five other standard botany textbooks, including *The Anatomy of Seed Plants* (1960), *Vascular Differentiation in Plants* (1965), and *The Phloem* (1969). One professor of plant biology, William Lucas, said, "Her prose is elegant and precise; each word is carefully chosen. When you read her publications, you're at the microscope with her—you see what she's seeing."

Esau was also highly respected for her teaching ability and her sincere interest in students. She had total command of the subject, a gift for storytelling, and a keen sense of humor, evidenced by a lecture entitled "The Saga of Vladimir-the-Virus and the Sad Fate of Norman-the-Nucleus," in which she personified the components of a viral infection. She often began her lectures with the words "Once upon a time . . . ," leading students to refer to her lectures as "Esau's fables."

For most of her career at UC-Davis, Esau worked in a garage with no air-conditioning, yet she was still able to conduct research that earned her election to the National Academy of Sciences in 1957, only the sixth woman to receive that honor. Finally, in 1960, she moved into a "real" building when the university erected Robbins Hall. That year, too, she began using an electron microscope for her work. In 1963 she moved to the Santa Barbara campus of the University of California, and in 1969, with a grant from the National Science Foundation, she acquired her own electron microscope. Amazingly, she continued working until 1982, when, at age 84, she gave her last lecture. She still was not done, though. Two years later, she began to write a new edition of *Plant Anatomy*. To aid in the process she bought a personal computer and, at age 86, took computer lessons.

In 1989 Esau received her highest honor when President George Bush awarded her the National Medal of Science. After she died at her home in Santa Barbara in 1997 at age 99, Peter Raven, director of the Missouri Botanical Garden, commented that she "absolutely dominated the field of plant anatomy and morphology for several decades. She set the stage for all kinds of modern advances in plant physiology and molecular biology." ◆

# Faber, Sandra

DECEMBER 28, 1944– ● ASTRONOMER

Sandra Moore, who took the name Faber when she married in 1967, was born in Boston, Massachusetts. As a child she was interested in all kinds of science, and she often spent evenings in the yard with her father, looking at the night sky. She did not study astronomy seriously, though, until she was a student at Swarthmore College, where she graduated with a degree in physics in 1966.

Faber then enrolled in the graduate program in astronomy at Harvard University. After two years of classes she followed her husband to Washington, D.C., where she continued to work independently on her Ph.D. thesis out of an office at the Carnegie Institution. In that thesis, she used spectrographic analysis to detail her discovery of a correlation between the size of a galaxy and the strength of the absorption lines in its spectrum, which in turn is related to the production of elements within the galaxy's stars. With the completion of her Ph.D. in 1972, Faber began a distinguished career studying science on the grandest possible scale. Her goal was no less than to understand the formation and evolution of galaxies and the evolution of the structure of the universe.

In 1972 Faber moved to California, where she accepted a position as an assistant professor at the Lick Observatory at the University of California at Santa Cruz. In 1977 she was promoted to associate professor, then just two years later to full professor. In 1996 she became one of just four nonemeritus

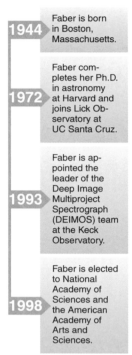

**1944** Faber is born in Boston, Massachusetts.

**1972** Faber completes her Ph.D. in astronomy at Harvard and joins Lick Observatory at UC Santa Cruz.

**1993** Faber is appointed the leader of the Deep Image Multiproject Spectrograph (DEIMOS) team at the Keck Observatory.

**1998** Faber is elected to National Academy of Sciences and the American Academy of Arts and Sciences.

professors in the University of California system to be appointed to the rank of University Professor, the highest honor the system awards to recognize excellence in teaching and research.

Over nearly three decades at the Lick Observatory, Faber emerged as one of the leading cosmologists in the world. She investigated the nature, composition, and motion of stars within a galaxy as related to their ages. She made important contributions to astronomers' understanding of the structure and formation of elliptical galaxies. Working with a graduate student, Robert Jackson, she discovered a method for determining how far away elliptical galaxies are. Called the Faber-Jackson relation, the method is based on the correlation between the brightness of an elliptical galaxy and the width of its spectral lines.

Faber also joined six other astronomers—a group that came to be known in the profession as the Seven Samurai—to show that in the earth's part of the universe, a large-scale flow of galaxies is moving at a speed of about a million miles an hour toward the constellation Centaurus. This flow is caused by the gravitational pull of an unusually large supercluster of galaxies, which the group nicknamed "the Great Attractor."

Faber was closely involved with two major telescope ventures in the 1980s and 1990s. From 1985 to 1997 she was a member of the wide field/planetary camera team of the Hubble Space Telescope. She was one of three astronomers who diagnosed a flaw in the telescope and reported their findings to the National Aeronautics and Space Administration. She then served on the Hubble Refurbishment Mission to fix the telescope. Additionally, from 1987 to 1992 she helped plan and develop the Keck Observatory in Hawaii, home to the world's largest optical and infrared telescopes. Beginning in 1993 she was the leader of the Deep Image Multiproject Spectrograph (DEIMOS) team at the Keck Observatory. Her work made possible large surveys of the distant universe for the first time by increasing spectrographic power trained on distant galaxies by a factor of 10.

Using these telescopes, Faber concentrated on three areas of research. One was to measure the large-scale motion of nearby galaxies and use the data to measure the total mass and density of the universe. A second was to measure the mass-to-light ratios and the star populations of elliptical galaxies. This effort led to methods to determine the age and the metallic makeup of stars, and she discovered that many elliptical star

## The Association for Women in Science

The Association for Women in Science (AWIS), located in Washington, D.C., was founded in 1971 to help achieve greater participation for women in science, mathematics, engineering, and technology. Its activities are carried out through the national organization and at the chapter level, with the strength of over 5000 members, the majority of whom are Ph.D.-trained scientists in academia, private industry, and government. Nationally, AWIS provides expert speakers—for example, to appear before Congress during policy discussions—and publishes AWIS's magazine and other literature about science and issues of importance to girls and women. The national organization is led by a national office staff, board of directors, and national committees.

Since its founding, AWIS has sponsored or cosponsored a number of activities. These include: using educational programs in schools and communities to encourage the participation of girls and women in science, preparing a study suggesting ways for institutions of higher learning to improve the working conditions of women science faculty, and improving community mentoring programs for undergraduate and graduate students. Several conferences have also been convened, including the 1997 conference on career advancement and leadership.

In 2000, AWIS was working with funding from the Office of Naval Research to build a database of women scientists in the U.S. The database will be a tool for companies recruiting for jobs, award-granting agencies and employers looking for qualified applicants, and news outlets needing contacts and spokespersons.

populations are surprisingly young. A third area, using the Hubble telescope, involved studying star populations in nearby globular clusters, elliptical galaxies, and distant clusters of galaxies. Using the Hubble's Faint Object Spectrograph, she also searched for nuclear black holes in space.

In addition to her research, Faber was an active and widely honored member of the astronomy profession. In 1998 she joined an elite group of scientists when she was elected to both the National Academy of Sciences and the American Academy of Arts and Sciences. Among other positions, she served on the California Council on Science and Technology, the President's Advisory Panel of the National Academy of Sciences, and the National Academy's Committee on Astronomy and Astrophysics. She also served on the board of trustees of both the Carnegie Institution of Washington and the SETI Institute.

In addition to her research, Faber was also a highly respected teacher. She served as a visiting professor and guest lecturer at numerous colleges and universities. Many of her students noted in evaluations that she was the best teacher

> **"By all accounts she is one of the leading cosmologists in the world."**
>
> David S. Kliger, Dean of Natural Sciences, University of California, Santa Cruz, 1999

they ever had, and over the years she maintained collaborative relationships with many former graduate students. In 1999 her teaching excellence was recognized when she received the "Outstanding Faculty Award" from UC Santa Cruz. ◆

# Fossey, Dian

JANUARY 16, 1932–DECEMBER 26, 1985 ● ZOOLOGIST

Dian Fossey

**B**orn just outside San Francisco in Fairfax, California, Dian Fossey had a difficult childhood. Her father drank heavily, and her parents divorced when she was three years old. Her mother later married a cold and distant man who did not treat her well. A lonely child, Dian found a sense of connection with other children and often with animals.

Fossey's interest in animals led her to enroll in a pre-veterinary program in college, but she was not very good at the hard sciences, so she switched her major to occupational therapy. After completing her degree at San Jose State College, she took a job as a therapist in Kentucky. She longed to work with animals, though, and after reading the work of George Schaller, a naturalist who studied mountain gorillas in Africa, she borrowed money to finance a six-week trip there in 1963.

In Africa, Fossey made arrangements to meet Dr. Louis Leakey, a renowned paleoanthropologist who studied mountain gorillas in the Virunga Volcanoes in central Africa and was excavating an archeological site at Olduvia Gorge. While this meeting proved to be the starting point of Fossey's career as a naturalist, it did not get off to a very promising start. Leakey had just uncovered a fossil, and in her enthusiasm to see it, Fossey slipped, fell into the excavation site, damaged the fossil, and—in pain from a twisted ankle—vomited on the fossil. Leakey, though, admired Fossey's determination and convinced her that mountain gorillas, which were in danger of becoming extinct, needed further study.

Fossey returned to the United States determined to organize a research program to study mountain gorillas in Africa. Her chief obstacle was funding, which she found hard to get because she did not have credentials or training as a zoologist. With Leakey's support, her efforts finally paid off in 1966 when the National Geographic Society and the Wilkie Foundation agreed to fund her research.

In January 1967 Fossey arrived in Zaire, but almost immediately she faced a difficult problem when civil war broke out and her research station was shut down. In July, though, a new location was found in neighboring Rwanda, where Fossey spent most of the next 18 years studying mountain gorillas at the Karisoke Research station. She displayed enormous patience in allowing the gorillas to get used to her presence. Her efforts were finally rewarded in 1970 when Peanuts, an adult male, touched her hand—the first friendly contact between a gorilla and a human ever recorded.

Eventually, Fossey earned the complete trust of all the gorilla groups she studied. Her work dispelled notions that gorillas were cruel, savage beasts. Through detailed study of their habits, she showed that they were gentle, lived in close-knit, structured family units, and resorted to violence only when necessary to protect themselves.

Knowing that she needed academic credentials to attract funding, Fossey began studying for a Ph.D. at England's Cambridge University in 1970. After completing her degree in 1980, she accepted a position at Cornell University, where she wrote *Gorillas in the Mist* (1983), a widely read book that was made into a major motion picture in 1988. Her efforts drew worldwide attention to the plight of the gorillas, whose numbers had dwindled to about 250 largely because so many had been killed by poachers or seized by profiteers who sold them to zoos.

In her determination to protect them, Fossey became a lightning rod for controversy. She was critical of "theoretical conservationists" who wanted to protect the gorillas indirectly and avoid confrontation with Rwandans. Instead she practiced what she called "active conservation," confronting the problem

1932 — Fossey is born in Fairfax, California.

1963 — Fossey travels to Africa for the first time.

1967 — Fossey begins her 18-year study of gorillas.

1983 — Fossey publishes *Gorillas in the Mist*.

1985 — Fossey is murdered in Rwanda.

of poaching head-on. She organized antipoaching patrols to capture poachers and destroy their traps. When Digit, a gorilla Fossey felt particularly attached to, was brutally killed by poachers in 1978, Fossey persuaded CBS to announce his death on the evening news. She then launched the Digit Fund to collect money she used to step up her efforts. She raided villages to find poachers, burned their belongings, and aggressively questioned them to gather information about other poachers. Some villagers claimed that she tortured them. She circulated stories that she was a sorceress who could curse people. She required her assistants to carry guns. Her actions led Paul Schindler, president of the African Wildlife Fund, to remark that "her dedication got in the way of common sense." Some observers even questioned her sanity.

Fossey also opposed efforts to introduce tourism into the area as a way of raising hard currency for the Rwandan government, which would then presumably see value in protecting the gorillas. She believed that tourists were insensitive to the gorillas and that many gorillas contracted diseases from the trash and waste tourists left behind. One organization that sponsored such tours, the Mountain Gorilla Project, tried to convince the Rwandan government to shut down Karisoke and convert it into a tourist center. This placed Fossey directly at odds with corrupt members of the Rwandan government, who hated Fossey because they saw her as an obstacle in the way of profits from gorilla poaching.

On top of these political challenges, Fossey faced severe physical hardships. Her friends and relatives lived far away. Her research assistants could endure only a few months at the primitive research station. Fossey suffered from asthma, and she often needed oxygen to breathe at the high altitudes. Rainy conditions often left her fighting pneumonia, and spider bites were common. She had to hike miles to study the gorillas, despite painful sciatica and broken ankles and ribs. On top of it all, Fossey was afraid of heights, a problem she had to fight daily in the mountains. Money was a nagging worry. In later years, after the National Geographic Society and other organizations withdrew their support, she had to fund her efforts out of her own pocket.

Fossey had made enemies. She knew that her life was in danger when in October 1985 she found on her doorstep a wooden image that had been placed there by a Rwandan and that represented a curse of death. On December 26, 1985, Fossey was found murdered in her cabin. She had been killed with a panga, a machete-like weapon used by poachers. The murderer was never found.

In the years that followed, the Atlanta-based Fossey Fund continued to send researchers to Rwanda, and the mountain gorilla population in the region made steady, significant gains. ◆

# Franklin, Rosalind Elsie

JULY 25, 1920–APRIL 16, 1958 ● BIOCHEMIST AND GENETICIST

Rosalind Elsie Franklin, a biochemist known widely for *not* winning the Nobel Prize, was born in London, England, the second of five children. Her Jewish ancestors had lived in England since 1763 and not only acquired wealth in banking but established a tradition of public service and commitment to social causes. Her father, for example, helped numerous Jews escape Nazi Germany, and an uncle once served six weeks in prison for attacking Winston Churchill with a whip because of Churchill's early opposition to the right of women to vote.

As a child Franklin attended the St. Paul's Girls' School in London, a demanding school for the daughters of affluent families. The school offered excellent physics and chemistry classes, sparking Franklin's interest in science. She became an avid amateur astronomer and studied star maps published in the *London Times*. She passed the entrance examination for Cambridge University, but her mother and an aunt had to pressure her reluctant father to agree to pay to educate a daughter. She enrolled in Newnham College, the women's college of Cambridge University, and graduated with a degree in chemistry in 1941. She then worked for a year doing research with Nobel Prize–winning chemist Ronald Norrish.

The war effort contributed to Franklin's later high reputation as a research scientist. She took a job with the British Coal Utilization Research Association, where her work focused on ways England could use its wartime coal and charcoal more efficiently. Over the next four years she published five major papers on the structure of carbon fibers. Doing all the research herself, she designed elegant experimental methods and produced reams of experimental data. Her work earned her a Ph.D. from Cambridge in 1945. Just 26 years old, she was one of the leading industrial chemists in England.

**1920** ▶ Franklin is born in London, England.

**1941** ▶ Franklin gradu-ates from Cambridge University.

**1945** ▶ Franklin earns a Ph.D. from Cambridge University.

**1951** ▶ Franklin begins her ground-breaking work that would un-lock the mys-teries of DNA

**1958** ▶ Franklin dies.

**X-ray crystallography:** procedure enabling researchers to look within the structure of crystals and their formations.

After World War II ended, Franklin found a job in a chemistry lab in Paris. There she began to learn about a new field called **X-ray crystallography**, a technique for using X-rays to photograph molecules and thus examine their structure. While most scientists were applying the technique to regularly shaped crystals, Franklin pioneered its use in examining large, disorderly molecules, including biological molecules. Starting in 1947, Franklin enjoyed three carefree years in Paris, forging friendships, debating science with her colleagues, and savoring all that France had to offer. She knew, though, that her professional future was in England, so in 1950 she returned.

In 1951 she accepted a job at King's College at the University of London. There she worked under John Randall, a physicist who had assembled a team of scientists to study DNA, the molecules that encode and pass on hereditary information in living organisms. Franklin was put in sole charge of analyzing X-ray photographs of DNA that were taken by Raymond Gosling, a graduate student. Franklin, though, had a strong personality, and she interacted with colleagues through confrontation rather than polite collaboration. Gosling once said, "She scared the wits out of me." Nonetheless, Franklin, with Gosling's help, gathered extensive data and published five papers about the structure of DNA.

In time Franklin learned, using what she called the B-form of DNA molecules, that DNA is in the shape of a helix—although she refused to affirm this conclusion because she was unable to get useable photos of the A-form. (The two forms differ primarily in their moisture content; A is the "dry" form, B is the "wet" form.) She later learned that DNA molecules consist of two phosphate strands wound together; that they are oriented in opposite directions; and that each step in the strand is composed of two particular bases. In essence, Franklin unraveled the mystery of DNA, though she did not know it to her own satisfaction because of the nagging problem of photographing the A-form.

In late 1951 Franklin gave a talk at King's College to explain her work to date. Sitting in the room was James Watson, an American geneticist who had been working on DNA with his graduate student, Francis Crick. Watson essentially ignored Franklin's data; in his own later account of the discovery of DNA, it is apparent that he spent the time critiquing "Rosy's" physical appearance and personality. Watson, though, understood enough to know that he was in a horse race with Franklin, and for the next two years it was an open question who would win the DNA sweepstakes. Unfortunately, Franklin lost opportunities to team up with others who could have contributed to—and speeded up—her research. One was Linus Pauling, the eminent American chemist unfairly barred from foreign travel because of charges that he was a Communist. The other was Crick, who at one point wanted to join Franklin. He had a reputation for eccentricity, though, and Franklin ignored him.

The missing piece of information in DNA research at that time had to do with base pairings in DNA molecules. Franklin's records show that she solved the problem in February; she typed a manuscript of an article announcing her findings on March 17, 1953. But on March 6, the science journal *Nature* received a 1,000-word article announcing the same finding. The authors were Watson and Crick, and in the annals of science history it was Watson and Crick who crossed the finish line first. They won the Nobel Prize (in 1962), Watson published the best-selling book *The Double Helix* (1968), and every high school biology student "knows" that Watson and Crick discovered DNA. What those students likely do not know, however, is that in the view of some respected scientists, the two used Franklin's data and DNA photographs—especially one key photo removed from her desk and turned over to Watson—without her permission and without acknowledging her. Many scientists continue to believe that Franklin deserved the Nobel Prize.

Franklin left King's College, but her work was not done. She accepted a job at the University of London's Birkbeck College, where she produced important work on RNA-containing viruses and virtually created the field of structural virology. She later moved her lab to Cambridge University, where she continued to work on the structure of viruses. Her model of a virus molecule, the first of its kind, was exhibited at the 1958 World's Fair in Brussels, Belgium.

In 1956 Franklin was diagnosed with ovarian cancer. She underwent treatment and carried on with her work for two years. She died in 1958 at the age of 37. ◆

> "Quick, fierce, and fun-loving, Rosalind Franklin was a commanding leader, an idealist about science, and in her time the supreme experimentalist analyzing the molecules of heredity."
>
> Quoted in *Nobel Prize Women in Science*, 1993

# Freud, Anna

## DECEMBER 3, 1895–OCTOBER 8, 1982 ● CHILD PSYCHOANALYST

The youngest of Sigmund Freud's children, Anna Freud was born in Vienna and developed a very special relationship with her father, acting as his secretary, nursemaid, and eventually becoming his successor. The only one of

Anna Freud

his six children to follow in his footsteps, she became a leading figure in the fields of psychoanalysis, ego psychology, research methodology, and child analysis, all with no formal education in the field.

Her interest in the field may be said to have begun in her youth, for as a 14-year-old she was to be found "sitting on a little library ladder in the corner" at the meetings of the Vienna Psychoanalytic Society. Nonetheless when she graduated from the Cottage Lyceum, it was to school teaching and not psychoanalysis that she turned. She remained close to her father and, as she never married, lived at home with him, caring for him assiduously after he developed cancer of the palate in 1923. In 1918 when she was 22 years old, she was psychoanalyzed by him. This seems to have been a turning point in her gravitation toward the field of psychoanalysis.

Anna Freud came to take a particular interest in child analysis after hearing a paper in 1920 by Hermine von Hug-Hellmuth, the first child analyst. That year her father also sent her for analysis to Lou Andreas-Salomé, with whom she was to maintain a lifelong correspondence. Anna Freud also developed a relationship with Dorothy Burlingham, who brought her son to Vienna from America for analysis with Anna Freud, and eventually became a close friend, companion, and colleague.

In 1922 Anna Freud was accepted to the Vienna Psychoanalytic Society and in 1923 established a private practice in Vienna. Two years later she was on the executive committee of the society, and by 1925 she was its chairman. In 1926 she opened a private school in Vienna with Dorothy Burlingham. Her Seminar on Children (1926 and 1927) and a series of lectures on child analysis at the Vienna Psychoanalytic Institute established her as reputation as a leading figure in the field of child analysis, as did her book *Introduction to the Technique of Child Analysis* (1929).

Her investigations into the subject of ego psychology were published in *The Ego and the Mechanisms of Defence* (1936), a seminal work on ego psychology that moved the emphasis of psychology from conflicts in the unconscious toward a study of the mechanisms by which the ego protects itself from anxiety. Such mechanisms (among them repression, projection, sublimation, and rationalization) have remained key concepts in the practice of psychoanalysis.

Adolf Hitler's rise to power signaled the culmination of Anna Freud's career in Vienna and as the specter of Nazism enveloped Europe she insisted that her father leave Austria with her. They moved to London, settling in Hampstead. There she was instrumental in the reestablishment of psychoanalysis after its destruction in Europe. She brought as many analysts as possible out of Europe and opened the Hampstead Wartime Center for the study and treatment of young war victims. The facility, described in *Young Children in War-Time* (1942), *War and Children* (1943), and *Infants Without Families* (1944), eventually developed into the Hampstead Center for the Psychoanalytical Study and Treatment of Children, which she directed until her death. She also helped found and served as editor of *The Psychoanalytic Study of the Child*. After the war she often lectured in the United States and published the classic *Normality and Pathology in Childhood* (1965). Her writings, collected in *The Writings of Anna Freud*, fill seven volumes. ◆

**1895** Freud is born in Vienna, the youngest child of Sigmund Freud.

**1922** Freud is accepted into the Vienna Psychoanalytic Society, and establishes a private practice the next year.

**1929** Freud publishes *Introduction to the Technique of Child Analysis*.

**1936** Freud publishes *The Ego and Mechanisms of Defence*.

**1945** Freud develops the Hampstead Center for the Psycholanalytical Study and Treatment of Children in London, and directs it until her death.

**1982** Freud dies.

# Friend, Charlotte

### MARCH 11, 1921–JANUARY 13, 1987 ● MICROBIOLOGIST

The third of four children and the youngest of three daughters, Charlotte Friend was born on Houston Street in Manhattan to Russian immigrant parents, Morris Friend, a businessman, and Cecilia Wolpin, a pharmacist. Friend was only three when her father died. After his death, the family moved to Boston Post Road in the Bronx to be closer to her mother's relatives and lived on the inheritance Morris Friend had left. Following the stock market crash of 1929, the inheritance funds diminished, and the family existed on relief from the city. Despite such conditions, Friend's mother urged the children to continue their education.

Charlotte Friend

**hematology:** the study of the configuration of the blood and blood forming tissues.

**microbiology:** the study of organism such as bacteria, yeasts, and viruses which are too small for viewing with the naked human eye.

As a child Friend loved to read books about bacteriologists such as Louis Pasteur. She dreamed of working at the Pasteur Institute, a dream that came true later in her life. At the age of 10 she wrote a homework composition titled "Why I Want to Become a Bacteriologist." Science continued to draw her interest when she attended Hunter College High School on a scholarship.

After graduation Friend worked at a doctor's office during the day and attended night classes at Hunter College, receiving a B.A. degree in 1944. Following graduation she enlisted in the U.S. Navy and in April 1944 was commissioned as an ensign. Promoted to lieutenant junior grade, she served as second in charge in the **hematology** laboratory of the naval hospital in Shoemaker, California. Laboratory exposure convinced her to pursue a career in **microbiology**. After her discharge in 1946, she enrolled as a graduate student in microbiology at Yale University, where she received her Ph.D. in 1950.

Accepted for a postdoctoral position at Sloan-Kettering Institute for Cancer Research by the director, Cornelius P. Rhoads, Friend worked under the virologist Alice Moore. In 1952 Friend entered a joint program of the institute and Cornell University in Ithaca, New York, where during the same year she became an associate professor of microbiology. While examining carcinoma cells of a mouse under a microscope, she unexpectedly saw particles that had a similar appearance to small sections of what she called "virus-infected cells." This prompted Friend to delve deeper over the next four years.

Friend had only a few studies to guide her, since little research on a link between viruses and cancer had been done. Peyton Rous, the one scientist who had written a paper on the subject, had been ridiculed. Starting without much prior documentation, Friend took tissue from leukemia-infected mice, removed the cells, and injected the tissue into healthy adult mice. The mice developed leukemia. Under the high magnification of an electron microscope, Friend found the virus she thought had caused the leukemia and photographed it.

Friend recorded her discovery in the *Journal of Experimental Medicine* and prepared to present her findings to the annual meeting of the American Association for Cancer Research in 1956. Her conclusions met with a furious outburst and ridicule from the scientific audience, which called her conclusions "absurd." She stood her ground, however, convinced that her research was correct.

After the initial controversy, Friend's arguments gained credibility when a renowned scientist, Jacob Furth, found her experiment to be correct. In 1957 Rous helped Friend carefully document her research and present a paper, which met with approval from the scientific community. Friend at last gained recognition, and the Friend virus became a model that benefitted research and researchers in numerous fields. Twenty years later she addressed the American Association for Cancer Research as its president, telling her audience that she had been one of the "surfers on the tide of history," experiencing each day as a "new adventure."

In 1962 Friend received the Alfred F. Sloan Award for Cancer Research, which allowed her to spend three months at a time visiting various institutes all over the world. The same year she also received the American Cancer Society Award, and in 1970 she was awarded the Hunter College Presidential Medal Centennial Award. Elected to the Hunter College Hall of Fame in the same year, she received the Virus-Cancer Progress Award from the National Institutes of Health in 1974. In 1976 she was elected to the National Academy of Sciences, and in 1978 she became president of the New York Academy of Sciences.

In 1966 Friend left Sloan-Kettering and became director of and professor at the Center for Experimental Cell Biology at the Mount Sinai School of Medicine in New York City. A laboratory for research into viruses and tumors, the center had many specialists working as a team. By 1972 Friend had made another dramatic discovery: when she used certain drugs on a mouse leukemia cell, it then differentiated, becoming nearly normal. Friend's test-tube cells became another model in the study of cancer.

Friend's laboratory was her playground, where she often lingered in the evening to speak to colleagues about work or personal affairs. She never married, nor did she have children. She loved the Manhattan skyline and her vantage point from her apartment in the Stuyvesant Town complex on East 14th

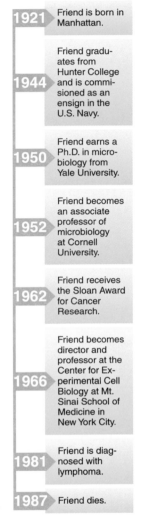

**1921** Friend is born in Manhattan.

**1944** Friend graduates from Hunter College and is commissioned as an ensign in the U.S. Navy.

**1950** Friend earns a Ph.D. in microbiology from Yale University.

**1952** Friend becomes an associate professor of microbiology at Cornell University.

**1962** Friend receives the Sloan Award for Cancer Research.

**1966** Friend becomes director and professor at the Center for Experimental Cell Biology at Mt. Sinai School of Medicine in New York City.

**1981** Friend is diagnosed with lymphoma.

**1987** Friend dies.

Street in Manhattan, where she lived for most of her adult life. Visitors called it "the Friend Hotel" because Friend always welcomed anyone who needed a place to stay. A soft-spoken, fair-haired woman, she surrounded herself with friends and family. Her leisure was spent in the classical pursuits of theater, music, opera, and reading. She also loved to travel.

In 1981 Friend was diagnosed with lymphoma. While undergoing extensive treatment, she kept researching, writing, and sending out grant applications. During her career Friend was rarely exposed to sex discrimination and was respected for her opinions. She stood by her convictions, even when they were unpopular. A firm believer in the women's movement, she readily agreed to speak out when asked. She wrote extensively, publishing 49 abstracts and 113 original papers, reviews, and book chapters, many of them composed on her own rather than collaboratively. Friend finally lost her battle with **lymphoma** in New York City. She is buried in New Montifiore Cemetery in Farmingdale, New York.

**lymphoma:** a condition called by a tumor of the lymphoid tissue.

Described by associates as a woman with a "brilliant and imaginative mind," Charlotte Friend provided pathways to new discoveries. She laid the groundwork for studies that assisted in the development of cancer research, the characterization of the human immunodeficiency virus (HIV), and the explanation of how viruses can interrupt the process of cell growth. She encouraged young scientists and inspired many young women scientists by sharing her knowledge of viruses and cells without hesitation. The Friend virus contributed to the search for the causes of cancer, and her legacy lives as a new generation of scientists continues to probe the Friend virus under the microscope. ◆

# Galdikas, Biruté

MAY 10, 1946– ● ANTHROPOLOGIST

Biruté Galdikas was born in Germany when her parents were en route from their native Lithuania to Canada, where Galdikas grew up. As early as age five, Galdikas wondered where human beings came from; although she knew that they evolved from a common ancestor of monkeys and apes, she wanted to know more. As an adolescent she foreshadowed her professional career when she played in High Park in Toronto, Ontario, Canada. She would venture into the wilder portions of the park and pretend that she was a member of an Indian tribe. She spent hours quietly roaming the woods, at one with nature as she secretly observed animals in the park.

To further her goal of working with animals, Galdikas enrolled at the University of California at Los Angeles, where she earned a bachelor's degree in psychology and biology in 1966, a master's degree in anthropology in 1969, and a Ph.D. in anthropology in 1978. She later taught part-time at Simon Fraser University in Vancouver, British Columbia, but for three decades she spent half of each year in Borneo, where her research made her the world's foremost authority on orangutans, a word that means "person of the forest."

Galdikas's career journey began in 1969 when she attended a lecture at UCLA by Dr. Louis Leakey, the anthropologist who gained fame not only for his own research on human fossils in Africa but also for becoming a mentor to well-known primate

**1946** Galdikas is born in Germany.

**1971** Galdikas begins research on orangutans in Borneo.

**1978** Galdikas publishes her Ph.D. thesis on the behavior of orangutans.

**1986** Galdikas founds Orangutan Foundation International.

field researchers Jane Goodall (who studied chimpanzees) and Dian Fossey (who studied mountain gorillas). She approached him after the lecture, and he quickly recognized that she had the ability and enthusiasm to follow in the footsteps of Goodall and Fossey. She thus became the third of what came to be called his "three angels" and the "Trimates." Leakey raised funds from several sources, and in 1971 he sent Galdikas and her husband to the Tanjung Puting wildlife reserve in central Borneo.

Studying orangutans was no easy feat. They are solitary creatures, and Galdikas had to slog through the rainforests for a week before she saw her first orangutans, a mother and her infant. The animals seldom mingle, and they live in high trees, rarely coming down to the swampy ground beneath. One adult needs an area of about 40 square kilometers for foraging, making the orangutan population of a given area low. Further, they live slow-paced lives; a female, for example, does not bear an infant until she is 15 years old, and Galdikas discovered that the reproductive cycle of an orangutan is about eight years.

Because orangutans are so solitary, they did not welcome Galdikas's presence. At first they threw branches at her and defecated on her from the trees above when she approached. She displayed an enormous amount of patience, though, never pressing them in her efforts to help them get used to her presence. It took her 12 years to get one orangutan to tolerate her presence. More typical was the behavior of one male she stumbled across while tracking down a female in the area. The orangutan, which had been fighting with another male over the female, grabbed a vine, swung down to within a yard of her head, and glared into her eyes. For Galdikas the message was clear: Leave me alone.

Galdikas's work formed the basis for her highly praised Ph.D. thesis. Using modern data collection and statistical techniques, she recorded her observations of the orangutans in meticulous detail. She observed adolescents traveling together and sometimes forcing themselves on females, she observed the lengthy courtship rituals of adults, she identified their calls, and she catalogued the plants and insects they ate. Like Fossey and Goodall, she added much to the limited store of knowledge scientists had about humans' nearest relatives, and she inspired a generation of young researchers to follow her into the field to learn more.

After a divorce in 1979, Galdikas married an Indonesian and became devoted to the preservation of Indonesian culture. As time went on, she became less concerned with academic research and more concerned with conservation. At Camp Leakey in the Tanjung Puting reserve, a research station Galdikas founded in 1971 and named in honor of her early mentor, she led efforts to preserve the rainforests and save the orangutans from the encroachments of civilization and from black marketeers who captured and sold them outside the country. In 1986 she founded the Orangutan Foundation International to fund her work and protect orangutans around the world. She publicized her efforts through articles in *Life*, *The New York Times*, and *National Geographic* and appearances on network television morning shows and newsmagazines. In 1995 she published an autobiography, *Reflections on Eden: My Years with the Orangutans of Borneo*.

While Galdikas's stature in the field of primate research was unquestioned, and while she received numerous awards from conservation groups for her work, she did not escape controversy. Some professionals criticized her for not publishing more and claimed that later publications recycled data from her Ph.D. thesis. Earthwatch, an ecotourism group that sent volunteers to Camp Leakey, broke off relations with her for this reason. Galdikas, who published more than 50 scientific articles, responded, "Those who say I haven't published haven't been in the swamps up to their armpits."

More significantly, many professionals were critical of her efforts to rehabilitate orangutans that had been captured by black market traders but later returned to Indonesia, largely through her efforts. The Indonesian Forestry Ministry, for example, investigated allegations that she kept as many as 100 infants at her residence illegally, and that many died because of poor conditions. Charges were also made that she ignored the research reports of her volunteers, mistreated staffers, and was obsessive about caring for baby orangutans. Galdikas denied these charges, and her supporters hotly disputed them.

Commenting on the significance of her work, Galdikas said, "What I have learned from orangutans is that we humans must not turn our backs on our own biological heritage, ... living and working in family groups and communities.... Otherwise we are just stressed out 'orangutans' in an urban setting." ◆

"I've always wanted to study the one primate who never left the Garden of Eden. I want to know what we left behind."

Dr. Biruté Galdikas on her research

# Germain, Sophie

April 1, 1776–June 27, 1831 ● Mathematician

Undaunted by
her parents' dis-
approval, Ger-
main continued
her studies at
night wrapped in
a blanket and
reading by the
light of candles
she had hidden.

Marie-Sophie Germain was born in Paris, France, the daughter of an affluent silk merchant who later became a director of the Bank of France. As revolution was brewing in France and America, her childhood home became a gathering place for people interested in political reform, and she was exposed to wide-ranging philosophical and political conversation.

Germain's interest in mathematics began at the height of the French Revolution, when she was 13. She was reading in her father's library and came across an account of Archimedes, the Greek mathematician who was killed by a Roman soldier because he was too engrossed in a geometrical figure to respond to the soldier's commands. Moved by the story, she concluded that she wanted to be a mathematician. Her parents, though, like many middle-class parents of the time, did not believe that her interest was appropriate for a girl. In an effort to pry her away from her studies, they took away her clothes after she was in bed and deprived her of heat and light. Undaunted by her parents' disapproval, Germain continued her studies at night wrapped in a blanket and reading by the light of candles she had hidden. She mastered Greek and Latin and studied the works of such scientists as Isaac Newton and Leonhard Euler. Eventually, her parents gave in and allowed her to continue her studies openly.

In 1794 the École Polytechnique was founded in Paris to train mathematicians and scientists. As a woman, Germain was not allowed to enroll, but she obtained lecture notes from a number of courses. She was particularly interested in the work of J. L. Lagrange and submitted a paper to him under the pseudonym M. LeBlanc. He was so impressed with the originality of the paper's analysis that he sought out its author. He was surprised to learn that the paper was written by a woman, but he recognized her abilities and agreed to become her mentor. The two frequently corresponded, and the relationship gave her access to other leading mathematicians. For example, she wrote to Adrien-Marie Legendre about some problems raised by his 1798 *Essai sur le Théorie des Nombres*, and Legendre included some of her analysis in a second edition of the book.

Germain's most famous correspondence, though, was with the German mathematician Carl Friedrich Gauss. In response to Gauss's 1801 book, *Disquisitiones Arithmeticae*, she began corresponding with him about number theory in 1804, again using the pseudonym M. LeBlanc. Gauss praised her work in letters to colleagues and was delighted when he learned in 1807 that "M. LeBlanc" was really a woman. In 1808 Germain sent Gauss a letter in which she described her most important work in number theory, a theorem that was an important step in proving a nagging mathematical puzzle called Fermat's last theorem. Her solution, which came to be known as Germain's theorem, was the most important work on Fermat's theorem in a period spanning more than 100 years.

**1776** Germain is born in Paris.

**1808** Germain describes the theorem that is later named after her in a letter to Carl Gauss.

**1815** Germain wins a competition conducted by the French Academy of Sciences.

**1831** Germain dies in Paris.

At about this time, the French Academy of Sciences announced a competition based on the work of the German physicist Ernst Chladni, who had visited Paris and conducted experiments on vibrating elastic figures, the so-called Chladni figures. The academy solicited papers on the underlying mathematical law of Chladni's figures, and set a two-year deadline. Most mathematicians did not even attempt to solve the problem, primarily because Legrange had proclaimed that current mathematical methods were inadequate to do so. Germain, however, accepted the challenge and spent the next decade trying to develop a theory of elasticity. During those years she collaborated with some of Europe's most respected mathematicians and physicists.

In 1811 Germain submitted the only paper the academy received, but because the paper reflected her lack of formal training, she did not win the prize. Legrange, though, was one of the judges. Germain's work provided him with insights into the problem, and the two developed an equation that in part solved Chladni's figures. The contest deadline was extended, and two years later Germain resubmitted her work, this time winning honorable mention. She continued to work on the problem, and when the contest was reopened again in 1815, her paper won the prize, a kilogram of gold. Germain continued her work on the theory of elasticity, including a 1825 paper she submitted to the Institut de France, though rivals at the institute brushed aside her work. The theory she developed, on which future mathematicians and scientists built, raised elasticity to an important scientific topic.

By winning the prize, Germain helped to break down at least some of the barriers that women mathematicians faced.

She was introduced to the ranks of some of the day's most prominent mathematicians. With the sponsorship of Jean-Baptiste-Joseph Fourier, she was the first woman who was not the wife of a mathematician to attend the sessions of the Academy of Sciences. The Institut de France invited her to its sessions, the highest honor that body ever conferred on a woman. Gauss, who by this time was at the University of Göttingen in Germany, persuaded the university to confer on her an honorary degree. She died, however, before she could receive it.

Germain continued her work on mathematics and philosophy until her death. She outlined a philosophical essay, entitled *Considérations générale sur l'état des sciences et des lettres,* that was published after her death in the collected *Oeuvres Philosophique de Sophie Germain.* In 1829 she was stricken with breast cancer, but undeterred by the disease and by the 1830 revolution in France, she finished papers on number theory and the curvature of surfaces. She died in 1831, at the age of 55. Her death certificate listed her not as a mathematician or scientist but as a *rentier,* or property holder. ◆

# Gilbreth, Lillian Moller

May 24, 1878–January 2, 1972 ● Industrial Engineer

Lillian Moller was born in Oakland, California. The oldest of eight surviving children, she was the daughter of William Moller and Annie Delger. Her mother came from a prosperous family that had made its money in Oakland real estate, and her father was the proprietor of a thriving hardware retail business. As a result of her family's comfortable circumstances, Gilbreth enjoyed many early advantages.

A shy child, Gilbreth received her earliest education from her mother. The home tutoring came to an end at the age of nine when she was enrolled in the Oakland public school system. On completing her high school education in 1896, her parents were reluctant to honor her desire for more education. But eventually they allowed her to attend the University of California at Berkeley, where she majored in English. After receiving her undergraduate degree in 1900, she began working toward a master's degree in literature at Columbia University.

Her unhappiness there, however, prompted her to return to the University of California, Berkeley, where she completed the work for her degree in 1902. Shortly thereafter, she began working toward a doctorate in psychology.

In the spring of 1903, she interrupted her studies to make a tour of Europe. During a stopover in Boston she met Frank Gilbreth, who at age 35 was one of the country's leading building contractors and was rapidly making a name for himself as an industrial efficiency expert. On October 19, 1904, they were married. They settled in New York City, where Frank Gilbreth had his business.

Gilbreth had taken an interest in her husband's work even before

Lillian Gilbreth

their marriage, and she was soon playing an active role in it. Of special interest to her was Frank Gilbreth's preoccupation with increasing productivity in the construction industry by streamlining the motions required for workers to complete given tasks. In the process of collaborating with him on several publications devoted to that subject, she increasingly believed that their joint quests for what would later be dubbed "the one best way" was of far greater importance than her husband's building ventures. It was thus due in large part to her quiet encouragement that Frank Gilbreth finally gave up his construction business in 1911 to establish himself as a full-time management engineering consultant. The maiden venture of this new enterprise was a contract with the New England Butt Company in Providence, Rhode Island, where the Gilbreths lived until shortly after World War I, when they moved to Montclair, New Jersey.

While continuing to collaborate in her husband's business, Gilbreth began work on a doctorate in industrial psychology at Brown University, which she completed in 1915. At the same time, having given birth to her first child in 1906, she had the major responsibility for raising a growing brood of offspring. The Gilbreths had 12 children over a period of 17 years, 11 of whom

**Cheaper by the Dozen**

*Cheaper by the Dozen* (1948), a book by Frank B. Gilbreth, Jr. and Ernestine Gilbreth Carey, is one of the most enduring classics of family literature. The novel chronicles the family of Lillian Gilbreth and Frank Gilbreth, Sr. and their adventures in Rhode Island, New Jersey, and elsewhere. The parents' expertise in motion and efficiency studies comes in handy as they do their best to raise and educate their 12 children, sometimes using the children as test subjects for their own theories about effective teaching. The book's title derives from the father's words. When he would approach a situation (like passing a tollbooth) where the cost of the event was per person, he would often ask the money collector if his large group came "cheaper by the dozen."

A play adapted from the book remains popular as a high school and community production. A 1950 film version was produced by 20th Century Fox; Walter Lang directed, and Clifton Webb (*Laura*) and Myrna Loy (*The Thin Man*) starred. While not all elements of the story have aged well—some parts might strike readers today as racist or chauvinistic—it remains not only a funny and well-told story, but a vivid reminder of the personal life of scientists, and a testimony to their ability to integrate their private lives with their professional interests.

lived to adulthood, and their crowded household often served as a testing ground for their motion theories. Years later the story of this large family, headed by efficiency experts, became the subject of memoirs coauthored by two of the Gilbreth children, *Cheaper by the Dozen* (1948) and *Belles on Their Toes* (1950).

By the early 1920s the Gilbreths' business was a thriving enterprise, and Frank Gilbreth was numbered among the most highly paid industrial consultants in the world. After his sudden death in 1924, however, the prosperity came to an end. Though determined to carry on their business, the newly widowed Gilbreth quickly found that clients were distrustful of a female consultant, and most of the contracts that the Gilbreths had with various businesses were soon canceled.

To support her family, Gilbreth established in her home the Motion Study Institute, which offered instruction in promoting efficiency in the workplace; she ran the institute successfully for six years. At the same time, she began to apply motion theory to home management. Her work in this area eventually spawned many articles for women's magazines and two books, *The Home-Maker and Her Job* (1927) and, with Orpha Mae Thomas and Eleanor Clymer, *Management in the Home* (1954). It also led to her serving as a consultant to home economics departments of numerous colleges and universities and to contracts with companies such as General Electric, whose products catered to the needs of homemakers. Ironically, Gilbreth herself never fully mastered her teachings on home management. Left to her own devices, she was barely capable of preparing the simplest of meals.

A gifted and fluent speaker, Gilbreth became a professor of management at Purdue University in 1935. In that position, which she held until 1948, she helped to establish the school's time and motion laboratory, and as an adviser there on careers for women, she was credited with fostering a more positive attitude toward women in industry. She also taught at a number of other schools, including the University of Wisconsin and Newark College of Engineering.

One of the hallmarks of Gilbreth's career was her abiding concern for human well-being, and among her greatest achievements were her efforts to find ways to help the physically handicapped. In the 1940s, she collaborated with Edna Yost on *Normal Lives for the Disabled* (1944), and as a consultant to the Institute of Rehabilitation at the New York University Medical Center, she helped to develop a kitchen for the handicapped. Gilbreth's work with the disabled represented a continuation of her husband's efforts to rehabilitate disabled veterans of World War I; in 1968, the couple's contributions to the rehabilitation field were hailed as "phenomenal."

Gilbreth's distinction won her many honorary degrees and awards from professional societies. The recipient in the early 1930s of the first Gilbreth Medal granted by the Society of Industrial Engineers in memory of her husband, she was also the first woman to receive the Herbert Hoover Medal for distinguished service by an engineer. Blessed with a robust constitution, she remained professionally active practically until her death. At age 90, her public-speaking schedule sometimes included as many as five engagements per week. She died in Scottsdale, Arizona. ◆

**1878** Gilbreth is born Lillian Moller in Oakland California.

**1900** Gilbreth earns an undergraduate degree from the University of California at Berkeley.

**1904** Gilbreth marries Frank Gilbreth.

**1915** Gilbreth earns a doctorate in industrial psychology from Brown University.

**1935** Gilbreth becomes a professor of management at Purdue University.

**1940** Gilbreth and Edna Yost write *Normal Lives for the Disabled.*

**1972** Gilbreth dies.

# Godwin, Linda

JULY 2, 1952– ● PHYSICIST

Physicist Linda Godwin took part in the first American EVA aboard the Russian Mir space station. Godwin and fellow STS-76 mission specialist Rich Clifford exited the airlock of the orbiter Atlantis, which was docked to Mir, and installed several experiments on the exterior of the station.

Linda Godwin

STS-76 was Godwin's third spaceflight. Previously she was payload commander for STS-59, the April 1994 flight of the orbiter Endeavour that carried the first Shuttle Radar Laboratory. This $366 million imaging system was the most advanced ever devoted to Earth studies. During the 11-day flight the SRL imaged more than 70 million square kilometers of the Earth's surface and returned enough data to fill 20,000 encyclopedia volumes.

Godwin also served as a mission specialist aboard STS-37, the April 1991 flight of the orbiter Atlantis that deployed the Gamma Ray Observatory in low Earth orbit. The GRO, a $617 million element in NASA's "great observatory" program, was at 17.5 tons, the most massive object yet carried by the Shuttle. During deployment an antenna failed to unfold. Using the Atlantis's remote manipulator arm. Godwin positioned the GRO so that astronauts Jerry Ross and Jay Apt could perform a contingency EVA, freeing the stuck antenna. A day later Godwin assisted Ross and Apt in a second EVA, testing space station construction techniques.

Godwin was born July 2, 1952, in Cape Girardeau, Missouri She graduated from high school in nearby Jackson in 1970, then attended Southeast Missouri State University, receiving a B.S. in mathematics and physics in 1974. She later earned an M.S. (1976) and Ph.D. (1980) in physics from the University of Missouri at Columbia.

While working on her doctorate at Missouri Godwin taught physics and conducted research in low temperature solid state physics, publishing several papers. In 1980 she joined NASA as a flight controller and payload operations officer, working on several shuttle missions.

She is also a private pilot holding an instrument rating.

Godwin was one of the 13 astronaut candidates selected by NASA in June 1985. In July 1986 she qualified as a shuttle mission specialist, and has since done a tour in the Shuttle Avionics Integration Lab (SAIL) and worked on the development of inertial upper stage (IUS) and Spacelab missions. Between missions she served as chief of astronaut appearances and head of the astronaut office mission development branch. Since April 1993, she has been deputy chief of the astronaut office, with time off for STS-76 crew training and for a brief tour as acting deputy director of flight crew operations. ◆

# Goeppert-Mayer, Maria

JUNE 28, 1906–FEBRUARY 20, 1972 ● PHYSICIST

Maria Goeppert-Mayer was born in Kattowitz, Upper Silesia (now Katowice, Poland), the only child of Friedrich Goeppert, a professor of pediatrics at Georgia Augusta University in Göttingen, and Maria Wolff. Her father actively encouraged his daughter to develop her scientific curiosity. Goeppert-Mayer attended public school and a private preparatory school for girls before entering Georgia Augusta University in 1924 to study mathematics.

She switched from mathematics to physics under the influence of her first course in quantum mechanics, taught by one of the chief theorists of the subject, Max Born. Goeppert-Mayer developed a close relationship with Born, under whom she took her doctoral degree, and with whom she shared a preference for a strictly mathematical style of physics. Born later

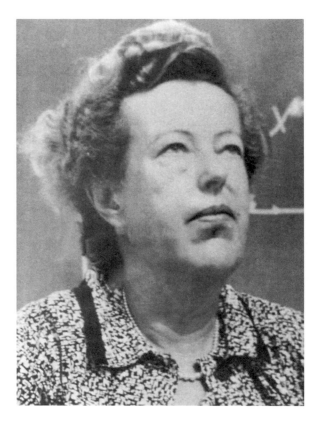

Maria Goeppert-Mayer

**benzene:** a colorless, flammable toxic used as a solvent.

described Goeppert-Mayer as one of his most talented students. The thrust of her doctoral dissertation (1930) extended Paul A. M. Dirac's theory of radiation and matter to the case of two-photon processes, using second-order time-dependent perturbation theory.

While completing her work at Georgia Augusta, she met Joseph Edward Mayer, an American chemist who completed studies with Gilbert Newton Lewis at the University of California at Berkeley. After their marriage in January 1930, the Mayers moved to Baltimore, where Joseph Mayer accepted an associated professorship of chemistry at The Johns Hopkins University. Goeppert-Mayer became an American citizen in 1933. The Mayers had two children.

For the first 30 years of Goeppert-Mayer's career, she had no regular paid appointment. Most of her research during the years 1930 to 1939 (at Johns Hopkins) was in chemical physics and physical chemistry. During this period, Mayer collaborated with her husband on several papers concerning the application of quantum mechanics to chemistry. This work gave Goeppert-Mayer a greater appreciation for the role of experimental data in the formulation of physical theory and taught her to apply her theoretical talents to a variety of specific experimental results.

Goeppert-Mayer also worked with Alfred Lee Sklar, a student of her colleague Karl Herzfeld, on calculating the energy levels of a complex molecule, **benzene**, from strictly theoretical principles; this pioneering work established her reputation as a specialist in the analysis of the spectra of complex systems. Goeppert-Mayer and her husband, in their final years at Johns Hopkins, completed the textbook *Statistical Mechanics* (1940), which became one of the standard texts. It had 10 printings by 1963; in 1977 a second edition was published.

The Mayers moved to New York City in 1939, when Joseph Mayer took a position in the chemistry department at Columbia University. Goeppert-Mayer gave occasional lectures in the same department (1939–1945) and took over Enrico Fermi's physics class in 1941 when he became involved in nuclear fission research in what would later become the Manhattan Project. After the start of World War II, Goeppert-Mayer joined Harold Urey's group, the Substitute Alloy Materials Laboratory (SAM), which was working on the difficulties of isotope separation for the Manhattan Project. Goeppert-Mayer made significant contributions toward the theory of both photochemical and chemical separation before beginning work on gaseous diffusion, the method eventually used.

In 1945 the Mayers accepted posts at the University of Chicago, where she became voluntary associate professor. They both joined the new Institute for Nuclear Studies, and Goeppert-Mayer also held a half-time position as a research physicist in the theoretical division of the new Argonne National Laboratory. Lacking a comprehensive background in nuclear physics, she developed her knowledge of the field through discussions with colleagues. Her lack of familiarity with many traditional beliefs proved to be an advantage and led to her most famous contribution to physics.

In 1945, Niels Bohr's compound-nucleus interpretation of nuclear reactions and the assumption that the nucleus behaves like a liquid drop prevailed, but early in 1947, Goeppert-Mayer found evidence that nuclei in some instances behave as collections of discrete particles. She noticed that nuclei with 2, 8, 20, 50, or 82 neutrons or protons or with 126 neutrons were particularly abundant and therefore unusually stable. This phenomenon could not be explained by the liquid-drop model.

Goeppert-Mayer interpreted these "magic numbers," as she called them, as providing evidence that individual nucleons have individual values of energy and angular momentum and that they can be viewed as occupying different energy levels, or "shells," like electrons in an atom. Quantum mechanics could not predict the magic numbers above 20. Two years later, as a result of a suggestion by Fermi, Goeppert-Mayer realized that the answer lay in an effect called "spin-orbit coupling," in which the **intrinsic** spin of each nucleon, when coupled with its orbital angular momentum, can affect its total binding energy enough to move some nucleons into the next energy level. Goeppert-Mayer first published the theory of the nuclear shell model in 1949. Goeppert-Mayer's shell model was of great value to experimental nuclear physicists because it could account for

**1906** Goeppert-Mayer is born in Poland.

**1924** Goeppert-Mayer enrolls in Georgia Augusta University to study mathematics.

**1930** Goeppert-Mayer earns a doctorate in mathematics.

**1930** Goeppert-Mayer marries Joseph Edward Mayer, an American chemist.

**1930** Goeppert-Mayer begins research at Johns Hopkins University in Baltimore, studying chemical physics and physical chemistry.

**1940** Goeppert-Mayer and her husband publish the textbook *Statistcal Mechanics*.

**1941** Goeppert-Mayer begins lecturing at Columbia University.

**1945** Goeppert-Mayer and her husband are offered positions at the University of Chicago.

**1960** Goeppert-Mayer dies of a stroke.

**intrinsic:** an essential internal part of an object or being.

many values of nuclear spin and magnetic momentum. The model was accepted readily by physicists who had previously believed that discrete particles could not exist in the nucleus, in part because the shell model was also proposed simultaneously and independently by Otto Haxel, J. Hans, D. Jensen, and Hans Suess in Germany. Goeppert-Mayer and Jensen subsequently collaborated on various theoretical aspects of the shell model, culminating in the publication of *Elementary Theory of Nuclear Shell Structure* (1955).

Goeppert-Mayer continued her work at the University of Chicago and Argonne Laboratory until 1960. In 1959, the University of California at San Diego offered both Mayers full paid professorships and they moved to La Jolla, near San Diego, the following year. Within weeks of their arrival, Goeppert-Mayer suffered a stroke. Although she continued to work, she never recovered her health, channeling her diminished energies into teaching. She died in La Jolla.

Goeppert-Mayer's work is remarkable in that her early theories, although mathematically derived, had a strong physical basis and in several cases foreshadowed later discoveries. Her early work served as a solid theoretical basis for subsequent developments in laser spectroscopy, double-beta decay, the theory of rare-earth elements, and photochemical isotope separation. In 1963, Goeppert-Mayer received the Nobel Prize for physics for her work with Jensen on the nuclear shell model. ◆

# Goodall, Jane

April 3, 1934– ● Zoologist

Jane Goodall, one of the world's most recognizable names in primate research, was born in London, England. When she was five years old, she and her family moved to France, but as World War II approached, the family returned to England and settled in Barnemouth in a home just blocks away from the English Channel.

As a child Goodall was fascinated by animals. Although she did well at her studies, she never liked school, preferring to spend the weekends horseback riding and, with a group of friends who called themselves the Alligator Club, observing animals and insects. She recalled once worrying her mother by disappearing to a hen house for five hours because she wanted to see how a chicken lays an egg. Her mother, author Vanne Goodall, recognized her patience with animals and encouraged her interest. Goodall first knew she wanted to go to Africa at age seven when she read Hugh Lofting's *The Story of Dr. Doolittle* about an Englishman in Africa who could talk to animals.

After graduating from high school, Goodall attended a secretarial school in London. She also worked for a studio at Oxford University that made documentary films. A turning point in her life came when a friend invited her to visit a farm in Kenya. To save money to make the trip, Goodall moved back home and worked as a waitress, and in 1957 she boarded a passenger ship bound for Mombasa,

Jane Goodall and friend.

Kenya. After visiting her friend, she found an office job in Nairobi, then was hired as an assistant to Dr. Louis Leakey, the famed anthropologist who at the time was the curator of Kenya's natural history museum. She even accompanied Leakey and his wife, Mary Leakey, on archeological digs on the Serengeti Plain.

After a few months, Leakey, who would gain fame not only for his research but for also sponsoring world-renowned primate field researchers Dian Fossey and Biruté Galdikas, asked her if she would like to study a group of chimpanzees along the Gombe stream on the shore of Lake Tanganyika. Goodall jumped at the opportunity, and over the next four decades she became the world's foremost authority on the behavior of chimpanzees.

Goodall, who at the time lacked formal training and academic credentials (though she would earn a Ph.D. from Cambridge University in 1965), returned to England to learn everything she could about chimps in labs and zoos. In the meantime, Leakey solicited funds for the project. In 1960, accompanied by her mother, she left Kenya for Tanzania in an old

Land Rover. When she arrived at the Gombe Game Reserve and came across a group of baboons, she knew that her dream had come true.

Goodall's enormous patience played a key role in her success. Months passed before she made any significant sightings of chimps. Finally she discovered what she called "the Peak," which provided her with a vantage point from which she could watch chimps in the valley below through binoculars. Over time they became less fearful of her and she was able to approach them. She even gave the chimps she studied names. Her breakthrough came about a year after her arrival. A chimp she called David Greybeard finally approached her without fear. Then another chimp, Flo, came close to her and allowed her infant to touch Goodall. Soon she was trekking with the chimps throughout the 30-square-mile protected area in which they lived.

Despite the physical hardships, including a bout of malaria, Goodall made meticulous observations about the chimps' behavior, which she recorded in documentaries, several articles in *National Geographic*, and her best-selling 1971 book, *In the Shadow of Man*. She was the first researcher to describe the ability of chimps to use tools, including long twigs from which they stripped the leaves and used to dig termites out of the ground to eat. She described the leadership struggles of the chief males in the groups and how the groups occasionally made war on one another.

Perhaps Goodall's most important discovery was that the behavior of chimps, whose DNA differs from that of humans by only about 1 percent, is remarkably similar to that of humans. Like humans, they learn over a long childhood. They develop close, affectionate bonds with one another that can span 50 years. They show unselfishness in their nonverbal communications. They kiss, embrace, hold hands, pat one another on the back, swagger, tickle—all with the same meaning these actions have for humans. As Dr. Roger Fouts, a psychologist who studies sign language in chimps, said, "She let the chimpanzees tell her about themselves. Her life is a progression of discovery after discovery."

Jane Goodall's life in Africa was as adventurous as that of a character in a novel. In 1961 she married a Dutch aristocrat, photographer Hugo Van Lawick, and she gave birth to a son. The two divorced in 1974, and Goodall soon after married Derek Bryceson, a Tanzanian government minister who was in charge of the nation's national parks. In the mid-1970s the Gombe project, which by this time was staffed by volunteers, was attacked by Zairian rebels, who kidnapped four of the volunteers and held them for ransom. Goodall and her staff fled to Bryceson's home on the Indian Ocean coast, the ransom was paid, the hostages were released, and Goodall returned to Gombe.

In later years Goodall, concerned about the shrinking population of chimps because of poachers, hunters, and the destruction of habitats, focused more on conservation rather than on research. In 1977 she founded the Jane Goodall Institute, which raised funds to support conservation. In 1991 she founded Roots and Shoots, an organization whose purpose was to teach children about the environment and the need to preserve living creatures. She further publicized her cause with the 1990 publication of *Through a Window: My Thirty Years with the Chimpanzees of Gombe* and through frequent television specials and arduous lecture tours. Her work had important implications not only for the growing field of ethology, or the study of animal behavior in groups, but for moral issues surrounding the use of animals such as chimps for human medical research, a practice she fought with some success. As Goodall noted, "They are so like us in so many ways that sometimes we seem to see our own behavior, the behavior of our remote ancestors mirrored in chimpanzee behavior." ◆

"They are so like us in so many ways that sometimes we seem to see our own behavior, the behavior of our remote ancestors mirrored in chimpanzee behavior."
Jane Goodall, from an address to the National Press Club in 1996, quoted at Jane Goodall Institute's Center for Primate Research web page

# Granville, Evelyn Boyd

MAY 1, 1924– ● MATHEMATICIAN

Evelyn Boyd was born in Washington, D.C., the second of two daughters of Julia Walker Boyd, a U.S. government employee, and William Boyd, an apartment building superintendent. William Boyd did not remain with the family; Granville was reared primarily by her mother and aunt. Granville attended Dunbar High School and won a partial scholarship to study at Smith College in Northampton, Massachusetts.

Granville excelled in mathematics, and in 1945 she graduated summa cum laude from Smith, where she was elected to Phi Beta Kappa. She won several grants that allowed her to enter a graduate program at Yale University, from which she

Evelyn Boyd Granville

**trajectory:** the curve that a body or object negotiates in space; a progression.

earned a Ph.D. with a specialty in functional analysis in 1949. She was one of the first two black female recipients of a doctorate in mathematics. She had a postgraduate fellowship at New York University and, in 1950, was appointed to the mathematics faculty of Fisk University in Nashville. She remained on the faculty for two years and inspired at least two young women to pursue a Ph.D. in mathematics. She left Fisk and spent 16 years working in government and private industry. Some of her employers included the National Bureau of Standards, IBM, the Computation and Data Reduction Center of the Space Technology Laboratories, the Diamond Ordinance Fuze Laboratories, and the North American Aviation Company. Her work involved primarily celestial mechanics, **trajectory** and orbit computation, and associated numerical and digital computer techniques.

In 1967 Granville was appointed to the faculty at California State University in Los Angeles. While there, she cowrote a book with Jason Frand, *Theory and Application of Mathematics for Teachers* (1975). She accepted a position in 1985 at Texas College in Tyler, where she had purchased a farm with her husband, Edward V. Granville. Granville left Texas College in 1988 and, in 1990, was appointed to the Sam A. Lindsey Chair at the University of Texas in Tyler. In addition to teaching at the university level, Granville has taught in secondary school programs in the California and Texas public school systems. ◆

# Hamilton, Alice

FEBRUARY 27, 1869–SEPTEMBER 27, 1970 ● PHYSICIAN

Born in New York City, Alice Hamilton, who became the leading name in American industrial medicine, grew up in Fort Wayne, Indiana, where she was part of an affluent and well-educated family. Her sister, Edith Hamilton, gained fame as a classicist and author of popular books on classical mythology. Craving independence, Hamilton decided as a teenager that she wanted to become a doctor, and to that end she earned a medical degree from the University of Michigan in 1893. Initially she worked as a practicing physician in an immigrant neighborhood in Boston, but she became so disturbed if one of her patients died that she thought her objectivity was compromised. For this reason she decided to become a laboratory researcher.

Hamilton moved to Chicago, Illinois, and for the next 12 years she worked as a medical researcher. She also taught pathology at Northwestern University. Still feeling the

Alice Hamilton

1869 Hamilton is born in Fort Wayne, Indiana.

1910 Hamilton is appointed head of the Illinois Occupational Disease Commission.

1919 Hamilton becomes the first woman faculty member at Harvard.

1970 Hamilton dies.

need to serve other people, she lived at Hull House, a settlement founded in 1889 by reformer Jane Addams to help the immigrant poor. In the basement of Hull House she started a clinic for children, and she also taught adult education classes.

A turning point in Hamilton's life came in 1910 when the governor of Illinois, concerned about the high rate of industrial illness in the state, asked Hamilton to head a team to investigate the problem. Hamilton spent a year as head of the Illinois Occupational Disease Commission, examining conditions in manufacturing plants and talking to owners and managers about working conditions. At that time few people in the United States knew much about the need for ventilation in manufacturing plants. The air in many of these plants was filled with toxic fumes and dust, particularly lead, a substance in which Hamilton was especially interested. In one plant that Hamilton studied, fully *half* of the workers developed lead poisoning over a six-month period. Many plant owners were willing to make changes, but only if Hamilton could prove that lead poisoning was really the cause of worker illness.

This demand raised a whole new set of problems for Hamilton. Many of the workers in these plants were immigrants who could not speak English and who worried that if they complained about working conditions, they would lose their jobs. Compounding the problem was that if a worker became ill and did not come to work, Hamilton had trouble finding him, for companies at that time paid their workers in cash and did not keep records on them. If Hamilton wanted to talk to such a worker, she had to learn his approximate whereabouts (and often his last name) from other workers, then comb through the neighborhood knocking on doors until she found him. She then had to track down hospital records and talk to the workers' doctors, but many of these doctors had failed to diagnose lead poisoning because they did not know what Hamilton knew—that lead poisoning could cause weight loss, weakness and shaking, paralysis, coma, mental problems, and even death.

In the meantime, other members of the commission studied other diseases linked to brass, coal, steel, rubber, and other materials used in industry. While some plant owners cooperated, others did not, and they could not be forced to make changes because there were no laws governing industrial working conditions. Due largely to Hamilton's efforts, that changed in 1911 when Illinois passed the first workers' compensation laws in the United States, requiring companies to compensate workers who were injured or made ill by work-related conditions. In the years that followed, other states followed suit.

Hamilton enjoyed the work so much that she never returned to the laboratory. In 1911 the federal Department of Labor hired her to study occupational disease throughout the nation. She continued to investigate the effects of lead, but she examined other occupational hazards as well, and she toured the country examining mines, factories, smelters, and forges. By the end of her career she was the leading authority on industrial toxicology and had published hundreds of studies and several books on the subject.

At the start of World War I, Hamilton grew concerned about workers who were exposed not only to munitions but to gases, acids, and other chemicals that were changing the face of warfare. While investigating the problem, she often placed herself in danger; in one plant, a number of vats of acid exploded, and Hamilton had to flee the building with other workers to escape a cloud of toxic gas. While her efforts often came too late to help workers during World War I, by World War II many of the hazards faced by workers in the war industries had been greatly reduced, and in some instances eliminated. The U.S. government established a special program to assist workers who had been harmed by industrial poisoning, and most states passed workplace safety laws. All of these changes came about as a result of the work of people like Alice Hamilton.

In 1919 Hamilton was appointed assistant professor of industrial medicine at the Harvard University Medical School, the first women to have faculty status at Harvard. In 1935, at the age of 67, Hamilton retired from Harvard, but the government and industry continued to hire her as an adviser and consultant. She lived to see the beginning of the nuclear age, and in an interview she gave at age 90, she warned that "new industries, new materials, new processes often create new dangers." One of the dangers she foresaw was the problem of storing and disposing of nuclear waste: "I worry about it, but I keep hoping. Maybe tomorrow or the next day will bring a solution."

Alice Hamilton died in 1970 at the age of 101. ◆

"I chose [medicine] because as a doctor I could go anywhere I pleased—to far-off lands or to city slums—and be quite sure that I could be of use anywhere."

Dr. Alice Hamilton, quoted at the National Women's Hall of Fame web site

# Hazen, Elizabeth Lee

AUGUST 24, 1885–JUNE 24, 1975 ● BACTERIOLOGIST

Elizabeth Lee Hazen, whose name survives primarily as that of the co-inventor of the antifungal antibiotic nystatin, was born in Rich, Mississippi. After her parents died when she was three years old, she and her two siblings were adopted by an aunt and uncle. She attended a rural public school in Lula, Mississippi, then graduated in 1910 from the Mississippi Industrial Institute and College (today called Mississippi University for Women) with a bachelor's degree and a certificate in dressmaking. As an undergraduate she developed an interest in bacteriology that she pursued for the remainder of her career.

After graduation Hazen worked for six years teaching high school physics and biology in Jackson, Mississippi. She continued to study bacteriology, and in 1917 earned a master's degree in **bacteriology** from Columbia University. From 1918 to 1923 she worked for the U.S. Army diagnostic laboratories and directed the Clinical and Bacteriological Laboratory of Cook Hospital in West Virginia. She then returned to school, earning a Ph.D. in microbiology from the medical school at Columbia in 1927.

Hazen joined the Division of Laboratories and Research at the New York State Department of Health—at that time an agency with a good record of hiring and promoting women—as the director of the Bacterial Diagnosis Laboratory. There she analyzed vaccines and serums and conducted research on a range of infectious diseases. She traced an outbreak of **anthrax** to its source, and she was the first person in North America to locate the organism implicated in deaths from eating canned fish. She became particularly interested in mycoses, or fungus diseases, while working with Dr. Ruth Gilbert researching a fungal infection called moniliasis.

At that time, medicine had no effective treatment for fungal diseases, which were particularly prevalent among children and members of the armed forces and were often fatal. Penicillin actually worsened fungal infections, and the substances that were known to attack fungi were too toxic to be used in humans. Hazen's goal was to correct that deficiency by discovering a naturally occurring antifungal antibiotic that would be safe for use by humans.

**bacteriology:** the study of bacteria, a single-celled organism which is too small to be seen with the naked human eye.

**anthrax:** a disease in warm-blooded animals which can be passed along to humans by handling infected products; characterized by lung lesions and external ulcerating nodules.

Encouraged by Dr. Rhoda Benham, cofounder of the Medical Mycology Laboratory at Columbia, Hazen assembled a collection of fungal cultures that she used for teaching, research, and medical diagnoses. She tirelessly screened soil samples for microorganisms called actinomycetes, which were known to have antifungal properties. A turning point came when she met a chemist, Dr. Rachel Fuller Brown, who worked in the Albany office of the New York State Department of Health, and the two began a long and fruitful collaboration. Brown's role was to extract, isolate, and purify antifungal substances and return them to Hazen for further testing. Working together, the two made their breakthrough discovery in 1948. That year Hazen found a soil sample near Warrenton, Virginia. From it she isolated a culture that produced two antifungal antibiotics. One turned out to be too toxic to test on humans, but the other, which Hazen and Brown called **fungicidin**, proved effective against a range of fungi. Brown presented their findings in a paper presented at the 1950 meeting of the National Academy of Sciences. Characteristically, Hazen stayed out of the spotlight.

E. R. Squibb and Sons, Inc., was the first drug company to contact Hazen and Brown about their discovery, which the women renamed nystatin after the New York State Division of Laboratories and Research. The company agreed to develop the drug, with Hazen and Brown consulting on the production process. After the drug won approval from the U.S. Food and Drug Administration, Squibb began production of nystatin in 1954 under the trade name Mycostatin, and for the first time in history, doctors had an effective weapon against oral, vaginal, skin, and intestinal fungal infections. The drug turned out to have other uses as well: It proved effective in fighting fungal infections in poultry, it helped in the fight against Dutch elm disease, it was used as a preservative in wine, it protected bananas during shipment, and it even helped restore valuable paintings and frescoes that had become mildewed after 1966 flooding in Florence, Italy.

In the meantime, Hazen and Brown established the Research Corporation of New York to secure a patent for the drug, which they obtained in 1957. The drug generated more than $13 million in royalties, and Hazen and Brown stipulated that half of those royalties should be used to fund research programs in biochemistry, microbiology, and immunology and to help advance the careers of women in science. This fund, which totaled nearly $7 million, lasted until 1976 and at the time was

> **"One of the most famous tales in the history of American medical science is the long-distance collaboration of Elizabeth Lee Hazen and Rachel Fuller Brown, who developed and patented a wonder drug of the 20th century: the world's first successful fungus-fighting antibiotic."**
>
> On Hazen and Brown's discovery of the drug nystatin, quoted at the Massachusetts Institute of Technology's Invention Dimension web site

**fungicidin:** an antifungal medicine designed by Elizabeth Lee Hazen which could be used on humans.

the single most important source of funding for research in medical mycology in the nation. Hazen and Brown used the other half of the money to continue their own research.

Hazen's work did not end with the discovery of nystatin. In 1958 she accepted a position as an associate professor at the Albany Medical College while keeping her position with the state of New York and continuing to collaborate with Brown. She resumed a long-term research project, begun in the 1940s, that help doctors alleviate ringworm and co-authored a reference text entitled *Laboratory Identification of Pathogenic Fungi Simplified* (1960). She also lectured at the Columbia University Medical Mycology Laboratory.

The professional and academic community recognized Hazen for her work. With Brown, she won the Squibb Award in Chemotherapy in 1955. In 1968 she and Brown received honorary doctorates from Hobart College and William Smith College. Again with Brown, she won both the Rhoda Benham Award given by the Medical Mycological Society of the Americas (1972) and the Chemical Pioneer Award from the American Institute of Chemists (1975)—the first time the latter award had been given to a woman or to a scientist who was not a chemist.

Hazen died in 1975 while visiting an ailing sister in Seattle, Washington. In 1994 she and Brown became the second and third women inducted into the National Inventors Hall of Fame. ◆

# Healy, Bernadine

AUGUST 2, 1944– ● PHYSICIAN

Bernadine Healy's appointment as president and chief executive officer of the American Red Cross in 1999 represented the culmination of a life devoted to public service and humanitarian ideals in the field of medicine. Born in New York City, Healy graduated from the prestigious Hunter College High School in New York. She received a bachelor's degree with highest honors from Vassar College in 1965 and a medical degree with honors from the Harvard Medical School in 1970. After completing her postgraduate training in internal medicine and cardiology at the Johns Hopkins School of Med-

Bernadine Healy

icine, she served from 1976 to 1984 as a faculty member at Johns Hopkins, where she taught cardiology and was director of the medical school's Coronary Care Unit.

Healy's career in public service began in 1984, when President Ronald Reagan appointed her deputy director of the White House's Office of Science and Technology Policy. This appointment placed her in the center of life science and regulatory issues at the federal level. She served as chair of the White

House Cabinet Working Group on Biotechnology, as executive secretary of the White House Science Council's Panel on the Health of Universities, and as a member of several advisory groups. These included the Councils of the National Heart, Lung, and Blood Institute and the White House Working Group on Health Policy and Economics.

In 1985 Healy accepted a position as chair of the Research Institute of the Cleveland Clinic Foundation. There she directed the research programs for a number of departments, including the molecular biology, artificial organs, cancer, immunology, neurobiology, and cardiovascular departments. She was also heavily involved in recruitment, fund-raising, and strategic planning for the institute. During her tenure, the Research Institute more than doubled in size and moved into new research facilities.

In 1991, a new opportunity opened for Healy when President George Bush appointed her director of the National Institutes of Health (NIH). There she led a federal agency with 19,000 employees, including 4,000 research scientists at the NIH campus in Bethesda, Maryland, and a budget of over $11 billion. During her years at the NIH, which is a major source of funding for biomedical research throughout the United States, she established the Shannon Awards to foster innovative approaches to biomedical research and to keep talented researchers working during gaps in their funding. She also established a major laboratory for studying human genetics, oversaw the establishment of the Institute for Nursing Research, and led the development of the NIH Women's Health Initiative, a $625 million program to study the causes, prevention, and cures for diseases affecting women.

In 1995 Healy accepted a position as dean of the College of Medicine and Public Health and professor of medicine at Ohio State University. Like the institutions at which Healy had previously worked, Ohio State benefitted from her leadership. She expanded programs in cancer research and tumor genetics, created the Heart and Lung Institute, and spearheaded both the school's recognition as a Center of Excellence in Women's Health and the public health program's accreditation. She also was chair of the Ohio State University Research Commission, a task force that reviewed research throughout the university. When Elizabeth Dole resigned her position as director of the Red Cross to campaign for the Republican presidential nomination in 1999, Healy seemed the obvious choice

## National Institutes of Health

The National Institutes of Health evolved from a series of U.S. government initiatives in public health dating from 1798, when President John Adams established the Marine Hospital Service for the relief of sick and disabled seamen. In 1887, a Laboratory of Hygiene was established in Staten Island, New York, for research into cholera and other infectious diseases. In later years, the laboratory, which would ultimately move to Bethesda, Maryland, expanded its mission to include leprosy, influenza, and other diseases that threatened public health. In 1930, the laboratory was renamed the National Institute of Health (NIH), and it came to be a center for grants, research, and the coordination of various governmental health initiatives. Today, the NIH is one of eight health agencies of the Public Health Services, organized within the Department of Health and Human Services. The NIH has allocated money for research at the forefront of the battle against diseases, and most recently has made the news for its involvement in human genome mapping. Notable achievements include research leading to the reduction in deaths from strokes and cancer, improved treatment of spinal cord injuries, and advances in the study of schizophrenia and depression.

Bernadine Healy became the NIH's 13th director, and first female director, in 1991. Her tenure saw continued expansion of the NIH, including the transfer of the National Institute on Alcohol Abuse and Alcoholism, National Institute on Drug Abuse, and National Institute of Mental Health into the NIH. She was instrumental in launching the $625 million Women's Health Initiative, a project affiliated with 16 university medical programs, to expand our knowledge of the most common causes of disease and death among women. Under her leadership, the NIH also instituted the Shannon Award for new discoveries in biomedical research. Before heading the NIH, Healy served on the advisory committee to the NIH director. At the end of her term as director in 1993, she returned to serve at the Cleveland Clinic in Ohio and at Ohio State University.

to succeed her. She became the 19th person to serve as the organization's director in its then 118-year history.

In addition to leading these major organizations, Healy gave generously to her profession. She served on the American Board of Internal Medicine, the Board of Governors of the American College of Cardiology, and as president of the American Federation of Clinical Research. In 1988–89 she served as president of the American Heart Association, where she started a Women and Minorities Leadership Task Force and a Women and Heart Disease program. In 1997 she became a medical consultant for CBS News, discussing health, medical, and public safety issues on network programs, and she was also a regular contributor to PBS's *Health Week*. Throughout her career she wrote or cowrote more than 220 papers on cardiovascular research and health and science policy. She also wrote a 1996 book, *A New Prescription for Women's Health*.

For her efforts, Healy was the recipient of numerous awards. She was elected to the Institute of Medicine at the National Academy of Sciences. She also won leadership awards from organizations almost too numerous to mention, including the Charles A. Dana Foundation, *Glamour* magazine, the Greater Cleveland Hospital Association, the National Women's Economic Alliance Foundation, the McDonough Center, the YMCA, and the League of Women Voters. Numerous colleges and universities recognized her work by awarding her honorary doctorates. In November 1997 she and her husband, Dr. Floyd D. Loop, were named Humanitarian of the Year by the Red Cross.

In accepting the position at the helm of the Red Cross, Healy said, "The most important aspect of the Red Cross to me is its mission—humanitarianism around the world. I've always been passionate about helping people in crisis and have aspired to make humanitarianism part of everyday life. I look forward to my new assignment in life as an exciting adventure." ◆

# Herschel, Caroline Lucretia

MARCH 16, 1750–JANUARY 9, 1848 ● ASTRONOMER

Caroline Lucretia Herschel was born in Hanover, a duchy that today is part of Germany. Her father, Isaac Herschel, was a professional military musician, and he brought up his four sons to follow in his footsteps. He also took an interest in astronomy and philosophy and tried to give his two daughters a good education as well. Herschel later recalled spending time with her father at night, looking at constellations in the sky. His chief obstacle to educating his daughters was their mother, who grudgingly accepted that the boys should be educated but thought that girls should not do anything other than household chores.

In 1757 the French occupied Hanover. Caroline's brother Wilhelm escaped to England, where he became a music teacher and, in 1766, an organist in the resort town of Bath. Her father went off to fight the French, leaving Caroline under the control of her mother. Isaac returned in 1760 in poor health, and until his death in 1767, Caroline was essentially a live-in servant, caring for her father and doing household work for her mother.

Realizing that she had to take control of her life, Herschel escaped her mother and joined Wilhelm in Bath in 1772. There she trained as a singer and took music lessons from her brother. In time she gave successful singing performances, including a part in Handel's *Messiah*, at Bath, Bristol, and other towns. Wilhelm, though, was also interested in mathematics and astronomy, and after long days at work he often read books about astronomy, including Maclaurin's *Fluxions*. He taught his sister algebra, geometry, and **spherical trigonometry** (as well as English), and, starting in 1777, she helped him in the process of grinding metal mirrors for the telescopes he was constructing. Over time the two began to devote more and more time to their astronomical pursuits. Herschel wrote, "Every leisure moment was eagerly snatched at for resuming some work which was in progress, without taking time or changing dress, and many a lace ruffle ... was torn or bespattered by molten pitch."

A turning point came in 1781, when Wilhelm discovered the planet that is now named Uranus. In recognition of his work, King George III gave him an annual salary and appointed him king's astronomer, enabling him to pursue astronomy as a full-time profession rather than as a hobby. The two gave up music and in 1782 moved to Dachet, where they remained until 1785, when they moved to Clay Hall near Windsor. By day Herschel helped her brother with his research, often performing lengthy mathematical calculations of data he compiled while observing the heavens the night before. At night she made her own observations, using a telescope Wilhelm had made for her. The two built larger and larger telescopes, enabling them to discover galaxies beyond the Milky Way. They also observed binary stars, providing the first confirmation of Newton's law of gravitation outside the Earth's solar system.

Caroline Herschel

**spherical trigonometry:** trigonometry as applied to the principles and functions of spherical triangles and polygons.

1750  Herschel is born in Hanover, Germany.

1786  Herschel is the first woman to discover a comet.

1798  Herschel publishes a star catalog.

1835  Herschel is elected honorary member of the Royal Society.

1848  Herschel dies in Hanover.

"Every leisure moment was eagerly snatched at for resuming some work which was in progress, without taking time or changing dress, and many a lace ruffle ... was torn or bespattered by molten pitch."

A description of Caroline Herschel's work habits, quoted at the Mac-Tutor History of Mathematics web site

In 1786 the two moved yet again to Slough and took up residence in a home called Observatory House. Herschel obtained a new telescope with a 27-inch focal length and a magnification power of 30. The telescope was mounted on the roof of the house. There, on August 1, 1786, Herschel recorded her observation of a comet, making her the first woman to discover a comet. As a result of her discovery she gained a certain amount of notoriety; articles were written about her, and in 1787 the king awarded her an annual salary as Wilhelm's assistant.

Between 1786 and 1797 Herschel discovered a total of eight comets. She then turned her attention to cross-referencing and correcting a star catalog that had been published by the astronomer Flamsteed. In 1798 she submitted to the Royal Society a work entitled *Index to Flamsteed's Observations of the Fixed Stars,* together with a list of 560 stars Flamsteed had omitted. During this period she also discovered 14 new nebulae.

In 1788 Wilhelm had married, and after the 1798 publication of the *Index,* Herschel devoted much of her time to the education of his son, John Herschel, who went on to attend Cambridge University and, as a noted mathematician and astronomer, become a member of the Royal Society. She continued to assist Wilhelm, but her own reputation was secure, and she was invited as a guest to the Royal Observatory in 1799 and was a frequent guest of the Royal Family in the years 1816–1818.

When Wilhelm died in 1822, Herschel returned to Hanover. She assisted her nephew John in his astronomical work, but she continued to conduct her own independent research. She completed a catalog of 2,500 nebulae, and in 1828 the Royal Society awarded her a gold medal for her work. Word spread that she was back in Hanover, and soon she received visits from some of the most eminent German scientists and mathematicians of the day, including Carl Gauss, Alexander von Humboldt, and others. She also received many honors for her work. In 1835 she and Mary Somerville were the first women elected to honorary membership in the Royal Society. In 1838 she was elected to membership in the Royal Irish Academy. On her 96th birthday she received a letter, written by von Humboldt, that stated, "His Majesty the King of Prussia, in recognition of the valuable service rendered to astronomy by you, as the fellow worker of your immortal brother, wishes to convey to you in his name the Large Gold Medal for science."

Caroline Herschel remained in good health despite her advanced age. John Herschel described her as "fresh and funny," and on her 97th birthday she even entertained the Hanoverian crown prince, singing a song Wilhelm had written. She died on January 9, 1848, at the age of 98. In 1889 a planet was named Lucretia in her honor. ◆

# Hodgkin, Dorothy Crowfoot

MAY 12, 1910–JULY 29, 1994 ● CHEMIST

One of the pioneers of X-ray crystallography, Dorothy Crowfoot Hodgkin was born in Cairo, Egypt, on May 12, 1910. During her childhood, which was disrupted by World War I, the high point of her education was an introduction to crystal-growing techniques when she was 10 years old. Finding chemistry fascinating, she pursued experiments in her home laboratory with the wholehearted encouragement and support of her mother. She had to catch up on several subjects in secondary school, but she worked hard and graduated in 1928.

After remedial work in Latin and botany, Hodgkin was able to pass the examination for entrance to Oxford University, where she studied chemistry and began experimenting with the technique of X-ray crystallography. Upon her graduation in 1932, she went to work at Cambridge University with John Desmond Bernal, who was using X rays to study biological crystals in an effort to use structure to explain function. Bernal was a firm believer in equal rights for women, and working in his laboratory allowed Hodgkin to develop her experimental and analytical skills. She developed a driving desire to solve problems that others viewed as impossible, and this characteristic helped her continue her scientific career despite severe rheumatoid arthritis that was diagnosed in 1934. She worked through the pain as her hands and feet

Dorothy Hodgkin

1910 — Hodgkin is born in Cairo, Egypt.

1932 — Hodgkin graduates from Oxford University and goes to work at Cambridge University.

1937 — Hodgkin marries Thomas L. Hodgkin.

1946 — Hodgkin determines the complete structure of penicillin.

1956 — Hodgkin yields the structure of the vitamin B12.

1964 — Hodgkin is awarded the Nobel Prize for chemistry.

became badly disfigured, always managing to retain the dexterity needed for her experimental work. Hodgkin then moved on to Oxford, where, relegated to dismal and vastly underequipped basement laboratories, she continued to develop her skills and build a reputation for insight into complex crystal structures.

In 1937, she married Thomas L. Hodgkin, and by 1946 they had three children. In 1940, she started work on the structure of penicillin, and after a mountain of calculations, she determined the complete structure of penicillin in 1946. In 1947 she was only the third woman elected to the Royal Society of London, and promotions and improved laboratory facilities followed at Oxford.

Hodgkin's research group was well-established by 1948 and attracted numerous women to chemistry who might otherwise not have been interested; future Prime Minister Margaret Thatcher was among her students. Hodgkin treated her students like family. She took pride in their accomplishments. Eight years of data collection and analysis by the group yielded the structure of vitamin B12 in 1956, the accomplishment for which she was awarded the Nobel Prize in chemistry in 1964. She went on to determine the three-dimensional structure of insulin in 1969 and retired from active research in 1977.

All her life, Hodgkin had been interested in world peace, and in 1975 she became the president of the Pugwash Conferences on Science and World Affairs. Being a Nobel Prize winner allowed her access to leaders across the globe, and she used this advantage to promote harmony and cooperation among the most powerful countries of the world. Throughout her retirement, she continued to participate in scientific and peace conferences. Hodgkin died on July 29, 1994, at her home in Ilmington, England. ◆

# Hoffman, Darleane Christian

November 8, 1926– ● Chemist

Darleane Christian Hoffman's roots ran deep in the state of Iowa. She was born in Terril, where her father, a mathematician, was the superintendent of the small local public school. After second grade, she and her family moved to Coon Rapids, where her father had been offered a new job, and she lived in Coon Rapids through the ninth grade. During these years she developed interests both in mathematics and in music, and she not only sang in choral groups but played the piano, the saxophone, the flute, and the oboe. After the ninth grade the family moved once again, this time to West Union, where Darleane was able to live near her Norwegian immigrant grandparents. When she graduated from high school in 1944 at the top of her class, she knew that she wanted to go to college but was uncertain whether to major in mathematics or a new interest, art.

Hoffman finally decided to enroll as an applied art major at Iowa State University, where she not only excelled academically but was a swimmer and tennis player and continued to participate in musical activities. During her freshman year, though, she was required to take chemistry, and she enjoyed the course and its teacher so much that she changed her major. She won a position as an undergraduate research assistant at the university's Institute of Atomic Research, and this early work with radioactivity set her on her future professional course.

Hoffman graduated in 1948, then entered graduate school at Iowa State in the fall of that year. That fall, too, she met her future husband, Marvin Hoffman, who was a student in nuclear physics. For her graduate thesis, she studied the behaviors of new isotopes of cobalt, platinum, and iridium formed by photonuclear reactions in the university synchrotron. After she completed the requirements for her Ph.D. in December 1951, she married Hoffman and took a position at the Oak Ridge National Laboratory in Tennessee. In 1953, though, she left Oak Ridge to join her husband at the Los Alamos Scientific Laboratory in New Mexico, where she took a job in the radiochemistry group. Her first three months at Los Alamos were frustrating because, while the authorities were unsuccessfully trying to locate her Oak Ridge security clearance, other scientists were discovering new elements in the debris left by the first thermonuclear bomb test conducted in 1952.

Hoffman went on to a distinguished career as a nuclear chemist. In 1964 she spent a year in Oslo, Norway, on a National Science Foundation postdoctoral fellowship. In 1971 she was named associate group leader of the radiochemistry group at Los Alamos, and in 1975 she was named a project leader at the Nevada nuclear testing facility, where she was the first woman to participate in the sampling of underground nuclear

**1926** Hoffman is born in Terril, Iowa.

**1951** Hoffman completes her Ph.D. at Iowa State University.

**1984** Hoffman joins the faculty of the University of California at Berkeley.

**1993** Hoffman confirms the existence of the heavy element seaborgium.

**1997** Hoffman wins the National Medal of Science.

Directing a staff of 160, Hoffman worked on projects ranging from nuclear medicine and nuclear fission research to nuclear waste isolation.

**transuranic elements:** elements which are heavier than uranium and decay to lighter elements in a matter of milliseconds.

testing sites. In 1978 she won a Guggenheim Fellowship to study nuclear fission at the University of California at Berkeley. Then in 1979 she returned to Los Alamos to become leader of the Division of Chemistry and Nuclear Chemistry.

Directing a staff of 160, Hoffman worked on projects ranging from nuclear medicine and nuclear fission research to nuclear waste isolation. In 1984 she left Los Alamos to accept a professorship in the chemistry department at Berkeley, where she also worked as a group leader in the Division of Nuclear Science at the Lawrence Berkeley Laboratory. Although she nominally retired in 1991, she stayed on at Berkeley as a professor in the graduate school and a senior scientist in the laboratory. From its inception in 1991, she was also director of the Glenn T. Seaborg Institute for Transactinium Science, a facility devoted to research in the heavy elements and named after the Nobel Prize winner and Hoffman's Berkeley colleague.

During her career, Hoffman emerged as an internationally known expert in the so-called **transuranic elements**. These are elements that are heavier than uranium and normally decay to lighter elements in seconds to milliseconds. At Los Alamos, for example, she became the world's leading authority on the spontaneous fission, or the sudden decay of heavy nuclei into "daughter" nuclei, of such elements as fermium. She also worked on radionuclide migration in the environment, work that had relevance for problems associated with nuclear waste storage and disposal.

After joining Berkeley, Hoffman continued her work on the heavy elements, using the university's 88-inch cyclotron to create rare heavy elements. Using the "atom-at-a-time" technique she and her colleagues pioneered, she was often able to generate just a few atoms per week for study. In 1993 she was part of a team of researchers that confirmed the existence of seaborgium (element 106), the heaviest element found so far. In the late 1990s she was part of an international collaboration that studied the chemistry of rutherfordium (element 104) and seaborgium. A list of her published articles in major professional journals runs to several pages. Throughout her career she also served on numerous advisory committees, and she often gave talks and conducted counseling sessions designed to encourage girls and young women to pursue careers in science.

Hoffman was widely honored for her work. She was a fellow of the American Institute of Chemists and the American Physical Society, as well as a member of the Norwegian Academy of

Science and Letters. In 1983 she was the first woman to receive the Award for Nuclear Chemistry from the American Chemical Society (ACS), and in 1990 she won the ACS's Garvan Medal, given to women chemists for outstanding contributions to the field. In 1996 she received Berkeley's highest award, the Berkeley Citation. Then in 1997 she received her highest honor, the National Medal of Science awarded by the National Science Foundation. A favorite daughter of Iowa, she received the Iowa State University Alumni Association's Distinguished Achievement Award in 1986. ◆

# Hogg, Helen Sawyer

AUGUST 1, 1905–JANUARY 28, 1993 ● ASTRONOMER

Helen Sawyer was born in Lowell, Massachusetts, where she attended the Lowell public schools. She enrolled at Mount Holyoke College with the intention of studying chemistry, but in 1925 she changed her mind and began studying astronomy. She knew that she had made the right decision a year later when noted astronomer Annie Jump Cannon visited the Mount Holyoke campus. Her admiration for Cannon was so great that when she graduated, with honors, from Mount Holyoke in 1926, she joined Cannon at the Harvard University Observatory, where she investigated star clusters. She completed her master's degree from Radcliffe College in 1928, then her Ph.D. from Radcliffe in 1931. She attended Radcliffe because at the time Harvard did not give graduate degrees to women.

Hogg would go on to spend most of the rest of her life in Canada. In 1930 she married Frank Hogg, who had studied astronomy at Harvard. In 1931 she accompanied him to Victoria, British Columbia, where he had obtained a job at the Dominion Astrophysical Observatory. Helen was unable to secure a paid job at the observatory, so from 1931 to 1935 she worked as his unpaid assistant. In Victoria she began work on variable stars—stars that grow bright, then dim, then bright again—in globular clusters. Of particular importance was a technique she developed for measuring the distance of galaxies outside the Milky Way. She took photographs of variable stars and catalogued the cyclical changes in their brightness. She then used

**1905** Hogg is born in Lowell, Massachusetts.

**1931** Hogg earns a Ph.D. in astronomy from Radcliffe College.

**1946** Hogg is named a fellow of the Royal Society of Canada.

**1964** Hogg is the first woman elected president of the Royal Canadian Institute.

**1993** Hogg dies in Richmond Hill, Ontario.

these changes to calculate their distance. Based on thousands of photographs, she published detailed observations that are still used today. Her work helped astronomers better understand not only the distance but the age and composition of remote stars in our galaxy.

In 1935 Hogg and her husband moved to Toronto, Canada, where Frank had obtained a job at the University of Toronto and where Hogg continued her work on variable stars and globular clusters. In Toronto Hogg obtained a job at the university's David Dunlop Observatory, though again she had to work for a year as an unpaid volunteer. In 1936 the university put her on the payroll, and in addition to working at the observatory, she began to teach at the university. In 1957 she was appointed professor. She held this position until 1974 when she was promoted to research professor. She retired as professor emeritus in 1976. She also served as a visiting professor and acting chair of the astronomy department at Mount Holyoke in 1940–41, and in 1955–56 she was a program director in astronomy for the U.S. National Science Foundation.

Although Hogg published more than 200 academic papers, most on the subject of variable stars and globular clusters, she was best known in Canada for making astronomy popular. For nearly 30 years she was a warm and enthusiastic teacher of elementary astronomy for students who were not majoring in science. Hogg wanted everyone to find the same enjoyment in the stars that she did, so from 1951 to 1981 she wrote a popular column called "With the Stars" for a Toronto newspaper—named, appropriately, the *Toronto Star*. In 1976 she published a book entitled *The Stars Belong to Everyone*. She also published dozens of articles on historical astronomy in the *Journal of the Royal Astronomical Society of Canada*. In the 1970s she hosted an astronomy television series.

In addition to her research and publications, Hogg made important contributions to the profession of astronomy. From 1939 to 1941 she was president of the American Association of Variable Star Observers. From 1955 to 1961 she was president of the International Astronomical Union. She also served as president of the Royal Astronomical Society of Canada from 1957 to 1959 and president of the Physical Sciences section of the Royal Society of Canada from 1960 to 1961. In 1964 she became the first woman president of the Royal Canadian Institute, and from 1965 to 1968 she was the first woman councillor of the American Astronomical Society. In 1971–72 she was the founding president and one of the first two female members of the Canadian Astronomical Society. She was also the first honorary president of both the Toronto Centre of the Royal Astronomical Society of Canada (1972–77) and the national Royal Astronomical Society of Canada (1977–81)

With this record of accomplishment, it is no surprise that Hogg became one of Canada's most highly honored scientists. She received six honorary doctorates from Canadian and American universities, including Mount Holyoke. In 1946 she was elected as a fellow to the Royal Society of Canada, the first woman in the physical sciences section. In 1950 the American Astronomical Society recognized her with the Annie Jump Cannon prize. The year 1967 was a banner one for her; that year she won the Rittenhouse Medal, the Service Award Medal from the Royal Astronomical Society of Canada, the Radcliffe Graduate Achievement Medal, and Canada's Centennial Medal.

The following year Hogg won the Medal of Service from the Order of Canada, and in 1967 she was made a Companion of the Order of Canada, one of the highest honors the nation bestows. In 1983 she was the first Canadian to be awarded the Klumpke-Roberts Award. In 1985 the city of Toronto awarded her the Order of Merit and the Royal Canadian Institute awarded her the Sandford Fleming Medal. In 1984 Asteroid 2917 was named Sawyer Hogg in her honor. Additionally, two observatories are named in her honor: the Helen Sawyer Hogg Observatory at the National Museum of Science and Technology in Ottawa and the University of Toronto's southern observatory in Chile.

Helen Sawyer Hogg died of a heart attack in Richmond Hill, Ontario, in 1993, bringing to an end a 60-year career as a leading authority on astronomy. ❖

> Hogg became one of Canada's most highly honored scientists.

# Hopper, Grace

DECEMBER 9, 1906–JANUARY 1992 ● COMPUTER SCIENTIST

Grace Brewster Murray Hopper was born on December 9, 1906, in New York. She earned her bachelor of arts degree in 1928 at Vassar College, where she was elected to Phi Beta Kappa. She did graduate work at Yale University

Grace Hopper

receiving both her master's (1930) and doctoral (1934) degrees in mathematics. Her dissertation, entitled "New Types of Irreducibility Criteria," was written under the supervision of the algebraist Oystein Ore.

Hopper returned to Vassar as an assistant in mathematics in 1931, becoming, successively, instructor, assistant professor, and associate professor. In December 1943, she entered the U.S. Naval Reserve, was commissioned Lieutenant (Junior Grade), and ordered to the Bureau of Ordnance Computation Project at Harvard University. Here she learned to program the Mark I computer.

In 1946, she resigned from Vassar and joined the Harvard Faculty as a Research Fellow in Engineering Sciences and Applied Physics at the Computation Laboratory, where work continued on the Mark II and Mark III computers for the Navy.

In 1949, Hopper joined, as senior mathematician, the Eckert-Mauchly Computer Corporation in Philadelphia, then building the UNIVAC I, the first commercial large-scale electronic computer. She remained with the company as a senior programmer when it was bought by Remington Rand (later to become Sperry Rand Corporation, Sperry Corporation, and Unisys Corporation). There she pioneered in the development of the COBOL (Common Business Oriented Language) compiler and later became one of the prime movers in the development of the COBOL programming language in the 1950s. COBOL was based on Hopper's FLOMATIC, the first English-language data processing language. Her reason for developing the business compiler was, simply, why start from scratch with every program you write when a compiler could be developed to do much of the basic work for you over and over again.

Throughout her business life, Hopper was affectionately anchored to the Navy. She chose to retire in 1966, but the Navy called her back to active duty a year later, when she was

60. She finally left the fleet with the rank of rear admiral in 1986 at the age of 79. Grace Hopper was one of the U.S. Navy's greatest public relations assets. She traveled widely, speaking about computers on the Navy's behalf, exhibiting an honest pride in the Navy and her country, and talking vividly and forthrightly about the work she loved. She encouraged people to be innovative. One of her favorite pieces of advice was, "It is easier to apologize than to get permission."

In her lectures, Hopper lashed out at the computer industry on several counts. Its lack of standards—for programming languages, computer architecture, data structure, and networks—was costing the government hundreds of millions of dollars a year in hardware and software that had to be thrown out because of incompatibility.

Hopper also condemned the notion that larger computers were automatically superior. As an analogy, she pointed out that when a farmer had to move a big, heavy boulder, and one of his oxen was not strong enough to do the job alone, he did not try to raise a bigger ox. He added another ox. Likewise, large volumes of data were better handled by multiple users than by a larger machine.

On September 1, 1986, just over two weeks after she retired from the Navy, she began working as a roving speaker for Digital Equipment Corporation. She died in January 1992.

Hopper's achievements in the design and preparation of problem solutions for digital computers distinguished her as one of the major contributors to program development throughout a period spanning three computer generations. She disseminated her thoughts and ideas not only through her writings, but also through numerous lecture tours. ◆

| | |
|---|---|
| **1906** | Hopper is born in New York. |
| **1928** | Hopper earns a bachelor of arts from Vasser College. |
| **1934** | Hopper earns a doctorate in mathematics from Yale University. |
| **1943** | Hopper enters the U.S. Naval Reserve. |
| **1946** | Hopper joins the engineering faculty at Harvard Univesity. |
| **1949** | Hopper is hired by the Eckert-Mauchly Computer Corporation and remained for years. |
| **1986** | Hopper, who had reamained active in the Navy, retires with the rank of rear admiral. |
| **1992** | Hopper dies. |

# Hyde, Ida Henrietta

SEPTEMBER 8, 1857–AUGUST 22, 1945 ● PHYSIOLOGIST

Ida Henrietta Hyde was born in Davenport, Iowa, to a German immigrant family that later changed its name from Heidenheimer to Hyde. In her late teens and early 20s, she was an apprentice to a milliner in Chicago and took classes at the Chicago Athenaeum, a school for working people. In 1881 she enrolled at the University of Illinois, but a lack of finances

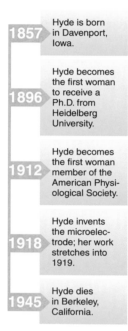

1857 — Hyde is born in Davenport, Iowa.

1896 — Hyde becomes the first woman to receive a Ph.D. from Heidelberg University.

1912 — Hyde becomes the first woman member of the American Physiological Society.

1918 — Hyde invents the microelectrode; her work stretches into 1919.

1945 — Hyde dies in Berkeley, California.

**summa cum laude:** graduating from an educational institution "with highest distinction."

forced her to leave after just a year and work for the next several years as a public school teacher in Chicago. When she accumulated enough money, she returned to college at Cornell University, where she completed her bachelor's degree in 1891. She then worked as a researcher for Jacques Loeb, a physiologist and embryologist, as well as for zoologist Thomas Hunt Morgan, who later won a Nobel Prize for his work on chromosomes. Her work earned her a biology fellowship at Bryn Mawr College in 1892, and in 1893 she was an instructor at the college.

Hyde spent much of the 1890s in Europe. Alexander Wilhelm Goette, a zoologist and physiologist, knew of her work, which supported his own theories, and invited her to conduct research with him at the University of Strassburg (now Strasbourg). Hyde was able to take him up on his offer with the help of a fellowship from an organization now called the American Association of University Women (AAUW). Hyde tried to obtain a Ph.D. on the basis of her work at the university, but she withdrew her application in the face of objections based on her sex. That would be the last time Hyde would ever back down in the face of such opposition.

Believing that conditions were more favorable for women at Heidelberg University in Germany, Hyde moved there in 1894. While many colleagues supported her work, the head of the physiology department threw many obstacles in her path, refusing, for example, to allow her to enroll in his classes. Hyde studied on her own, in the meantime petitioning the Grand Duke of Baden to allow women equal access to the university. The duke supported her petition, making Hyde a key figure in opening German universities to women. Hyde performed brilliantly on her doctoral examinations and in 1896 became the first woman to receive a Ph.D. from Heidelberg—though she was denied the **summa cum laude** designation many of her examiners thought she deserved, again because of the objections of the department head.

Apparently, the department head had a change of heart, for he was instrumental in helping Hyde secure her next two positions. The first was conducting research at the university's zoological station in Naples, Italy, one of the most advanced research facilities of its kind at that time. Hyde enjoyed the experience so much that she returned to the United States to establish the American Women's Naples Table Association to encourage scientific research by women. The second position enabled her to conduct research in physiology at the University of Berne in Switzerland.

Hyde returned to the United States at the end of 1896 as an Irwin Research Fellow in biology at Radcliffe College. She attained another first in 1897 when she joined William Townsend Porter, a renowned physiologist, to conduct research at the Harvard Medical School—the first woman ever to conduct research at the laboratories there. Additionally, she was an instructor at various college preparatory schools in the Cambridge, Massachusetts, area and was director of the biology department at the State Teachers College in Hyannis. From 1897 to 1899 and from 1901 to 1907, she spent her summers as a researcher and professor of physiology at the Woods Hole Marine Biological Station. Her research there and elsewhere centered on the anatomy and physiology of invertebrate and vertebrate animals, particularly their respiratory, circulatory, nervous, and sensory systems.

After all her travels, Hyde finally settled in the Midwest, and in 1898 she was appointed associate professor of physiology at the University of Kansas. Additionally, from 1900 to 1913 she was a faculty member at the university's college of medicine. In 1905 she was promoted to full professor and named head of the university's new Department of Physiology. She could not stay still, though. In 1904 she traveled to England to conduct research at the University of Liverpool, and from 1908 to 1912 she spent summers studying for a medical degree at the University of Chicago (though she fell just one semester shy of completing the degree).

Another first came Hyde's way in 1912 when she was named the first woman member of the American Physiological Society. When World War I hit, she was chair of the Women's Commission of Health and Sanitation of the State Council of National Defense, and, to work the farms in Kansas, she organized a unit of the Women's Land Army. In the meantime she was the author of two textbooks, *Outlines of Experimental Physiology* (1905) and *Laboratory Outlines of Physiology* (1910).

As a scientist, Hyde is best known for inventing the microelectrode, a tiny probe that enables researchers to electrically or chemically stimulate a cell and record the activity the stimulation causes. Hyde developed the invention in 1918–19 and described it in a 1921 article in the *Biological Bulletin*. Her invention, however, was not widely publicized and she failed to

As a scientist, Hyde is best known for inventing the microelectrode.

receive the credit due her when, in 1933, someone else "invented" the microelectrode.

Hyde retired from the University of Kansas in 1920, but she continued her work. In 1922 she returned to the University of Heidelberg to conduct research on the biological effects of radium. She worked tirelessly to encourage women to pursue careers in science and participated in the women's suffrage movement. In 1927 she endowed the Ida H. Hyde Scholarship at the University of Kansas, and in 1945, just before her death from a stroke at age 87, she established the Ida H. Hyde Woman's International Fellowship of the AAUW. ◆

# Hypatia

c. 370–MARCH 415 ● MATHEMATICIAN AND ASTRONOMER

Hypatia, who became the world's leading mathematician and astronomer of her time, was born in Alexandria, Egypt, which at that time was a Greek state and part of the declining Roman Empire. Historians dispute the year of her birth; while most place it at around 370, some argue that she was older and was born around 355. Hypatia's father was Theon, one of the most highly educated men in Alexandria. Theon studied and wrote about the mathematician Euclid and the astronomer Ptolemy, and he was a professor of mathematics at what we would call a university but was then called "the Museum."

Throughout her childhood Hypatia was surrounded by learning and the quest for knowledge. In addition to urging her to maintain a healthy body, Theon taught her the principles of oratory, and in future years Hypatia became an admired teacher and public speaker. He also taught her mathematics and astronomy, and records indicate that she collaborated with him on an astro-

Hypatia

nomical table and wrote commentaries on the work of earlier mathematicians, though these documents do not survive. She has been credited with inventing the astrolabe, a device used in astronomical research, but most historical sources suggest that the astrolabe had been invented about 100 years earlier. As a mathematician, she was best known for her work on conic sections. Building on the work of Apollonius, she edited a book called *On the Conics of Apollonius*. She divided cones into different parts by a plane, introducing to mathematics the concepts of **hyperbolas, parabolas,** and **ellipses.** While Hypatia may not have been the first woman mathematician, she was the first to have a major impact on the field, and Descartes, Newton, and Leibniz all expanded on her work.

Hypatia was respected as a philosopher as well as a mathematician. She based her teachings on the philosophy of Plotinus, who founded the Neoplatonist school of thought around the year 300. Following Plotinus, who in turn followed Plato, she taught that there is an ultimate reality, a Platonic ideal, that exists apart from physical reality, and that the goal of life was to see and understand this ultimate reality. In mathematics, numbers are a kind of Platonic ideal in that they exist apart from physical instances of numbers (the number 2 exists as an "ideal" apart from, say, a pair of socks), so Hypatia's philosophy was highly influenced by science and mathematics. By all accounts, Hypatia was a charismatic teacher.

Hypatia lived at a time when being a mathematician and a Neoplatonist was dangerous, and her tragic death was a direct outcome of her dedication to science. To understand why, it is necessary to understand the political and religious climate that surrounded her. In the late fourth century, Alexandria, like the rest of the Roman Empire, was officially Christian. However, there was a great deal of turmoil throughout parts of the empire as Jews, various heretical sects, Neoplatonists, and other so-called pagan groups contended both with one another and with Christians for spiritual domination.

Caught up in this contention were mathematicians and astronomers, who began to acquire a bad reputation. Because astronomy for the first time enabled people to predict, for example, an eclipse or the positions of the planets, it became associated with foretelling the future. Ordinary people, though, wanted science to foretell their own immediate futures, leading to the emergence of astrology, which argues that the positions of the planets—the province of astronomers—have an influence on

**c. 370** Hypatia is born in Alexandria, Egypt.

**413** Synesius, Hypatia's protector, dies.

**415** Hypatia is murdered in a church in Alexandria.

**hyperbola:** curve formed by the intersection of a double-right circular cone with a plane cutting both halves of the cone.

**parabola:** a plane curve generated by a moving point; its distance from a fixed point equals the distance from a fixed line.

**ellipses:** a plane section of a right circular cone, which is a closed curve.

people's day-to-day lives. In the minds of Christian authorities, legitimate mathematicians such as Hypatia and Theon were little different from charlatans who practiced astrology and numerology. In the middle of the fourth century, for example, the church Council of Laodicea forbade priests from practicing mathematics, and the Roman emperor Constantius passed a law that said "No one may consult a soothsayer or a mathematician." In the minds of many, mathematicians were just another breed of pagan.

Around 391 or 392 Theophilus, the Christian archbishop of Alexandria, razed the temple of Serapis, the god of many Alexandrian pagans, and some historians believe that this action put an end to the Museum where Hypatia's father taught. Theophilus left Hypatia alone, primarily because of her friendship with Synesius of Cyrene. Synesius had been one of Hypatia's admiring students, and by this time he had converted to Christianity and was the bishop of Ptolemais. (Synesius is credited with formulating the Christian doctrine of the Trinity based on Neoplatonist ideas he learned from Hypatia.) Theophilus died in 412 and was succeeded by his nephew, Cyril. Synesius died in 413, leaving Hypatia without her influential protector.

Cyril, backed by a militia, began to assert his spiritual authority and came into conflict with Orestes, the civil governor of Alexandria, and their violent confrontations escalated in 415. Hypatia was a close fiend of Orestes, and a rumor began to spread that Orestes resisted Cyril's spiritual authority because of Hypatia's influence. Worse, she was a "mathematician," one "devoted at all times to magic, astrolabes and instruments of music, [who] beguiled many people through her satanic wiles, and the governor ... through her magic."

Hypatia's fate was sealed. In 415 she was returning home when she was seized, dragged from her carriage into a church, and brutally murdered by Christian fanatics. Church historians to this day remain divided on the issue of Cyril's complicity in the murder, some arguing that he ordered her execution, others that members of his militia acted without his authority. Still others argue that she was simply murdered by Alexandrians who feared her knowledge and talent. Hypatia's murder set off an exodus of scholars from Alexandria, which led to the decline of the city as a center of learning. Cyril, who became an eminent church theologian and formulated the doctrine of the Incarnation, was later canonized as a Christian saint. Not until the 18th century would a woman be as preeminent in mathematics as Hypatia. ◆

J

# Jackson, Shirley Ann

AUGUST 6, 1946– ● PHYSICIST

Shirley Ann Jackson's life of achievement was headlined by a number of historic firsts, both for women and for African Americans: She was the first African American woman to earn a doctorate from the Massachusetts Institute of Technology (MIT), the first African American to serve as a commissioner for the U.S. Nuclear Regulatory Commission, the first woman to head the Nuclear Regulatory Commission, and the first African-American woman to lead a major research university.

Jackson was born in Washington, D.C. Her parents, Beatrice and George Jackson, encouraged her interest in science and even helped her prepare science projects for school. She graduated first in her class at Roosevelt High School, then, as a Martin Marietta Aircraft Corporation Scholar, she was one of only 30 women to enter the freshman class at MIT. In 1968 she earned her bachelor's degree from

Shirley Ann Jackson

165

**1946** Jackson is born in Washington, D.C.

**1973** Jackson is the first African-American woman to earn a Ph.D. at the Massachusett's Institute of Technology.

**1995** Jackson is appointed head of the U.S. Nuclear Regulatory Commission.

**1999** Jackson is named president of Rensselaer Polytechnic Institute.

MIT, then went on to complete a Ph.D. in theoretical high-energy physics in 1973—the first African American woman to earn a Ph.D. in any subject at that prestigious university and just the second African-American woman ever to earn a Ph.D. in physics in the United States. She organized the university's Black Student Union, and later, as a member of the MIT Educational Council and a life member of the MIT board of trustees, she worked to increase the number of African American students at the university. In just one year the number of entering African Americans rose from two to fifty-seven.

After graduating from MIT, Jackson joined the Fermi National Accelerator Laboratory in Batavia, Illinois, as a research associate, where she worked from 1973 to 1974, then from 1975 to 1976. Between these two stints she was a visiting scientist at the European Center for Nuclear Research in Geneva, Switzerland.

In 1976 Jackson left the Fermi lab and accepted a position with the AT&T Bell Laboratories in Murray Hill, New Jersey, where she was a research scientist for the next 15 years. There she conducted research in theoretical physics, investigating primarily the electronic, optical, magnetic, and transport properties of semiconductor systems. Describing her research interests, she said, "Of special interest are the behavior of magnetic polarons in semimagnetic and dilute magnetic semiconductors, and the optical response properties of semiconductor quantum-wells and superlattices." Her research earned her membership as a fellow of the American Academy of Arts and Sciences and of the American Physical Society. Based on her achievements, she was also asked to serve on the National Research Council of the National Academy of Sciences.

In 1991 Jackson joined Rutgers University in New Jersey as a professor of physics, though she continued her association with Bell Labs as a consultant in semiconductor theory. While still at Rutgers, she became the first African American to serve as a commissioner for the Nuclear Regulatory Commission. Then, in 1995, President Bill Clinton appointed her chair of the NRC—the first woman to head that federal agency. She enhanced the agency's regulatory effectiveness and conducted a thorough assessment of all its activities with an eye to public safety. In 1997 she also spearheaded the formation of the International Nuclear Regulators Association, and she was elected the group's first chair. The association comprises senior nuclear regulatory officials from the major industrialized nations, including Canada, France, Germany, Japan, Spain, Sweden, the United Kingdom, and the United States.

Jackson served as chair of the NRC until 1999. That year she accepted the position as the 18th president of the Rensselaer Polytechnic Institute in New York. With her appointment she became the first African American woman to head a major national research university.

In addition to her professional positions, Jackson served the nation and the scientific community in numerous other capacities. She was on the boards of directors of several major corporations, as well as on the board of trustees of Lincoln University. She was a member of the U.S. Department of Energy Task Force on the future of its multipurpose National Laboratories and a member of the advisory council of the Institute of Nuclear Power Operations. She was also a member of several high-level commissions in New Jersey, including the New Jersey Commission on Science and Technology. In all of these roles she worked to advance not only science but the role of women in science.

Jackson received numerous awards in recognition of her research and her public service. She was named an Outstanding Young Woman of America in 1976 and 1981. For her research and for her advocacy of education, science, and public policy, she was named to the National Women's Hall of Fame in 1998. In March 2000 she was given the Golden Torch Award for lifetime achievement in academia from the National Society of Black Engineers.

Jackson is married to Dr. Morris A. Washington, who is also a physicist, and she has one son. ◆

# Jemison, Mae C.

OCTOBER 17, 1956– ● PHYSICIAN AND ASTRONAUT

Mae C. Jemison was born in Decatur, Alabama, the youngest of three children. Her father, Charlie, was a maintenance worker, and her mother, Dorothy, was a schoolteacher. When Jemison was three years old, she and her family moved to Chicago, Illinois, where an uncle introduced her to science; and at an early age she was interested in anthropology, archeology, and astronomy. She graduated from Morgan

Mae C. Jemison

Park High School in 1973, and that year, at age 16, she enrolled in Stanford University. In 1977 she completed her bachelor's degree in chemical engineering and African American studies. She then entered the medical school at Cornell University, where she began to demonstrate her commitment to social welfare by becoming a volunteer and traveling to Cuba, Kenya, and a refugee camp in Thailand to provide primary medical care to people in need.

After completing her medical degree at Cornell in 1981, Jemison moved to Los Angeles, California, where she was a general medical practitioner for the INA/Ross Loos Medical Group. In 1983, though, she joined the Peace Corps and served for two years as an area medical officer for the West African countries of Sierra Leone and Liberia. There she supervised the pharmacy, the laboratory, and the medical staff, wrote self-care manuals, developed and implemented guidelines for health and safety issues, and worked with the Centers for Disease Control on vaccine research. After leaving the Peace Corps in 1985, she returned to Los Angeles to work as a general practitioner for the CIGNA Health Plans of California. She remained interested in engineering, though, and over the next two years updated her knowledge by enrolling in graduate classes in engineering.

Looking for new challenges, Jemison applied to the astronaut program of the National Aeronautics and Space Administration (NASA), though her first application was not accepted. In 1987, though, on her second application, she was one of just 15 out of 2,000 applicants accepted as an astronaut candidate. She completed her training in August 1988, becoming just the fifth African American and first African American woman astronaut in NASA history. Jemison made further history on September 12, 1992, when the space shuttle *Endeavor* blasted off with her aboard—the first African American woman in space. She was the science specialist on a joint U.S.–Japanese mission (she spoke fluent Japanese, as well as Swahili and Russian) and conducted experiments in life sciences, materials sciences, and bone cell research.

After six years with NASA Jemison resigned in 1993, though she continued her association with the space program as a member of the National Research Council Space Station Review Committee. She went on to become a professor in the environmental studies program at Dartmouth College in New Hampshire and the director of the Jemison Institute for Advancing Technology in Developing Countries. At Dartmouth she also founded a private company called The Jemison Group.

Jemison's goal in forming this company was to integrate science and technology with culture, health, the environment, and education for the benefit of everyone on the planet, including the 75 percent of the earth's population living in developing countries. In pursuit of this end, she teamed with universities, governments, agencies, foundations, and business to launch a number of projects. One, called Alafiya, was a satellite-based telecommunications system to help provide health care to West Africa. A second was the design of solar and thermal electricity generating systems for use in developing nations. A third was an effort to introduce a U.S. science curriculum into South Africa. A fourth was the development of real-time desktop computer simulations for pilots. Finally, she developed a program called The Earth We Share, an international camp that used an experiential curriculum to teach science to students ages 12 to 16. In addition to this work, Jemison traveled nationally and internationally to lecture on such topics as science literacy and education, achieving excellence, and the need to increase women and minority representation in mathematics and the sciences.

Jemison's endeavors did not go unnoticed. She was a member of the Women's Hall of Fame. *People* magazine named her one of the "World's 50 Most Beautiful People" in 1993. Johnson Publications gave her the Black Achievement Trailblazers Award. She won the Kilby Science Award. A number of universities awarded her honorary doctorates. She gave presentations to the United Nations on the uses of space technology. In 1994–95 she was the host and technical consultant for the *World of Wonder* series on the Discovery Channel. She was the subject of a Public Broadcasting System documentary, "The New Explorers." She even appeared in an episode of *Star Trek: The Next Generation.* She served on the boards of directors of Scholastic, Inc., The Aspen Institute, and Spelman College. An alternative public school in Detroit, Michigan, is named in her honor. ◆

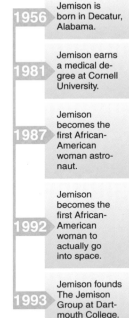

1956 Jemison is born in Decatur, Alabama.

1981 Jemison earns a medical degree at Cornell University.

1987 Jemison becomes the first African-American woman astronaut.

1992 Jemison becomes the first African-American woman to actually go into space.

1993 Jemison founds The Jemison Group at Dartmouth College.

# Joliot-Curie, Irène

SEPTEMBER 12, 1897–MARCH 17, 1956 ● PHYSICIST

Irène Joliot-Curie was born on September 12, 1897, the elder daughter of Marie Curie and Pierre Curie. Within a week of her birth, her mother returned to the laboratory. This was the beginning of a three-generation tradition of Curie women who were world-class scientists as well as wives and mothers.

Joliot-Curie was a stubborn child, who developed the grave look and masculine traits of her father. As an adult, she was very uneasy in social situations. The development of these personality traits may have been connected to the sudden death of her father when she was seven.

At the age of 11, Joliot-Curie completed her primary schooling. Rather than sending her to secondary school, her mother participated in the organization of a cooperative school for children of a faculty at the Sorbonne. This group of young people received lessons from some of the most brilliant scientific and mathematical minds of the day. After the cooperative school closed, Joliot-Curie was sent to a private secondary school, which she completed at age 17.

During World War I, Joliot-Curie served as an assistant to her mother in delivering and operating X-ray units for military hospitals. The technology was new, and Joliot-Curie found herself educating surgeons in the use of X-ray films to locate shrapnel fragments. At times, receiving instruction from a 17-year-old girl was not appreciated by the physicians. During these years Joliot-Curie and her mother continued to relate to each other more as professional colleagues than as mother and daughter.

Irène Joliot-Curie

In March 1925, Joliot-Curie received her doctorate from the Sorbonne, completing her dissertation research in her mother's laboratory. Joliot-Curie was given no special privileges at the Institut du Radium, but she had the advantage of the tutelage of Marie Curie.

Joliot-Curie met Frédéric Joliot at the Institut du Radium, where he also worked. The couple were married on October 4, 1926. Just as her parents had done, the Joliot-Curies worked closely together on research in nuclear chemistry. They had two children, Héléne and Pierre.

Research conducted by the Joliot-Curies resulted in the discovery of the neutron and the positron. Since they were unable to identify the chargeless particle emitted from the nucleus during the transmutation reactions, credit for the discovery of the neutron is not given to them. They reported the discovery of the **positron** at the Solvay Conference in October 1933. The report was treated coldly by the assembly, but was privately lauded by both Niels Bohr and Wolfgang Pauli after the meeting. In 1935, the Joliot-Curies received the Nobel Prize in chemistry for the discovery of artificial radioactivity. Their experiments produced new radioactive elements by alpha particle bombardment.

As Europe prepared for World War II, Joliot-Curie received a professorship at the Sorbonne, unusual for a woman. She also served briefly as the French undersecretary of state for scientific research. Her accomplishments identify her as a significant contributor to the advancement of the role of women in France. During the Second World War, Joliot-Curie and the children lived in Switzerland, while Frédéric remained in France as a member of the Resistance. After the war, she returned to collaborate with Frédéric on the design of the first atomic pile built in France. She used knowledge of geology acquired in early life to locate potential deposits of uranium in France.

Like her mother and husband, Joliot-Curie suffered the physical effects of working with radioactive materials on open lab benches. Even though the Institut du Radium developed safety procedures during Joliot-Curie's career, the effects of early exposure took their toll. Throughout her life she was plagued by diseases of various types, and she died of leukemia on March 17, 1956. ◆

In 1935, the Joliot-Curies received the Nobel Prize in chemistry for the discovery of artificial radioactivity.

**positron:** a positively charged particle.

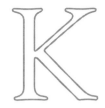

# Karle, Isabella L.

DECEMBER 2, 1921– ● CHEMIST

Isabella Karle was born Isabella Helen Lugoski to a Polish immigrant family in Detroit, Michigan. Though her family's income was meager, her parents were frugal, and even during the Great Depression Isabella and her siblings did not want for anything. Her parents and neighbors spoke Polish at home, so Isabella did not learn English until she started attending school, but by that time her mother had already taught her to read and write in Polish and to do arithmetic.

Karle was first exposed to science in high school, when by chance she took a course in chemistry to fulfill a college preparatory requirement. She found the course fascinating, and despite the counsel of her teacher, who told her that chemistry was not a proper field for girls, she determined that she wanted to be a chemist. Later in life she said simply, "I want to know how things work."

Karle enrolled in Detroit's Wayne State University as a chemistry major, but after one semester

Isabella L. Karle

**1921** Karle is born Isabella Lugoski in Detroit, Michigan.

**1946** Karle begins a lifelong career at the U.S. Naval Research Laboratory.

**1993** Karle becomes the first woman to win the Bower Award and Prize in Science.

**1995** Karle wins the Medal of Science from the National Science Foundation.

she transferred to the University of Michigan, which had awarded her a four-year scholarship and where she secured an undergraduate assistantship in the chemistry department. She graduated with the highest honors in 1941 and wanted to go on to graduate school, but she found her opportunities limited because graduate assistantships at Michigan were awarded only to men. With a fellowship from the American Association of University Women, though, she was able to begin graduate studies, then won a fellowship that enabled her to continue.

In 1942, Karle completed her master's degree and married Jerome Karle, a fellow graduate student with whom she went on to collaborate professionally throughout her career. She stayed at the University of Michigan to complete her Ph.D. in chemistry in 1944. She was just 22 years old.

After graduation, the Karles worked briefly in Chicago on the Manhattan Project, which led to the development of the atomic bomb. When World War II ended, they tried to secure academic employment at the same university, but the only organization that would offer both of them a job was the U.S. Naval Research Laboratory (NRL). When they arrived at the NRL in 1946, they found talented people and an exciting research atmosphere, and they both remained there throughout highly distinguished careers.

In 1964 Karle won the Navy Superior Civilian Service Award. In 1968, she won the Society of Women Engineers Achievement Award, and the following year she won the Hellebrand Award given by the American Chemical Society (ACS). In 1976 she won the Garvan Medal, given each year by the ACS to a woman chemist who has made important contributions to the field. In 1978 she became a member of the National Academy of Sciences.

Other awards followed: the Robert Dexter Conrad Award; the Pioneer Award given by the American Institute of Chemists; the Secretary of the Navy Distinguished Achievement in Science Award; the Gregori Aminoff Prize given by the Royal Swedish Academy of Science; the Bijroet Medal from the University of Utrecht in the Netherlands. In the 1990s Karle reached the summit of her profession. In 1993 she became the first woman to win the Franklin Institute's Bower Award and Prize in Science—an award that carried a prize of $250,000. Then in 1995 she won the prestigious Medal of Science, awarded by the National Science Foundation. By this time

Karle was a senior scientist and head of the X-ray Analysis Section at the NRL's Laboratory for the Structure of Matter.

Throughout her 50-plus-year career, Karle conducted research in crystallography, which, she explained, tried to determine "which atoms are connected to which, and how they are arranged in respect to each other in the crystal lattice." She became interested in crystallography in graduate school, where one of her professors was examining the crystal structure of gaseous molecules. The Karles, though, began to think about the crystal structures of solid matter. With Herbert Hauptman, Jerome Karle developed a theoretical mathematical model for X-ray crystallography of solid matter, and for their work the two shared the Nobel Prize in chemistry in 1985. Their model solved the problems that arose when the techniques used successfully to examine the crystalline structure of gases were applied to solid crystals. Isabella Karle translated the theoretical model into practical, experimental results.

In 1966 Karle and her husband published a joint article in which they described the theory and outlined a revolutionary technique for examining solid crystal structures, a technique they called the "symbolic addition procedure." Their findings led to greater understanding of the three-dimensional nature of matter and how this structure influenced a substance's physical and biological properties. Karle's experimental results were documented in nearly 300 scientific papers.

This work had important practical applications, for it made it much easier for scientists to understand the structure of a substance. For example, one of Karle's first major successes was to determine the crystalline structure of a frog venom; the venom was valued by medical researchers studying nerve transmission because it blocked nerve impulses. Karle's techniques allowed scientists to develop a synthetic form of the toxin. Similarly, her work had benefits for drug researchers by helping them synthesize therapeutic drugs without harmful side effects. The U.S. Navy was able to synthesize an agent found in a scarce type of wood that repels worms and termites and used the synthetic agent to treat the wood in its ships. The Karles' work made it possible to develop hundreds of such substances.

Karle was happily at work in her lab well into her 70s. She stayed fit by ice skating, swimming, hiking, and doing yard work. She became a vocal advocate for the value of basic (as opposed to applied) scientific research, pointing out that it

**"What she came up with is now being used by crystallographers throughout the world. We used to have to spend an inordinate amount of time trying to understand structures. Now our understanding occurs faster."**
Drake Eggleston, fellow at SmithKline Beecham, on Isabella Karle's discoveries, quoted in *The Scientist*, January 10, 1994

might take as much as 50 years for the results of basic research to find practical application: "The pool containing basic information must be constantly replenished, otherwise it will run dry." ◆

# King, Mary-Claire

FEBRUARY 27, 1946– ● GENETICIST

Mary-Claire King, best known for identifying and locating the gene implicated in some forms of breast cancer, was born in Evanston, Illinois. As a child she enjoyed solving problems and puzzles, and this inclination evolved into a mathematics major at Carleton College in Minnesota, from which she graduated in 1966 when she was just 19 years old.

In the 1960s, King dropped out of school for a period of time to serve as an anti–Vietnam War activist and work with consumer advocate Ralph Nader; throughout her career, science and political activism frequently intersected. She returned to school and earned a Ph.D. in genetics from the University of California at Berkeley in 1973, where she eventually became a professor in the School of Public Health and the Department of Molecular and Cell Biology. In the years that followed she remained committed to political causes and used her expertise in biological research to help groups that the biomedical field sometimes overlooked, including women, AIDS patients, and victims of South American political turmoil.

In 1975 the results of King's Ph.D. dissertation research earned her a cover story in the journal *Science*. With that research, she altered the direction of evolutionary biology by showing that the genomes of humans and chimpanzees are 99 percent identical. She based her work on a comparison of proteins and discovered that only one out of 100 proteins differ in humans and chimpanzees. Previously, scientists had used fossil records to conclude that humans diverged from apes about 15 million years ago, but King's research sparked a reassessment of that view and a different conclusion: that humans and apes diverged evolutionarily only about five million years ago. Her work proved in the lab something that field researchers such as chimp expert Jane Goodall had already known from observation: that in many ways humans and chimps are not all that different from one another. Her findings also had implications for ethical questions surrounding the use of chimps for human medical research.

Beginning in 1984 King found a unique way to use her knowledge of human genetics to solve a social problem. That year she traveled to Buenos Aires, Argentina, to begin work for the Committee for the Investigation of Disappearance of Persons. The purpose of this committee was to help a group called the Abuelas de Plaza de Mayo, a group of grandmothers who were trying to locate their kidnapped grandchildren. In 1975 a vicious civil war had broken out in Argentina. As fascist dictators tried to impose their rule on the country, they abducted pregnant women and women with small babies. They placed the children with military families and murdered the mothers.

Into this fray entered the grandmothers—mothers of the murdered women—who were determined to locate their missing grandchildren. First, however, they needed a way to prove that they were biologically related to the children and that the apparent "parents" were not. King played a major role in the development of a blood test that could show with 99.9 percent accuracy whether a child is related to a set of these grandparents. The test, based on specific genetic markers such as the human leukocyte antigen, could detect variations in DNA sequences between individuals. Combined with other techniques such as **mitochondrial sequencing**, this test helped King and her associates reunite 50 children with their families by proving that they were genetically related.

While still at UC Berkeley, King made the breakthrough discovery for which her name is best known. Scientists had always believed that inheritable diseases were the result of multiple genes interacting with environmental factors. They also believed that breast cancer was not a hereditary disease. Working with a team of researchers, King redirected thinking on this issue. She examined 1,500 family histories, looking for patterns of breast cancer occurrence. Out of this group she identified about 15 percent of families that showed a high incidence of breast cancer through multiple generations. Using blood tests as well as family histories, she began the daunting task of searching through 183 possible genetic markers for the one that might be linked to breast (and ovarian) cancer. In 1990 she announced that she had identified the gene, called BRCA1. The next step was to locate the gene by examining

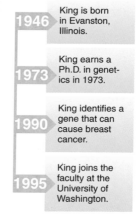

**1946** King is born in Evanston, Illinois.

**1973** King earns a Ph.D. in genetics in 1973.

**1990** King identifies a gene that can cause breast cancer.

**1995** King joins the faculty at the University of Washington.

**mitochondrial sequencing:** Ordering of studying energy reporduction and cellular respiration in organisms.

"Women tend to tackle questions in science that bridge gaps. We're more inclined to pull together threads from different areas, to be more integrative in our thinking."
Dr. Mary-Claire King, on women in science, quote in "The Search for a Breast Cancer Gene," in *Glamour* magazine, December, 1993

the DNA of healthy breast tissue cells and comparing it to the DNA of cancerous cells, where mutations were occurring. In 1994 King found it on chromosome 17. Scientists now had a more complete understanding of the role of genetics in breast cancer and could begin to develop more effective ways to fight it. King herself went on to conduct research at major cancer centers to study inherited susceptibility to breast cancer in specific populations, including Jewish and rural southern African-American women. With a team of researchers at Vanderbilt University she explored the use of gene therapy as a form of treatment for ovarian cancer. She also led a team that investigated how genetics and the environment interacted among 120,000 participants in the Harvard Nurses' Health Study.

In 1995 King joined the University of Washington in Seattle as a professor of medicine and genetics. There she focused on AIDS research. In particular, she investigated why people's immune systems can respond to the virus in markedly different ways. She also attempted to map and clone the gene responsible for certain types of inherited deafness.

In all, Mary-Claire King has contributed more than 150 articles to professional journals and is in frequent demand as a speaker about the impact of breast cancer on women's lives. She is not only a pioneer in genetic research but a tireless advocate for the view that basic science can improve the health and well-being of people. ◆

# Kittrell, Flemmie Pansy

DECEMBER 25, 1904–OCTOBER 1, 1980 ● NUTRITIONIST

Born in Henderson, North Carolina, Flemmie Kittrell attended local public schools and then Hampton Institute in Hampton, Virginia, from which she graduated in 1929. At Cornell University she received a master's degree (1930) and a doctorate in nutrition (1935). Kittrell's research interests included protein levels in adults, the nutritional requirements of black infants, and the education of preschool children. She taught nutrition and home economics at a number of colleges and universities including Benton College in Greensboro, North Carolina (1928–1940) and Hampton Institute (1940–1944). She later served as Head Nutritionist at Howard University (1944–1973), where she developed both master's and doctoral programs in the field of nutrition.

Kittrell began promoting international cooperation in home economics in 1950 when she received a Fulbright Award to help Baroda University in India establish a College of Home Economics. She returned to India in 1953 and again in 1960 to help complete the organization of the college and to assist with a nutritional survey of India and Thailand for the Food and Agriculture Organization of the United Nations. Kittrell also promoted cooperation in Africa, where in 1957 she researched nutritional practices in Liberia, Nigeria, and French West Africa for the U.S. State Department, and participated in cultural tours of West and Central Africa (1959) and Guinea (1961).

Kittrell was the recipient of numerous citations and awards, including the Scroll of Honor from the National Council of Negro Women for special services rendered to the U.S. government. She died in Washington, D.C., in 1980. ◆

# Kovalevskaya, Sofia

JANUARY 15, 1850–FEBRUARY 10, 1891 ● MATHEMATICIAN

Russian mathematician Sofia Kovalevskaya was born in Moscow. As the daughter of minor nobility, she grew up in affluent surroundings and was educated by tutors and governesses at the family's country estate at Palabino, then in St. Petersburg. She felt neglected as a middle child, caught between an admired older sister and a younger brother who was heir to the estate. This, combined with the attentions of a strict governess who took it as her duty to turn Sofia into a proper young lady, made her somewhat shy and withdrawn, traits she displayed for the rest of her life.

Kovalevskaya became interested in mathematics at a very young age, when an uncle discussed mathematical concepts with her. She could not understand these concepts, but under his influence she began to see mathematics as an "exalted and mysterious science." Because of a wallpaper shortage, her nursery was papered with her father's lecture notes from a course in calculus, and at age 11 she studied the notes, recognizing principles her uncle had discussed. Under a tutor, she

Sofia Vasilyevna
Kovalevskaya

became so enamored of mathematics that she neglected her other studies, and when her father stopped her mathematics lessons, she borrowed an algebra book and read it while the family slept. At age 14 she was reading a physics textbook written by a neighbor and taught herself trigonometry so that she could understand the optics section. The neighbor recognized her ability and persuaded her father to send her to St. Petersburg to continue her education.

The story of Kovalevskaya's adult life is one of doors closing in her face because she was a woman. After finishing her secondary education, she wanted to attend a university, but to do so she had to go abroad because no Russian university would accept her. In order to travel abroad at that time, a young Russian woman had to have the permission of a father or husband. She was 18, so in 1868 she entered into a marriage of convenience with Vladimir Kovalevsky, to whom she remained married until his suicide in 1883. With Vladimir's permission she arrived in Heidelberg, Germany, in 1869 to study mathematics and natural sciences, but she discovered that the university was not open to women. Her only option was to persuade university officials to allow her to attend classes unofficially, which she did for three semesters.

In 1870 Kovalevskaya decided that she wanted to study mathematics at the University of Berlin under Karl Weierstrass, one of the most eminent mathematicians of the day. Again, the university did not admit women, and at first Weierstrass did not take her seriously. Her failure to gain admission to the university actually worked to her advantage, for when she solved a complex problem Weierstrass put to her, he recognized her genius and agreed to tutor her privately. By 1874 she had written papers on partial differential equations, Abelian integrals, and Saturn's rings; the first of these papers was so significant that it was published in an influential mathematics journal, an almost unprecedented achievement for a woman at that time. Weierstrass, who had come to admire his gifted pupil, believed that these papers qualified her for a doctorate, and with his help, she was granted a Ph.D. with honors from the University of Göttingen in 1874.

Despite her degree and the sponsorship of Weierstrass, doors remained closed to Kovalevskaya and she was unable to obtain employment teaching mathematics. The only job she could find, which she did not accept, was teaching arithmetic to elementary-school girls, but, she observed wryly, "I was unfortunately weak in the multiplication table." She decided to return home, but shortly after she arrived at Palabino, her father died suddenly, and in her grief she neglected mathematics for the next six years. During these years she gave birth to a daughter and wrote fiction, theater reviews, and science articles for a newspaper. Her literary gifts were considerable, and later in life she wrote plays.

In 1880 Kovalevskaya resumed her study of mathematics. She presented a paper on Abelian integrals at a scientific conference. In 1882 she began work on the refraction of light and published three papers on the subject. Finally, in 1883 a door opened. One of Weierstrass's former students invited her to lecture at the University of Stockholm in Sweden. The position was only a temporary one, but Kovalevskaya was determined to use the position to make her mark when she arrived at the university in 1884. She taught courses in the latest mathematical topics. In 1885 she published a paper on crystals. She was appointed editor of a new journal, *Acta Mathematica*. She organized conferences with leading mathematicians from major European capitals.

Then, in 1888, Kovalevskaya entered a paper entitled "On the Rotation of a Solid Body about a Fixed Point" in a competition for the Prix Bordin sponsored by the French Academy of Science. The paper was so highly regarded that the academy actually increased the prize money from 3,000 to 5,000 francs. In 1889 she won a prize from the Swedish Academy of Sciences for further work on the same topic, and in the same year the Imperial Academy of Sciences in her native Russia changed its rules so that she could be elected a corresponding member. The University of Stockholm could not ignore these accomplishments. In 1889 the university granted her status as a professor.

Unfortunately, Kovalevskaya's triumph did not last long. At the summit of her career, she contracted influenza. Pneumonia

**1850** Kovalevskaya is born in Moscow.

**1874** Kovalevskaya is awarded a Ph.D. from the University of Göttingen.

**1884** Kovalevskaya is appointed a temporary lecturer at the University of Stockholm.

**1889** Kovalevskaya is appointed a professor at the University of Stockholm.

**1891** Kovalevskaya dies in Stockholm.

set in, and she died in Stockholm in 1891 at just 41 years of age. The scientific world mourned her loss, but her name survived not only for her ground-breaking discoveries but for stimulating the work of later mathematicians. ◆

# Kwolek, Stephanie L.

JULY 31, 1923– ● CHEMIST

Occasionally a scientific researcher's name becomes linked to a single important invention or discovery. Such is the case with Stephanie Kwolek. Kwolek was the DuPont research chemist who discovered KEVLAR, the superstrong fabric that found an enormous variety of applications in modern life.

Kwolek was born in New Kensington, Pennsylvania. In his free time her father, John Kwolek, was a naturalist, and she often tramped with him through the woods and fields surrounding their home, where she collected leaves, seeds, and flowers that she assembled into scrapbooks. From her mother she acquired a love of sewing and fabrics, and for a time considered a career in fashion design. When she was 10, her father died, forcing her mother to support her and her younger brother by working for the Aluminum Company of America.

Kwolek graduated from high school in 1942. Her original aspiration was to become a doctor, which led her to enter the Margaret Morrison Carnegie College, the women's college of Carnegie-Mellon University in Pennsylvania. She did, however, take science classes with men at the university's college of engineering and graduated in 1946 with a bachelor's degree in chemistry. She still planned to become a doctor, but she and her family lacked money to pay for tuition, so she applied for jobs with various chemical companies with the intention of saving money so that she could go to medical school. One of the jobs was at the DuPont Chemical Company. The research director who interviewed her told her that he would inform her of the company's decision in two weeks, but Kwolek had to respond to another job offer and told the director that she needed to know sooner. He offered her a job on the spot, and in time Kwolek became so excited by her work in polymer chemistry that she abandoned plans to go to medical school. She stayed at DuPont for four decades.

Kwolek spent her first four years in the company's rayon department in Buffalo, New York. She then moved to the Pioneering Research Laboratory in Wilmington, Delaware, where she remained for 36 years, steadily earning promotions to the level of research associate. Her first major accomplishment came as a member of a team that developed NOMEX, a fire-resistant fabric used by firefighters.

Kwolek then turned her attention to the condensation processes used to make polymer fibers such as nylon. At the time, these processes required high temperatures, but Kwolek devised a process that allowed polymer fibers to be condensed at low temperatures, and even at room temperature. In 1959 Kwolek and one of her colleagues published an article in the *Journal of Chemical Education* that showed schoolteachers the "nylon rope trick," a way to almost magically form a rope of nylon from a beaker solution in the classroom.

In 1964, Kwolek made the discovery that, in its own small way, changed the world. She had been assigned the task of developing a new high-strength fabric, one that would remain stable at high temperatures. She began her investigation with liquid crystals, or polymer solutions in which the molecules line up facing the same direction—unlike the molecules in most polymers, which flow in unordered chains. The problem she encountered, though, was how to spin these crystals into fibers, and for that she needed both a new solvent and a new way to spin the fibers. She finally developed a solution that was thin and milky rather than viscous and clear, as the brew for other fibers had been. She had to persuade the person who ran the spinning equipment to spin the solution, for he believed it would clog up the machine. When she spun the solution, there emerged fibers with properties so remarkable that Kwolek first thought that some kind of mistake had occurred.

In fact, what came out of the machine was KEVLAR, which the company began producing commercially in 1971. KEVLAR is five times stronger than steel. It has about half the density of fiberglass. It is flame resistant and does not conduct electricity. It is resistant to wear and tear. KEVLAR found application in hundreds of products, including radial tires, skis, sails, tennis rackets, fiberoptic cables, brake pads, suits for firefighters, helmets, parts of space vehicles and airplanes, and

**1923** Kwolek is born in New Kensington, Pennsylvania.

**1946** Kwolek begins a 40-year career with DuPont.

**1964** Kwolek develops KEVLAR.

**1996** Kwolek wins the National Medal of Technology.

cut-resistant gloves used by butchers and surgeons. Its most prominent application was in bulletproof vests, and it is estimated that KEVLAR has saved the lives of thousands of police officers who might otherwise have lost their lives from gunfire.

KEVLAR was not the only fiber Kwolek developed. By the time she retired from DuPont in 1986 she held 17 patents. She was also widely honored for her work. Among her many awards were the Howard N. Potts Medal, awarded by the Franklin Institute of Philadelphia; the Chemical Pioneer Award, given by the American Institute of Chemists; the Award for Creative Invention, given by the American Chemical Society; and the George Lubin Memorial Award, given by the Society for the Advancement of Material and Process Engineering. In 1995 she became only the fourth woman to be inducted into the National Inventors Hall of Fame, in 1996 she received the National Medal of Technology in a ceremony at the White House, and in 1997 she became the second woman to receive the Perkin Medal. In 1999 she won the Lemelson-MIT Lifetime Achievement Award.

In the years following her retirement, Kwolek remained busy. To celebrate her retirement, she bought herself a new sewing machine, but she also served as a consultant to DuPont as well as to the National Research Council and the National Academy of Sciences. Well into her 70s she traveled around the world speaking about her work to students and other scientists; she even made a television commercial for DuPont that credited her for the KEVLAR discovery. ◆

# Lawrence,
# Margaret Cornelia Morgan

AUGUST 19, 1914– ● PHYSICIAN

Margaret Morgan was born in New York City because her mother, Mary Elizabeth Morgan, a teacher, had traveled there in search of the better medical care available to black people in the North. Margaret's father, Sandy Alonzo Morgan, was an Episcopal minister, and the family followed him as he answered calls to minister in Portsmouth, Virginia; New Bern, North Carolina; Widewater, Virginia; and Mound Bayou, Mississippi, before settling in Vicksburg, Mississippi, when Margaret was seven.

Morgan was certain at a young age that she wanted to be a doctor. She persuaded her parents to allow her to live with relatives in New York City to take advantage of the better educational opportunities there. She attended Wadleigh High School for Girls in New York City, and entered Cornell University with a full scholarship in 1932. She was the only African American undergraduate studying there at the time. Barred from the Cornell dormitories because of her race, she boarded as a live-in maid to a white family. Although her grades and entrance examinations were more than satisfactory, Cornell Medical School refused her admission because she was black. She enrolled in Columbia University, where she earned her M.D. in 1940, and served her medical internship and residency at Harlem Hospital. In 1943, she received an M.S. in Public Health from Columbia.

**1914** Lawrence is born in New York City.

**1940** Lawrence earns a medical degree from Columbia University.

**1943** Lawrence receives a master's degree in public health from Columbia.

**1943** Lawrence becomes a professor at Meharry Medical College in Nashville.

**1951** Lawrence receives a Certificate in Psychoanalysis from the Columbia Psychoanalytic Clinic.

**1988** An award winning biography of Lawrence, written by her daughter, is published.

That year she moved with her husband, sociologist Charles Radford Lawrence II, and their baby son to Nashville, where she became a professor at Meharry Medical College. While in Nashville, she gave birth to two daughters 18 months apart, created a Well-Baby Clinic in East Nashville, and maintained a private pediatric practice at home. In 1947, the Lawrence family returned to New York, and Lawrence attended Columbia University's Psychiatric Institute. She was the first African-American trainee at the Columbia Psychoanalytic Clinic for Training and Research, from which she received a Certificate in Psychoanalysis in 1951. That year she moved with her family to Rockland County, New York, where she organized the Community Mental Health Center and had a private psychiatric practice. From 1963 until her retirement in 1984, Lawrence served as a child psychiatrist at Harlem Hospital, directing its Developmental Psychiatry Clinic, and an associate clinical professor of psychiatry at Columbia's College of Physicians and Surgeons.

Lawrence, one of the first black women psychiatrists in the nation, published two books on child psychiatry, *The Mental Health Team in Schools* (1971) and *Young Inner City Families* (1975). She was a Julius Rosenwald Fellow (1942–1943) and a National Institute of Mental Health Fellow (1948–1950). In 1991 her pioneering work developing the "ego-strength" of disadvantaged children was recognized as she received the Camille Cosby World of Children Award. In 1988, Lawrence's achievements were celebrated in an award-winning biography, *Balm in Gilead: Journey of a Healer,* written by her daughter, Sara Lawrence Lightfoot, a professor of education at Harvard University. ◆

# Leakey, Mary Douglas

FEBRUARY 6, 1913–DECEMBER 9, 1996 ● PALEONTOLOGIST
AND ARCHEOLOGIST

Mary Douglas Leakey, a renowned paleontologist and archaeologist, was born in London, England, on February 6, 1913, the only child of landscape painter Erskine Nicol and Cecilia Marion Frere. After World War I, the family made annual visits to Switzerland, France, and Italy. Leakey's father brought her with him to various archaeological locations such as Dordogne, France, where Cro-Magnon hunters had drawn cave paintings. These trips aroused Leakey's interest in early humans and prehumans. Unfortunately, the trips came to an abrupt end when her father died when she was 13.

An independent-minded teenager, Leakey was expelled from two convent schools, in one case for setting off an explosion in her chemistry class. Rather than attending a university, she studied drawing and archaeology on her own. By the early 1930s, she was earning money by drawing the stone tools of prehistoric humans; she was also participating from time to time in archaeological digs.

In 1933, the budding archeologist met Louis Leakey, a highly-regarded paleontologist and archaeologist who was searching for early human and prehuman fossils in East Africa. Even though he was married, the two began openly living together, which created a scandal. When his divorce came through in 1936, she and Louis got married. They then went to East Africa, where she lived for the rest of her life.

For more than 30 years, Mary Leakey labored in the shadow of her husband, but her work was crucial to his. Together, they rewrote the history of human evolution. Their efforts were crucial in establishing, for example, that the earliest humans evolved in Africa, not in Asia as had previously been thought; that humans did not evolve along a single line but that there were, rather, several types of prehumans; and that the time scale of human evolution was far longer than had been believed. More often than not, their conclusions were based upon her fossil discoveries, not his.

Leakey established her credibility just one year after their marriage with an excavation of an Iron Age site near Nakuru in Kenya, the results of which she published in the *Transactions of the Royal Society of South Africa*. In 1948, on Rusinga Island in Lake Victoria, Leakey discovered the skull of *Proconsul africanus*, an ape-like ancestor of apes and humans that lived some 16 million years ago. With great care and skill, she pieced it together from many small fragments.

In 1959 Leakey made a major fossil discovery at Olduvai Gorge in Tanzania, which was where the couple did much of their work. There, she found the skull of an erect human ancestor, later known as *Australopithecus boisei*, that was 1.75 million years old. Before this discovery, paleontologists had believed that human evolution began only 500,000 years ago. F. Clark

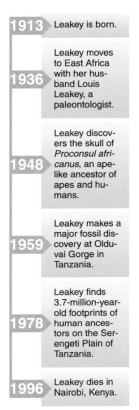

**1913** Leakey is born.

**1936** Leakey moves to East Africa with her husband Louis Leakey, a paleontologist.

**1948** Leakey discovers the skull of *Proconsul africanus*, an ape-like ancestor of apes and humans.

**1959** Leakey makes a major fossil discovery at Olduvai Gorge in Tanzania.

**1978** Leakey finds 3.7-million-year-old footprints of human ancestors on the Serengeti Plain of Tanzania.

**1996** Leakey dies in Nairobi, Kenya.

> **"For every vivid claim made by Louis [Leakey] about the origins of man, the supporting evidence tended to come from Mary, whose scrupulous scientific approach contrasted with his taste for publicity and enjoyment of personal battles."**
>
> Quoted in *The Times* of London, December 10, 1996

Howell, a paleoanthropologist at the University of California at Berkeley has said that this discovery represented the beginning of "the true scientific study of the evolution of man." This discovery brought great fame to the Leakeys, as well as major funding from the Washington-based National Geographic Society.

In the late 1960s, the Leakey's marriage began to come apart (although they did not divorce). At the same time, she became more independent and more willing to criticize her husband's work. She, and many others in the profession, believed that Louis Leakey was becoming too much a publicity seeker, too inclined to draw unwarranted conclusions from their discoveries, and too disposed toward turning professional differences into personal battles. She also could not help being disturbed by the fact that in his lectures, Louis gave the impression that her discoveries were actually his. "I ended by losing my professional respect for him," she later wrote. Many others eventually concluded that Mary was the key to their work. Gilbert Grosvenor, chairman of the National Geographic Society, remarked that "Louis could interpret finds, sometimes beyond the obvious, but it was Mary who really gave that team scientific validity."

Mary Leakey made her most important discovery in 1978, six years after Louis's death. At Laetoli on the Serengeti Plain in northern Tanzania, she discovered three trails of footprints made by human ancestors, set in wet volcanic ash that had subsequently hardened. At 3.7 million years old, they were the oldest such footprints to ever be found. The discovery showed that human ancestors had begun walking on two legs long before scientists had believed. Most significantly, the footprints demonstrated that erect posture preceded the development of an enlarged brain in the history of human evolution, a hotly debated issue until her discovery. For Leakey, these tracks had a personal meaning beyond their scientific significance. Describing one of the three trails, she wrote: "At one point she stops, pauses, turns to the left to glance at some possible threat or irregularity, and then continues to the north. This motion, so intensely human, transcends time."

Toward the end of her active career, Leakey wrote *My Search for Early Man* (1979), a popular account of her work. As averse to publicity as her late husband sought it, she agreed to write her autobiography—*Disclosing the Past* (1984)—only after winning assurance that a book of hers on cave paintings in Kenya would also be published. Because of her always gracious behavior, in contrast to the combative and quarrelsome style of many of her fellow paleontologists, she became known as the "grande-dame" of her profession.

Expressing her love of archaeological digs, Leakey once said, "Given the chance, I'd rather be in a tent than in a house." In 1982, however, she was forced by declining eyesight to end her fieldwork. Subsequently, she lived on a five-acre compound near Nairobi, Kenya, with her books and her beloved pack of dalmatian dogs as company. In her later years as earlier, she enjoyed smoking Cuban cigars and drinking bourbon, especially at sunset.

Leakey received many honors. The National Geographic Society in Washington, the Geological Society in London, and the Royal Swedish Academy all awarded her with medals. She also received honorary doctorates from many institutions of higher learning, including Cambridge University, where Louis Leakey had once taught; Yale University; and the University of Chicago. She had three sons, one of whom, Richard, became a famous paleontologist in his own right. Mary Leakey died on December 9, 1996, in Nairobi, Kenya. ◆

# Leakey, Meave

July 28, 1942– ● Zoologist and Paleontologist

Meave Leakey, who was born Meave Epps in London, England, always knew that she wanted to be a scientist. As a child she collected fossils and insects, and she took that interest in the natural world with her to the University of North Wales. Her initial goal was to pursue a career in marine zoology, but events led her away from the water to the parched, arid shores of Lake Turkana in Kenya—and from the study of living sea creatures to the excavation of some of the oldest human fossils on record.

That career path began in 1965, when Leakey, with an honors degree in zoology and marine zoology, took a position at the Tigoni Primate Research Centre outside of Nairobi, the capital of Kenya. Here her research focused on the evolution of east

Meave Leakey and two paleontologists pose with fossils.

African fossil mammals, including monkeys, apes, and hominids. She then returned to the University of North Wales, where she completed a Ph.D. in primate anatomy in 1968. When she returned to Kenya in 1969, Dr. Richard Leakey invited her to join his field expedition at the Koobi Fora paleontological site on the eastern shore of Lake Turkana, beginning her long-term association with the Turkana Basin research project.

In 1970 Meave and Richard married, and the couple had two children. With her marriage, she became a member of a clan whose members were devoted to "stones and bones" and were perhaps the most famous names in paleontological research. In the 1930s, Dr. Louis Leakey was responsible for exciting fossil finds that shed light on the origins of humans—in particular, the discovery of *Homo habilis*, or "Handy Man," the first human ancestor able to make and use tools. His research was carried on by his wife, Mary Leakey, and their son Richard represented the third generation of Leakeys whose fossil discoveries filled in missing parts of the human family tree and pushed back estimates of when intelligent human life evolved. From

1970 onwards Meave Leakey was able to participate as a partner in those discoveries.

One of the most significant of those discoveries came in 1972. Leakey had just given birth to her first daughter, Louise, at a Nairobi hospital. She was determined to continue her research, so she boarded a single-engine plane and, with her infant daughter safely in her arms, flew back to Koobi Fora. Just four days before her arrival, one of the Leakeys' assistants, Bernard Ngeneo, had been passing through a gully 13 miles northeast of the camp when he spotted some bone fragments close to the path. Examining them closely, he suspected that they were part of a hominid cranium.

In the days that followed, excitement ran high as the research team sifted through the sand and recovered fragments of the bones—most of them the size of a fingernail or smaller—and brought them back to the camp. Leakey was given the job of putting the pieces together, a job that required enormous patience and the ability to hold in her mind a three-dimensional picture of the slowly emerging skull. She traced her ability to do this kind of painstaking work back to her childhood, when she was adept at jigsaw puzzles: "I always liked jigsaws, and as a child I used to turn them upside down if I found them too easy." When Leakey's work was finished, palaeontologists had a nearly complete cranium—known prosaically as Skull 1470—from the genus *Homo*. Skull 1470—its catalog number in the Kenya Natural History Museum—provided crucial evidence supporting the view that *Homo* emerged at least two million years ago.

In 1984 Leakey was also on hand for a second significant discovery, the skeleton of "Turkana boy," a *Homo erectus* who lived about 1.6 million years ago. What made Turkana boy so significant was, first, that the skeleton was nearly complete, and second, that it showed that he walked upright. At five feet four inches in height and with a small cranium, Turkana boy demonstrated that, along the path of human evolutionary development, humans walked upright before they gained increased intelligence. Again, Leakey played a major role in reconstructing the skeleton from its fragments and in determining the boy's age, which was about nine.

Richard Leakey had been the director of Kenya's National Museums, but he left that position in 1989 to take over management of Kenya's wildlife parks. Meave, who had become director of the museums' Division of Palaeontology in 1982, took

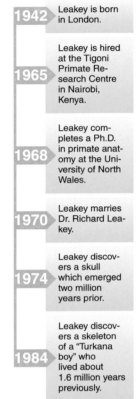

1942 — Leakey is born in London.

1965 — Leakey is hired at the Tigoni Primate Research Centre in Nairobi, Kenya.

1968 — Leakey completes a Ph.D. in primate anatomy at the University of North Wales.

1970 — Leakey marries Dr. Richard Leakey.

1974 — Leakey discovers a skull which emerged two million years prior.

1984 — Leakey discovers a skeleton of a "Turkana boy" who lived about 1.6 million years previously.

over management of field research in the Turkana Basin, and she continued to hold both positions in her late 50s. Under her management, the Turkana Basin yielded yet another important find in the late 1990s, a skeleton of *Australopithecus anamensis*, an early hominid that stood up and walked on two feet. While the more famous "Lucy" skeleton found in Ethiopia in 1974 suggested that hominids began walking upright about 3.2 million years ago, this more recent find pushed that estimate back to about 4 million years.

Throughout her time in Kenya, Leakey faced a certain degree of danger. In the early years the Kenyan government was repressive and corrupt and discouraged her and her husband's work. Richard later became the center of controversy when, as Kenya's wildlife director, he adopted a shoot-on-sight policy to discourage ivory poachers. Further, the large Muslim population in Kenya was vigorously opposed to the very notion of human evolution. While the climate improved in later years, Leakey still lamented the refusal of some Kenyans to make their nation's position as the cradle of humanity a point of national pride. ◆

# Leavitt, Henrietta Swan

JULY 4, 1868–DECEMBER 21, 1921 ● ASTRONOMER

Henrietta Swan Leavitt overcame both physical disability and the male biases of her profession to become one of the most noteworthy American astronomers of the early 20th century. She was born in Lancaster, Massachusetts, though shortly after her birth her family moved to Cleveland, Ohio. From 1885 to 1888, she attended nearby Oberlin College, majoring in music. She completed her education at the Society for the Collegiate Instruction of Women, now called Radcliffe College, with a bachelor's degree in 1892. During her senior year she took a course in astronomy that sparked her interest in the subject, and later she was able to do some graduate work in astronomy.

For the next three years Leavitt traveled throughout the United States and Europe. It was during this time that disaster struck, for she became seriously ill and lost most of her hearing. In spite of her hearing loss, she resurrected her interest in astronomy and volunteered as a research assistant at the Harvard College Observatory starting in 1895. Not until 1902 did she become a permanent member of the staff—at a wage of just 30 cents an hour.

Throughout her years at the Harvard Observatory, Leavitt was never able to carry out theoretical research, nor was she allowed to pursue research projects of her own. Instead, she did the work that was assigned to her by the director, Edward Charles Pickering, who did not want his employees wasting time doing anything else. Yet despite these limitations, she made several important discoveries, and her efforts laid important groundwork for other, later astronomers such as Ejnar Hertzsprung, Harlow Shapley, and Edwin Hubble.

Leavitt initially worked in the photographic photometry department and soon became head of that department. Her routine job was to ensure that telescopes were properly positioned and to examine photographic plates. She began, however, to work on the problem of determining the magnitude, or brightness, of a star from its photographic image—a difficult problem because photos did not always provide accurate readings of magnitude, and different telescopes could yield different magnitudes. Leavitt corrected this problem by developing a method of examining the north polar sequence of stars, enabling one to be compared to another. Using 299 photographic plates from 13 different telescopes, she applied logarithmic equations to classify stars into 17 orders of magnitude. After she published her findings in 1912, the International Committee on Photographic Magnitudes recognized the importance of her system and in 1913 adopted it as the standard for determining star magnitude. This standard, called the Harvard Standard, remained in effect until 1940.

Leavitt is also known for discovering what is called the period-luminosity relationship of stars. This discovery came about as a result of her work on variable stars, or stars that go through a regular cycle of brightness, dimness, and then brightness again. At the time of her death, there were about 2,400 known variable stars, and Leavitt had discovered 1,777 of them. She was primarily interested in the Cepheid variable stars in the Small Magellanic Cloud—a galaxy located in the Milky Way about 200,000 light-years from Earth. These stars were significant because they were known to all be about the same distance from Earth, meaning that if one star appeared brighter than others, it probably actually was brighter. As Leavitt put it,

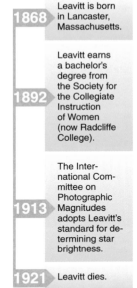

**1868** Leavitt is born in Lancaster, Massachusetts.

**1892** Leavitt earns a bachelor's degree from the Society for the Collegiate Instruction of Women (now Radcliffe College).

**1913** The International Committee on Photographic Magnitudes adopts Leavitt's standard for determining star brightness.

**1921** Leavitt dies.

## Williamina Paton Stevens Fleming

Williamina Paton Stevens Fleming (1857–1911) is best-known as the astronomer who discovered "white dwarf" stars. She was born on May 15, 1857, in Dundee, Scotland. There, she attended and taught at public schools until marrying James Fleming in 1877. Soon thereafter the couple moved to Boston, Massachusetts. Not long after, Fleming became pregnant, which caused James to abandon her. Finding herself in a foreign country and with another mouth to feed on the way, Fleming searched for employment and found a job as a maid working for Edward Pickering, director of the Harvard Observatory. Beginning in 1881, Pickering hired Fleming to work at the observatory; other brilliant women worked there as assistants to Pickering, including Henrietta Leavitt, his research assistant beginning in 1895. At the observatory, Fleming almost immediately excelled at the work and showed her stellar intelligence and creativity. Although she had no higher education, she tracked thousands of stars using her own method for classifying stars according to their spectra (prism light pattern). She presented these findings in *Draper Catalogue of Stellar Spectra* (1890).

While continuing her empirical observations, she also took on administrative tasks, including overseeing other employees and editing various observatory publications. In 1898 she became curator of astronomical photographs at Harvard. She continued to conduct and report on her own research, including a study of variable stars (1907) and, most remarkably, a claim for the discovery of "white dwarfs," which are hot dense stars nearing the end of their existence.

In 1906 she became the first American woman elected to the Royal Astronomical Society. Fleming died on May 21, 1911, in Boston, Massachusetts.

"Since the variables are probably at nearly the same distance from the earth their periods are apparently associated with their actual emission of light as determined by their mass, density and surface brightness." By intensely examining these stars, Leavitt determined that there is a direct correlation between the time it took for a star to go from bright to dim and its actual magnitude. Again in her words, "A straight line can readily be drawn among each of the two series of points corresponding to maxima and minima, thus showing that there is a simple relation between the brightness of the variables and their periods."

Leavitt's discovery of the period-luminosity relationship had practical implications for future astronomers. Until that time, astronomers could determine the distance of stars only up to about 100 light-years. Leavitt's discovery extended that distance to about 10 million light-years, for she showed that if two variable stars have equal periods but one is brighter than the other, the difference is the result of distance, and that distance could then be measured. Put differently, a nearly deaf, under-paid employee at the Harvard Observatory put into the hands of future astronomers the yardstick they needed to measure the size of galaxies.

For her work, Leavitt was named an honorary member of the Associated Variable Star Observers. She was also a member of the American Astronomical and Astrophysical Society, the American Association for the Advancement of Science, Phi Beta Kappa, and the American Association of University Women. Sadly, she died prematurely from cancer in 1921 at the age of 53. Later astronomers noted that had she not been cut off during her most productive years, she surely would have made additional important discoveries, for, as one said, she was "the most brilliant woman at Harvard" and she possessed "the best mind at the Observatory." As it was, Henrietta Swan Leavitt opened the door for future women astronomers who were able to achieve in life the recognition that she achieved largely after her death. ◆

# Lehmann, Inge

## MAY 13, 1888–FEBRUARY 21, 1993 ● SEISMOLOGIST

Inge Lehmann was born on May 13, 1888 in Copenhagen, Denmark, and died there on February 21, 1993. She is famous for her discovery of Earth's solid inner core inside its fluid core. Her father, Alfred Lehmann, was a scientific pioneer who introduced experimental psychology at the University of Copenhagen. They both loved outdoor activities such as hiking in the mountains.

Lehmann graduated from Hanna Adlers School in 1906. At the school, boys and girls were treated equally, which was unusual at the time. Later in life she found that such equal treatment was not the norm. She was not active in women's liberation, but, busy with her own work and with a fighting spirit, she achieved her own liberation.

In 1920 Lehmann received a master of science (M.S.) degree in mathematics from the University of Copenhagen. In 1925 she became attached to the geodetic institution that was in charge of measuring the meridian arc in Denmark. Her first major task was the installation of seismographs for the new

**1888** Lehmann is born in Copenhagen, Denmark.

**1920** Lehmann earns a Master of Science degree in mathematics from the University of Copehagen.

**1928** Lehmann is appointed chief of the seismology department at the Geodetic Institute in Copenhagen.

**1936** Lehmann discovers the inner solid core.

**1993** Lehmann dies in Copenhagen, Denmark.

**geodesy:** a branch of mathematics that determines the areas and figures of large portions of the earth's surface; also measures the curvature of the earth.

**seismology:** the study of earthquakes.

seismic station in Copenhagen. She went to Germany in 1927 and was introduced to seismology by Beno Gutenberg during a month stay in Darmstadt.

In 1928 Lehmann received an M.S. degree in **geodesy** and was appointed chief of the department of **seismology** at the newly established Geodetic Institute in Copenhagen. Her duties in that position were to run seismograph stations in Denmark and Greenland and to report the arrival times of seismic waves in bulletins. Such bulletins are used to determine earthquake epicenters. She installed seismograph stations at Ivigtut and Scoresbysund in Greenland. Scoresbysund, which started recording in 1928, is situated in such a remote area that ships can reach it only in late summer.

Lehmann became strongly interested in the fact that knowledge of Earth's interior can be obtained from the observations of the earthquake recordings from seismographs. One of the problems in doing that was that the estimates for epicenters were inaccurate because the travel time curves used to calculate them were inaccurate. A travel time curve is a curve showing the travel time of seismic waves from earthquakes as a function of the distance along the surface of the earth. Lehmann found a way to improve the knowledge of travel times because she could determine the slope of the travel time curve by using the European network of stations as an array. For this work she looked at copies of seismograms from these stations and ascertained that she was reading the same wave propagating through Earth to the different stations. These slopes were used by Sir Harold Jeffreys, with whom she corresponded extensively, while he calculated seismic travel time curves in cooperation with Keith Bullen. They used statistical methods to determine travel time curves from many observations of arrival time.

Lehmann's biggest contribution was the discovery of the inner (solid) core in 1936. She suggested the possibility of an inner core with a wave velocity higher than that of the rest of the core, and she showed that this assumption can explain some seismic phases observed in the shadow zone. This zone is the region from 102 to 142 degrees, where the direct wave from the earthquake is much reduced because Earth's core refracts seismic waves away from it. Only waves that are bent around the core will reach the zone. Such waves are called diffracted waves. They were expected to be weak, whereas she had observed strong phases. The assumption of an inner core was a bold assumption because at the time, good evidence showed that the Earth's core was a homogenous fluid. The suggestion of a core was immediately accepted by Gutenberg, and a few years later also by Jeffreys. This discovery is one of the most important advances in our knowledge of Earth's interior during the past 60 years.

Lehmann's retirement in 1953 did not mean she stopped working, but she did get relief from her day-to-day duties of station operation. She worked on the structure of the upper mantle, that is, the upper 600-700 km of the Earth. She found recordings of nuclear explosions to be very valuable for this work, but earthquake recordings were also used. She worked in her home in Copenhagen as well as at the Lamont Geological Observatory of Columbia University (now Lamont Doherty Earth Observatory), at the California Institute of Technology at Pasadena, at the Seismographic Station of the University of California at Berkeley, and at the Dominion Observatory (now Geological Survey of Canada) in Ottawa. She observed that clear differences in upper mantle structure existed between eastern and western North America, and that the upper mantle below Europe was different as well. She was respected for years as a leading authority on seismic evidence on upper mantle structure. Certain models of the Earth, used for free oscillation calculations, adopted the Lehman upper mantle structure. (A discontinuity she introduced at 220 km depth is included in the current PREM Earth Model.)

Lehmann's last publication (1987) summarizes, in an interesting way, works by the geophysicists Gutenberg, Jeffreys, and herself during the period 1925–1936. This paper was first written in Danish for the Danish Geophysical Society, but Bruce Bolt asked for a translation as an introduction to his paper. Lehmann was one of the founders of the Danish Geophysical Society, and she chaired that organization from 1941 to 1944.

In the summer she lived in a small cottage overlooking a quiet lake, where many scientists visited. Lehmann's last years were hard. Though blind and weak, her fighting spirit never changed. As late as the summer of 1992, she was able to enjoy a visit to her beloved cottage, located 20 kilometers from her apartment.

Lehmann received numerous awards: the German Geophysical Society's Emil-Wiechert Medal (1964), an honorary doctorate from Columbia University of New York (1964), the Royal Danish Academy of Science's Gold Medal (1965), an honorary doctorate from the University of Copenhagen (1968), and the American Geophysical Union's William Bowie Medal, given for outstanding contributions to fundamental geophysics and unselfish cooperation in research (1971).

Lehmann created a fund administered by the Academy of Science in Denmark, and now this fund has been given her entire fortune. It offers a travel award each year, which is given alternatively to psychologists and to geophysicists. ◆

# Levi-Montalcini, Rita

APRIL 22, 1909– ● PHYSICIAN AND BIOLOGIST

Rita Levi-Montalcini was born to an intellectual Jewish family in Turin, an industrial city in northern Italy. The Levi family had deep roots in the community, having migrated to the area during the time of the Roman Empire, and the family produced, before and since, a number of notable writers and professionals. As an adult Rita Levi added Montalcini, her mother's maiden name, to her name to distinguish herself from the rest of the family.

As a child and young adult Levi-Montalcini was dominated by her father, a passionate, imperious man who demanded obedience from his family; however, he was also a religious freethinker who encouraged his daughter to be the same. When Levi-Montalcini was a child, her father determined that she should abandon her academic education and attend a girls' finishing school so that she could become a good wife and mother. But at age 20 she summoned up the courage to tell him that she wanted to be a

Rita Levi-Montalcini

doctor instead and that she never wanted to marry. Her father disagreed with her choice, but he did agree to pay for the tutors she needed to pass the university entrance examinations. She entered the University of Turin medical school in 1930, one of just seven women in the class—all of whom had to fend off the advances of their male colleagues.

At the university, Levi-Montalcini became the protégée of Professor Guiseppe Levi (no relation), a brilliant histologist who approached life with the same passion and need for dominance that her father did. Professor Levi taught his student a new technique for studying nerve cells, using chrome silver to stain neurons from embryonic chicks so that their patterns would stand out in minute detail. Levi-Montalcini wrote a thesis in which she examined collagen reticular fibers, the supporting fibers in various types of tissue. When she completed medical school in 1936, she was uncertain whether to practice medicine or continue her research; for two years, she continued studying neurology with Professor Levi.

Then, the Italian fascist dictator Benito Mussolini made the decision for her. In 1938 he decreed that Jews were prohibited from pursuing academic or professional careers. With few options open to her, she practiced medicine secretly among the poor, but she could not write prescriptions. She then practiced medicine in Brussels, Belgium, for a year, but she returned to Italy just prior to the German invasion of Belgium.

Not knowing what to do with herself, she followed the advice of an old medical school friend and set up her own tiny research lab in a bedroom, later in a farmhouse, using primitive tools and begging farmers for fertilized chick eggs to use to continue her research. To the horror of her brother, who helped her with her work by finding or building equipment, she extracted the nerve cells she wanted from the embryos, then scrambled what was left of the eggs for dinner. With war raging around her and Allied bombers attacking Turin, she published several scientific papers in Swiss and Belgian journals about nerve cell death. Assisting her was Professor Levi, who joined the project after he was banned from the university.

After the war, Levi-Montalcini was invited to the United States by Viktor Hamburger, a prominent neurobiologist at Washington University in St. Louis, Missouri. Hamburger had read her papers and wanted her to join him, even though her theories differed from his own, so in 1946 she set sail for the United States. Levi-Montalcini described her 26 years at

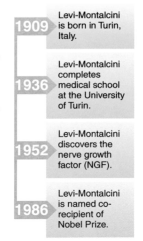

**1909** Levi-Montalcini is born in Turin, Italy.

**1936** Levi-Montalcini completes medical school at the University of Turin.

**1952** Levi-Montalcini discovers the nerve growth factor (NGF).

**1986** Levi-Montalcini is named co-recipient of Nobel Prize.

> "Great ideas are a dime a dozen. The great scientist is one who delivers. And Rita delivered."
>
> Robert Provine, Rita Levi-Montalcini's postdoctoral fellow, quoted in *Nobel Prize Women in Science*, 1993

Washington University as the "happiest and most productive years of my life. . . . I felt at home the day I landed. . . . And America is a society in which merit is genuinely rewarded—you cannot say the same for Italy."

During the late 1940s and early 1950s, Levi-Montalcini made her most important discoveries. She amputated embryonic limbs in chicks, then examined the growth of nerve cells at the point of amputation. She discovered that the nerve cells began to grow, then faded and died. She concluded that a developing neuron depended on some type of feedback signal or growth hormone from the missing limb. Then in 1950 she began experimenting with small mouse tumors, which she would place in the vicinity of chick embryo neurons. She was startled to discover that the tumors seemed to be secreting something that caused the nerve fibers to reach out and grow, producing a halo effect that is characteristic of NGF, or nerve growth factor—the discovery of which she announced in 1952.

In the years that followed, Levi-Montalcini teamed with other scientists to discover the precise makeup of NGF. The discovery of NGF had profound implications for the treatment of degenerative conditions such as Alzheimer's disease and Parkinson's disease, as well as for helping burn patients. Her discovery may also have implications for understanding the development of cancerous tumors, for it provided an important clue to understanding how embryonic cells differentiate and how cells in a growing organism work together.

Although she had to spend years trying to convince the scientific community that NGF actually existed, Levi-Montalcini eventually received acclaim for her work. In 1968 she was elected to the prestigious National Academy of Sciences. Then, in 1986, she and Stanley Cohen, a postdoctoral fellow at Washington University who had collaborated with her in her work in the 1950s, shared the Nobel Prize for Medicine and Physiology for the discovery of NGF. The prize, however, led to some controversy, for many neurobiologists believed that Hamburger, who had laid some of the foundations for Levi-Montalcini's work, should have been named a corecipient of the prize.

In her later years, Levi-Montalcini continued to direct research in Italy and to volunteer her time for agencies working toward cures for degenerative diseases. An elegant, charismatic woman, she became a national hero in her native land, where people often quipped that the Pope was instantly recognizable—provided that he appeared with Levi-Montalcini. She addressed the Italian parliament on issues that had scientific implications, and the media called on her for interviews when they wanted the views of women scientists. Even in her 80s and 90s, she tirelessly promoted Italian science and the careers of women in science. ◆

# Libby, Leona Wood Marshall

### AUGUST 9, 1919–NOVEMBER 10, 1986 ● PHYSICIST

The daughter of Weightstill Woods, an attorney, and Mary (Holderness) Woods, a teacher, Leona Libby was the second child of three girls and two boys. The family lived outside the city limits of Chicago on a farm in La Grange, Illinois. Hit hard by the Great Depression, the Woods family struggled financially. Although the parents had little money, their extremely bright children were expected to attend college. Ambitious and eager to compete with her older brother, Leona won scholarship money and, in addition, worked 20 hours a week to get through the University of Chicago. She received her B.S. degree in 1938 and her Ph.D. in chemistry in 1943.

Prior to her actual graduation, Libby was hired as a research associate for the Manhattan District, later called the Manhattan Project, which developed the first atomic bomb. She worked on a team headed by the Italian Nobel laureate Enrico Fermi, and she was the only woman present for the first nuclear chain reaction, which took place under the football stands at the University of Chicago on December 2, 1942. Although Libby was the only woman on the primary team, as many as 85 other women served in some capacity on the Manhattan Project.

Libby was selected because her dissertation research had familiarized her with the vacuum technology needed to build boron trifluoride counters. These counters measured neutrons in a pile of graphite and uranium blocks used to create a chain reaction, a necessary step in making the atomic bomb. A sense of urgency prevailed, as the team was ever mindful that the Germans might build the bomb before the Americans. The highly

classified project assumed the code name Chicago Metallurgical Laboratory. Libby explained to her family that her work was like Buck Rogers science. She worked so closely with the other physicists that she considered them family also. For leisure she swam in Lake Michigan almost daily during the summer, and she developed a friendship with Fermi, who consistently encouraged young women. In February 1943, the nuclear pile and the team were transplanted to new headquarters in Argonne, Illinois.

Extremely brilliant and attractive, the dark-haired Libby was not without admirers. John Marshall, Jr., a physicist on the project, caught her attention, and on July 3, 1943 the pair married. When Libby realized she was pregnant, she worried that she might be fired from the laboratory. She kept her pregnancy a secret by wearing loose denim overalls and jamming the pockets with tape measures, pliers, notebooks, and other necessary equipment. She worked until shortly before the birth of her son, and she returned to work within a week.

On a temporary assignment in New York, Libby was exposed to a large dose of radiation while she soldered a canister containing radium salt and beryllium metal, but the exposure was not problematic until later in her life. Leona and John Marshall's work at Argonne ended in 1944, and they went to Hanford Engineering Works in Washington State to oversee construction of artificial plutonium developed from production reactors. Libby worked with John Wheeler to help "solve the riddle of the Hanford xenon poisoning" and baby-sit the reactors, she said in an interview. Her work on the Manhattan Project from 1944 to 1946 is documented in her book *The Uranium People* (1979).

In 1946, Libby joined Fermi at the University of Chicago as a research fellow at the Institute of Nuclear Studies, where she was a member of a group of physicists researching the innovative field of fundamental particle physics. She advanced to research associate in 1947 and to assistant professor of physics in 1954. In 1949 her second son was born. She remained a consultant to Los Alamos Scientific Laboratory from 1951 until her death.

Following Fermi's death in 1954, the institute group members began dispersing. In 1957 Libby went to Princeton, New Jersey, to become a fellow at the Institute for Advanced Study, where she conducted research with J. Robert Oppenheimer. That year Libby also began work as a consultant for the

Rand Corporation in Santa Monica, California, performing analysis on foreign nuclear explosions and related national defense problems. She retained this position until 1970.

In 1958 she was a visiting scientist at Brookhaven National Laboratory in Upton, Long Island. She was an associate professor at New York University from 1960 to 1962 and a professor of physics from 1962 to 1963. She next became an associate professor of physics at the University of Colorado, Boulder, where she remained until 1972.

In 1966 Libby divorced John Marshall, who had been living in Los Alamos since 1957. In December of that year she married Willard Frank Libby, a Nobel laureate in physics whom she had met on the Manhattan Project. The couple had no children and alternated between their university jobs in Colorado and California. Both of the Libbys were partially responsible for developing the Environmental Science and Engineering Department at the University of California, Los Angeles, where scientists explored solutions to the effects of world pollution. A visiting professor for the department in 1970, Leona Libby became an adjunct professor in 1972. She also served as a consultant for TRW Space Systems Group, and from 1972 to 1976 she was a staff member at R & D Associates in Santa Monica.

Libby developed an interest in her husband's research of ancient climates. She studied tree rings to uncover the history of climates through the measurement of isotopes in trees and wrote *Carbon Dioxide and Climate* (1980) and *Past Climates: Tree Thermometer, Commodities, and People* (1983). Following her husband's death in 1980, she edited *Collected Papers Willard F. Libby* (1981). The author of more than 100 articles, many dealing with environmental issues and cosmology, she also published *Fifty Environmental Problems of Timely Importance* (1970).

In California, Libby lived at 129 Ocean Way in Santa Monica. Her scientific home was the Environmental Science and Engineering Department at UCLA. She enjoyed photography, swimming, and playing the piano. Although she had been raised in the Episcopal faith, she became an agnostic over the years. She died in St. John's Hospital in Santa Monica, from probable radiation-induced illness and liver failure. Her remains were cremated.

Described as having a dominant personality yet "kindhearted," Libby had high expectations of what could be accomplished. Beginning as a chemist, she branched into physics and then high-energy physics. She contributed to environmental concerns and supported nuclear power. Leona Marshall Libby never had regrets about her work on the atomic bomb. During an interview for *Newsweek* in 1967, she emphasized that "we saved lives in the long run." ◆

# Lloyd, Ruth Smith

JANUARY 25, 1917– ● ANATOMIST

1917 ▶ Lloyd is born in Washington, D.C.

1937 ▶ Lloyd earns an A.B. in zoology from Mt. Holyoke College.

1941 ▶ Lloyd receives a doctorate in anatomy from Western Reserve University.

1942 ▶ Lloyd is appointed assistant professor of anatomy at Howard University.

1955 ▶ Lloyd is named associate professor at Howard University, a position she held until her retirement in 1977.

Ruth Smith Lloyd was born in Washington, D.C., the daughter of Bradley Donald and Mary Elizabeth Morris Smith. A 1933 graduate of Dunbar High School, she attended Mount Holyoke College, where she earned a B.A. in zoology (magna cum laude) in 1937. On the urging of her zoology professors, she went on for graduate work at Howard University under the eminent black zoologist Ernest Everett Just. In 1938 she earned an M.S. in zoology, and Just motivated her to pursue doctoral studies. With the support of a Rosenwald Fellowship, she earned a Ph.D. in anatomy at Western Reserve University in 1941. Her thesis focused on adolescent development in macaques, a type of monkey. She was the first African American woman to receive a doctorate in anatomy.

Lloyd began her professional career in physiology at Howard (1940–41, 1942) and in zoology at Hampton Institute (1941–42). In 1942 she was appointed instructor in anatomy at Howard's college of medicine. She became assistant professor of anatomy in 1947 and associate professor in 1955, the position she held until her retirement in 1977. Lloyd's primary research interest was ovarian anatomy. She also assisted William Montague Cobb, head of the anatomy department at Howard, on a bibliography of physical anthropology, published in the December 1944 issue of the *American Journal of Physical Anthropology*. Among her numerous educational activities, she was a director of Howard's academic reinforcement program for medical students during the mid-1970s.

Lloyd was a member of the American Association of Anatomist, American Association of Medical Colleges, and New York Academy of Sciences. Her husband, Sterling Morrison

Lloyd (whom she married in 1939), was a physician. The couple had three children. ◆

# Logan, Myra Adele

1908–JANUARY 13, 1977 ● PHYSICIAN AND SURGEON

Myra Logan was born in Tuskegee, Alabama, where her father was treasurer of the Tuskegee Institute. She attended Tuskegee's laboratory school, the Children's House. A 1923 honors graduate of Tuskegee High School, she was the valedictorian of her graduating class at Atlanta University in 1927. She then moved to New York City where her sister, Ruth Logan Roberts, a nurse involved in public health issues, was already living. Logan received an M.S. in psychology from Columbia University in New York, and an M.D. from New York Medical College in 1933. (She went to medical school on a $10,000 four-year scholarship established by Walter Gray Crump, a white surgeon committed to helping African Americans advance in the medical profession.)

Logan did her internship at Harlem Hospital, and continued to practice there as a surgeon. She is generally regarded as the first woman to successfully operate on the heart, and was the first African American woman elected a Fellow of the American College of Surgeons. She did extensive research on the use of aureomycin and other antibiotics, publishing many articles on the subject in such medical journals as *The Archives of Surgery* and *The Journal of American Medical Surgery*. Along with her brother, the physician Arthur C. Logan, she was a founding member of an early health maintenance organization, the Upper Manhattan Medical Group of the Health Insurance Plan. She left the group in 1970 to join the Physical Disability Program of the New York State Workmen's Compensation Board. Logan was a member of many organizations, including the Planned Parenthood Association and the National Medical Association of the NAACP. She had been a member of the New York State Committee on Discrimination, but resigned in 1944 to protest Gov. Thomas E. Dewey's disregard of the anti-discrimination legislation the committee had proposed.

She died in New York City in 1977. ◆

**1908** Logan is born in Tuskegee, Alabama.

**1927** Logan is valedictorian of her graduating class at Atlanta University.

**1933** Logan earns a medical degree from New York Medical College and begins her residency at Harlem Hospital.

**1970** Logan joins the Physical Disability Program of the New York State Workmen's Compensation Board.

**1977** Logan dies in New York City.

# Lucid, Shannon

<small>JANUARY 14, 1943– ● CHEMIST AND ASTRONAUT</small>

**1943** — Lucid is born in Shanghai, China.

**1963** — Lucid graduates from the University of Oklahoma with a bachelor of sciences in chemistry.

**1973** — Lucid earns a doctorate in chemistry from the University of Oklahoma.

**1978** — Lucid, also a pilot, is chosen as an astronaut by NASA, and qualified as a space shuttle mission specialist the next year.

**1985** — Lucid makes her first shuttle flight on *Discovery*.

**1989** — Lucid flies on STS-34, and the Galileo space probe is launched towards Jupiter.

**1996** — Lucid becomes the American record holder for space endurance during a 188-day mission aboard the Russian *Mir* space station.

Chemist Shannon Lucid is the American space endurance record holder, including a 188-day tour aboard the Russian *Mir* space station in 1996.

Delivered to the Russian space station by the orbiter *Atlantis* and the crew of STS-76 in March 1996, Lucid joined the *Mir*-20 crew of Yuri Onufriyenko and Yuri Usachev for what was supposed to have been a 140-day mission. Problems with the shuttle's solid rocket boosters, and a hurricane at the Kennedy Space Center, delayed the launch of STS-79, her return mission, from July to September.

The 52-year-old mother of three, Lucid operated her own set of scientific experiments while also meeting the day-to-day challenges of living on orbit for weeks at a time: cooking meals and getting exercise, loading and unloading Progress supply vehicles, providing communications support while Onufriyenko and Usachev made EVAs.

In August 1996 Onufriyenko and Usachev were replaced by the *Mir*-21 crew of Valery Korzun and Alexandr Kaleri, who arrived at the station with French physician Claudie-Andre-Deshays. Lucid herself returned to Earth with the crew of STS-79 in September 1996. Her record-setting stay aboard *Mir* is chronicled in the 1997 IMAX film *Mission to Mir*.

Lucid has made four shuttle flights, all of them as a mission specialist, beginning with Shuttle Mission 51-G in June 1985. On this flight of the *Discovery* the seven-astronaut crew, which included Prince Sultan Salman al-Saud of Saudi Arabia and Patrick Baudry of France, deployed three communications satellites and the Spartan scientific satellite, which was later retrieved.

In October 1989 Lucid flew on board STS-34, during which the Galileo space probe was successfully launched on its way to the planet Jupiter. She later served in the crew of STS-43, an August 1991 flight of the orbiter *Atlantis*. During this nine-day mission the crew of five astronauts successfully deployed a Tracking and Data Relay Satellite (TDRS) while conducting numerous experiments for proposed space station missions.

Her most recent shuttle flight was STS-58, the second flight of the Life Sciences Spacelab, in October 1993. At 16

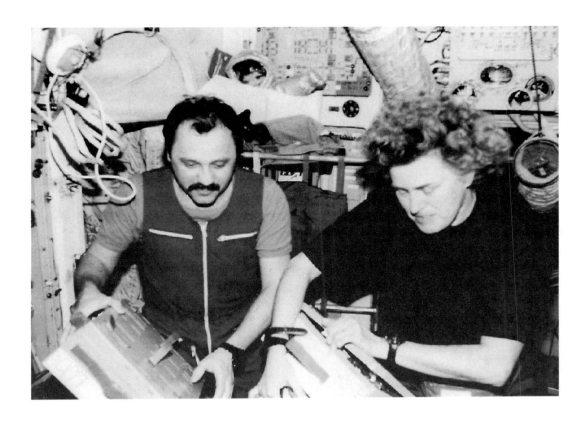

days, STS-58 was the longest medical mission flown to that time. Its crew of seven, including four physicians, also served as medical test subjects.

Lucid was born Matilda Shannon Wells on January 14, 1943, in Shanghai, China, where her parents were missionaries. The Lucid family was interned in a Japanese prison camp for a year, but was released in 1944, and eventually settled in Bethany, Oklahoma, where Lucid graduated from high school in 1960. She received a B.S. in chemistry from the University of Oklahoma in 1963, and an M.S. and Ph.D. in biochemistry from the same school in 1970 and 1973.

While working for her doctorate Lucid held a variety of jobs: teaching assistant at the University of Oklahoma Department of Chemistry (1963–64), senior lab technician at the Oklahoma Medical Research Foundation (1964–66), chemist at Kerr-McGee (1966–68), and graduate assistant at the University of Oklahoma Health Science Center's Department of Biochemistry and Molecular Biology (1969–73). When chosen by NASA she was a research associate with the Oklahoma

Shannon Lucid (right) and Russian cosmonaut Yuri Usachev preparing to eat a meal on the Russian space station Mir in 1996.

Medical Research Foundation, a position she had held since 1974. She is also a pilot with ratings in commercial, instrument and multi-engine flying.

Lucid was one of the 35 astronauts selected by NASA in January 1978. In August 1979, she completed a training and evaluation course which qualified her as a shuttle mission specialist. As an astronaut she worked in the Shuttle Avionics Integration Laboratory (SAIL), the flight software laboratory, and in the testing of payloads. From August 1985 to January 1986 she was a mission control capcom for shuttle flights. She has also served as chief of the mission support branch.

Lucid is currently astronaut office deputy for Shuttle-Mir. ◆

M

# Mahoney, Mary Eliza

MAY 7, 1845–JANUARY 4, 1926 ● NURSE

Mary Eliza Mahoney was born in Dorchester, Massachusetts. Little is known about her life before 1878, when
she was accepted into the professional nursing program at the New England Hospital for Women and Children in
Boston. After completing the highly competitive 16-month
program in 1879, Mahoney graduated and began a 40-year career as a professional nurse. Mahoney seems to have spent her
career as a nurse in private homes in Boston, probably because
of the general unwillingness of hospitals to hire black nurses.

At the turn of the century Mahoney became one of the first
African American members of the newly organized American
Nurses Association (ANA), even though most state and local
organizations excluded black nurses. In 1908 Mahoney supported the creation of the National Association of Colored
Graduate Nurses (NACGN), which was established in order to
integrate the profession and serve as a black alternative to the
ANA. The following year she gave the opening address to the
NACGN's first annual meeting in Boston where she was
elected national chaplain, responsible for the induction of new
officers. Mahoney was also active in the women's suffrage
movement and publicly supported the ratification of the 19th
Amendment in 1920.

Mahoney retired in 1922 and died four years later in Boston. In 1936 the NACGN established in her honor the Mary
Mahoney Medal in recognition of significant contributions to

1845 — Mahoney is born in Dorchester, Massachusetts.

1879 — Mahoney completes a nursing program at the New England Hospital for Women in Children in Boston.

1908 — Mahoney supports the creation of the American Nurses Association.

1922 — Mahoney retires.

1926 — Mahoney dies.

Beginning in 1936, the National Association of Colored Graduate Nurses (NACGN) conferred the Mary Mahoney Award, named in honor of the first African American graduate nurse in the United States. After the NACGN dissolved in 1951, the American Nurses Association (ANA) began overseeing the award. The award is now one of several given by the ANA to registered nurses both "to recognize their outstanding contributions to the nursing profession and the field of health care," and to help the general public better understand the role of nurses in health care. Related awards include the SNA Affirmative Action Award and the Barbara Thoman Curtis Award.

In keeping with Mahoney's legacy of enhancing the reputation and status of African American nurses, the Mary Mahoney Award honors nurses (individuals or groups) who have made significant contributions toward integrating the nursing profession. Eligible people include those who make a significant contribution to nursing, improve the presence, integration, and retention of minorities in nursing, and advance intergroup relations. A committee devoted to the award reviews all nominations, taking into account nominating forms, a nominee's curriculum vita, letters in support of the nominee, and narrative statements. The committee then recommends one person whose nomination is approved by the ANA Board of Directors.

integration in nursing. The award continued to be awarded annually by the ANA, which officially desegregated in 1948, after the NACGN was dissolved in 1951. ◆

# Margulis, Lynn

MARCH 5, 1938– ● MICROBIOLOGIST

Lynn Margulis was born Lynn Alexander in Chicago, Illinois, the oldest of four sisters. As a child she was so precocious that she enrolled as an undergraduate at the University of Chicago at age 14. The early 1950s were marked by the discovery of DNA, and in her sophomore year Margulis took a course that examined the question "What is Heredity?" from an interdisciplinary perspective. She was fascinated by the subject and went on to a distinguished career as a microbiologist. Though she knew more than virtually anyone else in the world about the role played by microorganisms during the 3.5 billion years of evolution, she never took a college course in microbiology.

Margulis completed her bachelor's degree in 1957. That year, too, she married Carl Sagan, the best-selling author who popularized the field of astronomy and who became a house-hold name for a generation of Americans. She went on to the University of Wisconsin, where she completed a master's degree in zoology and genetics in 1960. She then completed a Ph.D. at the University of California at Berkeley in 1965. She had two children with Sagan, but their marriage ended and she married Thomas Margulis in 1967. She accepted a position at Boston University in 1966, eventually rising to the rank of university professor in 1986.

In 1988 Margulis left Boston University to become Distinguished University Professor at the University of Massachusetts at Amherst. Throughout her career she was a member of a number of scientific societies, including the Russian Academy of Sciences, and she received six honorary doctorates. From 1977 to 1980 she was chair of the National Academy of Science's Space Science Board Committee on Planetary Biology and Chemical Evolution. In 1979 she was awarded a Guggenheim Fellowship to further her work. In 1998 she won the American Institute of Biological Sciences Distinguished Service Award.

No barebones summary of Margulis's professional career, no label such as "microbiologist," can begin to suggest the enormous impact she had on a variety of scientific disciplines. Within the scientific community, her name always struck a responsive chord. To some she was a gadfly, and many scientists greeted her views with a mixture of exasperation and amusement. One of her early correspondents even tried to "order" her out of the profession because her theories contradicted conventional wisdom. To others she was a brilliant thinker who productively challenged accepted notions about the fundamental nature of life on earth and shifted the ground on which biologists and evolutionists had stood for generations.

Margulis began to attract controversy while studying for her Ph.D. At that time it was assumed that the genetic makeup of a cell's offspring was determined entirely within the cell's nucleus. Margulis, though, challenged this assumption by looking for—and finding—genetic material in cells' **cytoplasm**, the area outside the nucleus, as well. She concluded that the two types of DNA had different origins in the evolutionary process. She then challenged conventional efforts to classify microbes as either animals or plants. She began with the notion that

1938 — Margulis is born in Chicago.

1970 — Margulis publishes *The Origin of Eukaryotic Cells*.

1974 — Margulis teams with James Lovelock to advocate the Gaia hypothesis.

1983 — Margulis is elected to the National Academy of Sciences.

**cytoplasm:** the protoplasm of a cell apart from its nucleus; is the site of most of a cell's chemical activites.

**"Some critics say she's off in left field. To me, she's one of the most exciting, original thinkers in the whole field of biology."**
Peter Raven, director of the Missouri Botanical Garden, on Lynn Margulis, quoted at the Kapiolane Community College web site

**eukaryotic cells:** cells of higher organisms containing a true nucleus bonded with a chemical membrane.

there are two types of cells, those with a nucleus and those without, and that while animals and plants are composed of nucleated, or "**eukaryotic**," cells, most microbes consist of non-nucleated cells. Margulis developed the radical theory that cells with nuclei evolved from a merger—a symbiosis—of two or more different bacterial cells that lacked nuclei. Put differently, at the level of microbiology, cooperation, not competition, was the basis of evolutionary development, and eukaryotic cells are actually communities of organisms that interact within the boundaries of the same cell membrane. She published an account of her ideas in her 1970 book, *The Origin of Eukaryotic Cells*.

Throughout the 1970s many members of the scientific community ignored Margulis's ideas. Others tried to prove her wrong, but they couldn't, and by the time she published a revision of her book in 1981, her radical theory had become accepted thought and was being incorporated into standard textbooks. In 1983 she shed her role as a professional outcast when she was elected to the prestigious National Academy of Sciences.

Throughout the 1980s and 1990s Margulis disseminated her ideas to a broader audience in a series of widely read and reviewed books. Several of these books were written with her son, Dorion Sagan, who often jokingly referred to his famous parents as "Earth mother" and "Space father." These books, which included *Microcosmos* (1986), *Origins of Sex* (1988), *Mystery Dance: On the Evolution of Human Sexuality* (1991), *What Is Life?* (1995), and *What Is Sex?* (1997), challenged scientists and nonscientists alike to think about evolution and the earth's biological systems in new ways. Together, these books—as well as Margulis's many articles in professional journals—argue that symbiosis, not a series of random mutations, drove evolutionary development and created new species. Margulis also contributed to the teaching profession with articles in *American Biology Teacher*, teachers' guides, educational films, slide sets, and videos.

In recent years, Margulis has continued to be a lightning rod for controversy because of her advocacy of the Gaia hypothesis, which seems a natural extension of her views. The Gaia hypothesis was first advocated by British chemist James Lovelock in the early 1970s, and in 1974 he and Margulis teamed up to become its major champions within the scientific community. The Gaia hypothesis, which some observers dismiss as fuzzy, New Age thinking, takes the view that the earth as a whole is alive, that it forms a single, interdependent, self-regulating symbiotic system. It thus tries to replace the older Darwinian view that life on earth is the product of brutal competition between organisms and species. Always the provocateur, Margulis wrote that the Darwinian view of life on earth will ultimately be seen as "a minor 20th-century religious sect within the sprawling religious persuasion of Anglo-Saxon biology." "Gaia," she wrote, "threatens everything they do." Many scientists remained skeptical, but they were often reluctant to attack her views. She had proven them wrong before. ◆

# Maury, Antonia C.

## MARCH 21, 1866–JANUARY 8, 1952 ● ASTRONOMER

Antonia Maury was one of a number of talented, independent women who worked at the Harvard College Observatory in the late 19th and early 20th centuries, and her innovations in star classification made her one of the most influential American astronomers during this exciting period.

Antonia Caetana de Paiva Pereira Maury was born in Cold Spring, New York, the daughter of a minister. Her grandfather was the distinguished chemist and physician Dr. John William Draper, who took an early interest in photography and who may have shot the oldest existing photograph in the United States. Her uncle was Dr. Henry Draper, a prominent physician whose name would play a role in his niece's future career. Both were amateur astronomers with an interest in astrophotography, and Maury would follow in their footsteps. A precocious child, she helped her famous uncle in his lab when she was just four years old, and by age nine, at the urging of her father, she was reading the classical writer Virgil in the original Latin.

At Vassar College, Maury studied under the noted astronomer Maria Mitchell, completing her bachelor's degree with honors in astronomy, physics, and mathematics in 1887. Her original goal was to teach chemistry and physics, but her father inquired about a position for her as a "computer" —one who did laborious mathematical calculations in the days before silicon computers—at the Harvard College Observatory, where

<table>
<tr><td>1866</td><td>Maury is born in Cold Spring, New York.</td></tr>
<tr><td>1887</td><td>Maury graduates with honors from Vassar College.</td></tr>
<tr><td>1889</td><td>Maury discovers the second binary star.</td></tr>
<tr><td>1943</td><td>Maury is awarded the Annie Jump Cannon Prize.</td></tr>
<tr><td>1952</td><td>Maury dies on January 8.</td></tr>
</table>

the director, Dr. Charles Edward Pickering, was known for hiring women. Maury gladly accepted the position, and though the work could at times be dull and routine, she worked at the observatory on and off for most of the rest of her career.

Maury arrived at the observatory during the Henry Draper Memorial project, which eventually led to the publication of the *Henry Draper Catalogue*. This project was funded by Draper's widow and Maury's aunt, Anna Draper—who ironically had given Maury a lukewarm recommendation when she applied for the job. The observatory had already done work on spectral classification using photographs. Pickering, though, had decided to reexamine the stellar spectra data in greater detail using better telescopes and spectroscopic equipment that had become available, and he placed Maury in charge of the stars of the Northern hemisphere. Despite obstacles created by Pickering himself—who hired women but who also became irritated when they showed initiative and strayed from the tasks assigned them—she reexamined existing spectral classes and concluded that the existing classification system was inadequate, for it did not take into account the spectral lines she was able to see with the newer equipment.

On the basis of her detailed examinations of star photographs, Maury developed a set of collateral series—a so-called second dimension—for classifying stars according to their spectra. In particular, she identified what she called a "c-characteristic" that could be used to classify a star according to its electromagnetic field and what later turned out to be the presence of helium. Pickering thought that her system was too cumbersome, and he did not use it in the catalogue. Several years later, though, the famed Danish astronomer Ejnar Hertzsprung used her classification to identify "red giant" stars, and puzzled by its exclusion from the catalogue, he wrote to Pickering saying that Maury's work was "the most important advancement in stellar classification" in many years. Hertzsprung later teamed with Princeton's Henry Norris Russell to develop what is known as the Hertzsprung-Russell diagram of dwarf and giant stars, still a fundamental document in stellar astrophysics. Their work would not have been possible without Maury's spectral classification system.

In 1891 Maury left the observatory to take a teaching position at the Gilman School in Cambridge, Massachusetts. In 1893 she returned to the observatory, where she worked for a year and a half. Again she left, this time to travel in Europe, but in late 1895 she contacted Pickering and offered to help with any loose ends in the preparation of the catalogue. In the years that followed she gave public lectures on astronomy to general and professional audiences, accepted private pupils, and from 1896 to 1918 taught physics and chemistry at Castle School in Tarrytown, New York. She did, however, continue to work part-time as a research associate at the observatory, and after Pickering's death in 1919 she worked on and off at the observatory under the new director, Harlow Shapley, until her retirement.

During these years, Maury returned to an early interest in binary, or double, stars that could be identified through irregularities in their spectral lines. In 1888 she had helped in the discovery of the first binary star, Mizar, in the Big Dipper, and that same year she herself discovered the second, Beta Aurigae. She was the first astronomer to find the orbital periods of these stars and the first to compute their orbits. One astronomer called her work on spectral binaries "one of the most notable advances in physical astronomy ever made."

Maury worked at the Harvard observatory until 1935, though she had other interests. She was a student of philosophy, an amateur ornithologist (bird watcher), and a gifted conversationalist about a wide range of topics. She was also outspoken in her advocacy of the preservation of historic sites. From 1935 to 1938 she worked as custodian of the Draper Park Observatory Museum in Hastings-on-Hudson, where she lived until her death in 1952. For her work on stellar spectra, the American Astronomical Society awarded her the 1943 Annie Jump Cannon Prize—named for one of Maury's contemporaries at the observatory—and a lunar crater was later named in her honor. ◆

> **"The single greatest mind that has ever engaged itself in the field of the morphology of stellar spectra."**
> Dr. W. W. Morgan on Antonia Maury, to whom he dedicated his version of an atlas of stellar spectra, quoted in *Notable Women in the Physical Sciences*, 1997

# McClintock, Barbara

JUNE 16, 1902–SEPTEMBER 2, 1992 ● GENETICIST

Barbara McClintock became one of the 20th century's most famous American scientists for discoveries that changed the course of genetic research. She was also one of the nation's best loved scientists. Though she never married, and though she conducted most of her research in isolation, her admirers pointed out that she had sparkling eyes, a wicked

Barbara McClintock at the microscope in her lab on Long Island, New York, in 1947.

sense of humor, and a gift for conversation. An amateur botanist, she enjoyed talking to a gardener or a groundskeeper as much as to a fellow scientist. Among her wide circle of friends late in life were many people who were much younger than she, and she enjoyed turning brief chats with them into lengthy discussions about science. When she accepted the Nobel Prize in Stockholm, Sweden, the normally reserved audience was so glad that *she* won that they erupted into thunderous applause.

McClintock was born in Hartford, Connecticut, though she grew up in Brooklyn, New York. Her mother opposed her decision to attend college, and with her father out of the country as a World War I medical officer, she worked as an employment counselor. When her father returned home, he agreed to let her attend Cornell University, where she earned a bachelor's degree from the College of Agriculture in 1923. She remained at Cornell to earn a master's degree in 1925 and a Ph.D. in 1928. From 1927 to 1931 she was a biology instructor at Cornell, then left to become a research fellow under a grant from the National Research Council until 1933.

McClintock continued her research as a Guggenheim Foundation fellow in 1933–34, then returned to Cornell as a research associate until 1936. From 1936 to 1941, she was an assistant professor at the University of Missouri, where she encountered what today seems an almost comical form of sex discrimination: Her dean threatened to fire her after he saw in the local newspaper a notice announcing the engagement of another Barbara McClintock. Miffed, she immediately packed up her Model A car and left Missouri. In 1942 she then settled into a job as a staff member for the Carnegie Institution of Washington in Cold Spring Harbor, New York, where she remained until 1967.

1902 McClintock is born in Hartford, Connecticut.

1970 McClintock wins the National Medal of Science.

1983 McClintock wins the Nobel Prize for Medicine.

1992 McClintock dies.

From her days as a graduate student, McClintock was regarded as a rising star in the field of genetic research, and from the 1920s through the end of her career. she produced a stream of new concepts that challenged accepted thinking in the field. Her primary achievement in the 1930s was to find chromosomes that formed rings, and she later discovered that these ring chromosomes were a special case of broken chromosomes that are now known to be implicated in the development of some forms of cancer and in the aging process.

Though she was unable to see them, McClintock predicted the existence of structures called telomeres on the ends of normal chromosomes. Telomeres help maintain the chromosomes' integrity and stability, but they are lost when the chromosomes are broken. Then, during the 1940s, she discovered what lay behind this instability—genetic material she called transposable elements, or "jumping genes." These were small genetic elements that could move from one place to another on a chromosome or even between chromosomes and that seemed to cause genetic breakage. McClintock went on to show that cells used these elements to regulate themselves, acting as switches to turn genes on and off. Already a respected geneticist, she was elected president of the Genetics Society of America in 1944, and in 1945 she was elected to the National Academy of Sciences.

McClintock published the results of her findings in 1950, but she had her first chance to sell her ideas in a paper she delivered to a group of eminent biologists at the 1951 Cold Spring Harbor Symposium. The paper presented breakthrough findings, but it met with a cool reception, and it seemed to many observers, especially looking back, that her work was ignored for years. McClintock, though, conducted most of her

## Cold Spring Harbor Laboratory

The Cold Spring Harbor Laboratory in Cold Spring Harbor, New York, is one of the most famous research centers of any kind in the world; many notable scientists have passed through its doors in its more than 100 years of existence. It began as a biological laboratory founded by the Brooklyn Institute of Arts and Sciences in 1890. Its early years were largely devoted to investigations of evolutionary theories. In the early 20th century, it began focusing on genetic research, including hereditary theory (influenced by Gregor Mendel), eugenics, plant hybrids, and multiple allele theory. The laboratory's preeminence in molecular biology came largely as a result of the efforts of Milislav Demerec, director of the biology laboratory from 1941.

The tumor virus program, spearheaded by James Watson, led to the development of advances in recombinant DNA, largely based on the work of Richard Roberts, who studied the ability of bacteria to destroy viral DNA. Later researchers were among the first to discover RNA splicing in genes. Recent advances include the discovery of telomeres, molecular clocks of sorts that could open to way to unlocking the mysteries of aging. Mike Wigler, with Nikolai Lisitsyn, conceived of representation difference analysis, a method for comparing sequences of DNA from various tissue samples and identify differences in viruses.

In the 1950s, Barbara McClintock discovered "transposable elements" or "jumping genes," genes that do not remain in a single location on chromosomes. This is the work for which she received the Nobel Prize. In later years, the research of other scientists at Cold Spring Harbor Laboratory, studying the genetics of brewer's yeast, bore out many of McClintock's key hypotheses.

research with corn, and in the early 1950s geneticists were more interested in bacteria and viruses than in corn, which was becoming "old-fashioned" in genetic research. Furthermore, geneticists in those days were expending much of their effort mapping the genes in the fruit fly. Until McClintock, they believed that genes were a static blueprint for an organism, but McClintock's work showed them that an organism's genes are a dynamic system that interacts with the environment.

By challenging the very notion that genes could be mapped, McClintock was in effect undermining the cherished work of a generation of researchers. To make matters worse, many of the attendees simply did not understand her dense, statistic-laden report. Her failure to ignite her audience at Cold Spring Harbor became part of a myth—that she went into seclusion, washed her hands of her hostile colleagues, and settled into the role of the neglected and misunderstood scientist.

In fact, it simply took time for McClintock's complex theories to take hold. With better equipment, scientists in the

1970s were finally able to actually see a transposable element—not just in corn but in fruit flies, bacteria, yeast, and even humans. Cancer researchers were beginning to investigate the role of telomeres. By this time, the awards and recognition McClintock deserved had begun to pour in. A partial list includes the Merit Award from the Botanical Society of America (1957), the Kimber Genetics Award from the National Academy of Sciences (1967), the prestigious National Medal of Science (1970), the Lewis S. Rosensteil Award for Distinguished Work in Basic Medical Research (1978), and the Thomas Hunt Morgan Medal from the Genetics Society of America (1981). Several universities awarded her honorary doctorates. She achieved the summit of her profession in 1983, when, more than 30 years after the fact, she won the Nobel Prize for Medicine for the work she published at the Cold Spring Harbor Symposium. Later she said that she hated the publicity and notoriety that accompanied the prize.

McClintock continued to reap honors until her death in 1992. In 1984 she won the Albert A. Michelson Award. She was named an honorary member of the American Medical Women's Association, the Medical Women's International Association, the American Society of Naturalists, and the New York Academy of Sciences, and she was named a "Foreign Member" of London's Royal Society. She continued to work until her death—though in her late 80s, she did slow down to an eight- or nine-hour workday. ◆

> "She's far ahead of her time and tries not to startle you with it.... She enjoys making things clearer. She's a passionate teacher. The passion of her existence is removing the fog."
> Guenter Albrecht-Buhler on Barbara McClintock, quoted in *Nobel Prize Women in Science*, 1993

# McManus, R. Louise

MARCH 4, 1896–MAY 29, 1993 ● NURSE AND EDUCATOR

R. Louise McManus, one of the most forward-thinking nursing educators of the 20th century, was born Rachel Louise Metcalfe in North Smithfield, Rhode Island. Her higher education began at the Pratt Institute in Brooklyn, New York, where she received a diploma in institutional management in 1916. She then went on to earn a diploma in nursing from the Massachusetts General Hospital School of Nursing in 1920. In 1925 she received a bachelor of science degree from the Columbia University Teachers College, where she remained to complete a master's degree in student personnel administration in 1927.

**1896** McManus is born in North Smithfield, Rhode Island.

**1947** McManus is appointed director of the Division of Nursing Education at Teachers College, Columbia University.

**1953** McManus founds the Institute for Nursing Research in Nursing Education.

**1996** McManus dies on May 29.

During her years at Columbia, McManus was also a member of the Teachers College staff, and she foreshadowed the direction her career would take with the publication of a 1928 article, "Research in Nursing Education," in *The Nursing Education Bulletin*, the first research journal in nursing. Eventually, McManus earned a Ph.D. in educational research and psychology from Columbia in 1947, making her the first nurse in the country to receive a Ph.D.

In the meantime, she met John McManus, a successful salesman, on a Mediterranean cruise in 1929. After a brief courtship, the two married, and McManus stayed at home with her husband's six children from a previous marriage. In 1934, however, John McManus died. Not long after, Isabel Stewart, head of the Teachers College nursing school, invited McManus back to the college to work as a research assistant on a major curriculum study the nursing school was undertaking. McManus accepted the position, moved to Manhattan, and at age 41, began a 24-year career dedicated to nursing and nursing education at Teachers College. In 1947 she succeeded Stewart as director of the Division of Nursing Education, but, always known for her quiet, unassuming manner, she never sought the position, expressed surprise at her appointment, and initially thought that it was only temporary. She held the position until her retirement in 1961.

Under McManus's leadership, the Division of Nursing Education changed the face of the nursing profession in the United States. The program not only elevated nursing to the status of a profession but charted a path for the enormous growth of the number of college- and university-based schools of nursing throughout the country. As an administrator McManus was adept at identifying the challenges that nursing faced, and her visionary solutions to these challenges—which she often literally pulled full-blown from her lower right-hand desk drawer—represented a series of "firsts" for nursing education.

One challenge was the need for nursing schools to create a foundation of basic research knowledge about the field, and to this end McManus founded and directed the Institute for Nursing Research at Teachers College, which in 1953 became the first university center for research in nursing. As part of this effort, she established curricula for graduate-level nursing programs for nursing teachers and supervisors.

A second challenge was the burgeoning need for nurses in the post–World War II era. Nursing schools—which had usually been connected to hospitals—simply were not turning out enough graduates to meet the needs of the medical profession. McManus foresaw the role that two-year colleges could play in filling this need and put her considerable fund-raising skills to work to spearhead the Cooperative Research Project in Junior and Community College Education for Nursing. That project led to the development of a new level of nurse, the nursing technician, who could perform many of the functions of a registered nurse.

As the number of nurses began to grow, McManus identified a third challenge: the need to develop a standardized national approach to licensing nurses. McManus worked with state boards of nursing, state legislators, and national nursing organizations to develop such standards. Finally, McManus saw the need to protect the interests of patients, so she developed a "Patient Bill of Rights" that was adopted by the Joint Commission in Accreditation of Hospitals.

McManus's contributions to the nursing profession did not go unnoticed.. Among her many awards were the Columbia University Bicentennial Award, the Florence Nightingale International Red Cross Society Citation and Medal, and the Mary Adelaide Nutting Award for Leadership. In 1964 Teachers College named its Nursing Education Alumni Medal after her. But McManus was more than the sum of her résumé.

Throughout her career she was highly admired by administrators, faculty colleagues, and students. Many recalled with amusement her somewhat eccentric approach to paperwork, for rather than using files, this institutional management graduate had her own system. In fact, a national nursing organization sent to Columbia for an accreditation visit learned all about McManus's filing methods when she presented them with all the documents they needed—in a shopping bag, her preferred method of storage. McManus also loved to knit, and her knitting bag accompanied her wherever she went. On fund-raising trips at national meetings, donors would hand her a check, or even cash, and into her knitting bag the money would go—always without question on the part of the donor.

After her retirement from Columbia in 1961, McManus moved to Massachusetts, where she died after a brief illness in Natick at age 97. ◆

# Mead, Margaret

DECEMBER 16, 1901–NOVEMBER 15, 1978 ● ANTHROPOLOGIST

Margaret Mead was born in Philadelphia, Pennsylvania, one of five children of Edward Sherwood Mead, an economics professor at the Wharton School of the University of Pennsylvania, and Emily Fogg, a feminist and sociologist. Her parents raised their children in various towns in New Jersey and Bucks County, Pennsylvania, from which her father commuted to his work in Philadelphia. Mead graduated from the New Hope School for Girls in Pennsylvania and enrolled at DePauw University in Greencastle, Indiana, in 1919. After an unhappy year, she transferred to Barnard College in New York City. There, in her senior year, she discovered her life's work, under the influence of anthropology professor Franz Boas and his assistant, Ruth Benedict, for whom Mead's affection was intense, reciprocal, and unending. At the same time she carried on a placid courtship with her fellow Pennsylvanian, Luther Sheeleigh Cressman, a theology student who had secretly been her fiancé since her teens. They were married on September 3, 1923, a few months after Mead received her B.A. degree from Barnard. She received both her M.A. degree (1924) and Ph.D. (1929) from Columbia University.

Partly at Mead's urging, Cressman left the clergy for sociology, then anthropology, and eventually became a distinguished archaeologist. For Mead, marriage was less compelling than her work, which in 1925 took her across the world to American Samoa. Boas sent her there on her first field trip, to undertake "a study in heredity and environment based on an investigation of the phenomenon of adolescence among primitive and civilized peoples." Her task, as she described it, would "involve working almost entirely with women, and should therefore add appreciably to our ethnological information on the subject of the culture of primitive women."

En route home after five and a half months of fieldwork, Mead fell into a shipboard romance. Reo Franklin Fortune was a brilliant young New Zealander, bound for graduate studies in psychology at Cambridge University in England (and destined to switch professions and become an anthropologist). He and Mead corresponded when Mead was back in New York, joylessly reunited with Cressman. In 1926, Mead became an assistant curator at the American Museum of Natural History, an association that lasted until her death. She completed her doctorate and finished the manuscript for *Coming of Age in Samoa* (1928), the first and best known of her 32 books, which asserted that there were ways not only of getting through puberty but of doing almost anything. If Samoans could get through adolescence without pain and clumsiness, then so might Americans and Europeans.

Mead and Cressman were divorced in the summer of 1928. She proceeded with plans to return to the South Seas to do more fieldwork, in partnership with Fortune, whom she married in Auckland, New Zealand, on October 8, 1928. Together they headed for the Admiralty Islands, where they began work that led to his *Manus Religion* and her *Growing Up in New Guinea* (1930). In 1930 they returned to New York, then went to Nebraska on an assignment from the American Museum of Natural

Margaret Mead

**1901** Mead is born in Philadelphia, Pennsylvania.

**1923** Mead marries Luther Cressman.

**1923** Mead receives a bachelor's degree from Barnard College.

**1926** Mead becomes an assistant curator.

**1928** Mead publishes *Coming of Age in Samoa.*

**1928** Mead divorces Cressman and marries Reo Franklin Fortune.

**1929** Mead earns a doctorate from Columbia University.

**1940** Mead begins teaching at Vassar College.

**1978** Mead dies in New York City.

History to do a summer of fieldwork with a tribe of native Americans, the result of which was *The Changing Culture of an Indian Tribe* (1932). Mead and Fortune received grants in 1930 that allowed them to begin work in the Pacific the following fall.

Studying the different ways sex roles were stylized in three Melanesian tribes—the Arapesh, Mundugumor, and Tchambuli—Mead took decreasing pleasure in her teamwork with Fortune. The strain between the two had grown acute by Christmas of 1932, when they encountered British ethnographer Gregory Bateson, who was doing fieldwork of his own in the Pacific. Fortune was the odd man out in the ensuing romantic triangle. The three returned to their native countries, and Mead and Fortune divorced in 1935. Mead wrote *Sex and Temperament in Three Primitive Societies* (1935), a report of her studies of the New Guinea cultures; taught her first course at Columbia University; and kept in close touch with Bateson, whom she married in Singapore on March 13, 1936.

For two years their collaboration was idyllic. First they worked in Bali (1936–1938), where they devised new research methodologies using film and photography, and then with a New Guinea tribe called the Iatmul in 1938. As World War II loomed, the couple returned to New York, where Mead gave birth to her only child, Mary Catherine Bateson. Motherhood, she was determined, would not conflict with her and Bateson's writing or with their work on the applications of social science to international crises.

Mead somehow managed to balance her domestic life with an ever-expanding array of outside commitments. In 1940 she began a two-year teaching stint at Vassar College in Poughkeepsie, New York. During World War II she commuted to Washington, D.C., to work on the National Research Council's Committee on Food Habits and went to England for the Office of War Information to study the relationships between British citizens, especially young women, and American troops. She and Benedict launched an ambitious postwar project sponsored by the United States Navy called Research on Contemporary Cultures at Columbia. All this was hard on her marriage, and she and Bateson were divorced in October 1950.

Setting up housekeeping in Greenwich Village with Rhoda Métraux, a widowed fellow anthropologist who also had a child, Mead did her best to keep up with old and new friends, her own large family, and all her former in-laws. Once a protégée, she became more and more a mentor to her students and her assistants at the Institute for Intercultural Studies, which she had established in 1944 at the American Museum of Natural History. In 1953, around the time she coined the term "post-menopausal zest," she returned with two young fieldworkers to Peri village in Manus. In *New Lives for Old* (1956), she described how World War II had affected the people she and Fortune had studied 25 years earlier.

Mead continued to write books and articles, give speeches, and agree to more responsibilities. She continued the teaching she had been doing since 1934 at Columbia University (and would do all her life) and was a visiting lecturer at the University of Cincinnati School of Medicine's Department of Psychiatry (1957–1978) and at the Menninger Foundation in Topeka, Kansas (1959). She also taught at Fordham University in New York City (1968–1970). A devout Episcopalian, always ecumenical and interdisciplinary, she took on roles with the World Council of Churches, Planned Parenthood, the United Nations, the World Federation of Mental Health (president, 1956–1957), the National Academy of Sciences, the American Anthropological Association (president, 1960), and the American Association for the Advancement of Science (president, 1975, and chairman, 1976). She spoke out for various environmental causes, made appearances on late-night television talk shows, and wrote a monthly column, one of many collaborations with Métraux, for *Redbook* magazine. As the 1970s waned she was physically thin and quite irritable, which turned out to be symptoms of pancreatic cancer, of which Mead died in New York City.

Five years after her death Mead's reputation was subjected to a severe attack from Derek Freeman, a New Zealand-born professor at the Research School of Pacific Studies at the Australian National University. Freeman based his charges on fieldwork he had conducted over six years, beginning in 1940, in Western Samoa. He asserted in *Margaret Mead and Samoa: The Making and Unmaking of an Anthropological Myth* (1983) that Mead had seriously misrepresented her first subjects' culture and character. Mead's research, Freeman contended, had been conceived as part of Boas's philosophical struggle against biological determinism and was conducted in unscholarly haste. Mead's young natives, said Freeman, had duped her. Her champions rose to Mead's defense, in print and in a series of spirited colloquia, but Freeman still challenged her reputation. Other posthumous critics, particularly indigenous scholars in the islands Mead had studied, regarded her as a coconspirator

Mead took on roles with the World Council of Churches, Planned Parenthood, and the United Nations.

in neocolonialism. By portraying South Pacific natives in terms of savagery, cannibalism, and wanton sexuality, they asserted, she reinforced belief in Western colonialist supremacy and in a distortedly romanticized view of the Pacific Islands.

Mead's early fieldwork may have been hurried and imperfect, but in the mid-1920s, when she went off to Samoa, little formal training in field methods existed anywhere. Several years later, when Columbia University offered its first course in the subject, she was one of its first teachers. If in her early travels she was guilty of some wrong answers, she kept on asking what many strongly felt were the right and most urgent questions. The question one colleague said Mead took to Samoa was one she kept asking all her life: "How can we understand ourselves?," not "How can we understand others?" ◆

# Meitner, Lise

NOVEMBER 7, 1878–OCTOBER 27, 1968 ● PHYSICIST

Lise Meitner

Lise Meitner's work spanned the development of the 20th century atomic physics from radioactivity to nuclear fission. Albert Einstein called her "our Marie Curie." It is true that Meitner, like Curie, was a brilliant experimental physicist of exceptional prominence.

She was born to intellectual, politically liberal parents, the third of eight children of Philipp (a lawyer) and Hedwig Meitner. Although the family background was Jewish, Judaism played no role in the children's upbringing, and all were baptized as adults, Lise as a Protestant in 1908.

At the time, schooling for Austrian girls ended at age 14, but in 1897 Austria opened its universities to women. Lise attended university from 1901 to 1906, the second woman to receive a physics doctorate in Vienna (the first was Olga

Steindler in 1903). There she learned physics from Ludwig Boltzmann, a brilliant teacher who gave her the "vision of physics as a battle for ultimate truth" (Frisch, 1970, p. 406). Her doctoral research was experimental; she was introduced to radioactivity by Stefan Meyer in 1906.

There were no jobs for women physicists, however, in 1907 Meitner went to Berlin to study under another great theoretical physicist, Max Planck, who became her mentor and friend. For research she found a partner in Otto Hahn, a radiochemist just her age. Berlin became her professional home, and she stayed 31 years.

With Hahn she found new radioactive species, studied beta decay and beta spectra, and in 1918 discovered protactinium, element 91.

Between 1920 and 1934 Meitner, independent of Hahn, pioneered in nuclear physics. From studies of beta-gamma spectra, she clarified the radioactive decay process by proving that gamma radiation follows the emission of alpha (or beta) particles; her studies of the absorption of gamma radiation verified the formula of Oskar Klein and Yoshio Nishina and indirectly the relativistic electron theory of P. A. M. Dirac. Meitner was among the first to determine the mass of neutrons and to observe the formation of electron-positron pairs.

In 1934 Meitner began studying the products formed when uranium is bombarded with neutrons; the investigation, led by Meitner and including Hahn and chemist Fritz Strassmann, culminated in the discovery of nuclear fission in December 1938. Five months earlier, however, Nazi racial policies forced her to flee Germany, and although she conducted an intense scientific correspondence with Hahn from exile in Stockholm, she was not credited with her share of the discovery. In early 1939 she and her physicist nephew Otto Robert Frisch published the first theoretical explanation for the process and named it fission. Hahn was awarded the 1944 Nobel chemistry prize alone, an injustice that clouded Meitner's reputation in later years.

Meitner had a talent for friendship and a deep love for music and the outdoors. She served in the Austrian army as an x-ray nurse in World War I and retained her Austrian citizenship all her life. In 1943 she was asked to join the atomic bomb project at Los Alamos but refused on principle; years later she said that her "unconditional love for physics" had been damaged by the knowledge that her work had led to nuclear weapons. ◆

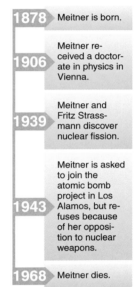

**1878** Meitner is born.

**1906** Meitner received a doctorate in physics in Vienna.

**1939** Meitner and Fritz Strassmann discover nuclear fission.

**1943** Meitner is asked to join the atomic bomb project in Los Alamos, but refuses because of her opposition to nuclear weapons.

**1968** Meitner dies.

# Mexia, Ynes

May 24, 1870–July 12, 1938 ● Botanist

Ynes Mexia launched her career as a distinguished botanist at an age when most people look forward to retirement. In a burst of activity over the last years of her life, she collected thousands of botanical specimens and made herself an expert in the plant ecosystems of Mexico and South America.

Mexia was born in the Georgetown district of Washington, D.C. Her father was an agent for the Mexican government, and her mother already had six children from a previous marriage. When Mexia was three years old, her parents separated and she moved to Texas with her mother. At age 15, she returned to the East Coast to attend Saint Joseph's Academy in Maryland for a year. She then spent the next 10 years living with her father in Mexico City, inheriting his plantation after his death.

Mexia married in 1897 but lost her husband seven years later. She established a successful poultry and stock-raising business at her Mexico City plantation and married a man 16 years her junior. But in 1909 she had to go to San Francisco, California, for medical reasons, and in her absence her husband nearly bankrupted the business. She made the decision to remain in San Francisco, sold what was left of the business, and divorced her husband. Though she did part-time social work, she was depressed and felt that her life lacked direction.

That lack of direction ended in the late 1910s and early 1920s when she began to take field trips with the local Sierra Club and discovered a love of botany. In 1921 she enrolled in natural science classes at the University of California at Berkeley, then in 1925 took a course in flowering plants at the Hopkins Marine Station in Pacific Grove, California. In the fall of that year, she went on her first major botanical expedition, accompanying Roxanna Stinchfield Ferris, a botanist at Stanford, to western Mexico. In her mid-50s, Mexia had finally found her calling in life.

From 1925 until her death in 1938, Mexia logged thousands of miles of arduous travel; obtained, catalogued, and preserved over 137,000 plant specimens; and lived a life so filled with harrowing adventure that she could be described as the "Indiana Jones" of botany. That first field trip to western Mexico with Ferris was cut short by a fall from a cliff that resulted in several broken bones, so she returned to San Francisco to recuperate. There, ever the businesswoman, she decided to fund future expeditions by selling plant samples to various institutions. She returned to western Mexico in 1926, exploring the mountains, the coastlines, and three Mexican states—all the while contending with gnats, ticks, and panthers and traveling by horseback, canoe, a steamer, and a packtrain. She returned with 33,000 specimens, including 50 new species and a new genus named in her honor, *Mexianthus mexicanus*. On her next expedition, Mexia traveled to Mount McKinley in Alaska in the summer of 1928, adding 6,100 specimens to her collection.

1870  Mexia is born in Washington, D.C.

1921  Mexia enrolls in natural science classes at Berkeley.

1925  Mexia takes her first botany field trip, to western Mexico.

1938  Mexia dies in California.

Then in 1929 Mexia began her conquest of South America, where she spent much of the rest of her career. In October she traveled to Rio de Janeiro, Brazil, and from there to the highlands of Minas Gerais, a state in east Brazil, where she stayed for a year and a half collecting specimens. She returned to Rio, then embarked on a 3,000-mile expedition to the interior of South America, a journey she described for the readers of the *Sierra Club Bulletin* in a 1933 article.

The journey began on August 28, 1931, when she boarded the steamer *Victoria* and started up the Amazon River, often stopping along the way to explore the dense rain forests that lined the river. Twenty-four days later, the steamer arrived at Iquitos, Peru, but Mexia was not done with her journey. She repacked her gear, hired three men and a launch named *Alberto*, and traveled westward on the Rio Maranon, a tributary of the Amazon. Seven days later the party abandoned the launch for four canoes.

When the Andes Mountains blocked the their movement westward, they set up camp at the mouth of the Rio Santiago, a tributary of the Rio Maranon, and for three months Mexia collected specimens and bartered for goods—including the toucans, monkeys, and parrots that she ate—with local Indians. In January 1932 she loaded a raft made of balsa logs and headed back to Iquitos with 65,000 plant specimens. Still not done with her journey, she sent her specimens back to California, then made her way across South America by hydroplane, airplane, car, and train to the Pacific Coast. Two and a half years after arriving in Rio de Janeiro, she fulfilled her dream of traveling across the continent at its widest point.

Mexia returned to California, where for the next two years she took trips with the Sierra Club throughout the American Southwest. But South America continued to beckon, and in 1934 she set out for Ecuador, where she hoped to study a rare wax palm tree that grew at higher altitudes and cooler temperatures than most palm trees, meaning that the tree might be suitable for cultivation in California. With the help of an Indian guide, she endured dense forests, steep slopes, and a blistering sun until she found and photographed the tree, as well as adding 5,000 specimens to her collection. Then in October 1935—after just three days' rest in Tulcan, Equador—she joined an expedition led by T. Harper Goodspeed from the botany department at the University of California. Until January 1937 she traveled with Goodspeed south from Peru to the Straits of Magellan, adding 15,000 specimens to her collection.

Mexia returned to Mexico at age 67. She began to complain of chest pains, but she continued to collect specimens, adding 13,000 to her collection before returning home to California in May 1938, where she died of lung cancer on July 12. In his book *Plant Hunters in the Andes*, Goodspeed described her as "a true explorer type and happiest when independent and far from civilization." ◆

# Mitchell, Maria

AUGUST 1, 1818–JUNE 28, 1889 ● ASTRONOMER

America's first woman astronomer, Maria Mitchell, was born on Nantucket Island, 48 kilometers off the southern coast of Massachusetts, on August 1, 1818. She was the third of 10 children of Quaker parents. Mitchell's father, William, was a liberal, cultured gentleman, a teacher in the Nantucket schools, and from 1836 to 1861-cashier of the local bank. He was an ardent amateur astronomer and close confidant of the first two directors of Harvard College Observatory, William and George Bond. Mitchell received her basic training in astronomy from her father and at an early age became his assistant. At the age of 12, during the annular solar eclipse in 1831, she timed the contacts for him. Cyrus Peirce, before he accepted the directorship of Horace Mann's first normal school in Lexington in 1839, taught at a school for young ladies on Nantucket. One of his students was Mitchell, whose aptitude for mathematics he recognized and encouraged. By means of stellar observations William Mitchell checked the accuracy of the rates of chronometers for whaling captains. One time, when

William was not at home, a whaler brought his chronometer and Mitchell volunteered to check it, having learned by watching her father. The whaler was skeptical but let her try; to his amazement she accomplished the task perfectly.

In 1835, at age 17, Mitchell started a private school for girls age six and older. It was the first school on Nantucket to admit children of all races, color, or religious preference. (At that time the public school would not accept black children.) Unfortunately this experiment did not survive because the following year she was appointed the librarian at the Atheneum, Nantucket's public library, a position she held for 20 years. Mitchell went to work early every morning to study some of the books under her care before the doors opened to the public. She surveyed Nantucket for her father for the purpose of making a map of the island. This was arduous work, as much of the land had previously been explored only long ago by native Indians. William Mitchell published their map in 1838.

Maria Mitchell

On clear nights, after Mitchell's work at the Atheneum, William and Maria scanned the skies for interesting objects, searching for comets, observing variable stars, planets, and their satellites, and timing lunar occultations. One memorable evening, on October 1, 1847, working alone with their 7.5 cm Dollond telescope, Mitchell discovered a new comet. For this discovery she received a gold medal established by the King of Denmark to be awarded to anyone who first sighted a telescopic comet (one invisible to the naked eye at the time of discovery). Mitchell became the first woman and the first American to receive the medal, and this catapulted her to international fame. She declared, however, that she could not claim the comet as her own unless she could compute its orbit. Her earlier mathematical studies under Cyrus Peirce paid dividends. Her orbit for the comet indicated that it was traveling in a parabolic orbit and would not return—a conclusion confirmed much later by one of her Vassar students, Margareta Palmer, at Yale. In 1859, a group calling itself "The Women of

## The Maria Mitchell Association

The Maria Mitchell Association (MMA) was established on Nantucket Island in honor of Maria Mitchell, the brilliant astronomer and America's first woman professor of astronomy. Mitchell believed that the best way to teach students was to have them conduct actual research, not simply read textbooks. Accordingly, the MMA devotes itself to encouraging student research and advancing the presence of women in science, as well as fostering scientific research on Nantucket Island. The MMA boasts a first-rate astronomy research program, an aquarium, a natural science museum, writer/lecture series, class and field programs for children and adults (with special attention to the birds and flora of Nantucket), and a year-round library housing Mitchell's manuscripts, along with a variety of books, from lavishly illustrated 19th-century science texts to recent scientific journals and titles in natural science. The MMA also maintains the house where Mitchell was born. This house, which is open for tours during the summer months, features the brass telescope used by Maria Mitchell to discover a comet in 1847.

Since 1997, the MMA has also offered an annual prize of $10,000 that is called the Maria Mitchell Women in Science Award. It is given to people or programs that have a record of achievement and that also help girls or women advance in their careers in the natural and physical sciences, mathematics, engineering, computer science, and technology. Award winners include the Women in Engineering Program at Purdue University, and the Graduate Research Program for Women at Bell Laboratories/Lucent Technologies.

People interested in learning more about the MMA can visit its website at http://www.mmo.org/

America" presented Mitchell with a 12.5 cm Alvan Clark telescope with which she might discover more comets. Indeed, she discovered three more, and computed their orbits, but others anticipated her in these discoveries. The telescope is still in active use at the Nantucket Maria Mitchell Obsererected in 1908 in her memory. In 1848 she became the first woman to be made a member of the American Academy of Arts and Sciences, indeed the only woman inducted for nearly a century, when five women were admitted in 1943.

While a librarian, Mitchell was given the opportunity to compute ephemerides of Venus for the *American Ephemeris and Nautical Almanac*, a task she continued along with her other duties from 1849 through 1868. Alexander Bache, director of the U.S. Coast Survey, lent the Mitchells a transit instrument for them to contribute observations for the determination of the figure of Earth.

Vassar College for women was opened in 1865 with Mitchell as the first American woman professor of astronomy, a post she held until 1888. In Nantucket she had lived in a community where a large percentage of the male population were whalers, spending years at a time at sea. Hence the women of the island experienced greater responsibilities and greater freedom of decision than most women at that time. At Vassar Mitchell recognized discrimination for the first time when she discovered that the men in other departments, with responsibilities similar to her own, were being paid more. Henceforth she became an ardent advocate of women's rights, and in 1870 she was elected president of the American Association for the Advancement of Women.

Mitchell proved to be an outstanding teacher. One of her ablest students, Mary Whitney, who became her successor, reflected that Mitchell's gift as a teacher was her ability to provide stimuli, not drills. Few teachers were more inspiring. Among her students were later prominent woman astronomers, including Antonia Maury (1866–1952) at Harvard, noted for her pioneering work in stellar spectroscopy, and Margareta Palmer (1862–1924), the first woman in the United States to earn a Ph.D. in astronomy, at Yale in 1894 (see Hoffleit, 1983).

Although Mitchell was a diligent observer, she published very little: one article in the *Astronomical Journal* (1856) on her observations of minima of the eclipsing star Algol; one in the *American Journal of Science* in 1863 on observations of 36 double stars and four articles between 1873 and 1879 on the satellites of Jupiter and Saturn; and a few less technical articles elsewhere, notably in Nantucket's weekly newspaper.

Although she was primarily an astronomer, Mitchell's work on **chronometry**, **celestial navigation**, **cartography**, and her determination of the latitude and longitude of the Vassar College Observatory (Furness, 1934) constituted relevant contributions to earth sciences. ◆

**1818** Mitchell is born on Nantucket Island, Massachusetts.

**1835** Mitchell establishes a private girls school on Nantucket.

**1836** Mitchell is appointed librarian at the Atheneum.

**1847** Mitchell discovers a new comet and wins a gold medal from the King of Denmark.

**1865** Mitchell becomes the first American female professor of astronomy at Vassar College.

**1889** Mitchell dies.

**chronometry:** the science of measuring time.

**celestial navigation** moving on the earth by observing the positions of celestial bodies.

**cartography:** map making.

# Morawetz, Cathleen Synge

MAY 5, 1923– ● MATHEMATICIAN

When the National Organization for Women honored Cathleen Synge Morawetz for successfully combining a career with family, she quipped, "Maybe I became a mathematician because I was so crummy at housework." That

**1923** Morawetz is born in Toronto, Ontario, Canada.

**1951** Morawetz completes her Ph.D. at New York University.

**1984** Morawetz is appointed director of New York University's Courant Institute of Mathematical Sciences.

**1998** Morawetz wins the National Medal of Science.

she was "crummy" at housework was fortunate, for Morawetz became one of the nation's most distinguished mathematicians and served as a role model for a generation of young women interested in following in her footsteps.

Morawetz was born Cathleen Synge in Toronto, Canada, the daughter of Irish immigrants. Her father, John L. Synge, was a mathematician at the University of Toronto, and her mother had also studied mathematics, so both supported her decision to pursue a career in mathematics—though her father worried that he and his daughter might wind up at odds with each other over mathematical theories. In 1943 she earned her bachelor's degree in mathematics at the University of Toronto, where a family friend and teacher, Cecilia Krieger, encouraged her to pursue her master's and her Ph.D. After a year working as a technical assistant for inspection at the Board of the United Kingdom and Canada, she enrolled at the Massachusetts Institute of Technology (MIT), where she completed her master's degree in 1946. In the meantime she had married chemist Herbert Morawetz, a Czech immigrant, in 1945.

Originally Morawetz planned to get a job with a corporation, but she discovered that most of the best corporate jobs were not open to women. Instead, she moved to New York, where she edited a book by Richard Courant and Kurt Friedrichs of New York University called *Supersonic Flow and Shock Waves*. She then enrolled in the Ph.D. program at New York University (NYU), where, she later said, she found mentors who judged her on the quality of her work rather than on her gender. She completed the degree in 1951, conducting her thesis research on imploding shock waves. In the meantime, she became a U.S. citizen in 1950.

Morawetz returned to MIT, where she worked as a research associate for a year. She then returned to NYU, and there she remained for the rest of her career. For the first five years she was a research associate, after which she became an assistant professor in 1957, an associate professor in 1960, and a full professor in 1965. She was a Guggenheim Fellow in 1967–68 and again in 1978–79. In 1978 she was appointed deputy director of the university's Courant Institute of Mathematical Sciences, then made deputy director in 1981. In 1984 she became the first woman to head up a major mathematical institute when the Courant Institute appointed her director, a position she held until 1988.

Morawetz is best known for her pioneering developments in **partial differential equations** and in **wave propagation** applications. In the 1950s she made new estimates for the solution of mixed nonlinear partial differential equations, work that had implications for aircraft designers. In examining shock wave propagation, she showed that shock waves are inevitable as a plane moves close to the speed of sound, no matter how the wings are designed. Her mathematical models again had application for the aviation industry, for they led to improvements in airplane wing design that focus on minimizing rather than eliminating shock waves. Morawetz also did important work on geometrical optics and the mathematical theory of scattering, which describes how waves interact with obstacles. Based on this work she developed mathematical models that had applications for improvements in remote sensing, including ultrasound, radar, and sonar.

Throughout her career Morawetz was the recipient of many honors, and she gave generously of her time to her profession. She was a fellow for the American Association for the Advancement of Science and for the American Academy of Arts and Sciences. She was a member of the mathematical sciences advisory committees of the National Science Foundation and of the National Bureau of Standards. She was the first woman to belong to the applied mathematics section of the National Academy of Sciences. In 1981 she was the first woman to give the Gibbs Lecture to the American Mathematical Society, in 1982 she gave the Invited Address to the Society for Industrial and Applied Mathematics, and in 1983 she gave the Emmy Noether Lecture to the Association for Women in Mathematics. In 1993 the Association of Women in Science named her its Outstanding Woman Scientist. In 1995–96 she served as just the second woman president in the 105-year history of the American Mathematical Society, and later she was chair of the AMS's Committee on Science Policy. In 1997 she received the Krieger-Nelson Award, given by the Canadian Mathematical Society to outstanding female mathematicians. She also received four honorary doctorates.

Morawetz's highest distinction came in 1998, when she became the first female mathematician to receive the National Science Foundation's National Medal of Science, the nation's highest scientific honor. Commenting on the medal, she said, "… I hope it will draw attention to the idea that women can do

**partial differential equations:** a differential equation which contains at least one partial derivative.

**wave propagation:** an increase in the amount of wave lengths in the movements of objects.

math and will have some influence on women all the way from grade school to graduate school and beyond."

Somehow, Morawetz also managed to raise four children, all of whom became successful professionals. Her ability to combine work and family life led to her 1990 recognition by the National Organization for Women Legal Defense Fund for raising children with a "committment to equality at home." ◆

# Neufeld, Elizabeth F.

SEPTEMBER 27, 1928– ● MOLECULAR BIOLOGIST

Elizabeth Fondal Neufeld was born in Paris, France, the daughter of Russian immigrant parents. When World War II broke out, the family emigrated again, this time to New York. Neufeld's parents strongly supported her desire to pursue a higher education, and the roots of her career as a leading international authority on human genetic diseases extended back to her interest in biology as a high school student. In 1948 she completed her bachelor's degree at Queens College in New York, then went on to complete a Ph.D. in comparative biochemistry at the University of California at Berkeley in 1956.

Neufeld began her career as a plant biologist, and after completing the Ph.D. she conducted research in cell division in sea urchins. Later she examined the biosynthesis of plant cell wall polymers, and although she discontinued plant research in her future career, her work in this area provided

Elizabeth F. Neufeld

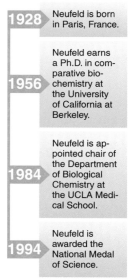

**1928**  Neufeld is born in Paris, France.

**1956**  Neufeld earns a Ph.D. in comparative biochemistry at the University of California at Berkeley.

**1984**  Neufeld is appointed chair of the Department of Biological Chemistry at the UCLA Medical School.

**1994**  Neufeld is awarded the National Medal of Science.

her with insights that led to some of her most noteworthy discoveries.

Neufeld's career took a new direction in 1963 when she began a two-decade-long stay at the National Institutes of Health (NIH), joining a relatively large number of women from that era who did pioneering work for the NIH and numerous other federal agencies. Often faced with discrimination in the private sector and in academia, many women sought refuge in government jobs during that era. From 1963 to 1973 she was a research biochemist for the NIH's National Institute of Arthritis, Metabolism, and Digestive Diseases. In 1973 she was appointed chief of the NIH section on Human Biochemical Genetics. Then in 1979 she was promoted to chief of the National Institute of Arthritis, Diabetes, and Digestive and Kidney Diseases (NIADDK), part of the NIH's Genetics and Biochemistry Branch. In 1981 she also took on duties as deputy director of the NIADDK Division of Intramural Research. In 1984 she left the NIH to become the first female department head at the University of California at Los Angeles School of Medicine, where she accepted a position as chair of the Department of Biological Chemistry. She remained at UCLA for the rest of her career.

Neufeld later said that she joined the NIH at just the right time, for interest was running high in the development of treatments for a group of inherited diseases called MPS disorders. MPS is short for mucopolysaccharidoses, a term that refers to lysosomal storage diseases, which include Hurler, Hunter, and Sanfilippo syndromes. While the diseases are not well-known to the general public, they are very serious. Patients with these and other related syndromes suffer neurological breakdown because their cells lack lysosomal enzymes, which are needed to break down complex sugars. As a result, the sugars accumulate in their cells, causing the cells to grow and putting pressure on nerve tissues. As the nerve tissues die because of too much pressure, the patients suffer from motor deterioration, mental problems, loss of hearing and vision, and premature death, often before puberty. Better known diseases such as Tay-Sachs are related to the MPS diseases.

Research in Europe had recently proven the importance of lysosomal enzymes in cell metabolism, and in the 1960s the NIH was conducting clinical trials of various enzymes that could be used in the production of drugs to treat these diseases.

Neufeld's research, along with that of her colleagues, provided critical information needed to treat patients with MPS disorders. At the time, she and her colleagues were assuming that patients' cells were producing more complex sugars than they could metabolize. Neufeld tried to use her research with plant cell wall polymers to determine what was wrong with the cells, and although that earlier research proved to be a dead end, it provided her with the basic science she needed to unlock the cells' secrets.

Together with colleague Joseph Fratantoni, Neufeld focused on Hunter syndrome, mixing normal cells with cells from a Hunter syndrome patient. Purely by accident, they mixed cells from a Hunter patient and a Hurler patient, and they made the startling discovery that the cultures actually "cured" each other, resulting in nearly normal cells. On that basis, they isolated the problem: that the cells were actually metabolizing complex sugars, but they were doing so at an extremely slow rate because of a defective gene. With further research they were able to identify the enzymes that were missing in patients with Hunter and Hurler syndromes.

On the basis of Neufeld's work, researchers were able to develop not only improved treatments for the diseases, but also prenatal tests for MPS and related disorders, leading to improved genetic counseling for parents. Neufeld's research also became one important piece in a large puzzle that may lead to gene replacement therapies and more effective bone marrow transplant treatments for patients with a variety of disorders.

Neufeld was widely recognized for her work. In 1977 she became the first female NIH researcher to be elected to the National Academy of Sciences. That year, too, she was elected to the American Academy of Arts and Sciences. In 1982 she was a co-recipient of the Albert Lasker Clinical Medicine Research Award. In 1988 she won the Wolf Prize in Medicine and became a fellow of the American Association for Advancement in Science. In 1992 she was elected to a one-year term as president of the American Society for Biochemistry and Molecular Biology. Her most prestigious award came in October 1994, when President Bill Clinton hosted a White House ceremony at which he awarded her and seven other researchers the nation's highest honor for scientific achievement, the National Medal of Science. ◆

# Nightingale, Florence

MAY 12, 1820–AUGUST 13, 1910 ● NURSE

Florence Nightingale received her first name from the Italian city her wealthy parents were visiting when she was born. Nightingale's upbringing was privileged and comfortable, imbued with the earnest humanitarian, cultural, and Christian religious commitments of her family. Her parents could not find a tutor for their daughters who matched their exacting standards and consequently the father undertook the task of educating them. The range of subjects they were taught was broad, embracing the classics, French, Italian, history and philosophy.

In 1837 Nightingale felt the first of what she believed were four divine calls to dedicate herself to holy works but initially she did not know in what field. She was free meanwhile to continue a busy social life and made an excellent impression on Paris society as a cultured and well-bred young lady. The social round continued with her presentation at Queen Victoria's court in 1839 and participation in all the other events that a lady of marriageable age was expected to patronize. She even had two suitors during the early 1840s, but neither won her favor. She had decided her mission demanded total commitment and that she must forgo marriage for she was taking upon herself the devotion of the Roman Catholic nuns whose medical missions she studied and admired.

By 1844 Nightingale had decided that nursing was to be her vocation. She had some experience from looking after sick family, friends, and some of the local villagers and wanted to get training working at Salisbury Infirmary. Her parents thought this was no place for a young lady of her class; hospi-

Florence Nightingale

### Florence Nightingale Museum

St. Thomas's Hospital, on Lambeth Palace Road in London, England, has collected information and memorabilia on Florence Nightingale for several decades. These items include her clothing, books and letters, furniture, and relics and nursing material from her service during the Crimean War. In 1983, the Florence Nightingale Museum Trust was established. It aimed to support the training of nurses and the study of Nightingale in various ways, such as offering facilities for research on Nightingale and the field of nursing, permitting her artifacts to be displayed, and awarding grants for nurses to begin graduate study in the U.K. and elsewhere.

In February 1989 the museum fulfilled a central part of its mission, opening its doors to the public and making the collection more widely accessible. In addition to displays of Nightingale's memorabilia, museum visitors can make use of the gift shop, which features books related to Nightingale, and hear talks offered by the museum staff. The museum is open year-round.

Another museum related to the legacy of Florence Nightingale is located in the Claydon House, in Middle Claydon, near Buckingham in England. Nightingale often stayed at this house when visiting her sister, Lady Verney. The Museum Room houses mementos of her personal life and nursing career. The museum, owned by the National Trust, is closed during winter months.

tals in their view, were unhealthy places and nurses had a poor moral reputation. Frustrated by family opposition, Nightingale toured Europe, visiting a model hospital at Kaiserswerth, Germany, where there she found an institution run on high moral principles, though staffed by nurses who were "only peasants—none of them gentlewomen." Eventually, persistence met with success and her father granted her an allowance of 500 pounds a year and did not oppose proposals to make her superintendent of the Institution for the Care of Sick Gentlewomen in Distressed Circumstances in London. With typical enthusiasm she began to make improvements in hospital organization, saving a considerable sum of money.

In 1854 the Crimean War began and the British public was dismayed when it learned of the incompetence with which the war was being managed. Disease was a far greater danger to the troops than Russian bullets: a fifth of the expeditionary force went down with cholera. There was a national outcry and Nightingale was approached and volunteered to lead a party of nurses to the Crimea under War Office sponsorship. However, her arrival was unwelcome by the army medical establishment, which resented female interference in their traditional preserve.

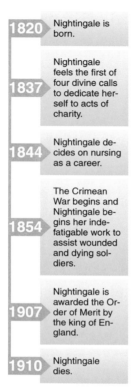

The nurses were housed in cramped and unsanitary quarters that lacked the most basic amenities. To complete the unpleasant reception there was a Russian general whose dead body nobody had bothered to remove from the nurses' living quarters!

Nightingale was deferential toward the authorities and made do with the appalling living conditions. The state of the hospital was even worse, and following the Battle of Inkerman (1854), an influx of wounded overwhelmed the primitive facilities and the army medical men were forced to turn to Nightingale and her nurses for help. She was not intimidated by the dreadful conditions, but found herself moved by the character of the ordinary soldiers, who had long been considered the lowest of the low. She recorded how "these poor fellows bear pain and mutilation with unshrinking heroism and die without complaint. Not so the officers."

The task was daunting. Nightingale ensured that the patients had clean linen and were bathed regularly, not just once in 80 days as had been the norm. Other innovations included scrubbing the floors of the wards, the distribution of literature and lectures for the wounded soldiers, as well as facilities for sending money home. Where necessary equipment was not forthcoming from the government supplies, she drew on a fund raised by the British public and used her own personal allowance toward these purchases. To the nurses working under her she could appear as a harsh, intimidating figure, convinced nobody had a right to oppose her will. For the soldiers, as she toured the hospital at night with her lantern, she became a comforting figure—the legend of "the Lady with the Lamp" was born.

When the war ended in 1856, Nightingale returned to Great Britain a national heroine. Physically and emotionally exhausted, she took to her bed as an invalid, which she remained for the rest of her long life. Incapacity did not prevent her from using her considerable influence to press for further reforms in the army medical services. She met Queen Victoria and Prince Albert and enlisted their support for a thorough investigation of military hospitals to prevent the "scene of '54" from ever being reenacted. Queen Victoria commented of her: "Such a *head*! I wish we had her at the War Office."

Nightingale also took a deep interest in improving sanitary and medical conditions for the troops in India and invested a vast amount of time in promoting the development of professional training for nurses and the betterment of treatment of the sick in the workhouse infirmaries of London. Some of her attitudes became outdated—she refused to accept the germ theory of the spread of disease—but in other ways her views were in advance of the time. She argued that the sick in the workhouses were not the indolent poor to be punished but merely "poor and in affliction" and that every step necessary to their recovery should be taken.

In 1907 this elderly blind lady became the first woman to be awarded the Order of Merit by the king. ◆

# Noether, Emmy

### MARCH 23, 1882–APRIL 14, 1935 ● MATHEMATICIAN

Emmy Noether, who was christened Amalie, was born in the quiet town of Erlangen in the plains of southern Germany. Like many mathematicians, she seemed to have had a genetic predisposition for the subject, for her father was Max Noether, an eminent mathematician at the University of Erlangen. Unlike many mathematicians, though, she showed little interest in the subject in her youth, and in fact was not an exceptional student. Despite the mathematical discussions that swirled around her at home, she showed more aptitude for languages, and after completing secondary school she passed examinations that qualified her to teach English and French. In the meantime she lived a life typical of that of many young women at the time, cooking, helping with household chores, shopping at the local stores, and flirting with young men from the university at dances.

At age 18, though, Noether embarked on a lifelong quest for official recognition of her devel-

Emmy Noether

1882 ▷ Noether is born in Erlangen, Germany.

1907 ▷ Noether completes her Ph.D. at University of Erlangen.

1916 ▷ Noether moves to Göttingen, Germany, to pursue a career in mathematics.

1934 ▷ Noether joins the faculty of Bryn Mawr College.

1935 ▷ Noether dies.

oping genius. She entered her father's university in 1900, one of just two women out of approximately 1,000 students, and she was only allowed to audit classes for no credit (instead of taking them for grades and credit as men did). Women at the time were not allowed to enter German universities as regular students, and just two years earlier the Erlangen faculty had declared that the presence of women "would overthrow all academic order."

For three years, Noether's intention remained to teach languages at a girls' school, but her plans changed in 1904 after the universities were opened to women and she passed the examination that finally granted her status as a regular student— one of just six women at Erlangen and 80 throughout all Germany. At this point she began to study mathematics more seriously, and in 1907 she completed a doctoral dissertation titled, "On Complete Systems of Invariants for Ternary Biquadratic Forms," written under the guidance of a family friend, Max Gordon. Over the next eight years she often substituted for her father, giving his lectures when he was ill. She also published several mathematical papers, lectured internationally, and began to acquire her own reputation.

Noether's family situation changed when her father retired, her mother died, and her brother Fritz, who became a prominent applied mathematician, joined the army, so in 1916 she moved to Göttingen, the center of mathematical thought in Germany at the time. She had been invited there by renowned mathematician David Hilbert, and in the years that followed she worked with Hilbert, Felix Klein, and Albert Einstein on the general theory of relativity, to which she made crucial mathematical contributions.

Of particular importance was Noether's work on invariants, which are important to the theory of relativity and the foundation stone of 20th-century quantum physics because they have a bearing on the question of what changes and what does not change based on the perspective of an observer. She also began to investigate the axiomatic theory of ideals, in effect reshaping the nature of algebraic thought. Future mathematicians continued to hold in awe her ability to for abstract thought, for her skill at seeing remote connections and extracting the core of a problem from its complicated whole. Early in her career, her work built on that of others, including her father, and she was often referred to as "Max Noether's daughter." By the end of her career, Max Noether was "Emmy Noether's father."

Although Noether was recognized as a mathematical genius, she struggled to gain paid employment and professional recognition. Göttingen granted doctoral degrees to women, but resistance remained high to granting them employment, and Noether carried on her work there with no salary and no official appointment. Hilbert tried to convince the faculty to grant her an official position, but his efforts were in vain. Although Noether lectured at the university, she delivered her lectures under Hilbert's name, and she was not paid.

Finally, in 1919, the social climate changed. Germany had lost World War I, the kaiser was out of power, and the more liberal Social Democrats were in power. They had given women the right to vote, women held seats in parliament, and the university regulations were relaxed so that Noether was given what was called an "unofficial associate professorship." At first the job carried no duties and no salary, but in time she was able to earn a modest salary teaching algebra. Though she was never known for her classroom skills, her almost feverish mathematical imagination often sparked similar creativity in her devoted students, who came to be called "the Noether boys."

Despite her irregular position, Noether brought recognition to the University of Göttingen and helped elevate its already impressive stature in mathematics. She spread the university's renown with a lecture series at Moscow University; in Frankfurt, Germany; and at the 1932 International Mathematical Congress in Zurich, Switzerland.

In 1933, though, life changed dramatically for Noether, as it did for many of Germany's most noted mathematicians and scientists. That year the Nazi Party consolidated its power, and for the Nazis, Noether's talent was less important than the fact that she was a political liberal, an intellectual woman, and Jewish. Further, though she had never taken part in partisan politics, she had become a pacifist as a result of World War I and the turmoil that followed in Germany, and in the early 1920s she had belonged to Social Democratic organizations. When the Nazis withdrew her position and salary (though the regime's scientists used her mathematical theories) and forced her to leave the country, she set sail for the United States, where she accepted a position at Bryn Mawr College. She also frequently lectured at the Institute for Advanced Studies at Princeton University.

For the first time in her life Noether had a regular faculty appointment. At Bryn Mawr she continued to win the devotion of her students, who often accompanied her on Saturday

"**Fraulein Noether was the most significant creative mathematical genius thus far produced since the higher education of women began.**"
Albert Einstein on Emmy Noether, quoted in *New York Times*, May 4, 1935, from the book *Women in Mathematics*, 1974

afternoon jaunts and who often had to protect their eccentric, absent-minded professor from traffic because she would become so intensely absorbed in mathematical discussions that she would not watch where she was going. She displayed the same warm, unassuming, unselfish personality that she had as a young woman—though she had a loud, disagreeable voice, atrocious table manners, and a tendency to mutter in German during her lectures. As one biographer wrote, "She looked like an energetic and near-sighted washerwoman."

Sadly, Noether taught at Bryn Mawr for only a year and a half. At the height of her powers, she died in 1935 from complications following routine surgery. ◆

# Novello, Antonia

AUGUST 23, 1944– ● PHYSICIAN

Antonia Coello Novello became the first woman, first Hispanic, and first Puerto Rican to hold the office of United States Surgeon General when she replaced the distinguished C. Everett Koop in 1990. She made her mark in the position by bringing a new level of warmth and compassion to the health concerns of minorities, women, and young people.

Novello was born on August 23, 1944, in Fajardo, Puerto Rico, to Antonio and Ana Coello. She was the eldest of three, and her father died when she was eight years old. From birth, Novello suffered from an oversized colon, an illness that sent her to the hospital at least two weeks each year. Finally, at age 18, Novello received surgery to correct her defect, but the surgery caused serious problems that required several more surgeries. Novello's experiences as a patient created her desire to become a doctor. She felt cared for by her pediatrician (children's doctor) and her gastroenterologist (doctor of stomach and intestines), of whom Novello later said, "His was the hand I saw—soothing and caring." Her nurse was her favorite aunt, who encouraged Novello to be a doctor. Encouraged also by her mother, a junior high school principal, Novello attended the University of Puerto Rico and received a B.A. in 1965. She received an M.D. from the university's School of Medicine in 1970.

Antonia Novello

On May 30, 1970, Antonia married Dr. Joseph Novello, a navy flight surgeon stationed at a base near Fajardo. Together they went to the University of Michigan in Ann Arbor, where Joseph studied psychiatry and Antonia completed her internship and residency in pediatrics. She worked in the university hospital's pediatric nephrology (kidney) unit. Watching children who needed kidney transplants, Novello recalled her own

For most Americans, "Surgeon General" is synonymous with the author of the warning posted on cigarette ads and products, stating the dangers of smoking. In fact, the surgeon general's office has a rich history of promoting public health. The surgeon general is the head of the Public Health Service Commissioned Corps within the U.S. Department of Health and Human Services. The office began as the Supervising Surgeon, head of the national hospital system established in 1870. John Woodworth was the first person to hold this position (1871). The precise functions of the surgeon general have changed many times over the years. Today it is less an administrative office and more of a prominent position for respected medical personnel to give voice to pressing public health issues. In the 1980s, C. Everett Koop was instrumental in bringing renewed attention to the office, in particular by using his position to help educate people about the emerging AIDS crisis in the United States. Antonia Novello, the first woman and first Hispanic to hold the position (1990–1993), continued the tradition of using the surgeon general's office to fight health problems associated with smoking, including public criticism of tobacco companies. She also focused on teenage drinking, urging wine and beer producers to remove advertising aimed at young people. Jocelyn Elders was the second woman and first African American to hold the post of surgeon general. During her often controversial tenure in the 1990s, she fought to educate people about a number of pressing health issues often ignored in public discourse, including sexually transmitted diseases and teen pregnancy.

childhood medical problems. She developed a strong concern for people who must struggle with the health care system to obtain needed care.

In 1974 the Novellos moved to Washington, D.C., where Antonia worked two years in a pediatric nephrology unit at Georgetown University Hospital. She then spent two years in private practice, but she quit when she found she became too emotionally involved. Her gifts lie in influencing public policy. Novello began working for the National Institutes of Health (NIH), a branch of the U.S. Public Health Service (PHS). The PHS is a division of the U.S. Department of Health and Human Services. Her first position was as a project officer working with kidney patients. She held two more positions at the NIH while earning her master's degree in public health from Johns Hopkins School of Medicine, which she received in 1982. By 1986 Novello had risen to deputy director of the NIH's National Institute on Child Health and Human Development.

In 1989 the administration of President George Bush discovered in Novello their ideal candidate for surgeon general of the United States. The surgeon general serves as the nation's chief health adviser. In that capacity, he or she authorizes research about important health issues and warns the public about health dangers. The surgeon general is appointed by the president, and the U.S. Senate must approve the appointment. The surgeon general ranks among the top PHS officials.

The Senate easily approved Novello, and she was sworn into office as the 14th surgeon general on March 9, 1990. Novello brought an immediate contrast to her predecessor, Koop, who had become famous speaking forcefully on such issues as AIDS. Novello became noted for a more diplomatic and nurturing approach. However, Koop had brought the surgeon general's position into the limelight, teaching Americans how to live healthier lives. Novello built on this example. She spoke out on health care for the needy. She also made a national priority of the problems of domestic violence, alcohol abuse, and smoking among women and young people.

In 1992 Novello joined the American Medical Association to publicly challenge the R. J. Reynolds Tobacco Company to stop an extensive advertising campaign that featured a cartoon character known as Joe Camel. Research had shown that most American youngsters recognized and liked Joe Camel. This began a long and vigorous fight by public health officials to stop tobacco advertising aimed at young people, who are particularly vulnerable to start smoking. Novello also denounced alcohol advertising for encouraging underage drinking. In spite of Novello's excellent performance and outstanding achievements, when Democratic president Bill Clinton replaced Republican Bush, he moved to appoint a new surgeon general. Novello left the position in June 1993, making way for Dr. Joycelyn Elders, an African American woman from Arkansas.

The hardworking Novello did not miss a beat in her career, and that year she became a special representative for health and nutrition for the United Nations Children's Fund (UNICEF). The position allowed her to address the needs of women and children all over the world. She remained in Washington with her husband, where he worked as a child psychiatrist. Having never become parents, both Antonia and Joseph achieved a great deal in their lives by committing their careers to the care of children. In 1999, Novello was appointed Health Commissioner of the State of New York. ◆

The Senate easily approved Novello, and she was sworn into office as the 14th surgeon general on March 9, 1990.

# Nüsslein-Volhard, Christiane

OCTOBER 20, 1942– ● BIOCHEMIST

Christiane Nüsslein-Volhard was born in Magdeburg, Germany, the second of five children. Her father was an architect, and her mother came from a family of talented artists and musicians. As a child she attended a prestigious girls' school, where she showed aptitude in a variety of subjects, including literature, history, and music, and as an adult she continued to sing and play the flute. She gave a commencement address at her school on the subject of communication among animals, and she once claimed to have developed her own theory of evolution at age 18. She was the only member of her family to show an interest in science, and she later pointed out that, although her parents were unable to provide her with help in the study of science, they supported her endeavors.

Nüsslein-Volhard's path to the Nobel Prize and her position as Germany's most famous scientist began at age 12, when she already knew that she wanted to be a scientific researcher. She later enrolled at the Johann-Wolfgang-Goethe University in Frankfurt as a biology major, but she quickly found biology to be a little dull so she branched out into physics and chemistry, completing her bachelor's degree in all three subjects in 1964. She then learned that a new program in biochemistry was being established at the University of Tübingen, so she left her family and friends for the first time and enrolled at that school. She was disenchanted with the program, so she did much of her work at the nearby Max-Planck Institute. She completed her degree from the University of Tübingen in 1968.

The late 1960s and 1970s were an unsettled time for Nüsslein-Volhard. She continued her graduate education at the University of

Christiane Nüsslein-Volhard

Tübingen, where she received a Ph.D. in biology and genetics in 1973. She also worked as a research associate at the Max-Planck Institute for Viral Research from 1972 to 1974. There, working with Heinz Schuller, she conducted research in virology and received a solid grounding in molecular biology. She then won a postdoctoral fellowship from the European Molecular Biology Organisation (EMBO) to study in 1975–76 at a new lab being set up by Walter Gehring in Basel, Switzerland.

In 1977 Nüsslein-Volhard accepted another postdoctoral fellowship, this time to study under Klaus Sander at the University of Freiburg. Then in 1978 she returned to the EMBO, where for three years she was head of a research group. Finally, in 1981 she landed back at the Max-Planck Institute, where she spent the remainder of her career. From 1981 to 1985, she was a group leader at the institute's Friedrich-Miescher Laboratory. From 1986 to 1990, she was the director of Developmental Biology. In 1990, she was appointed director of the Department of Genetics.

Throughout her career, Nüsslein-Volhard studied genetics using the fruit fly. The fruit fly (*Drosophila*) was an ideal subject for genetic researchers because of its small number of chromosomes, the existence of large chromosomes on its salivary glands, and its rapid rate of reproduction. In graduate school and in her early research positions, she was primarily interested in the embryology and **morphogenesis**—the differentiation of tissues and organs—in the fruit fly. At the EMBO she developed innovative techniques for studying the insect's early embryonic development, and her study of the development of mutant fruit flies led to a revolution in developmental genetics. In later research she discovered much of what is known about the process of fertilization, and she identified 120 "pattern genes" that enable an organism to begin its existence.

Nüsslein-Volhard conducted her most important research in collaboration with Princeton University's Eric F. Wieschaus, with whom though she began working when both were researchers at the EMBO. Their goal was to build on the work of Edward B. Lewis of the California Institute of Technology, who had identified genetic flaws that led to mutations in fruit flies, by discovering all the genes that determine embryo development in the fruit fly. Working in Nüsslein-Volhard's lab, they created 40,000 inbred families of fruit flies, each with a mutation of a particular gene. Some had no muscles; others had skin composed of nerve cells. Eventually they were able to identify

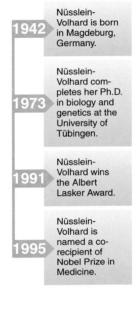

1942 — Nüsslein-Volhard is born in Magdeburg, Germany.

1973 — Nüsslein-Volhard completes her Ph.D. in biology and genetics at the University of Tübingen.

1991 — Nüsslein-Volhard wins the Albert Lasker Award.

1995 — Nüsslein-Volhard is named a co-recipient of Nobel Prize in Medicine.

**morphogenesis:** the process of cell formation and produce the complex shapes of adults from the simple ball of cells derving from the division of the fertilized egg.

## Lasker Awards

The Albert and Mary Lasker Foundation seeks to eradicate life-threatening diseases and disabilities. To pursue its vision, it supports medical research, especially as it affects national and international policies. Since the late 1940s, the foundation has awarded the Albert Lasker Medical Research Awards to those who have assisted in the progress of "the understanding, diagnosis, prevention, treatment, and even cure of many of the great crippling and killing diseases of our century." The awards are given in several categories, including basic research, clinical research, public service, and special achievement.

Contributions that have been recognized by the award include the development of the polio vaccine (Jonas E. Salk), discovery of the double helix structure of DNA (M. H. E Wilkins, E. H. C. Crick, and James D. Watson), discovery of moving genetic elements (Barbara McClintock), and identification of HIV as the cause of AIDS (Luc Montagnier). Christiane Nüsslein-Volhard won the Basic Research Award in 1991 for her discovery of most of the genes responsible for organizing basic body patterns. Other recipients include Janet D. Rowley (for patient-oriented research in cancer diagnosis), Elizabeth F. Neufeld (diagnosis of hereditary lysosomal storage disorders), and Rita Levi-Montalcini (various discoveries, including discovery of Nerve Growth Factor).

the specific genes that determine body shape and arrangement. Their work was an important contribution to the worldwide effort to discover the genetic plan in all life forms, including humans, for many of the genes that control development of fruit fly embryos are the same in humans. Scientists believed that their work would eventually help explain birth defects and miscarriages in humans. Because of researchers like Nüsslein-Volhard, thousands of distraught parents facing problem pregnancies may get help from the humble fruit fly.

The scientific community recognized the profound importance of Nüsslein-Volhard and her colleagues' work, and in 1995 she, Wieschaus, and Lewis were awarded the Nobel Prize in Medicine. This was not the first major prize she had won, though. In 1991, she received the Albert Lasker Award, second in prestige only to the Nobel. In 1992, she won the Gregor Mendel Medal from the Genetical Society of Great Britain. That year too she won the Louis Jeantet Prize for Medicine, the Alfred P. Sloan, Jr., Prize, and the General Motors Cancer Research Prize. She also received honorary doctorates from Yale, Princeton, and Harvard, as well as from Utrecht University and the University of Freiburg.

Nüsslein-Volhard was concerned about the issue of women in science. She said that Germany needed to give "much more encouragement to women who really dare to be a scientist." She even used some of her prize money to help the Max-Planck Institute establish a day-care center so that the women there could more easily pursue their careers. ◆

# Ochoa, Ellen

May 10, 1958– ● Astronaut and Electrical Engineer

Ellen Ochoa, the first Hispanic American woman to orbit the earth in space, was born in Los Angeles, California. Together with her sister and three brothers, she grew up in La Mesa, which is near San Diego. Her mother served as a role model for the value of education, and as a child Ochoa was an excellent student who showed aptitude in science and mathematics and even won the San Diego County spelling bee. She was also an accomplished musician and played the flute in her high school and college orchestras.

Ochoa graduated from Grossmont High School in La Mesa in 1975. She then enrolled at San Diego State University, but she had a difficult time deciding on a major. She explored music, business, computer science, and journalism, but she eventually settled on physics, completing her bachelor's degree in 1980. She was still considering a career in either music or business, but she went on to study electrical engineering at Stanford University, receiving a master's degree in 1981 and a Ph.D. in 1985. She first began to think about becoming an astronaut in 1983, when Sally Ride became the nation's first woman to fly in space.

After completing her Ph.D., Ochoa took a job as a research engineer at the Sandia National Laboratory in Albuquerque, New Mexico. There she continued work she had begun at Stanford designing optical systems that analyzed and drew conclusions about the objects they saw. She was awarded three patents

Ellen Ochoa

for optical devices she co-invented: one that inspects objects, one that recognizes objects, and one that removes "noise," or distortion, in an object's image. During these years she also learned to fly a plane.

When several of Ochoa's friends from Stanford applied to the National Aeronautics and Space Administration (NASA) to become astronauts, Ochoa decided to apply too. In 1988 NASA hired her, but not as an astronaut. Instead, she was hired as a researcher, and she quickly rose to become chief of NASA's Intelligent Systems Technology Branch at the Ames Research Center in Mountain View, California. There she supervised the work of 35 other scientists who researched and developed computational systems for aerospace missions. In the meantime, she wrote numerous papers presented at technical conferences and published in professional journals.

Ochoa's engineering and research ability caught the attention of the NASA space program, and in 1990 she was admitted as an astronaut trainee. In July 1991 she completed her training and joined the U.S. astronaut corps, and in the years that followed she had a number of technical assignments. She was responsible for flight software verification, and she was the crew representative for flight software and computer hardware development and for robotics development, testing, and training. She was also a spacecraft communicator at NASA's Mission Control.

Like any astronaut, though, Ochoa wanted to get into space. She achieved that goal on April 4, 1993, when the space shuttle *Discovery* blasted off with Ochoa aboard as mission specialist, making her the first Hispanic American woman to fly in space. *Discovery*'s nine-day mission was to conduct atmospheric and solar studies to help scientists better understand the effects of solar activity on the earth's climate and environment. Ochoa photographed the earth's oceans and continents, and she used the Remote Manipulator System, the robotic arm of the space shuttle, to release and later recapture the Spartan satellite, which had collected data on the solar corona and solar winds.

In November 1994, just a year and a half after her first flight, she was the payload commander on the *Atlantis* space shuttle flight. The main mission of that flight was to study the energy of the sun during an 11-year solar cycle and learn how changes in the sun affect the earth's climate and environment. Again Ochoa used the shuttle's robotic arm to retrieve a satellite that had mapped ozone and other gases in the earth's atmosphere. The one hitch in the mission came when Hurricane Gordon forced *Atlantis* to land at California's Edwards Air Force Base rather than in Florida.

Ochoa was then involved in the international study of damage to the earth's ozone layer. She also spent two years working on the international space station project, leading to her third space mission in May–June 1999. With Ochoa

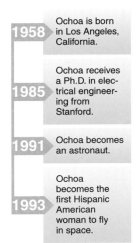

**1958** Ochoa is born in Los Angeles, California.

**1985** Ochoa receives a Ph.D. in electrical engineering from Stanford.

**1991** Ochoa becomes an astronaut.

**1993** Ochoa becomes the first Hispanic American woman to fly in space.

aboard, *Discovery* became the first space shuttle to actually dock with the space station, and, working 200 miles above the earth during an eight-hour space walk, Ochoa transferred four tons of supplies in preparation for the arrival of a crew to live on the station.

In all, Ochoa logged a total of 719 hours in space. Her third mission alone covered over four million miles. Back on earth, she continued to conduct research, and she kept up with robot arm technology and trained other astronauts in its use. She also saw herself as a role model, particularly to young Hispanic women, and she traveled the country giving talks on the importance of education. She was the recipient of numerous honors, including the NASA Exceptional Service Medal, the Women in Aerospace Outstanding Achievement Award, the Albert Baez Award for Outstanding Technical Contribution to Humanity, the Hispanic Heritage Leadership Award, and the San Diego State University Alumna of the Year award. She was also a member of the Presidential Commission on the Celebration of Women in American History. Married with one son, she enjoys flying planes, bicycling, and playing volleyball, and she continues to play the flute. ◆

# Patrick, Ruth

NOVEMBER 26, 1907– ● LIMNOLOGIST

Ruth Patrick was born in Topeka, Kansas. Her father, Frank Patrick, was a banker and lawyer, but he had a degree in botany from Cornell University, and he shared his love of science and nature with Ruth and her younger sister when the family went on weekend outings. After he and his daughters collected specimens of **algae**—especially the single-celled algae called diatoms—from local streams, he would encourage them to look at them under the four microscopes he kept in his rolltop desk at home. He gave Patrick her first microscope when she was seven years old, and throughout her childhood he encouraged her interest in science. That encouragement paid off when she became one of the nation's most prominent limnologists (scientists who study freshwater ecosystems).

When it came time for Patrick to attend college, her mother insisted that she attend Coker College, a small women's school in Hartsford, South Carolina. Her father, though, was concerned that the college was too small to provide extensive science facilities, so he arranged for her to attend summer courses at the Woods Hole Oceanographic Institute on Cape Cod, Massachusetts, and at the Cold Spring Harbor Laboratory on Long Island, New York. At Cold Spring Harbor, she met her future husband, Charles Hodge, but professionally she kept her maiden name in deference to her father, who had always wanted to be a scientist and longed to see the

**algae:** a term which groups several pyhla of the lower plants, including Rhodophyta, Cholorphyta, and Chrystopyhta.

259

Ruth Patrick

Patrick name on her books and scientific articles. Patrick completed her bachelor's degree in 1929. She then attended graduate school at the University of Virginia, completing her master's degree in 1931 and her Ph.D. in 1934. In graduate school she also studied in the summer at the Biological Laboratory at the University of Virginia at Mountain Lake, where she pursued her early fascination with diatoms and developed an interest in the ecology of aquatic organisms.

After completing her graduate studies, Patrick moved to Philadelphia with her husband, an entomologist (and direct descendant of Benjamin Franklin) who had found a job teaching zoology at Temple University. Here she gave birth to a son. It was the 1930s, and the United States was in the grip of the Great Depression. Patrick was unable to find a job, so she volunteered at the Academy of Natural Sciences, where she became a curator in the microscopy department in 1939. In 1947 she founded the academy's Department of Limnology and served as its chair—by now with pay—until 1973. After 1973 she was the Francis Boyer Research Chair at the academy, and in 1976 she became the first woman to chair the academy's board of directors. In the meantime she began lecturing on limnology in the biology department at the University of Pennsylvania in 1950. In 1970 the university made her a full professor.

Patrick spent her distinguished career either peering at tiny organisms through a microscope or journeying throughout the world to examine aquatic ecosystems; her work laid important scientific groundwork for environmental protection laws passed in the late 20th century. In graduate school she applied her knowledge of diatoms—an important link in the food chain in freshwater ecosystems—to the study of the Dismal Swamp between Virginia and North Carolina. By examining the diatoms in the layers of rock, she was able to chart changes in the condition of the water over time and concluded that at one time the area had been invaded by seawater. Using similar techniques she later determined that the Great Salt Lake in Utah had once been a freshwater lake. She also invented a device called the diatometer, which enables scientists to plot the size and growth of diatoms.

Patrick's career took a new direction in the late 1940s. An oil company executive heard her lecture about how different types of diatoms flourish—or fail to flourish—in different water conditions. He was interested in the question of whether diatoms could be used to determine whether a body of water had been harmed by pollution. He raised money to fund a study and insisted that Patrick direct it. She assembled a team of zoologists, biologists, and bacteriologists to study the Conestoga River Basin in Pennsylvania and to compare diatom populations in unpolluted areas with those in areas that were polluted by agricultural runoff or industrial chemicals.

Using the diatometer, Patrick developed techniques for using diatoms to determine the type and extent of pollution in a body of water, and she became the first scientist to demonstrate the relationship between water pollution and the health of the water's aquatic community. In this way she became an expert in water pollution, and she conducted limnological research not only in the United States, but in Mexico, Peru, and Brazil. She helped translate her findings into national water policy by serving on the National Academy of Science Committee on Science and Public Policy, the general advisory committee of the Environmental Protection Agency, and on the advisory council of the Renewable Resources Foundation. She also served as a member of the boards of directors

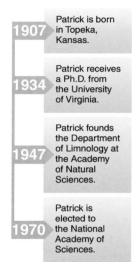

1907 ▸ Patrick is born in Topeka, Kansas.

1934 ▸ Patrick receives a Ph.D. from the University of Virginia.

1947 ▸ Patrick founds the Department of Limnology at the Academy of Natural Sciences.

1970 ▸ Patrick is elected to the National Academy of Sciences.

of Pennsylvania Power and Light and the DuPont Chemical Company.

Patrick received widespread recognition for the importance of her work. She was elected to the National Academy of Sciences in 1970 and to the American Philosophical Society in 1974. In 1975 she received the John and Alice Tyler Ecology Award—at the time the most lucrative scientific prize in the world thanks to its $150,000 cash award. She also received the Benjamin Franklin Medal for Distinguished Scientific Research from the American Philosophical Society and awards from the Ecological Society of America and the Botanical Society of America. In 1983 the Academy of Natural Sciences renamed the laboratories where she had worked the Patrick Center for Environmental Research. In addition, the University of South Carolina established The Ruth Patrick Science Education Center, a multipurpose facility designed to promote scientific education in elementary and secondary schools.

Clearly, Frank Patrick's early wish to see the Patrick name in print was granted, as his eminent daughter put her name on more than 140 scientific articles and several books, including a 1992 book (published when she was 85) examining the effectiveness of U.S. water laws. ◆

# Payne-Gaposchkin, Cecilia Helena

May 10, 1900–December 7, 1979 ● Astronomer

Cecilia Helena Payne-Gaposchkin was born in Wendover, England, the eldest of three children of Edward John Payne and Emma Leonora Helena Pertz. Her father, a lawyer, musician, and Oxford scholar, died when Payne was four years old. After seeing her first meteor at the age of five, she declared both her intention to become an astronomer and her haste, in case there should be no research left when she grew up. In 1923, Payne received her B.A. degree from Newnham College, Cambridge University, where she studied astronomy under Edward A. Milne. There she was also introduced to the Bohr atom by the Danish physicist Niels Bohr himself, and in accordance with the university regulations for women, she was seated in his advanced course, by herself, in the front row. Awarded a National Research Fellowship to do graduate work, she came to the United States, having been told by Leslie J. Comrie, who was going to teach at Swarthmore College, that a woman would have a better chance to win a research post in astronomy in America than in Britain.

Studying at Radcliffe College, Payne joined the Harvard College Observatory, which, under the directorship of Edward C. Pickering, was known for having encouraged the research of such famous women astronomers as Annie Jump Cannon, Williamina Paton Fleming, Antonia Maury, and Henrietta Leavitt. In 1925, Payne received the first astronomy Ph.D. from Radcliffe. Her dissertation on stellar atmospheres, described by Edward A. Milne as an "attractive story and a work of reference," sold out as a book. In the early 1900's, Henrietta S. Leavitt had made the important discovery of the relation between a star's magnitude and its period of **luminosity**. It was a critical astronomical yardstick, and Payne sought to explain the variations. In their history book *Astronomy in the 20th Century* (1962), Otto Struve and Velta Zebergs termed Payne's dissertation "undoubtedly the most brilliant Ph.D. thesis in astronomy." Payne was the first astrophysicist to determine the high dominance of hydrogen and helium in the cosmos, a theory that Henry Norris Russell at first discouraged but later supported. In 1926 she became the youngest astronomer ever "starred" in Jacques Cattell's *American Men of Science* (1947).

After obtaining American citizenship in 1931, Payne married Dr. Sergei I. Gaposchkin on March 6, 1934, and took the name Cecilia Payne-Gaposchkin. They had three children. Before her marriage, Payne-Gaposchkin had developed new ways of determining stellar magnitudes from photographic plates. With her husband, a Russian astronomer whom she had met in Germany in the early 1930's, she focused on the study of variable stars and contributed significantly to the understanding of novae, variable stars that suddenly increase in brilliance by thousands of times over the original and then decrease in brightness over a period of months, and their relationships to the life histories of stars. Together they examined 1,500 specimens in several million observations and published their conclusions in *Variable Stars* (1938), which became a standard source for researchers.

In 1938, Payne-Gaposchkin received her first Harvard rank under the presidency of James Bryant Conant when she was

**1900** ▶ Payne-Gaposchkin is born in Wendover, England.

**1923** ▶ Payne-Gaposchkin earns a bachelor's degree from Newnham College at Cambridge University.

**1925** ▶ Payne-Gaposchkin is awarded the first astronomy doctorate from Radcliffe College.

**1938** ▶ Payne-Gaposchkin is named Phillips astronomer and lecturer at Harvard.

**1956** ▶ Payne-Gaposchkin is the first woman to obtain the rank of full professor at Harvard.

**1979** ▶ Payne-Gaposchkin dies.

**luminosity:** the relative quantity of light an image or body gives off.

named Phillips astronomer and a lecturer at the Harvard College Observatory; she had been a permanent member of the staff since 1927. The appointment, however, was not a faculty position except in its duties; the courses Payne-Gaposchkin taught were not listed in the Harvard catalog until after World War II, in keeping with President Abbott Lawrence Lowell's longstanding policy that no female could receive an appointment from Harvard. Indeed, she had even experienced difficulties observing on Harvard-owned telescopes, for male directors of astronomical observation stations, usually located in isolated areas, believed it was too dangerous to have women observe alone, and improper for them to spend the night in the company of men. Regardless of her formal university status, Payne-Gaposchkin participated in numerous research projects conducted by the observatory's staff, and she worked independently. In addition to her study of variable stars and stellar atmospheres, she discovered the exploded nova of Hercules and photographed the fragments, and she worked on spectroscopy and the structure of the galactic system. For her outstanding scientific achievements, she was honored in 1952 by Radcliffe College with an Award of Merit. Her books include *Stars in the Making* (1952), *Introduction to Astronomy* (1954), *Variable Stars and Galactic Structure* (1954), and *Galactic Novae* (1957).

The first woman to achieve the rank of full professor at Harvard through regular faculty promotions, Payne-Gaposchkin was named a professor of astronomy in 1956, and from 1956 to 1966 she served as chair of the university's astronomy department. The American Association of University Women honored her in 1957 for her significant contributions to "the broadening of our understanding of the ages and lifetimes of stars and stellar systems." She was appointed astronomer at the Smithsonian Astrophysical Observatory in 1965, and in 1976 she received the Henry Norris Russell Prize, the most distinguished honor of the American Astronomical Society, which in 1934 had awarded her the Annie Jump Cannon Medal. Smith College, Western College for Women, Wilson College, and Cambridge University conferred honorary degrees on her. She died of lung cancer in Cambridge, Massachusetts, in 1979.

Throughout her life, Payne-Gaposchkin advocated a balanced life of career and homemaking for women. In *Cecilia Payne-Gaposchkin: An Autobiography and Other Recollections* (1984), she reflected on the past discrimination she had experienced as a female scientist, "a tale of low salary, lack of status, slow advancement," but she also exulted in her achievement of having, through dogged persistence, reached professional heights that were beyond her wildest dreams. In these same recollections, her daughter, Katherine Haramundanis, described Payne-Gaposchkin as a "Renaissance woman": at once scholar, linguist, generous neighbor, cultivated traveler, playgoer, musician, clever wit, political independent, keen scientist, and warm mother. ◆

# Pennington, Mary Engle

### OCTOBER 8, 1872–DECEMBER 27, 1952 ● CHEMIST

Many scientists devote their careers to theoretical research, making important discoveries about how and why things work in the natural world. Others devote their careers to the practical applications of science, using their know-how to help improve people's day-to-day lives. Mary Engle Pennington definitely fell into the second group. Today, when people open a can of vegetables or reach into the refrigerator for a fresh egg or glass of milk, they owe their confidence in the safety and wholesomeness of the product in large part to Pennington, whose scientific discoveries made such conveniences possible.

Mary Engle Pennington

Pennington was born in Nashville, Tennessee, though her family soon after moved to Philadelphia, Pennsylvania, to be near her mother's Quaker family. She shared with her father an interest in gardening, but her career path became apparent when she was 12 years old and stumbled across a medical book that sparked her interest in chemistry. Her parents and schoolteachers were shocked that she wanted to become a chemist, but her parents supported her, so in 1890 she began

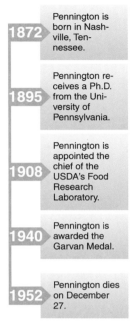

1872 ▶ Pennington is born in Nashville, Tennessee.

1895 ▶ Pennington receives a Ph.D. from the University of Pennsylvania.

1908 ▶ Pennington is appointed the chief of the USDA's Food Research Laboratory.

1940 ▶ Pennington is awarded the Garvan Medal.

1952 ▶ Pennington dies on December 27.

studying chemistry, biology, and hygiene at the University of Pennsylvania. At the time, the university did not award degrees to women, so even though she had completed the requirements for a bachelor's degree, she received instead a certificate of proficiency.

Determined to be a scientist, Pennington continued her studies and received a Ph.D. from the university in 1895, conducting thesis research on the elements columbium and tantalum. For two years she was a research fellow in chemical botany at the university, then for one year she was a research fellow in physiological chemistry at Yale University. At Yale she conducted research on the effect of colored light on plants.

Pennington began putting her extensive knowledge of chemistry to work in 1900 when she returned to Philadelphia. Throughout the next five decades, she had a hand in changing the face of modern life. Unable to find a job as a chemist, in 1901 she cofounded a private laboratory that analyzed medical tests for doctors. She began to lecture at the Women's Medical College of Pennsylvania and became director of the college's clinical laboratory. In 1904 she was appointed head of the bacteriology laboratory of the Philadelphia Department of Health, where she developed milk inspection standards that were later adopted throughout the country.

In 1905 Pennington took a job as a bacteriological chemist with the Bureau of Chemistry at the U.S. Department of Agriculture. Her work caught the attention of the bureau's chief, who urged her to apply for the position as chief of the USDA Food Research Laboratory, an agency newly established to enforce the 1906 Pure Food and Drug Act. He knew, though, that the USDA was unlikely to hire a woman for the job, so he suggested that she take the required civil service examination under the name "M. E. Pennington." She received the top score on the exam and was hired before anyone knew she was a woman.

From 1908 to 1919, Pennington and her growing staff, using what she knew about biological chemistry and the growth of such food enemies as bacteria and molds, devised refrigeration and other storage methods for eggs, poultry, and fish. She determined the correct temperature and humidity levels for storing and transporting eggs (even developing new egg packaging) and invented a new method for slaughtering and storing chickens safely. During World War I, when the nation faced food shortages and many women scientists worked in various jobs whose goal was to expand the nation's food supply, she actually traveled on refrigerated railroad cars, constantly checking the temperature level to ensure that the food did not spoil. She developed standards for railroad refrigerator cars, and as one of the nation's foremost experts on food refrigeration, she received the presidential Notable Service Medal in 1919.

Pennington left the USDA in 1919 and took a job as director of research and development with the American Balsa Company, which manufactured insulating materials and refrigerated boxcars. She later applied for two patents for strawboard insulating materials. She then launched her own business once again, this time in New York City, and from 1922 until her death in 1952, she was a consultant to packing companies, shipping firms, and warehouses, repeatedly solving problems connected with the storage, preservation, and transportation of food.

In the late 1920s, Pennington became interested in the frozen-food industry—which had been launched by Clarence Birdseye—and investigated issues surrounding the freezing of food, including ways to package the food to eliminate freezer burn. She wrote and published numerous technical articles and reports, as well as such books as *The Care of Perishable Food Aboard Ship; Food and Food Products;* and the two-volume *Eggs.* She was one of the few women scientists of the time who was able to achieve financial success in her field.

Pennington was widely honored for her work. Her most significant award was the 1940 Garvan Medal, given by the American Chemical Society specifically to women chemists for their achievements. In 1947 she was elected a fellow of the American Association for the Advancement of Science and was the first female fellow of the American Society of Refrigerating Engineers, of which she was serving as vice president at the time of her death. She was also a U.S. delegate to numerous international congresses on refrigeration held in Vienna, Paris, Copenhagen, Chicago, and Washington.

Given the nature of her work, it was almost inevitable that Pennington would acquire the nickname "the Ice Woman," but her admirers pointed out that she was a warm, gracious, hospitable woman who demonstrated excellent public relations skills in working with business and the government. She was living in New York City overlooking the Hudson River, where she enjoyed sewing and knitting with the help of her Persian cat, when she was stricken with a heart attack and died. Perhaps as testimony to her wide-ranging knowledge, *The New York Times* notice of her death listed her as an "engineer." ◆

# Pert, Candace B.

JUNE 26, 1946– ● PHARMACOLOGIST

> "I've come to believe that science, at its very core, is a spiritual endeavor. Some of my best insights have come to me through what I can only call a mystical process. It's like having God whisper in your ear. . . . It's this inner voice that scientists must come to trust."
>
> Candace B. Pert,
> *Molecules of*
> *Emotion*, 1997

**pharmacology:** a
medical science dealing
with the discovery,
chemistry,
manufacturing, effects,
and uses of drugs.

One weekend in 1972, a young researcher was working in a lab at the Johns Hopkins University pharmacology laboratory. Her young daughter played on the floor nearby. The researcher had recently been removed from the project on which she was laboring, but she disobeyed her boss, determined to conduct one last experiment that, if successful, might erase months of frustration. Later, the researcher said that during that last weekend she discovered the so-called opiate receptor, the chemical "lock" on nerve cells that binds with natural opiates in the body to determine a person's behavior, mood, and health. Her discovery altered the course of pharmacological and neurological research and led to a new understanding of the connection between the mind and the body.

The researcher was Candace B. Pert—a flamboyant, emotional woman who combined laboratory research with an almost mystical approach to science to become an internationally recognized pharmacologist and a leader in alternative medicine's mind-body movement. Pert was born in Manhattan in New York City. In 1970 she received her bachelor's degree in biology from Bryn Mawr College. From 1971 to 1974 she was a research assistant in the Johns Hopkins University Department of Pharmacology, and after receiving her Ph.D. in **pharmacology** from the university in 1974, she remained there for a year as a postdoctoral fellow.

In 1975 Pert joined the National Institute of Mental Health (NIMH) in Bethesda, Maryland, where she remained for 12 years. She began as a staff fellow in the NIMH Section on Biochemistry and Pharmacology, then was promoted to senior staff fellow (1977), research pharmacologist (1978), and chief of the Section on Brain Biochemistry (1982). In 1987 she left the NIMH to found and serve as the scientific director of Peptide Design L.P., a private firm in Germantown, Maryland, that created and tested new drugs. At the same time she was chairman of the board of Integra Institute, a nonprofit medical

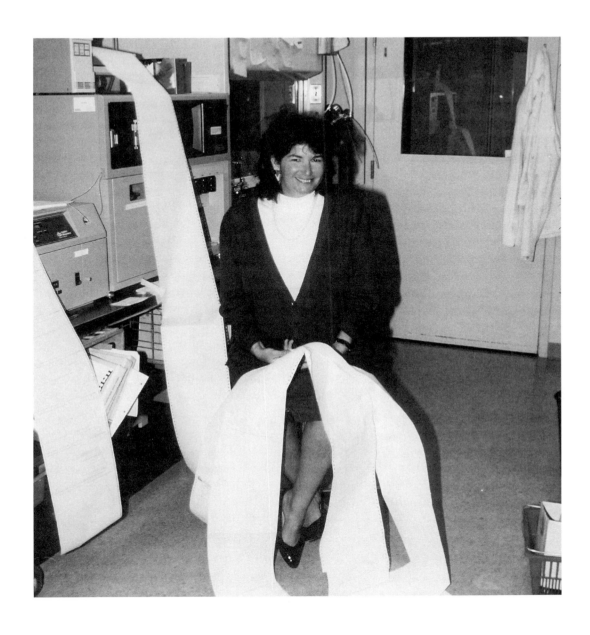

Candace Pert

research organization in Bethesda devoted primarily to AIDS research. From 1992 to 1994 she was a visiting professor at the Center for Molecular and Behavioral Neuroscience at Rutgers University in New Jersey. Then in 1994 she landed at Georgetown University in Washington, D.C., where she was a research professor in the Department of Physiology and Biophysics at the School of Medicine. She was a member of numerous professional organizations and on the editorial

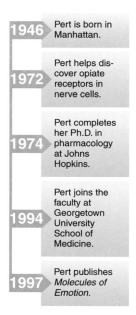

1946 ▸ Pert is born in Manhattan.

1972 ▸ Pert helps discover opiate receptors in nerve cells.

1974 ▸ Pert completes her Ph.D. in pharmacology at Johns Hopkins.

1994 ▸ Pert joins the faculty at Georgetown University School of Medicine.

1997 ▸ Pert publishes *Molecules of Emotion*.

**opiates:** any drug that induces sleep.

**endorphins:** large opioid peptides.

boards of at least 10 major research journals, and as of mid-2000 her résumé listed her as the author or co-author of nearly 250 research articles.

The work of Pert and her colleagues had profound significance for a number of fields, ranging from psychiatry and traditional medicine to AIDS and Alzheimer's disease research, immunology, virology, and molecular biology. By locating the opiate receptor on nerve cells—actually millions of receptors on each nerve cell that bind to other molecules that wander by—she in effect demonstrated that moods, behaviors, and emotions have a biochemical source and showed that the brain is wired to react to the body's own internal opiates. Her work led to further discoveries, including the identification of the body's natural **opiates**, called **endorphins**. Researchers believed that endorphins explain, for example, the "runners' high" that joggers often get, or the fact that depressed people are more likely to get sick, for their relative lack of endorphins allow viruses—the "evil twins" of endorphins—to lock onto nerve cells in their place.

Pert's later research focused on a class of proteins called peptides, which includes the natural opiate serotonin, that regulate emotions. Pert believed that one of these proteins, called peptide-T (for the amino acid threonine), might prove effective in combating a range of health problems, including psoriasis, AIDS, and Alzheimer's disease. Other peptides might improve the condition of patients with chronic fatigue syndrome, stroke, and head trauma.

As a natural extension of her research, Pert became a kind of "guru" in the alternative medicine movement, which bases treatment on the direct connection between emotions and health. She rose to prominence in this area in 1985, when the *Journal of Immunology* published the text of a speech she had given, "Neuropeptides and Their Receptors: A Psychosomatic Network." Later she joined the staff of the Institute of Human Potential and Mind/Body Medicine, a San Diego–based organization founded by best-selling author Deepak Chopra. She traveled around the world giving lectures on the mind-body connection in health, and her 1997 book, *Molecules of Emotion: Why You Feel the Way You Feel*, brought her theories to the attention of a wide popular audience.

The essence of Pert's views runs as follows: Peptide receptors are located not only in the brain but in other organs and glands, the spinal cord, and other tissues throughout the body.

These peptide receptors form a kind of communication network in which emotions and memory are stored. The network can be accessed at any point in the body, explaining why many alternative therapies, including yoga, chiropractic, massage, and therapeutic touch, often bring relief to people with emotional and physical disorders. It explains why deep breathing, important in yoga and meditation, has a calming effect, for it changes the types of peptides released by the brain stem. It even explains why the notion of a "gut reaction" may have a genuine physiological basis, for the stomach is dense with peptide receptors. Put simply, she said, "Peptides are the biochemical correlate of emotion."

Pert's theories were not universally accepted by the medical establishment. Some dismissed her as a "faith healer," but her supporters pointed out that the male establishment historically resisted the more intuitive approach to science that some women take, an approach that Pert described in *Molecules of Emotion*. ◆

# Picotte, Susan LaFlesche

### 1866–1915 ● PHYSICIAN

Native American physician, reformer, and civic leader Susan LaFlesche Picotte was born on the Omaha Indian reservation in Nebraska. The daughter of Joseph LaFlesche, "progressive" chief of the Omaha Indians, and his wife Mary Gale, Susan LaFlesche was educated at the reservation mission school, a young lady's academy in New Jersey, and at the Hampton Institute in Virginia. With the help of the Connecticut branch of the Women's National Indian Association, a philanthropic reform group, she then attended the Woman's Medical College in Philadelphia, from which she graduated in March 1889 as the first Indian woman physician in the United States.

After LaFlesche's graduation, she returned to the Omaha reservation where she planned to open a hospital. In 1894, she married Henry Picotte, a French Sioux, with whom she had two sons; after her husband died in 1905, she moved to the newly incorporated town of Walthill, Nebraska.

LaFlesche-Picotte created for herself a unique role as civic leader, doctor, missionary, and spokesperson for the Omaha Indians. She was an avid supporter of prohibition; a founder of

Walthill's Presbyterian church; president of the local board of health; and a member of the local women's club, the Thurston County Medical Association, the State Medical Society, and the Nebraska Federation of Women's Clubs. Her major satisfaction, however, always came from her work for the Omahas. In addition to treating as many as 100 patients a month, she assisted countless people with financial or personal problems. She made maximum use of her contacts to cut through government red tape and always blended her concrete assistance with advice firmly rooted in Protestant Christianity and Victorian morality.

In 1913, LaFlesche-Picotte saw her dream realized when the Presbyterian Board of Home Missions established a hospital in Walthill. When she died two years later at the age of 49, the hospital was renamed in her honor. ◆

# Ray, Dixy Lee

SEPTEMBER 3, 1914–JANUARY 3, 1994 ● ZOOLOGIST

Dixy Lee Ray, who was known not only as a scientist but also as a controversial political figure in the 1970s, was born in Tacoma, Washington, the second daughter of Alvin and Frances Ray. At her birth, her parents could not decide what to name her, so her birth certificate read "Baby Ray, female." As a child her parents called her "the little Dickens," which in time was shortened to "Dick." She chose her own name at age 16 when she changed "Dick" to "Dixy" and added "Lee" in memory of her Southern grandmother, a descendant of Confederate general Robert E. Lee.

Ray excelled in high school and received several scholarship offers. She decided to attend Mill's College, a women's school in Oakland, California, where she paid her way by waiting on tables and painting fences and houses. Initially she majored in drama and theater, but she had always been interested in marine biology—an interest sparked by her fascination with the tide pools around Puget Sound in Washington—so she changed her major to zoology. She graduated Phi Beta Kappa in 1935, and the following year she earned a master's degree and completed a teaching certificate. She then accepted a job teaching in the Oakland public schools, where she remained until 1942, working part-time on a doctoral degree at nearby Stanford University and spending weekends working at Stanford's Hopkins Marine Biological Station in Pacific Grove, California. In 1942 she left the Oakland schools

273

Ray remained at
the University
of Washington
for 27 years.
There she gained
a reputation as
a prominent
authority on
environmental
issues pertaining
to the sea.

when she received a fellowship that enabled her to study for her doctorate full-time. After completing her Ph.D. in 1945, she accepted a faculty position in the zoology department at the University of Washington in Seattle.

Ray remained at the University of Washington for 27 years. There she gained a reputation as a prominent authority on environmental issues pertaining to the sea. She was a member of a number of scientific panels that dealt with oceanography, and she was the chief scientist aboard the Stanford University research vessel *Te Vega*, which sailed on the International Indian Ocean Expedition. She was appointed director of the Pacific Science Center in Seattle in 1963, and under her leadership the center became a multipurpose organization that included a museum and laboratories and served as a center for scientific meetings. During these years Ray also became something of a local media celebrity; her local television series, *Animals of the Sea*, attracted a wide viewership throughout the state. In 1967 the city of Seattle named Ray its "Maritime Man of the Year" in recognition of her efforts to popularize science.

Ray's career took a radically different direction in 1972, when President Richard Nixon appointed her head of the Atomic Energy Commission (AEC), the federal agency that oversaw the nation's nuclear energy program. To many observers Ray seemed to be an odd choice for the post because she was a marine biologist, not a nuclear physicist. Ray, however, was deeply concerned about the nation's energy supply—the early 1970s was dominated by talk of an "energy crisis," and the first Arab oil embargo was just around the corner. On her way to Washington, D.C., to accept her appointment, she demonstrated her commitment to nuclear power by driving across the country so that she could inspect the nation's nuclear power facilities.

Ray began serving as head of the AEC in 1973, and in her new post she was both colorful and controversial. Convinced that nuclear energy could be not only plentiful but safe, she advocated expansion of the nation's nuclear energy supply and the construction of more nuclear power plants—a stand that often placed her at odds with environmentalists who opposed nuclear power. Known for her blunt outspokenness, she was a maverick in the nation's capital. She lived in a camper parked on the outskirts of the city along with her dogs—a 100-pound deerhound and a miniature poodle. She rarely conformed to the niceties of Washington behavior; not only on the street but in professional meetings, she dressed more for comfort than for fashion. A strong, sturdy woman, she did not conform to stereotypical views of "feminine" behavior and appearance.

In 1974 the AEC was abolished. Ray moved to the State Department, where she was appointed assistant secretary of state for oceans and international environmental and scientific affairs. She became frustrated, though, with the limitations placed on the diplomatic role of scientists, so after just six months she resigned, packed up her camper, and drove back to Washington State. Based on her conviction that scientists should play a more active role in politics, she ran in the 1976 gubernatorial primary as a Democrat. Lacking funds but bristling with energy, she barnstormed the state during her campaign. She narrowly won the Democratic primary, then went on to become the first woman governor in Washington's history.

Unfortunately, though, Ray continued to provoke controversy. Her belief in the safety of nuclear power, her support of economic growth and development throughout the state, and her belief that oil tankers should be allowed to dock in Puget Sound led environmentalists to call her "Ms. Plutonium," and bumper stickers saying "Nix on Dixy" were a common sight. An open feud with one of the state's U.S. senators cost her support, and in her 1980 bid for reelection she was defeated in the Democratic primary.

Ray retired to a 60-acre farm on Fox Island, but she continued to write and speak about environmental issues, often attacking environmentalists when she believed that their views were based on unsound science. She wrote two books and numerous magazine articles, and she frequently granted television interviews. She died in 1994 as a result of complications following a bronchial infection. ◆

# Rees, Mina

AUGUST 2, 1902–OCTOBER 25, 1997 ● MATHEMATICIAN

Although Mina Spiegel Rees was born in Cleveland, Ohio, she grew up in New York City. There she attended the prestigious Hunter College High School, and she maintained her association with Hunter College

Mina S. Rees

through much of her professional career. After graduating as valedictorian of her high school class, she went on to study mathematics at Hunter College, graduating *summa cum laude* in 1923. She then enrolled in the graduate program at Columbia University while teaching at Hunter College High School.

Rees's goal was to earn a Ph.D., but after completing most of her course work she was shocked to learn, through unofficial channels, "that the Columbia mathematics department was really not interested in having women candidates for Ph.D.'s." As a result, she left the mathematics department and completed her master's degree at the Columbia University Teacher's College in 1925. She accepted a position teaching mathematics at Hunter College, but she still wanted to earn a Ph.D., so she obtained a leave of absence from the college and enrolled at the University of Chicago. There she studied under Leonard Dickson and received her Ph.D. in 1931. Her thesis, "Division Algebras Associated with an Equation Whose Group Has Four Generators," was published in the *American Journal of Mathematics* in 1932. Some historians of mathematics believe that Rees missed an opportunity to conduct important future research, for her adviser failed to recommend her for a postdoctoral fellowship that would have allowed her to study under the eminent German mathematician Emmy Noether, who at the time was doing ground-breaking work in algebra that complemented Rees's.

After completing her Ph.D., Rees returned to Hunter College. She was promoted to assistant professor in 1932, then to associate professor in 1940. At this point in her career, World War II intervened, and Rees took another leave of absence from the college to make a contribution to the war effort at the Applied Mathematics Panel in the Office of Scientific Research and Development. Her job titles there were "technical aide" and "executive assistant," but these titles understate her level of responsibility. Her job was to study technical problems submitted to the panel by the various military branches, identify the underlying mathematics of the problems, and bring together mathematicians to work on the problems—often with the help of seven-figure grants that she controlled. For her work during the war, Rees received the President's Certificate of Merit and, from Great Britain, the King's Medal for Service in the Cause of Freedom.

When the war ended, Rees remained in government service when the U.S. Navy invited her to become head of the mathematics branch of the Office of Naval Research (ONR), whose mission was to support scientific and mathematical research. In 1949 she became director of the ONR's Mathematical Sciences Division, and in 1952–53 she served as the ONR's deputy science director. Her achievements in these roles were recognized in 1953 by the American Mathematical Society, which adopted a resolution that read, in part, "... the whole postwar development of mathematical research in the United States owes an immeasurable debt to the pioneer work of the Office of Naval Research and to the alert, vigorous and far-sighted policy conducted by Mina Rees."

After more than 10 years of government service, Rees returned to Hunter College in 1953, where she was appointed professor and dean of the faculty. In the years that followed she served on numerous public-policy committees for such organizations as the National Research Council, the National Bureau of Standards, and the National Science Foundation. She was also a consultant on the machine handling of data for the 1960 U.S. census.

Rees remained at Hunter College until 1961, when she was appointed professor and the first dean of graduate studies in the newly established City University of New York—making her possibly the first woman dean of a graduate school in the United States. She then went on to become provost of the graduate division in 1968 and president of the graduate school and university center in 1969, where she remained until her retirement in 1972. In 1971 she became the first woman president of the American Association for the Advancement of Science.

Rees contributed greatly to a profession that was slowly attracting increasing numbers of women. Reflecting on her role as dean of graduate studies, she wrote in 1965, "Ours is proving

**1902** Rees is born in Cleveland, Ohio.

**1931** Rees completes her Ph.D. at the University of Chicago.

**1961** Rees appointed dean of graduate studies at City University of New York.

**1971** Rees becomes first woman president of the American Association for the Advancement of Science.

"[Mina Rees's] ability to attach realisable pieces of basic research to mission-oriented applications of mathematics did much to develop a broadened base of support for mathematicians' work."
Uta Merzbach quoted in "Mina Spiegel Rees," at the St. Andrews MacTutor History of Mathematics web site

## American Association for the Advancement of Science

The American Association for the Advancement of Science (AAAS) was founded in 1848, from members of the former Association of American Geologists and Naturalists. Its purpose was to establish greater contact among scientists scattered across the United States and to give greater direction to scientific inquiries. From the beginning, the AAAS tried to expand the kinds of disciplines under its broad umbrella, and while many specialized societies have spun off from the society over the years, it continues to be the world's premiere society for scientists of all interests, with over 130,000 members worldwide. To the general public, AAAS is best known as the publisher (since 1946) of *Science* magazine.

Throughout AAAS history, its leaders have tried to focus greater media attention on the findings of scientists. They have also sought to influence policymakers—for example, when fighting for the freedoms of scientists in oppressive regimes, and when commissioning a study (led by Matthew Meselsonon) on the U.S. government's widespread use of defoliants in Vietnam in the late 1960s. Another goal has been to increase the presence of women and minorities in the sciences, as well as establishing Project 2061, a massive effort to achieve "science literacy" for all Americans by reforming science, mathematics, and technology education in grade schools. Key AAAS scientific contributions include giving voice to T. H. Morgan's genetic research on fruit flies and broadcasting Albert Einstein's formulation of the principle of gravitational lensing. In addition, a 1959 New York City United Nations' conference on oceanography was a pivotal moment in that field's growth.

Astronomer Maria Mitchell was AAAS's first female member, and Mina Rees its first female president (1969). Since that time, several women have served as its president, including anthropologist Margaret Mead (1975) and astronomer Margaret Burbidge (1983).

an ideal university to draw into advanced graduate work the most obvious source of unused talent in a society that desperately needs additional numbers of persons with training through the doctorate, namely women." In 1962 she was the first recipient of the Award for Distinguished Service to Mathematics from the Mathematical Association of America, given for contributions that "influence significantly the field of mathematics or mathematical education on a national scale." In 1983 she won the National Academy of Sciences Public Welfare Medal for her contributions to the application of mathematics to the public welfare. Additionally, she received honorary doctorates from a number of colleges and universities, and the graduate center library at the City University of New York is named in her honor. ◆

# Ride, Sally Kristen

MAY 26, 1951– ● PHYSICIST AND ASTRONAUT

Physicist Sally Ride became the first American woman space traveler on June 27, 1983, when she was one of five astronauts launched aboard the shuttle *Challenger* on STS-7. During the six-day STS-7 flight she served as flight engineer and took part in the deployment of two communications satellites and in the deployment and retrieval of the German built Shuttle Pallet Satellite (SPAS-01).

She went into space a second time aboard shuttle Mission 41-G in October 1984. On this mission she deployed the Earth Radiation Budget Satellite and took part in scientific observations of the Earth made with the OSTA-3 pallet and the Large Format Camera. It was during 41-G that Kathryn Sullivan, who had attended the same first grade class as Ride, became the first American woman to walk in space.

Ride was born May 26, 1951, in Encino, California. She attended Westlake High School in Los Angeles, where she was a nationally ranked tennis player, and graduated in 1968. She went on to attend Stanford University, earning a B.A. in English and a B.S. in physics in 1973, and an M.S. (1975) and Ph.D. (1978) in physics.

She was a teaching assistant and researcher in laser physics at Stanford when selected by NASA as an astronaut in January 1978. In August 1979 she qualified as a shuttle mission specialist while assigned to the Shuttle Avionics Integration Laboratory. She served as capcom for STS-2 and STS-3 prior to being assigned to the STS-7 crew in April 1982.

Prior to the explosion of the shuttle *Challenger* and the suspen-

Sally Ride

**1951** Ride is born in Encino, California.

**1983** Ride becomes the first American woman to fly in space as part of a mission on the shuttle *Challenger*.

**1989** Ride becomes a professor of physics at the University of California at San Diego and director of the university's California Space Institute.

sion of all shuttle flights, Ride was training for her third mission, 61-m, scheduled for launch in the summer of 1986. Instead she served as the astronaut office representative to the presidential commission investigating the tragedy. In 1987 she coauthored a report on future options for the U.S. space program.

She resigned from NASA in August 1987 to join Stanford University as an arms control scholar. In June 1989 she left Stanford to become head of the Space Science Institute at the University of California at San Diego. In addition to her duties with the institute, Ride served as a member of the President's Committee of Advisors on Science and Technology, and teaches physics at the University of California at San Diego.

Ride is the coauthor of two books for children, *To Space and Back* (1986) and *Voyager: An Adventure to the End of the Solar System* (1992). ◆

# Robinson, Julia Bowman

DECEMBER 8, 1919–JULY 30, 1985 ● MATHEMATICIAN

Julia Bowman Robinson was the second of two daughters born to Ralph Bowers Bowman and Helen Hall Bowman. Neither of her parents had gone to college, but her mother had attended a business school after graduating from high school. Ralph Bowman owned a successful tool and equipment shop in St. Louis.

When Robinson was two years old, her mother died. Robinson and her sister, Constance, were sent to live with their grandmother in a small desert community outside Phoenix, Arizona, near Camelback Mountain. After the death of his wife, Ralph Bowman lost interest in his business. He sold the shop and moved with his new wife, Edenia Kridelbaugh, to join his children in Arizona in 1923. In 1925 the family moved to Point Loma on San Diego Bay so that the girls, now ages five and seven, could attend school. Robinson, from infancy, had been slow to speak, and when she did talk, others had difficulty understanding her. Her older sister became her "interpreter." The small school they attended housed several grades together, enabling the younger students to learn from the older ones.

In 1928 Robinson, now nine years old, contracted scarlet fever followed by rheumatic fever and chorea, a nervous disorder. She was quarantined and missed more than two years of schooling. Her parents hired a private tutor, and in one year she covered the syllabuses for grades five through eight. In 1932 she entered the ninth grade at Theodore Roosevelt Junior High School in San Diego, and the following year she entered San Diego High School. She was introduced to algebra, and her two women math teachers soon discovered that she excelled in math and science. She was hampered in her studies, however, since at this time there were not accelerated or advanced-placement courses. Robinson was shy by nature, an avid baseball fan who was particularly adept at keeping box scores of the games she attended, and also exhibited an interest in horseback riding and enjoyed target practice with her father.

Robinson graduated from San Diego High School in 1936 with honors in math and science. She entered San Diego State College (now San Diego State University) that year, at age 16. E. T. Bell's *Men of Mathematics*, published in 1936, gave Robinson a glimpse into the world of mathematicians, about which she knew nothing. San Diego State was largely a teacher-preparatory college with few Ph.D.s (and none in math) and no research mathematicians. For this reason Robinson transferred to the University of California at Berkeley in 1939. For the first time in her life, she experienced a sense of belonging, as there were other bright women at Berkeley who were as excited about mathematics as she was. She received her B.A. degree in 1940 and remained at the university to complete her M.A. degree in 1941.

Julia Robinson met her future husband, Raphael Mitchel Robinson, a number theorist who had been one of Julia's professors at Berkeley. They were married in Berkeley on December 22, 1941. Meanwhile, Julia continued to take courses and joined other faculty wives in the statistics laboratory at Berkeley, working to fulfill the government contracts that the university received during World War II. During this period she learned that she had a weakened heart, a residual effect of the rheumatic fever that she had suffered as a child. Because of the heart condition she was unable to have children.

In 1947 Robinson began work on her Ph.D. at Berkeley under the direction of Alfred Tarski, the noted Polish logician who had joined the Berkeley faculty during the war. Her thesis, "Definability and Decision Problems in Arithmetic," was accepted in 1948. In that same year she began to work on a problem connected with David Hilbert's Tenth Problem, one of 23

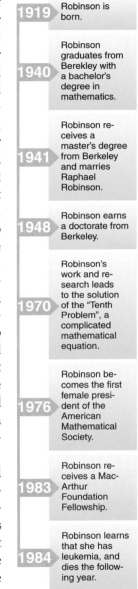

**1919** Robinson is born.

**1940** Robinson graduates from Berekley with a bachelor's degree in mathematics.

**1941** Robinson receives a master's degree from Berkeley and marries Raphael Robinson.

**1948** Robinson earns a doctorate from Berkeley.

**1970** Robinson's work and research leads to the solution of the "Tenth Problem", a complicated mathematical equation.

**1976** Robinson becomes the first female president of the American Mathematical Society.

**1983** Robinson receives a MacArthur Foundation Fellowship.

**1984** Robinson learns that she has leukemia, and dies the following year.

unsolved problems proposed by Hilbert at the Second International Congress of Mathematics in Paris in 1900. The Tenth Problem involved devising a general method of determining by a finite number of operations whether a given Diophantine equation has a solution in rational integers. This problem consumed most of Robinson's professional career, but she found time to work on other projects, such as one on elementary game theory in 1950. Her solution and the theorem she developed proved that a fictitious game problem has a convergent solution.

Many mathematicians had attempted to find a solution to the Tenth Problem, but it was Robinson's work (and she was given credit for it by the world of mathematics) that led to the ultimate solution in 1970, by Yuri Matijasevi , that there is no universal method for deciding the solvability of a Diophantine equation. The solution made Robinson famous and earned her a full professorship at Berkeley in 1975. The following year she became the first woman mathematician elected to the National Academy of Sciences, and in 1983 she became the first woman president of the American Mathematical Society. Other honors included an honorary degree from Smith College in 1979. In 1980 Robinson was the second woman in 50 years to deliver the prestigious Colloquium Lectures of the American Mathematical Society. In 1983 she was awarded a MacArthur Foundation Fellowship for five years in recognition of her contributions to mathematics.

In the summer of 1984, Robinson learned that she had leukemia. After a brief period of remission, she died in Oakland, California. Her cremated remains were buried in Santa Cruz, California. ◆

# Rowley, Janet Davison

APRIL 5, 1925– ● PHYSICIAN

Janet Davison Rowley's discovery of chromosomal "translocations" in cancer cells has revolutionized cancer research, diagnosis, and treatment. Translocation occurs when a piece of one chromosome breaks off and becomes associated with another chromosome.

Born on April 5, 1925, in New York City, Janet Davison was the only child of Hurford, a college educator, and Ethel (Ballantyne) Davison, a high school English teacher and librarian. Her parents were very supportive, encouraging her in any kind of intellectual activity. Her mother thought she was gifted and was not being challenged enough in school, so she transferred her to a junior high school in New Jersey. It was there that her interest in science first became apparent.

In 1940, when Davison was 15, she received a scholarship to the "Four Year College" at the University of Chicago, where she completed her last two years of high school and her first two years of college. She considers this an "important experience" because, as she later recalled, "we were taught to question and to read primary materials not just what you'd see in a textbook." Davison originally considered studying physiology, but she found that she really enjoyed her college biology classes and decided to become a pre-med student. Davison earned her Bachelor of Philosophy degree in 1944 and her Bachelor of Science degree in 1946, both from the University of Chicago. Davison applied to the university's medical school, but, as the quota of three female students (in a class of 65) had already been filled, Davison had to wait nine months before she could start. Despite this, Davison never felt she had suffered from any gender bias. Unlike many other women pursuing higher education in the sciences, Davison had several female professors in medical school who served as role models for her. Davison also found a role model in Dr. Charles B. Huggins, who would later win a Nobel Prize for his work with hormones and prostate cancer.

Davison received her medical degree in 1948, and, the day after graduation, married fellow doctor Donald Rowley. The couple would eventually have four children, and, as Rowley wanted to be home with them while they were growing up, she practiced medicine on a part-time basis, working two or three days a week for more than 20 years. Rowley was an attending physician at well-baby clinics at the Department of Public Health in Montgomery County, Maryland, from 1953 to 1954, and from 1955 to 1961 she was a part-time research fellow at a clinic for retarded children in Chicago. Rowley also worked as a part-time clinical instructor in neurology at the School of Medicine at the University of Illinois from 1957 to 1961.

In 1961, Rowley and her husband went on sabbatical in England. Rowley received a fellowship from the Public Health Service of the U.S. National Institutes of Health to work as a trainee in the radiobiology laboratory of Churchill Hospital at the University of Oxford. There she studied cytogenetics, the investigation of the role of cells in evolution and heredity.

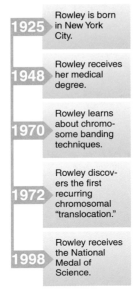

**1925** Rowley is born in New York City.

**1948** Rowley receives her medical degree.

**1970** Rowley learns about chromosome banding techniques.

**1972** Rowley discovers the first recurring chromosomal "translocation."

**1998** Rowley receives the National Medal of Science.

> "In general, Rowley's research indicates that translocations and deletions of genetic material occur in malignancy, and that cancer is caused by a complex series of events within a single cell, making some genes overactive (tumor producing) and eliminating other genes that would normally suppress growth."
>
> On Janet Davison Rowley's groundbreaking cancer research, quoted in *Notable Twentieth-Century Scientists,* 1996.

**bone marrow:** the spongy tissue found in the center of most large bones that produces the cellular components of blood white cells, red cells, and platelet.

During her stay, she collected slides of blood from patients who had a specific kind of chromosomal abnormality. After her year at Oxford, Rowley realized she preferred research to clinical work.

After her return to the United States in 1962, Rowley approached a former professor of hers at the University of Chicago, Dr. Leon Jacobson, about the possibility of continuing her research. Even though Rowley lacked research credentials, Jacobson agreed to hire her to work three days a week as a research associate and assistant professor in the Department of Hematology. She was given three feet of bench space and a microscope, and began studying the slides she brought from England. Jacobson remained supportive of Rowley's effort, although it was several years before her research would produce significant results.

In 1970, Rowley took a sabbatical to return to Oxford to learn the newly developed techniques of chromosome banding—a means of illuminating segments of chromosomes. Returning to Chicago, she applied these techniques to **bone marrow** samples from leukemic patients. Two years later, Rowley discovered the first recurring "translocation" of a chromosome to be identified for a disease in any species: the exchange of DNA between chromosomes 8 and 21 in patients with myeloblastic leukemia, a form of blood cancer. This discovery demonstrated that specific types of cancer are caused by specific chromosomal alterations. As a result of Rowley's discovery, scientists worldwide began looking for other translocations or "deletions," wherein chromosomes lose genetic material entirely. Rowley has also studied the chromosomal translocations seen only in patients who have been previously treated with particular drugs.

Rowley holds honorary degrees from several universities and has received many awards throughout her career, including the Dameshek Prize in 1982 from the American Society of Hematology, the Kuwait Cancer Prize in 1984, and the Charles S. Mott Prize in 1989 from the General Motors Cancer Research Foundation. In 1998, Rowley was a co-recipient of the Albert Lasker Clinical Research Award, and was named, along with her husband, Donald, a fellow in the American Association for the Advancement of Science. That same year, Rowley was awarded the National Medal of Science, the nation's highest scientific honor. Rowley considers receiving the medal a "fantastic honor" and one that "recognizes the critical importance of chromosomal (genetic) changes in cancer."

Since 1984, Rowley has been the Blum-Riese Distinguished Service Professor in the Department of Medicine and

Since 1959, the President of the United States has awarded the National Medal of Science (NMS) to citizens who have made significant contributions to the sciences. Initially, pioneers in biological, engineering, mathematical, and physical sciences were considered for the award; later, social and behavioral scientists were added. The 12 members of the nominating committee seek to evaluate an individual's overall contribution to science, including the value of their research and innovation, leadership, and impact on the education of others. The number of medals given each year varies. The Science Medal and its companion, the Technology Medal, are promoted by the National Science and Technology Medals Foundation (1991).

Janet Rowley received the award in 1998 for her breakthrough cancer research and her leadership in the study of oncology. Other NMS recipients discussed in this volume are: Darleane C. Hoffman (for many studies, including her discovery of primordial plutonium in nature, and for science education leadership), Isabella L. Karle (x-ray analysis of crystal and molecular structures), Cathleen S. Morawetz (partial differential equations and wave propagation), Elizabeth F. Neufeld (lysosomal storage diseases), Ruth Patrick (diatom research and the link between aquatic biodiversity and pollution), and Vera C. Rubin (dark matter and observational cosmology).

the Department of Molecular Genetics and Cell Biology at the Franklin McLean Memorial Research Institute at the University of Chicago. She is a cofounder and co-editor of the journal *Genes, Chromosomes and Cancer* and serves on the editorial boards of several other journals. In addition, Rowley has helped to initiate and organize workshops and symposia on genes, chromosomes, and cancer, and has served on the boards of various organizations, including the National Cancer Advisory Board of the National Cancer Institute and the Medical Advisory Board of the Leukemia Society of America. ◆

# Rubin, Vera Cooper

JULY 23, 1928– ● ASTRONOMER

V era Rubin's childhood fascination with stars would eventually lead her as an adult to make discoveries that have altered the ways scientists look at the universe. Born Vera Cooper in Philadelphia, Pennsylvania, on July 23, 1928, Rubin was the second daughter of Philip and Rose

(Applebaum) Cooper. She grew up in Washington, D.C., and dates her interest in astronomy to when she was 12 years old and would stare out her bedroom window, captivated by the stars. Her parents were supportive of her interest, although at first her father, an electrical engineer, encouraged her to do something more practical, such as mathematics. Still, he helped her build a telescope and went with her to meetings of a local amateur astronomers club.

For her undergraduate studies, Rubin chose to attend Vassar College in Poughkeepsie, New York, in part because most other colleges did not accept women into their astronomy programs. Rubin also choose Vassar because one of her heroes, Maria Mitchell, had taught there. As a child, Rubin had read about Mitchell's 1847 discovery of a comet and of her becoming the first woman elected to the American Academy of Arts and Sciences. Vassar was still an all-women's college when Rubin attended it, and she was the lone astronomy major. "If I hadn't done my homework or if I hadn't done it right or hadn't done enough," Rubin later recalled, "the personal interaction with the teacher was very difficult." Despite that, Rubin completed her undergraduate work in three years, receiving her bachelor's degree in 1948.

Following graduation, she met and married Robert Rubin, a physicist, and went with him to Cornell University in Ithaca, New York, where he was working on his doctoral degree. She was interested in attending graduate school at Princeton University, only to learn that Princeton did not admit women to its astronomy program. Instead, she enrolled in the graduate program at Cornell. Her master's thesis suggested that galaxies might have their own motion, or rotation, in addition to the expansion described in the widely accepted "big bang" theory. In 1950, three weeks after giving birth to her first of four children, she presented her theory at a meeting of the American Astronomical Society. Her findings were heavily criticized and received a great deal of negative publicity.

Rubin received her doctorate from Cornell in 1951, after which the Rubins moved to Washington, D.C., where her husband had been offered a job; she enrolled in the doctoral program at Georgetown University. Rubin did not know how to drive a car, so she took night classes for the next two years, with her husband driving her to class and waiting for her in the car while her parents babysat the children. Her doctoral dissertation focused on the distribution of galaxies in the universe, finding that they were not evenly distributed. Once again, her research ran counter to the "big bang" theory of an evenly distributed universe and was largely ignored. As with her master's thesis, her doctoral conclusion would be validated by other researchers in time.

Rubin graduated from Georgetown in 1954 and spent the next year teaching mathematics and physics at a local community college. A year later she returned to Georgetown to conduct research and teach, and remained there for 10 years. In 1965, Rubin joined the Department of Terrestrial Magnetism at the Carnegie Institution of Washington, in Washington, D.C., and remains there today as a senior researcher. That same year, Rubin became the first woman permitted to observe at the Palomar Observatory in California.

After joining Carnegie, Rubin worked with colleague Kent Ford to conduct additional research on the rotation of galaxies. The two reached the same conclusions that Rubin had reached earlier with her master's thesis, and again, the results were questioned. Rubin and Ford then turned their attention to why spiral galaxies vary in their brightness, theorizing that it was related to their rotations. Using a spectrograph Ford developed, the two began studying the rotations of galaxies and discovered that stars at the edge of the galaxy were traveling at the same rate of speed as stars close to the center. This ran counter to the Newtonian laws of gravity which held that, just as with the planets orbiting around the sun, stars farther out in the galaxy would travel at a slower speed than those closer to the center. Although its existence had been suggested by others, Rubin and Ford's work helped convince astronomers that there must be some other invisible mass, termed "dark matter," exerting the gravitational force needed to keep the stars in their orbits in these galaxies. Scientists now estimate that 90% or more of the universe consists of this "dark matter."

At the start of the year 2000, Rubin was busy observing with the Hubble Space Telescope. Her most recent discovery, at age 63, was of a galaxy with a disk in which half the stars were moving clockwise and the other half were moving counterclockwise. She is particularly proud of this discovery because, she said "it came when I was senior and beginning to wonder if there would be any more discoveries...." In 1997, Rubin published *Bright Galaxies, Dark Matter*, a collection of less technical papers and articles aimed at the general public.

**"Her careful observations with both terrestrial instruments and the Hubble Space Telescope have made significant contributions to the understanding of the behavior of stars in galaxies."**
On Vera Cooper Rubin's important astronmical discoveries, quoted in *Scientific American*

Rubin has received many honors during her career. She holds honorary degrees from a number of institutions, including Harvard University and Yale University. She was elected to membership in the National Academy of Sciences in 1981 and received the National Medal of Science in 1993. She now serves on the committee to select new winners of that science medal. Despite the accolades, Rubin believes that fame is short lived. "My numbers," she said, "mean more to me than my name. If astronomers are still using my data years from now, that's my greatest compliment." Accomplishments and honors notwithstanding, Rubin is most proud of her marriage and her four children, each of whom holds a Ph.D. in a scientific field. ◆

S

# Sabin, Florence Rena

NOVEMBER 9, 1871–OCTOBER 3, 1953 ● PHYSICIAN AND ANATOMIST

In a career spanning nearly half a century, anatomist Florence Rena Sabin left her mark as a teacher, researcher, and public health official, achieving many "firsts" for women along the way. She was born in Central City, Colorado, on November 9, 1871, the second daughter of George and Serena (Miner) Sabin. Her father was originally from Vermont and had moved to Colorado to work as an engineer in the gold mines; her mother was a school teacher. When Florence was four, the family moved to nearby Denver so that her older sister, Mary, could attend school. Following the death of their mother on Florence's seventh birthday, the girls were sent to boarding school in Denver and then later to live with relatives, first in Chicago and then in Vermont. In 1885 both girls were placed in boarding school in Vermont.

After graduating from high school in 1889, Sabin decided to follow her sister to Smith College in Northampton, Massachusetts. It

Florence Rena Sabin

289

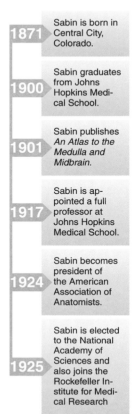

**1871** Sabin is born in Central City, Colorado.

**1900** Sabin graduates from Johns Hopkins Medical School.

**1901** Sabin publishes *An Atlas to the Medulla and Midbrain.*

**1917** Sabin is appointed a full professor at Johns Hopkins Medical School.

**1924** Sabin becomes president of the American Association of Anatomists.

**1925** Sabin is elected to the National Academy of Sciences and also joins the Rockefeller Institute for Medical Research

was at Smith that Sabin discovered her love of science, particularly zoology, and it is likely that she also developed her commitment to equal rights for women while there. She graduated from Smith in 1893 with a Bachelor of Science degree. Sabin had decided to pursue a career in medicine, and to earn the money for tuition, she taught mathematics in Denver and zoology at Smith. In 1896, she entered Johns Hopkins Medical School in Baltimore, Maryland, one of the first women to do so.

Sabin excelled as a student at Johns Hopkins. She found a mentor there in her anatomy professor, Franklin Mall. He encouraged her interest in anatomy at a time when the field was becoming more investigative rather than just descriptive. His approach to teaching was to let the student experience the satisfaction of discovery on her own, with limited direction from the instructor. He believed this approach would provide the incentive for the student to conduct additional research. This approach suited Sabin well, and she would employ the same method herself as a teacher. Her association with Mall, first as a student and then as a researcher, lasted 20 years. In 1936, she published his biography, which was called, *Franklin Paine Mall: The Story of a Mind.*

While a student at Johns Hopkins, Sabin began investigating the structure and function of the brain. She produced a model of the brain stem of a newborn infant that was reproduced and used as a teaching model in several medical schools. Sabin received her M.D. from Johns Hopkins in 1900, becoming the first female student to graduate from the institution. A year later she published *An Atlas to the Medulla and Midbrain*, covering her research on the brain. It remained a standard medical text for 30 years.

In 1901, Sabin won one of four coveted internships at Johns Hopkins Hospital. She spent a year there before deciding to return to the medical school to conduct research under a fellowship from the Baltimore Association for the Advancement of University Education of Women. The following year, Johns Hopkins dropped its policy of not appointing women to its faculty, and Sabin was named an assistant in anatomy. In 1917, she was appointed professor of histology, becoming the first female to achieve the rank of full professor at the medical college.

She focused her studies on embryology and the origins of the lymphatic system. "When I began my work," she said, "it was the accepted theory that lymphatics arose from the tissue spaces and then grew toward the veins." By injecting black or colored materials into the lymphatic channels of very small pig embryos, Sabin was able to demonstrate that lymphatics develop as buds growing out of the vein and continue to grow outward as continuous channels by further budding.

Sabin was now established as a leading researcher in her field and, in 1924, she became the first female president of the American Association of Anatomists. A year later, she became the first woman elected to the National Academy of Sciences. Sabin's reputation extended beyond the scientific community, as evidenced by a 1931 poll conducted by *Good Housekeeping* magazine naming her one of America's 12 most eminent living women.

Sabin left Johns Hopkins in 1925 to head the Department of Cellular Studies at Rockefeller Institute for Medical Research (now Rockefeller University) in New York City, becoming the first woman to be a full member of the institute. Her department's efforts were focused on the fight against tuberculosis, which was the leading killer in the country at that time. She also became a member of the Research Committee of the National Tuberculosis Association. Under her direction, the committee sought to integrate the bacteriological, chemical, and biological research being done on tuberculosis by various institutions. Sabin's work, through both the institute and committee, made important contributions to scientific knowledge about the disease.

Sabin retired from the Rockefeller Institute at age 67 in 1938 and returned to Denver to live with her sister Mary, now a retired school teacher. Sabin was looking forward to a quiet retirement, but it was not to last long. In 1944, six years after she moved to Denver, Colorado, governor John Vivian asked Sabin to come out of retirement to accept the chair of a subcommittee on health. At that time, Colorado was ranked among the least healthy states in the nation, and its health laws were 70 years old. Sabin undertook a tour of all of Colorado's 63 counties to investigate existing health and sanitation conditions. Sabin knew what had to be done to limit the incidences of diphtheria, tuberculosis, and other diseases. "The knowledge," she said, "of how to prevent them must be given to every parent. It is their children who die unnecessarily. If parents know the conditions causing these diseases, they will demand a change. I'm taking the truth to the people of my

## National Academy of Sciences

The National Academy of Sciences (NAS), Washington, D.C., was established by act of Congress in 1863 so that the U.S. government could have reliable official advisers in debates concerning technology and science. Membership in the NAS is lifelong and elected, not voluntary, and is given for outstanding achievement in scientific research. Today the NAS numbers about 1,800 regular members. In 1950, the NAS was combined with the National Research Council (NRC), which had been founded in 1916 to encourage interaction among scientists in academia and the public and private sectors; the NRC is responsible for most of the NAS committee work. The NAS currently helps scientists exchange information, meet at conferences, confer on regular committees, and meet to address special problems. In addition to member services, the NAS occasionally represents the U.S. scientific community in international assemblies such as the International Geophysical Year (1957–1958). The Institute of Medicine was founded in 1970 to carry out the NAS mandate with special attention to American health services; the National Academy of Engineering is also connected to the NAS.

Florence Sabin was the first woman member of the NAS, elected in 1925 in recognition of her research on the lymphatic system and tuberculosis. While some have been critical of the NAS's record for electing women, the gender balance has been improving since a 1986 report that showed that more than 96 percent of the group's members were men. The Committee on Women in Science and Engineering (1991) was established to encourage greater participation of women in science and engineering at various levels of training.

state." The resulting recommendations, called the Sabin Health Laws, completely revamped Colorado's public health system and were passed by the state legislature in 1947. These laws lead to improvements in Colorado's maternal death and infant mortality rates.

Following the passage of the bills, Sabin was asked to perform the same type of task for the City of Denver. In 1948 she became the city manger of health and charity, then chairwoman of the new Department of Health and Hospitals. She launched a war on "flies, rats and dirty milk." Following her reforms, Denver's death rate for tuberculosis fell and incidences of syphilis dropped dramatically. When told by the mayor that she must take a salary for her work, Sabin did so but donated it to the Colorado General Hospital to be used for medical research.

Sabin retired again in 1951 and died of a heart attack in Denver on October 3, 1953. During her lifetime, Sabin was awarded more than a dozen honorary degrees and a host of other awards from various groups. The State of Colorado honored her posthumously by selecting her as one of its two representatives in the Statuary Hall of the U.S. Capitol. ◆

# Scharrer, Berta

DECEMBER 1, 1906–JULY 23, 1995 ● NEUROENDOCRINOLOGIST

Together with her husband Ernst, Berta Scharrer helped to establish **neuroendocrinology**—the study of the physiological interaction between the central nervous system and the endocrine system—as a scientific discipline, a remarkable accomplishment considering that for the first 25 years of her 65-year career she held no academic position and received no salary.

**neuroendocrinology:** the study of functional and anatomical relationships between the nervous system and the endocrine system.

Scharrer was born Berta Vogel on December 1, 1906, in Munich, Germany, one of four children of Karl Phillip Vogel, a judge who served as a vice president of the federal court in Bavaria, and Joanna (Weiss) Vogel. The Vogels were a prosperous family, and Berta enjoyed a happy childhood. Berta developed her interest in biology while a young student. She decided to pursue a career as a research scientist, even though she knew that as a woman, her prospects for success were slight.

Berta attended the University of Munich, where she became interested in the work of bee behavioral biologist Professor Karl von Frish, who went on to win a Nobel Prize. She joined his laboratory to conduct her doctoral work comparing the taste and nutritive quality of various sugars of the honeybee. She received her Ph.D. in biology in 1930 and published her thesis the following year. While at the laboratory, she met Ernst Scharrer, and the two began a personal and professional partnership that would last until his death.

Scharrer and her husband moved together to the Research Institute of Psychiatry in Munich. There, Ernst Scharrer earned an additional degree in medicine, and she focused her studies on spirochete (i.e., spiral-shaped bacteria) infections of the brain in birds and amphibians. In 1934, Ernst was appointed director of the Edinger Institute for Brain Research at the University of Frankfurt. With Ernst's salary, the two could now

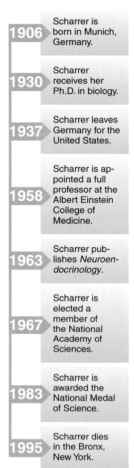

**1906** Scharrer is born in Munich, Germany.

**1930** Scharrer receives her Ph.D. in biology.

**1937** Scharrer leaves Germany for the United States.

**1958** Scharrer is appointed a full professor at the Albert Einstein College of Medicine.

**1963** Scharrer publishes *Neuroendocrinology*.

**1967** Scharrer is elected a member of the National Academy of Sciences.

**1983** Scharrer is awarded the National Medal of Science.

**1995** Scharrer dies in the Bronx, New York.

afford to get married. Berta worked as a research associate at the university, but, to avoid charges of nepotism, she received neither title nor salary. Berta took this in stride, later stating, "An academic career at that time did not look promising at all for a woman. I must say that I could not have done what I have if I had not been married to a biologist who gave me a chance to do my work."

While at the institute, the Scharrers conducted further research on Ernst's 1928 discovery that certain hypothalamic neurons in fish, which he called "nerve-gland cells," secreted substances that he hypothesized were hormones. Ernst's theory was not well received because, at that time, most scientists believed that nerve function was an electrical phenomenon and that nerve cells did not secrete any substances. Ernst continued his study of vertebrates, while Berta took up the study of nerve cells in invertebrates.

With the rise of Nazism in Germany, pursuing their scientific work became difficult for the Scharrers, as Nazi philosophy began to permeate the academic world. They were appalled by the Nazi policies against the Jews and were under pressure to join Nazi organizations. As a physician, Ernst would have had to accept a military position. Finally, the Scharrers could take no more. "We decided that it was impossible for us to be a part of this system any longer," Berta later said. And so in 1937, the Scharrers left Germany, leaving behind all their research materials. Officially, they were to return one year later after Ernst completed a fellowship in the Department of Anatomy at the University of Chicago. In reality, they did not plan to return.

Berta Scharrer obtained a small research space at the University of Chicago, but, once again, she had neither academic title nor salary. With little money available to buy lab animals or space to keep them, she made due with the cockroaches she found in the basement of her building. She would continue to study cockroaches and related insects for the rest of her career.

In 1938, Ernst accepted a position as a visiting investigator at the Rockefeller Institute for Medical Research (now Rockefeller University) in New York City. Once, again, Berta served as an unpaid research associate, continuing her studies on cockroaches. She and Ernst presented a well-received paper on neurosecretion at the 1940 annual meeting of the Association for Research in Nervous and Mental Disorders.

The Scharrers were on the move again in 1940, this time to Western Research University (now Case Western Reserve University) in Cleveland, Ohio, where Ernst was appointed assistant professor in the Department of Anatomy. As usual, Berta did not receive an academic position or salary. She continued her research, conducting experiments on a breeding colony of the South American woodroach she had established. The Scharrers left Cleveland in 1946 when Ernst was appointed associate professor for the Department of Anatomy at the University of Colorado in Denver. Berta was still without an academic appointment, but was awarded a Guggenheim Fellowship and then a Special Fellowship of the National Institutes of Health.

In 1955, the Scharrers accepted positions at the new Albert Einstein College of Medicine in the Bronx, New York. Ernst was appointed chair of the Department of Anatomy, and Berta, receiving her first academic position, was appointed a full-time professor, although she was paid only half the regular salary. She was appointed course leader for histology at the college, and this role took time away from her research work for several years. In 1963, however, the Scharrers published *Neuroendocrinology*, which became a leading text in the field.

Tragedy struck in 1965 when Ernst drowned while swimming on vacation. For the first time in her career, Berta was without Ernst. "I had to show that I could go it on my own," she said. She was offered her husband's position at the college, but turned it down, although she did serve as acting head until his successor was named. During the last 15 years of her career, Scharrer incorporated the use of the electron microscope into her research and then turned her attention to the new field of neuroimmunology. She continued her research and teaching and, in 1978, was appointed Distinguished University Professor Emerita. She continued working until shortly before her death on July 23, 1995, in the Bronx.

In recognition of her contributions to science, Berta Scharrer was awarded 11 honorary degrees and a number of other awards. In 1967 she was elected a member of the National Academy of Sciences, and in 1983 she was awarded the National Medal of Science for her "pioneering contributions to establishing the concept of neurosecretion and the demonstration of the central role of neurosecretion and neuropeptides in the integration of animal function and development." ◆

# Shiva, Vandana

1952– ● ENVIRONMENTALIST

Vandana Shiva has traveled far from her Himalayan birthplace to become an internationally known environmentalist and feminist. She is a strong opponent of globalization, which she sees as the exploitation of Third World nations—largely those in the southern hemisphere—by male-dominated corporations in western countries—primarily those in the northern hemisphere. Her efforts are focused on supporting grassroots organizations worldwide in their struggles to protect natural resources.

Vandana Garewal Shiva was born in 1952 in the Himalayan forest region of India. Her father was a forester conservator, and Shiva spent much time with him in the forests as she was growing up. She is grateful for those early experiences. "Ever since I was a child," she said, "love and knowledge of nature have given me my deepest satisfaction." Shiva credits her mother, an educated woman who was once a school inspector in the education department, with providing a strong, positive female role model and of being "…a feminist, ahead of her time." Her mother was also a strong believer in the teachings of Mahatma Gandhi and raised her children in that tradition. Shiva employs Gandhian philosophies in own activities, believing that "civil disobedience is a way to create permanent democracy, perennial democracy, a direct democracy."

Shiva attended Punjab University, receiving her bachelor's degree in physics in 1972 and her master's in physics two years later. She had originally planned a career in atomic research at the Atomic Research Institute of India, but several factors caused her to re-evaluate her plan. First, while still working on her master's, she began to realize that although she was learning how to create nuclear power, she was not being taught about potential radiation hazards. Later, after Shiva graduated and was working at a nuclear reactor, her sister, a doctor, did not want Shiva working there and told her of the potential impact of radiation on Shiva and any children she might have.

Shiva's growing concerns were dismissed by senior physicists, which she considered "…an exclusion and a violation of my search for knowledge" and an example of the male dominance in the field. At this point, Shiva decided to leave the institute and moved to Canada, where she entered the Foundations of Physics program at the University of Western Ontario and studied the foundations of quantum theory. She received her Ph.D. in 1979.

Returning to India in 1980, Shiva joined the Indian Institute of Management in Bangalore. Once again, a couple of what Shiva terms "triggers" caused her to change her professional focus. The first occurred when she returned to her favorite spot in the mountains where her father had often taken her as a child, only to discover that the stream she use to swim in no longer existed. With financing from the World Bank, the area had been converted into an apple orchard.

The second trigger occurred in 1981 when she was working on a forestry study and discovered that the World Bank was "...basically financing the conversion of food-growing land to timber-growing, pulp-growing land with huge subsidies." The study was the catalyst for peasants and farmers to challenge the World Bank, the first such major challenge to the bank in India. Later, when the World Bank visited the institute, its director, fearful of losing future consultancies from the bank, was apologetic about Shiva and other of the institute's young, enthusiastic researchers.

"That's the day," Shiva said, "I decided that I had to follow my mind and heart. I couldn't be working for the bosses who were apologizing for the fact that I was following my conscience." Shiva returned home and started the Research Foundation for Science, Technology, and Ecology, what she calls an "extremely elaborate name for a tiny institute" that was started in her mother's cow shed.

By that time, Shiva had become involved in the Chipko movement, a grassroots movement begun in the Alakananda Valley in the Himalayan foothills. Started by the Chipko Indian women, the movement fought against logging in the area, which was having a devastating effect on the local environment and, thereby, on their ability to earn a livelihood. To prevent the loggers from felling trees, the women would wrap themselves around the trees. The movement spread by word of mouth from village to village, and although at first dismissed by the government, the Chipko movement was ultimately successful in instituting a ban on logging above 1000 meters in the Himalayas. This movement very much inspired Shiva, and her research initiatives became less academic and more activist in nature.

Shiva has also fought against the efforts of foreign corporations to patent and market indigenous natural resources. One

1952 — Shiva is born in India.

1979 — Shiva receives her Ph.D. in physics.

1980 — Shiva joins the Indian Institute of Management.

1981 — Shiva starts the Research Foundation for Science, Technology, and Ecology.

1993 — Shiva and Maria Mies co-author the book *Ecofeminism*.

1994 — Shiva receives the Right Livelihood Award.

such example is the attempt by Western corporations to obtain a patent to market Indian Neem leaves as a natural pesticide, even though local farmers have used the leaves for generations. The problems as Shiva sees it is that "The West does not see technologies that are developed by non-Western cultures and indigenous communities as technologies evolved by human societies, but as a part of nature."

Shiva served as India's representative to the 1992 International Earth Summit in Rio de Janeiro, Brazil, and now gives presentations at other national and international conferences. Since 1982, Shiva has been a consultant to the United Nations University, and she is the Science and Environment Advisor to the Third World Network, an independent, nonprofit international network of organizations and individuals interested in issues relating to development, the Third World, and North-South relations. In addition, Shiva is a prolific author of articles and books on environmental issues, including *Staying Alive: Women, Ecology and Survival in India*, *Monocultures of the Mind: Perspectives on Biodiversity and Biotechnology*, and *Stolen Harvest: The Hijacking of the Global Food Supply*. In 1993, she wrote, with German sociologist Maria Mies, *Ecofeminism*, a term that she calls "…good… for distinguishing a feminism that is ecological from the kind of feminisms that have become extremely technocratic." She is also a contributing editor to *Third World Resurgence*, a journal of the Third World Network covering issues confronting the Third World, such as the environment, health, and international affairs.

Shiva has received a number of awards throughout her career, including the 1992 Global 500 Award from the United National Environmental Program and 1993 Earth Day International Award. In 1994 she was awarded, along with four other women, the $2 million Right Livelihood Award, considered an alternative Nobel Prize for peaceful environmental and social activism. ◆

# Simpson, Joanne

MARCH 23, 1923– ● METEOROLOGIST

Joanne Simpson was told that it was impossible for a woman to earn a Ph.D. in meteorology. In 1949, she proved the doubters wrong by becoming the first woman in the world to do so.

The oldest child of Russell and Virginia (Vaughn) Gerould, Joanne Simpson was born in Boston, Massachusetts, on March 23, 1923. She grew up in what she termed "an intellectual but unhappy" home. Her mother had been trained as a journalist, but, following her marriage and the birth of her children, was forced to give up her career. Although her mother later worked in the birth control movement, she was never able to support herself. That left a lasting impression on Simpson. As a young girl she decided that, "No matter what happened, I was going to put myself in the position to make my own living, and to provide for whatever children I might have without having to depend on anybody else."

Simpson attended private school in Boston, but when it came time to select a college, she rebelled against the "Eastern Seaboard Syndrome" by choosing to attend the University of Chicago instead of one of the "Seven Sisters" girls' colleges. At first, her interests were in political and social sciences. However, involvement with the university's student flying club lead her to her first course in **meteorology**, which she needed to obtain her pilot's license. With the outbreak of World War II, she considered dropping out of college to enlist in the military, but a professor told her about the need to train people in meteorology who would then train Air Force cadets in basic weather forecasting. In 1942, she received a scholarship from the U.S. National Weather Bureau for the university's meteorology program and, upon her graduation the following year, began teaching cadets at New York University and then students at the University of Chicago.

The end of the war brought changes that affected Simpson's life. As she later recalled, "when the war was over and the men came home and were demobilized, it was generally expected of women that they go back like 'Rosie the Riveter' to their mops and babies." Although this may have been what was expected, it was not what Simpson wanted to do. She was determined to pursue further studies in meteorology. Simpson returned to the University of Chicago and earned her master's degree in 1945. She wanted to continue and get her Ph.D., but met with resistance from the faculty there. She was told by advisors that no woman would ever get a Ph.D. in meteorology, so she should not even bother trying. Simpson was unable to find a faculty member who would agree to be her Ph.D. advisor, and, despite her good grades, she could not obtain funding for additional studies. Finally, a professor did agree to serve as advisor for her work on

1923 ▸ Simpson is born in Boston, Massachusetts.

1949 ▸ Simpson earns her Ph.D. in meteorology.

1965 ▸ Simpson heads an experimental meteorology laboratory.

1981 ▸ Simpson heads the Severe Storms Board at Goddard Space Flight Center.

1988 ▸ Simpson is named Chief Scientist for Meteorology at Goddard Space Flight Center.

1989 ▸ Simpson becomes the first female president of the American Meteorological Society.

1997 ▸ Simpson is honored by NASA, which names a supercomputer after her.

**meteorology:** the science of the atmosphere and its phenomena, particularly focusing on variations of heat and moisture, winds and storms.

"Told that because the job required working at night and flying in airplanes to do research, it was 'totally inappropriate for a woman to be a meteorologist,' she disregarded the advice."

On Joanne Simpson choosing meteorology as a career, quoted in a College Report, University of Chicago, February 1999

cumulus clouds. While working on her degree, Simpson taught physics and meteorology at the Illinois Institute of Technology to support herself. In 1949, she earned her doctorate.

While Simpson was at the University of Chicago, the meteorological program was headed by Carl-Gustaf Rossy, now considered to be the greatest meteorologist of the 20th century. He offered her some advice. "He told me," she said, "that I would look both ridiculous and pathetic if I didn't really make it big after making such an unconventional spectacle of myself in my fight to become a meteorologist." Years later, she would be honored by the American Meteorological Society with its highest honor—the medal that bears his name.

It was also at the University of Chicago that Simpson took a class on tropical meteorology from instructor Herbert Riehl, who would become her mentor. It was beginning of her "most important collaboration with anyone." The two developed the "hot tower theory," which deals with the source of the energy that drives atmospheric circulation. They also applied the theory to hurricanes.

After earning her doctorate, Simpson continued to teach at the Illinois Institute of Technology, leaving in 1951 to accept a position as meteorologist at the Woods Hole Oceanographic Institution on Cape Cod, Massachusetts, where she had spent summers while working on her Ph.D. She left Woods Hole in 1961 with her first husband for the University of California at Los Angeles, where each had been offered positions in the meteorology department; they were the first married couple to have professorships in the same department at UCLA. In the academic world, there had long been a ban on married couples working as professors in the same department, which often resulted in women taking less prestigious positions as research assistants or being forced out altogether. "I believe," Simpson would comment later, "I have suffered more grief and loss of potential from this source [nepotism] than from any other sex related restriction."

After divorcing her first husband, Simpson was hired in 1965 by the U.S. Weather Bureau to head the experimental meteorology laboratory in Coral Gables, Florida. She also taught at the University of Miami. The same year, she married Robert H. Simpson, who, along with her collaborator Riehl, had formed the National Hurricane Research Project in the 1950s. Bob Simpson would later serve as the director of the National Hurricane Center.

Simpson returned to full-time teaching at the University of Virginia at Charlotte in 1974. Two years later she became the first woman there to be named the W. W. Cocoran professor of environmental sciences. Simpson left teaching in 1981 to become head of the Severe Storms Board of the U.S. National Aeronautics and Space Administration's Goddard Space Flight Center (GSFC) in Greenbelt, Maryland. In 1988, she was named GSFC's Chief Scientist for Meteorology. Simpson was also involved during this time with the Tropical Rainfall Measuring Mission (TRMM), a new satellite dedicated to measuring tropical and subtropical rainfall through microwave and visible infrared sensors. She served as TRMM science director from 1992–1998. It was at GSFC that Simpson pioneered the use of computers in cloud modeling. She produced the first one-dimensional model and the first cumulus model, and lead research into multicloud modeling.

Throughout her career, Simpson has served as a role model for women in science, as evidenced by the *Ms.* Foundation naming her one of its top female role models in 1998. Although Simpson was happy to serve as such, later in her career she said that since she had "carried the burden of being a role model for women for so many years that I decided 5 or 10 years ago that since there are now so many brilliant young women who have won awards who are in the 40s and 50s, that I have simply retired from being a role model. It's somebody else's turn now."

During her career, Simpson has earned many honors and awards, some of them "firsts" for women. In 1975 she was elected to the council of the American Meteorological Society and became its first female president in 1989. She was elected to the National Academy of Engineering in 1988, received the Women in Science and Engineering Lifetime Achievement award in 1990, and was the awarded the Department of Commerce's Gold Medal in 1992. She was the first recipient of the William Nordberg Memorial Award for Earth Science in 1994. Simpson was also asked to contribute her autobiography and papers to the History of Women in America Project at the Schlesinger Library at Radcliffe College.

Simpson received a unique honor from NASA in 1997. Its fastest supercomputer, the CRAY T3E was named "jsimpson" in recognition for her pioneering work in using computers in meteorological research. Supercomputers are rarely named for a living person, and Simpson considered it a "great honor." She said, "When seeing things like comets named after people, that is glamorous. But a computer, particularly one of this power and capability, is an enabler for many people to do exciting work."

Despite her many accomplishments, Simpson has misgivings about the price she paid for them. "I am not," she said, "convinced that either the positions, rewards or achievements have been worth the cost. My personal and married life and child raising [she has three children from her first marriage] have surely suffered from the professional attainments I have achieved." Still, the work remains important. "I'm never going to retire," she asserted, "I like the work too much." ◆

# Singer, Maxine

FEBRUARY 15, 1931– ● GENETICIST

Maxine Singer

Geneticist Maxine Singer was at the forefront of controversy over the use of "recombinant" deoxyribonucleic acid (DNA) techniques—taking DNA fragments from one organism and inserting them into the living cells of another—to alter genetic characteristics. She advocated a cautious approach to the use of these techniques, seeking to strike a balance between conducting research and protecting public safety. To that end, she helped develop guidelines that established practices for constructing and handling recombinant DNA (rDNA) molecules, and organisms and viruses containing rDNA molecules.

Maxine Frank Singer was born on February 15, 1931, in New York City, to Hyman, an attorney, and Henrietta (Perlowitz) Frank, a hospital admissions officer, children's camp director, and model. Maxine Singer attended New York City public schools and then received her bachelor of arts degree, with high honors, from Swarthmore College in Pennsylvania. Singer did her graduate work at Yale University in New Haven, Connecticut, receiving her Ph.D. in biochemistry in 1957. Several years earlier, in 1952, she married Daniel Singer, and the couple would eventually have four children.

In 1956, Singer began her long professional relationship with the U.S. National Institutes of Health (NIH). She was a postdoctoral fellow at the NIH's National Institute for Arthritis, Metabolism and Digestive Diseases and, in 1958, received a staff appointment as a research chemist in the section on enzymes and cellular biochemistry. In 1974, Singer assumed the new position of chief of the Section of Nucleic Acid Enzymology of the Division of Cancer Biology and Diagnosis at the National Cancer Institute, conducting DNA-related research on tumor-causing viruses and on **ribonucleic acid (RNA)**. She became chief of the division's Laboratory of Biochemistry in 1980, leading 15 research groups conducting a variety of biochemical investigations. Singer left the NIH in 1988 to become president of the Carnegie Institution of Washington, in Washington, D.C., although she remains affiliated with the NIH as scientist emeritus—the only woman to gain that status at the NIH—where she continues to conduct research on human genetics.

While Singer was at the NIH, scientists had learned to how create rDNA, which could then direct the production of proteins in the foreign organism as if the DNA was still in its original organism. While the process of "gene splicing" held great potential as a means of discovering cures for serious diseases, developing crops, and providing other benefits to humanity, it also held out the frightening prospect of creating hazardous new organisms.

In 1972, Paul Berg of Stanford University, who was both a colleague and personal friend of Singer's and who would later win the Nobel Prize in Chemistry for his work with DNA, became the first scientist to create rDNA molecules. He was conducting related experiments involving DNA manipulation in the genes of tumor-causing viruses, but voluntarily stopped when some scientists voiced fears that a virus of unknown properties could potentially escape and spread into the general population.

The debate over gene-splicing continued to grow, and at the 1973 Gordon Conference, an annual, high-level research meeting of which Singer was co-chair along with Dieter Soll of

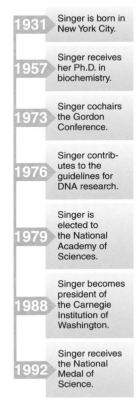

1931   Singer is born in New York City.

1957   Singer receives her Ph.D. in biochemistry.

1973   Singer cochairs the Gordon Conference.

1976   Singer contributes to the guidelines for DNA research.

1979   Singer is elected to the National Academy of Sciences.

1988   Singer becomes president of the Carnegie Institution of Washington.

1992   Singer receives the National Medal of Science.

**ribonucleic acid (RNA):** a nucleic acid found in all living cells which plays a role in transferring information from DNA to the protein-forming system of the cell.

Yale University, Singer was approached by several nucleic acid scientists suggesting that the conference include discussion of safety issues related to gene-splicing. Singer agreed, and opened the discussion by acknowledging that although DNA manipulation offered great hope in combating health problems, the process raised moral and ethical concerns. Those present decided that the best course of action would be to draft a public letter about the safety risks of rDNA to the president of the National Academy of Sciences and to request that the magazine *Science* publish it. Singer and Soll wrote the letter, suggesting that the academy study the problem and recommend guidelines.

The Singer-Soll letter generated concern that led 100 leading scientists to gather for the 1975 Asilomar Conference, of which Singer was one of the organizers. At the conclusion of the conference, a committee of the NIH began formulating guidelines for rDNA research. Singer played an important role in the development of the guidelines. She advocated a careful, analytic approach and submitted four principles to be used by the committee in drafting the guidelines: experiments posing serious hazards should be banned altogether; experiments with lesser or no potential hazards should be permitted if their benefits would be unobtainable through conventional methods and if proper safeguards were employed; the more risk an experiment carried, the stricter the safeguards should be; and the guidelines should be reviewed annually. Throughout the ensuing public debate, Singer remained a staunch advocate of the responsible use of biochemical genetic research. The resulting guidelines for research involving rDNA molecules were issued by the NIH in 1976 and have been updated periodically since then.

Following the implementation of the guidelines, Singer wrote in *Science* magazine that "under the Guidelines work has proceeded safely and research accomplishments have been spectacular." She has continued to promote the benefits of rDNA techniques. In the early 1990s she wrote an article encouraging the public to try the "Flavr Savr" tomato, the first genetically engineered food available to American consumers, pointing out that "almost all the foods we eat are the product of previous genetic engineering by cross-breeding."

In her current role as president of the Carnegie Institution, Singer leads biologists, astronomers, and earth scientists of the institution's 15 scientific departments. Singer has said that the "best part" of working at the institution is that she has "…thought about areas of science I haven't thought about since

**"As a scientist at the National Institutes of Health 30 years ago, Maxine Singer was present at the creation of modern genetic research. Her lab work helped decipher the genetic code, and she helped set the ethical agenda on DNA research."**

On Maxine Singer's role in advancing genetic research, quoted in *U.S. News & World Report*, August 26/September 2, 1991

## Carnegie Institution of Washington

The nonprofit Carnegie Institution of Washington (CIW), which is located in Washington, D.C., was founded in 1902. Andrew Carnegie provided the initial $10 million endowment and subsequent funding. His vision was "to encourage, in the broadest and most liberal manner, investigation, research, and discovery, and the application of knowledge to the improvement of mankind." CIW supports the education of predoctoral and postdoctoral students by offering them residency training; much of CIW's funding is also used for investigations conducted at its own research departments.

In addition to providing resources for professional scientists, CIW also offers programs for elementary school children. First Light is a weekend program for inner-city children with an interest in science but little access to science classes in their own schools. The program combines instruction, hands-on work, and field trips. Elementary school teachers can also attend a six-week summer program, sponsored by the Carnegie Academy for Science Education (CASE), where they can learn new ways to teach effectively.

Over the years CIW has focused more on promising, innovative work than on any single field of research, and as a result the most prominent areas of research have changed over time. Throughout the early 1900s, it was a leader in astronomy, where it continues to be prominent. To name just two achievements: Allan Sandage is an innovator in observational cosmology; Stephen Shectman has investigated the use of fiber optic systems in the simultaneous observation of many galaxies. In recent decades the institute has been at the forefront of plant biology and embryology (including pioneering advances in prenatal care) and geophysics (led by the Center for High Pressure Research). In the past, CIW supported Barbara McClintock's discovery of movable genetic elements; more recently, other notable women have been associated with CIW, including Marilyn L. Fogel, who has been a pioneer in stable isotopic chemistry in fossils.

Maxine Singer is the institute's eighth president (1988). She initiated the CASE program and the First Light program and has been a persuasive voice for bringing science education to women and minority groups traditionally left behind in science training.

I was in college. I haven't thought about physics, I haven't thought about real chemistry since I was a graduate student. I certainly never thought about astronomy. Now, suddenly, I'm really connected to people who are doing front line work in earth sciences, geochemistry, geophysics, extragalactic astronomy." Concerned with the quality of science education, Singer initiated two programs at the institution to help address the problem. The First Light program is a Saturday science school for inner-city children in Washington, D.C. The Carnegie Academy for Science Education is a program for the district's public school elementary teachers that includes six-week summer institutes and other programs throughout the school year.

Singer is a prolific author, with more than 100 books, articles, and papers to her credit. Together with her colleague and friend Paul Berg, she compiled *Genes and Genomes: A Changing Perspective*, a graduate-level textbook on molecular genetics, which received good reviews for its explanations of difficult concepts. The two also collaborated on *Dealing With Genes: The Language of Heredity*, a book for the layperson on genetic engineering, and *Exploring Genetic Mechanisms*, a genetics textbook. Singer has also served on the editorial board of *Science* magazine.

As a leading scientist in the field of human genetics, Singer has been called upon to testify before the U.S. Congress, and she has served on a number of advisory boards in the United States and abroad, including an advisory board to the Pope and the Committee on Human Values of the National Conference of Bishops. She was also a member of a Yale University committee that investigated the university's investments in South Africa, and she currently serves on the board of directors of Johnson & Johnson.

Throughout her career, Singer has earned many honors and awards, including honorary degrees from Brandeis University, Dartmouth College, Harvard University, New York University, Swarthmore College, Yale University, and others. She was elected to membership in the National Academy of Sciences in 1979, and received the National Medal of Science, the nation's highest scientific honor, in 1992 "for her outstanding scientific accomplishments and her deep concern for the societal responsibility of the scientist." ◆

# Solomon, Susan

JANUARY 19, 1956– ● CHEMIST

Born on January 19, 1956, in Chicago, Illinois, to Leonard and Alice (Rutman) Solomon, Susan Solomon knows exactly what got her interested in science. "It was," she said, "the airing of Jacques Cousteau on American TV when I was nine or ten years old." As a child she watched programs on natural history, but watching the Cousteau program sparked her interest in biology. She decided "right then that science was the most wonderful thing you could do in the world." Later, she would turn from biology to chemistry, preferring the quantitative nature of chemistry over biology. This change in focus would ultimately lead her to the relatively new field of atmospheric chemistry and her key role in discovering the cause of the "hole" in the earth's ozone layer, which protects the earth from the sun's deadly ultraviolet radiation.

For her undergraduate studies, Solomon attended the Illinois Institute of Technology, majoring in chemistry. A senior class project on measuring the reaction of ethylene and hydroxyl radical—a process that occurs in the atmosphere of Jupiter—sparked her interest in atmospheric chemistry. On her own, she read additional materials on the subject. It was while she was at the institute that she realized "you don't have to do chemistry in a test tube; you can do it in the real world." The summer following her graduation in 1977, Solomon worked at

Susan Solomon

the National Center for Atmospheric Research (NCAR) in Boulder, Colorado. Here she met Paul Crutzen, a research scientist who introduced her to the study of the ozone in the upper atmosphere.

In the fall of 1977, Solomon entered the master's program in chemistry at the University of California at Berkeley. While there, she met chemistry professor Harold Johnston, who had conducted pioneering work on the effect of the supersonic transport (SST) on the atmosphere. He, as had Crutzen, encouraged Solomon's interest in atmospheric chemistry. Solomon received her master's degree in 1979 and completed her Ph.D. coursework, also at Berkeley, returning to NCAR to conduct her thesis research with Crutzen. She received her Ph.D. in 1981.

After receiving her doctorate, Solomon joined the Aeronomy Laboratory of the U.S. Department of Commerce's National Oceanic and Atmospheric Administration (NOAA) in Boulder. Initially her efforts focused on developing computer models of ozone in the upper atmosphere, but her focus would

**1956** Solomon is born in Chicago, Illinois.

**1981** Solomon earns her Ph.D. from the University of California at Berkeley.

**1986** Solomon serves as the lead project scientist on an expedition to Antarctica.

**1987** Solomon conducts further research in Antarctica.

**1992** Solomon is elected to membership in the National Academy of Sciences.

**2000** Solomon wins the highest award given by the American Meteorological Society.

**"Now her work in chemistry is bringing her to the question of life's survival on earth."**

On Susan Solomon's important research, quoted in *Fortune* magazine

soon switch from the theoretical to the experimental. In 1985, scientists with the British Antarctic Survey discovered a "hole" in the ozone layer there. The 50 percent rate of depletion observed by the survey's scientists was much greater than the rate scientists had been predicting. Although scientists suspected that chlorofluorocarbons (CFCs)—man-made gases used in refrigerators, to power aerosol spray bottles, and in the production of semiconductors—were the cause of the problem, the reason for the drastic rate of depletion was unknown.

In an effort to solve this mystery, Solomon volunteered to be the head project scientist on the 1986 United States National Ozone Expedition to the Antarctic, spending three months—August, September, and October, or what is considered "spring" there—at the McMurdo Station. Solomon's team measured the amounts of chlorine dioxide and other atmospheric components.

Following her return to the U.S., Solomon wrote a research article theorizing that the ozone hole developed in the Antarctic because CFC derivatives react on the surfaces of polar stratospheric clouds, which are more extensive there than anywhere else on the Earth. Her theory is now generally accepted by scientists and helped to bring world attention to the threat to the ozone layer. As a result, many countries have now stopped the production and use of CFCs.

Solomon returned to Antarctica again in 1987 and thinks it's a "fantastic place" and a "scientist's playground." In addition to her research in Antarctica, Solomon is studying the ozone layer in the Arctic and at the middle latitudes where most of the world's population lives, the possible role of chemistry in climate changes, and the affects of volcanic eruptions on the ozone layer in middle latitude locations, such as the United States and Europe. Also, as a leading authority on the ozone layer, she has testified before several congressional committees.

Solomon has received a number of honors throughout her career. In 1985, she won the American Geophysical Union's J. B. MacElwane Award, which recognizes significant contributions to the geophysical sciences by an outstanding young scientist. The U.S. Department of Commerce awarded her a gold medal in 1989 for her "impeccable science in the cause of mankind." The American Meteorological Society presented her with its Henry G. Houghton Award in 1991 for her "outstanding theoretical and observational research on atmospheric

**National Oceanic and Atmospheric Administration**

The National Oceanic and Atmospheric Administration (NOAA), established in 1970, is one agency of the U.S. Department of Commerce. It has several mandates centered around the study of the environment. The National Ocean Service is responsible for research and data collection on marine physical conditions. The NOAA Corps commands and runs sea vessels. The National Weather Service has several roles. It operates weather data collection stations (largely manned by volunteers), which generate large volumes of extremely detailed daily weather data that must be managed and analyzed to spot long-term climate trends. It also reports the weather in the United States and issues severe weather warnings. The National Marine Fisheries Service is responsible for administering federal regulations for marine commercial fisheries, as well as for the protection of marine mammals and threatened or endangered marine fish, and for conducting research on estuarine and marine biology. NOAA also oversees the National Sea Grants, which are given to help institutions undertake marine research.

Susan Soloman works at NOAA's Aeronomy Lab modeling the effects of aerosol on the environment. Her findings will help researchers plan for more effective ways to preserve the atmosphere from harmful effects of pollutants. She is one of many scientists at NOAA combining its dual goals of environmental assessment/prediction and environmental stewardship.

constituent structure and for significant contributions to understanding the Antarctic ozone hole."

The following year she was elected to membership in the National Academy of Sciences. In recognition of her work there, an Antarctic glacier was named for her in 1994. Solomon's most recent honor, in 2000, is the Carl-Gustaf Rossby Research Medal, the highest award given by the American Meteorological Society. It cited her "for fundamental contributions to understanding the chemistry of the stratosphere and unraveling the mystery of the Antarctic ozone hole." ◆

# Somerville, Mary

DECEMBER 26, 1780–NOVEMBER 29, 1872 ● MATHEMATICIAN

In a lifetime spanning almost a century and in an era when it was deemed unnecessary for a women to be educated, Mary Fairfax Somerville made important contributions to the fields of science and mathematics.

Mary Fairfax Somerville

The daughter of William George Fairfax, a lieutenant and later a vice-admiral in the British navy, and his second wife, Margaret, Somerville was born on December 26, 1780, in Jedburgh, Scotland. She was born at the home of her maternal aunt Martha, who would later become her mother-in-law, and Martha's husband Thomas Somerville. "I was," she later recalled, "born in the house of my future husband and nursed by his mother—a rather singular coincidence." Her father was at sea at the time of her birth, and his position in the navy often took him away from his family. She was the fifth of seven children, although three died young, leaving her with an older brother and a younger brother and sister. Somerville spent time as a child exploring the seaside in her hometown of Burntisland in County Fife, Scotland. "I never cared for dolls," she would later relate, "and had no one to play with me. I amused myself in the garden, which was much frequented by birds. I knew most of them, their flight and their habits."

As was typical of the era, Somerville's brothers received a good education, while she and her sister did not. She was taught to read the Bible, but it was not considered necessary for girls to learn to write. When Somerville was about nine years old, her father returned from one of his long sea voyages only to be shocked at finding her to be, as she said, "such a savage," unable to write and able to read only at a basic level. As a result, when she was 10, she was sent to Miss Primrose's boarding school. Although she spent only one unhappy year there, she did learn basic reading and writing and was exposed to mathematics for the first time. After her return from school, Somerville began to educate herself by reading the books she found in her home. She taught herself some Greek and Latin, learning enough Latin by age 13 to read Caesar's *Commentaries*. Somerville was criticized by some family members for engaging in such an unladylike pursuit, although not by her uncle Thomas

Somerville. When she stayed with the Somervilles in Jedburgh, the two would read Latin together.

When Somerville was 13, her family rented a house in Edinburgh, spending the winter months there and the summer months in Burntisland. She continued her self-education and also learned more accepted pursuits such as painting, needlepoint, and playing the piano. At about age 14, she became interested in algebra through a fashion magazine, which as was typical of women's magazine of that era, contained puzzles. As she explained, she "…read what appeared to me to be simply an arithmetical question; but on turning the page I was surprised to see strange looking lines mixed with letters, chiefly *x*'s and *y*'s, and asked, 'What's that?'" All she could learn was that the symbols were part of some kind of mathematics called 'algebra.'

In addition to finding the algebra puzzle in the magazine, Somerville had also heard her painting teacher discussing with another student how Euclid's *Elements* formed the basis for perspective in painting as well as the basis for understanding the various sciences. Since it was considered improper for a lady to ask for a copy of the book in a bookshop, she secretly convinced her brother's tutor to buy it and other algebra texts for her. When Somerville's father discovered that she was studying mathematics, he forbid her to continue, although she did so in secret.

When Somerville was 24, in 1804, she married her cousin Samuel Greig, a captain in the Russian navy and a distant relative on her mother's side of the family. As her parents did not want her to move to Russia, they insisted that Samuel obtain an appointment in London before allowing the couple to wed. Her husband did not encourage her studies, nor did he try to stop her. Somerville continued studying math and began taking French lessons. She later wrote of her husband, "He had a very low opinion of the capacity of my sex, and had neither knowledge of, nor interest in, science of any kind." Somerville gave birth to two sons before Samuel died in 1807.

Following her husband's death, Somerville and her sons returned to Scotland, and with her inheritance she had the funds to openly pursue her own interests. Her family remained concerned that her continuing studies could injure her health. However, she had a group of friends who remained supportive. It was through her friend John Playfair, a professor of natural

1780 ▸ Somerville is born in Jedburgh, Scotland.

1826 ▸ Somerville publishes *The Magnetic Properties of the Violet Rays of the Solar Spectrum.*

1831 ▸ Somerville publishes *Mechanism for the Heavens.*

1848 ▸ Somerville publishes *Physical Geography.*

1872 ▸ Somerville dies in Naples, Italy.

philosophy, that Somerville became acquainted with William Wallace, a former student of Playfair's and a professor of mathematics. Somerville and Wallace began a correspondence, discussing problems in *The Mathematical Repository*, a popular mathematical journal. In 1811, Somerville won a silver medal from the *Repository* for her solution to one of the problems it had published.

Somerville was married again in 1812, this time to her cousin Dr. William Somerville, a hospital inspector who had recently returned from 15 years abroad in the army medical department. William was interested in science and supportive of Somerville's studies. Together they studied geology, and Mary, advised by Wallace, read mathematical and other texts. The Somervilles lived in Edinburgh where William was head of army hospitals in Scotland. The couple had four children, although in 1814 her only son from her second marriage died, as did her oldest son from her first marriage.

In 1816, William was appointed Inspector to the Army Medical Board, and the family moved from Edinburgh to London. As they had been in Edinburgh, the Somervilles were active socially, and they met many of leading scientists and mathematicians of the day. After William's job was eliminated in 1817, the couple decided to travel, spending most of the next year in Pairs, again meeting with scientists and mathematicians. The Somervilles moved again in 1824, this time to Chelsea, on the edge of London, where William had been appointed a physician in the Royal Hospital.

In the summer 1825 Somerville began conducting experiments on magnetism in her garden. A year later she published *The Magnetic Properties of the Violet Rays of the Solar Spectrum* in the proceedings of the Royal Society. Her paper was well received and was only the second paper by a woman to be read at the society and published in its proceedings. Although her theory was later proved wrong, she had established herself as a scientific writer.

In 1827, Lord Henry Bougham, an old friend from Edinburgh, asked Somerville on behalf of the Society for the Diffusion of Useful Knowledge to translate Laplace's *Mechanique Celetes* and Newton's *Principia*. He wanted to reach a wider audience by providing not only a translation but a detailed explanation of the mathematics. She agreed to undertake the project, but in secrecy. If she failed, the manuscript was to be destroyed and only a few would ever know it had existed. Somerville finished the work in 1831, and the book, *The Mechanism for the Heavens*, was too large for the society to publish and so another publisher was found. The book was an instant success. Somerville spent most of the next year abroad with her daughters, working on her second book, *On the Connexion of the Physical Sciences*, which was published in 1834.

Because of William's declining health, the family moved to the warmer climate of Italy in 1838, where William would live another 22 years and Mary would spend most of the rest of her life. Over the next decades, she published several additional works. *Physical Geography*, published in 1848 when she was 88, was her most successful work and went through seven editions. It would remain in use in schools and universities for the next 50 years. In 1869, she completed *On Molecular and Microscopic Science* as well as her autobiography, *Personal Recollections, from Early Life to Old Age, of Mary Somerville*, some heavily edited parts of which were published after her death by her daughter Martha.

Somerville supported the causes of women's suffrage and women's education, although she did express doubts about the intellectual abilities of women. She was conscious that she had not made a discovery on her own, rather that she reported on the discoveries of others. "I have," she said, "perseverance and intelligence but no genius; that spark from heaven is not granted to the sex." Indeed, she felt she may have contributed to her daughter Margaret's death at age nine by encouraging the girl's intellectual abilities. Nevertheless, when British philosopher and economist John Stuart Mill organized a petition on women's suffrage to be presented to parliament, he requested that Somerville's signature be the first on one on the petition, and she complied. After her death, Somerville College, one of the first two women's colleges at Oxford, was named in honor of her support of women's education.

Somerville died at age 92 on November 29, 1872, in Naples, Italy. She remained interested in mathematics and science until the end of her life, writing shortly before her death that although she was deaf and her memory of ordinary events was failing, she was "…still able to read books on the higher algebra for four or five hours in the morning, and even to solve the problems." Throughout her life, she received many awards and honors. In 1835 she was elected, along with astronomer Caroline Herschel, to the Royal Astronomical Society, the first two women to become honorary members. She was elected to a number of European and American organizations, including the Royal Irish Academy, American Geological and Statistical Society, and the Italian Geological Society. In 1870 she received the Victoria Gold Medal from the Royal Geographical Society. ◆

# Spurlock, Jeanne

JULY 21, 1921–NOVEMBER 25, 1999 ● PSYCHIATRIST

Jeanne Spurlock, the eldest of seven children, was born in Ohio and grew up in Detroit. A dedicated student during high school and college, she was interested first in journalism and then in history. However, she had wanted to become a physician since the age of nine. It was during this year that she had an unpleasant hospital experience that led to her desire to try and make patients, especially young patients, feel comfortable about being in a hospital.

Spurlock received her medical degree from Howard University College of Medicine, Washington, D.C., in 1947. She did her internship at Provident Hospital in Chicago from 1947 to 1948 and continued to reside in Chicago, where she completed a two-year residency at the Cook County Psychopathic Hospital. Spurlock chose psychiatry as her field of interest and received a fellowship in child psychiatry at the Institute for Juvenile Research in 1950. She acquired additional experience in adult and child psychoanalysis at the Chicago Institute for Psychoanalysis from 1953 to 1960.

Some of the positions Spurlock held include staff psychiatrist at the Mental Hygiene Clinic of Women's and Children's Hospital in Chicago, from 1951 to 1953; consultant for the Illinois School for the Deaf in Jacksonville, from 1951 to 1952; and clinical assistant professor of psychiatry, from 1960 to 1968 at the University of Illinois College of Medicine.

Spurlock moved to Nashville when she became chair of the department of psychiatry at Meharry Medical College in 1968. In 1973, she moved to Washington, D.C., to set up a private practice and to become clinical professor of psychiatry at Howard University College of Medicine. She held the post of deputy medical director of the American Psychiatric Association from 1974 to 1991. Although retired from her post, Spurlock

**1921** Spurlock is born in Ohio.

**1947** Spurlock earns a medical degree from Howard University College of Medicine.

**1950** Spurlock receives a fellowship at the Institute for Juvenile Research.

**1968** Spurlock is named chair of the department of psychiatry at Meharry Medical College.

**1973** Spurlock becomes a clinical professor at Howard University College of Medicine.

continued to participate in the organization as a consulting member on the council of national affairs.

Her honors include the Edward A. Strecker M.D. award in 1971 from the Institute of the Pennsylvania Hospital. Spurlock was the first African American and the first woman to receive the latter award.

The American Academy of Child and Adolescent Psychiatry sponsors a research fellowship for minority medical students in Dr. Spurlock's name. Spurlock died in Washington, D.C., on November 25, 1999 following surgery. ◆

# Steitz, Joan Argetsinger

JANUARY 26, 1941– ● BIOCHEMIST

Biochemist Joan Argetsinger Steitz discovered small nuclear ribonucleoproteins, the cellular complexes that play an important role in translating genetic instructions contained in deoxyribonucleic (DNA) into proteins.

Argetsinger was born on January 26, 1941, in Minneapolis, Minnesota, to Glenn, a high school guidance counselor, and Elaine (Magnusson) Argetsinger, a speech pathologist. Argetsinger's interest in science developed at an early age. She attended Antioch College in Yellow Springs, Ohio, majoring in chemistry. As part of the college's work study program, she conducted research at a MIT laboratory and it was there that she first became interested in molecular biology. Argetsinger received her bachelor's degree in 1963.

Although interested in molecular biology, Argetsinger originally planned to go to medical school, believing this would offer her greater flexibility for combining a career with marriage and a family. However, after spending the summer before she was to start medical school working on her own research project under the direction of embryologist Joseph Gall, then at the University of Minnesota, she opted instead to enter the graduate program at Harvard University.

Unlike many other women graduate students in the sciences, Argetsinger found mentors. At Harvard she became the first female graduate student to work with James D. Watson, who, along with Francis Crick and Maurice Wilkins, discovered the DNA double helix in 1953. She received the highest grade

**1941** Steitz is born in Minneapolis, Minnesota.

**1968** Steitz receives her Ph.D. from Harvard.

**1970** Steitz accepts a position at Yale University.

**1979** Steitz discovers snRNPs.

**1983** Steitz is elected to membership in the National Academy of Sciences.

**1986** Steitz receives the National Science Medal.

**1994** Steitz is the first recipient of the Weizmann Women and Science Award.

in his course during her first year. Argetsinger received her master's from Harvard in 1967 and her Ph.D. in biochemistry and molecular biology a year later, also from Harvard.

In 1966, Argetsinger married fellow scientist Thomas Steitz, and the next year the two went to England, where each had a position at the Medical Research Council (MRC) Laboratory of Molecular Biology at Cambridge University. Here she worked with Francis Crick, who, as had Watson, would serve as a mentor to her. After arriving at the MRC, though, Steitz realized that she had been accepted there only because her husband had been given a postdoctoral position at the laboratory. As there was no research space available for her, Crick first suggested she conduct a literature project so that she could work in the library. "I knew," she later said, "I wasn't going to be any good at thinking theoretical biology thoughts in the library. I wanted to do research. Luckily a couple of the younger staff members took pity on me and came up with a little bench space."

Before the Steitzs returned to the United States in 1970, they were both offered jobs by various educational institutions. At this time, the women's movement was gaining momentum in the United States, and universities were now interested in appointing women to their faculties. "At the time I was a graduate student, there were no women professors in the biological sciences at any major university," she later said. "There were [women] who worked in research positions for many years who were later appointed to professorships but didn't follow the traditional career path of assistant to associate to full professor...." Consequently, these offers were "such a scary prospect because there were no [women] role models out there." But, with of the support and encouragement of her husband, friends, and mentors, Steitz decided that "it was my responsibility to do it [accept a faculty position]." She became assistant professor in the Department of Molecular Biophysics and Biochemistry at Yale University in New Haven, Connecticut.

In 1979, Steitz was studying the antibodies of patients with rheumatic disease to try to learn more about a certain nuclear particle. Although she was not able to isolate this other particle, she and graduate student Michael Lerner discovered small nuclear ribonucleoproteins, or snRNPs, which Steitz pronounces as "snurps." She defined the role snRNPs play in removing unimportant information contained within genes during the protein synthesis process. Her discovery has helped science gain a greater understanding of the actual mechanics of basic cell functions, and her research has also translated directly into clinical application by improving the diagnosis and treatment of rheumatic diseases and other autoimmune disorders.

Steitz was made a full professor at Yale in 1978 and is the chair of her department. She has been an investigator at Howard Hughes Medical Institute since 1986 and the Henry Ford II Professor since 1988. She is a prolific author, having published more than 170 articles and papers, and her works are often cited in other sources. Steitz serves on the editorial boards of several journals and, since 1994, has been an associate editor of the journal *Genes and Development*.

Steitz has received numerous awards throughout her career, many of them "firsts" for women, including the American Chemical Society's Eli Lilly Award in Biochemistry in 1976, the Award in Molecular Biology from the National Academy of Sciences in 1982, and the Warren Triennial Prize in 1989. In 1994, she was the first recipient of the Weizmann Women and Science Award, which honors a woman researcher in the United States who has made a significant contribution in either basic or applied science. Steitz is particularly proud of this award. It is, she said, "very special because there aren't any [other] significant prizes targeted to women in science." Steitz was elected to membership in the National Academy of Sciences in 1983 and received a National Science Medal in 1986. She also holds honorary degrees from a number of institutions.

Of her career, Steitz has said, "I never envisioned myself as being what I am today. I thought I would be a research associate in someone else's lab. I never thought that I would teach; I never thought that I would mentor graduate students; I never thought that I would be an active and prominent faculty member at a prominent institution." ◆

> **"She even saw certain advantages to being a woman because women were suddenly in demand, and if, as a woman, you achieved good results, you were noticed and did not blend in with the crowd. Today she is a leader in her field."**
>
> Joan Argetsinger Steitz's feelings on being a female scientist, quoted in *The Door in the Dream: Conversations with Eminent Women in Science*, 2000.

# Stevens, Nettie Maria

### July 7, 1861–May 4, 1912 ● Biologist and Cytogeneticist

At a time when few women considered college, and even less earned advanced degrees, the American biologist Nettie Maria Stevens proved that it is never too late to pursue your dreams. Having begun her research career in her mid-30s, Stevens was an early-20th-century cytogeneticist (a

**1861** Stevens is born in Cavendish, Vermont.

**1883** Stevens graduates from Westfield Normal School in Massachusetts.

**1899** Stevens receives her B.A. from Stanford University.

**1900** Stevens receives her M.A. from Stanford University.

**1903** Stevens receives her Ph.D. from Bryn Mawr College.

**1905** Stevens publishes a paper on X-Y chromosomes and receives the Ellen Richards Research Prize.

**1912** Stevens dies in Baltimore, Maryland.

scientist who studies chromosomes in relation to genetics) who started her professional life as a school teacher and went on to graduate school to study under the accomplished geneticist Thomas Hunt Morgan. Her role in Morgan's lab was key to the development of genetics, and Stevens achieved an incredible milestone during her short career: she proved that the particular arrangement of "accessory chromosomes" that scientists had been seeing in insects were in fact determining sex, thus ushering in the first evidence of a biological difference directly linked to differences in chromosomes.

Stevens was born in Cavendish, Vermont, in 1861 to Ephraim Stevens, a carpenter of English heritage, and Julia Adams Stevens. Historians know little about her family or early life, except that she attended public schools in Westford, Massachusetts, and displayed exceptional scholastic talent. Upon graduation, Stevens taught a variety of subjects (including physiology and zoology) at the high school in Lebanon, New Hampshire. Between 1881 and 1883, Stevens attended a teacher's college called the Normal School (now Westfield State College) in Westfield, Massachusetts, completing the four-year course in just two years. Like women who worked in that era, Stevens was employed as a school teacher, and then as a librarian for a number of years after she graduated. Striving to accomplish more, in 1896 she enrolled at Stanford University in California, where her work in the sciences flourished and she received her bachelor's degree in 1899.

Stevens found the atmosphere of Stanford refreshing, and began studying physiology, where she was encouraged by her professor, Oliver Peebles Jenkins. She spent summers studying at the Hopkins Seaside Laboratory, in Pacific Grove, California, pursuing her quickly developing interest in biology. During this time, Stevens decided to change careers and focus on scientific research. While at Hopkins she researched the life cycle of *Boveria*, a parasite of sea cucumbers, and published her findings in the 1901 *Proceedings of the California Academy of Sciences*. While Stevens' research runs the gamut from her early work in morphology (structure and form) and taxonomy (plant and animal classification) to her later work in cytology (the formation, function, and structure of cells), her most important research was done with chromosomes.

Thanks to the discoveries of the Austrian botanist Gregor Mendel, who showed how the genetic traits of pea plants are inherited, scientists knew a lot about how chromosomes acted during cell division. However, scientists had yet to trace an inherited trait from the parents' chromosomes to those of the offspring. In addition, no scientific studies had yet linked one chromosome with a specific characteristic. Stevens' experiments proved to be a breakthrough. Working with the mealworm, Stevens determined that the male produced two kinds of sperm: one with a large X chromosome, and the other with a small Y chromosome. Unfertilized eggs, however, had only X chromosomes. Stevens suspected that the sex of an organism was determined by the inheritance of a specific X or Y chromosome: if an egg were fertilized with sperm carrying the male's X chromosome, it would produce a female; if it were fertilized with the male's Y chromosome, it would produce a male. Stevens performed experiments to confirm this hypothesis, expanding her studies to other species.

After earning her master's degree in physiology in 1900, Stevens began her doctoral studies at Bryn Mawr College in Pennsylvania, the first school of higher learning in the
United States to offer graduate studies for women. During this time, she studied at the Zoological Station in Naples, Italy, and then at the Zoological Institute of the University of Würzburg, Germany. Back at Bryn Mawr, she obtained her doctorate in 1903. She was made a research fellow in biology at Bryn Mawr and then was promoted to a reader in experimental morphology in 1904. In 1905, she was promoted again to associate in experimental morphology. That same year, after experiments with the *Tenebrio molitor* beetle, Stevens published her paper regarding the X and Y chromosomes as sex determinants.

The story of Stevens' career is a testimony to the human ability to accomplish much in a short amount of time. She wrote dozens of papers, and was awarded the Ellen Richards Research Prize in 1905, given to promote scientific research by women. Although the X-Y theory as it relates to sex determination was considered far-fetched by some scientists, it later proved profoundly important to the field of genetics and to an understanding of the determination of gender. Before assuming her professorship, Stevens died of breast cancer. Although Nellie Stevens shares credit for her discoveries with the well-known biologist Edmund Beecher Wilson (who was working independently yet simultaneously on the same type of chromosomal research), historians recognize her as one of the first American women to contribute to scientific research. ◆

> **"Stevens had a share in a discovery of importance and her name will be remembered for this."**
> Thomas Hunt Morgan, Nobel Prize-winning geneticist, on Nellis Stevens research, quoted in *Science,* 1912

# Sullivan, Kathryn

1951– ● Oceanographer and Astronaut

**oceanographer:** a scientist who studies the history, lifeforms, and characteristics of the earth's oceans.

Former **oceanographer** Kathryn Sullivan became the first American woman to walk in space when she spent 3.5 hours outside the orbiter Challenger on October 11, 1984. Sullivan and astronaut David Leestma successfully conducted a satellite refueling test. In addition, the seven astronauts of Mission 41-G, the largest crew sent into space in a single spacecraft to that date, deployed the Earth Radiation Budget Satellite and conducted observations of the Earth's surface.

In April 1990 Sullivan was a mission specialist aboard STS-31, which deployed the Hubble Space Telescope. During this five-day mission Sullivan took part in a series of unique Earth observations made possible by the record altitude of 380 miles reached by the orbiter Discovery.

Sullivan went into space a third time in March 1992, as mission specialist and payload commander in the crew of STS-45. This flight of the orbiter Atlantis carried the Spacelab ATLAS, a scientific package devoted to studies of the Earth's atmosphere.

Sullivan was born October 3, 1951, in Paterson, New Jersey, and grew up in Woodland Hills, California. She and future astronaut Sally Ride were briefly classmates in the same elementary school. Sullivan graduated from Taft High School in Woodland Hills in 1969 and went on to attend the University of California at Santa Cruz, where she received a B.S. in Earth sciences in 1973. She later earned her Ph.D. in geology from Dalhousie University in Halifax, Nova Scotia, in 1978.

As a graduate student at Dalhousie Sullivan took part in a number of oceanographic expeditions by the U.S. Geological Survey, visiting the Mid-Atlantic Ridge, the Newfoundland Basin, and fault zones off the coast of Southern California. She also taught at Dalhousie and worked for Geological Survey of Canada. In 1985 Sullivan became an adjunct professor of Geology at Rice University in Houston, Texas.

Sullivan was one of the 35 astronauts selected by NASA in January 1978. In August 1979 she qualified as a mission specialist on future Shuttle crews, then worked on the support crews of STS-3 through STS-8. She also continued her research in

geoscience by making high-altitude flights in the NASA WB-57F aircraft and being coinvestigator of the Shuttle Imaging Radar system flown on Mission 41-G.

Kathryn Sullivan (third from left) with fellow astronauts.

She was assigned to the Hubble Space Telescope mission, then known as Mission 61-J, in April 1985. The flight was delayed five years by the Challenger disaster. During the hiatus Sullivan accepted an appointment by President Reagan to serve on the National Commission on Space, a year-long study to determine goals for U.S. civilian space programs for the next 25 years. In 1988 she was appointed to the Chief of Naval Operations Executive Panel. (Sullivan was an oceanography officer in the Naval Reserve, with the rank of lieutenant commander.)

In October 1992 Sullivan became chief scientist for the National Oceanographic and Atmospheric Administration in Washington.

Since 1996 Sullivan has been president of the Center of Science and Industry (COSI), a museum in Columbus, Ohio. ◆

# Taussig, Helen

May 24, 1898–May 21, 1986 ● Pediatric Cardiologist

Raised in an academic atmosphere, Helen Taussig was the youngest of four children born to Frank William Taussig, a Harvard economics professor, and Edith Guild, one of Radcliffe College's first female students. Although Taussig was dyslexic, which made reading difficult, she persevered to achieve good grades. Her interest in the sciences may well have been inspired by her mother, who had studied botany and natural sciences. After her mother's death of tuberculosis when Taussig was 11, Taussig grew closer to her father, who taught her the value of compassion and positive thinking.

Taussig spent her summers with the family on Cape Cod and in the academic year attended Cambridge School for Girls. In 1917 a blue-eyed, five-foot, ten-inch tall Taussig entered Radcliffe, where she played on the tennis and basketball teams. In 1919 she transferred to the University of California at Berkeley and graduated in 1921 with a B.A.

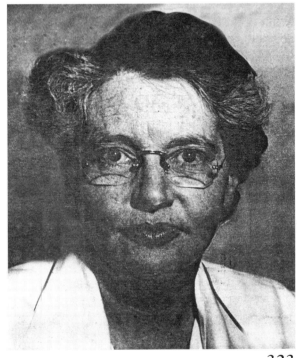

Helen Taussig

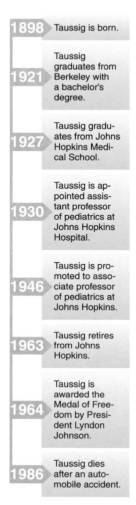

1898  Taussig is born.

1921  Taussig graduates from Berkeley with a bachelor's degree.

1927  Taussig graduates from Johns Hopkins Medical School.

1930  Taussig is appointed assistant professor of pediatrics at Johns Hopkins Hospital.

1946  Taussig is promoted to associate professor of pediatrics at Johns Hopkins.

1963  Taussig retires from Johns Hopkins.

1964  Taussig is awarded the Medal of Freedom by President Lyndon Johnson.

1986  Taussig dies after an automobile accident.

**rheumatic fever:** a disease involving the inflammation of the joints and damage to heart valves preceded by a streptococcal infection.

**pulmonary stenosis:** a defect of heart valves which can either be acquired or congenital.

degree. When she returned to Cambridge her father encouraged her to enter the new public health program being offered at Harvard University. Because Taussig discovered that women were required to have two years of medicine prior to attending and after admittance to the program would not be eligible for degrees, she entered medical school instead.

The medical field was also discriminatory toward women, and Taussig had to receive special permission to attend bacteriology and histology classes at Harvard Medical School, where she sat apart from male students. Her professor recognized her potential and encouraged her to transfer to Boston University, where she could earn one year of credit. At Boston University Medical School, which she attended from 1921 to 1924, her hard work and accurate observations caught the attention of the professor of gross anatomy. Upon his suggestion she enrolled in Johns Hopkins Medical School and graduated with her M.D. in 1927.

Although Taussig lost out on the one medical internship open to women, she was fortuitously awarded a cardiology fellowship. She interned in pediatric cardiology from 1928 until she was appointed assistant professor of pediatrics at the Johns Hopkins Hospital in 1930. The following year Dr. Edward Park named her the physician-in-charge of the Pediatric Cardiac Clinic of the Harriet Lane Home, a division of the hospital.

Infant patients came to the clinic with **rheumatic fever** and an almost always fatal condition called **pulmonary stenosis**. Challenged by Park to learn about this congenital heart problem, Taussig faced another hurdle when she suddenly suffered an almost complete hearing loss, probably due to an attack of whooping cough, in 1930. Her deafness prevented her from using a stethoscope, and thenceforth she listened to tiny heart vibrations through the gentle probe of her hands. With the acquisition of a fluoroscope and electrocardiograph, Taussig was able to see certain patterns and similarities, and she found that because of heart defects very little blood circulated through the baby's lungs, where the blood picked up oxygen. Without the oxygen these babies turned a bluish color, often died or suffered brain damage, and were referred to as "blue babies." Taussig thought that if the blood could be rerouted past the heart's defective area through an artificial passage, the blood would be shunted into the lung.

In 1943 Taussig consulted Alfred Blalock, chairman of the Johns Hopkins Department of Surgery. After conferring, Taussig, Blalock, and his assistant, Vivian Thomas, teamed to devise a surgical procedure to create a ductus arteriosus using a subclavian artery that normally went into the arm. After Thomas tried the bypass on 200 dogs, surgery was successfully performed on a 11-month-old girl on November 29, 1944. More surgeries followed and by 1951, the Blalock-Taussig shunt, as it became known, had been done on 1,037 patients and the mortality rate lessened to under 5 percent.

Taussig was promoted to associate professor of pediatrics at Johns Hopkins in July 1946 and continued studying various anomalies of the heart, especially rheumatic fever. Her research led to *Congenital Malformations of the Heart* (1947), a textbook that became the bible for pediatric cardiologists. New cardiac care centers opened using Blalock-Taussig procedures as a model, and Taussig's success inspired interns to study under her. Throughout the 1950s she taught, researched, and cared for patients. In 1959 she was promoted to a full professor, the first woman at the Johns Hopkins Medical School to hold the position.

In 1962 reports surfaced about infants with severe birth defects born to European women who had used the new drug thalidomide for nausea during pregnancy. Taussig traveled to Germany visiting clinics, questioning mothers and doctors, and seeing infants born without limbs. She reported her findings before a meeting of the American College of Physicians, to the medical community, and in journals. As a result of her investigation, thalidomide was permanently banned for American use.

Taussig retired from Johns Hopkins and the clinic in 1963 but continued to research, write, and commute to the hospital daily. She was the first recipient of the National Foundation of the March of Dimes $40,000 fellowship for scientists, which she used to do a long-term follow-up study of Blalock-Taussig patients. Although Taussig received her first honorary degree from Boston University in 1948, full recognition came slowly. In 1964 President Lyndon B. Johnson presented her with the Medal of Freedom. The following year she was elected the first female president of the American Heart Association, and in 1971 she was made a master of the American College of Physicians. She received more than 20 additional honorary degrees, and her work was published in numerous journals.

Taussig spent her leisure time gardening, reading poetry, and sailing during summers on Cape Cod. Her religious affiliation was with the Unitarian church. After moving to Crosslands, a retirement community near Philadelphia, she studied the deformed hearts of birds to find the initial cause of defects. She died as the result of an automobile accident that occurred as she was driving fellow retirees to the election polls and her car was struck. She died within an hour at Chester County Hospital in Philadelphia.

Taussig never married and once remarked that the only children she ever had were "the thousands I've taken care of." To her small patients she was a friend to whom she devoted all of her emotion, observation, and concern. Watching "blue babies" turn pink, she once explained, gave her gratification because she knew she had helped "a child live a more normal life." Taussig's career in medicine was strewn with obstacles and biases, but each detour led her toward the best direction. Taussig's persistence resulted not only in life-saving surgery but also brought her visions of remedies for other heart deficiencies. ◆

# Taussky-Todd, Olga

AUGUST 30, 1906–OCTOBER 7, 1995 ● MATHEMATICIAN

"In the work of others and in my own I look for beauty, and not only for achievement," Olga Taussky-Todd once said. That's quite a challenge to live up to from what scholars have called one of the world's most accomplished 20th-century female mathematicians. As a woman pioneer in mathematics, Taussky-Todd's kudos include revelations in number and matrix theory, the authoring of close to 300 papers, research and teaching posts at distinctive universities, and a bevy of honors, including the Cross of Honor for Science and Art, the highest recognition granted by her native Austria. Amongst a sea of accomplishment, Taussky-Todd is best known for her influential work in the field of matrix theory, which she used to design airplanes and spacecrafts, although she also made important contributions to algebraic number theory. What is less known about her, however, is that she was an inspirational role model, who made it her personal pledge to mentor young women entering the field.

Olga Taussky was born in Olmutz (now Olomouc), then part of the Austro-Hungarian Empire and today part of the Czech Republic. Just before she turned three, Taussky-Todd and her family moved to Vienna, Austria. Midway through World War I, the family moved again, this time to Linz in upper Austria. Her father, an industrial chemist, was the director of a vinegar factory there, and often asked his daughter to help calculate how much water to add to mixtures of various vinegars to achieve the right acidity. Taussky-Todd's interest in mathematics was piqued. However, at this time Taussky-Todd was more interested in essay writing and poetry—a hobby that would continue throughout her lifetime.

Taussky-Todd claimed high school as the time when her interest turned to science in general and then mathematics specifically. In the book *Mathematical People*, Taussky-Todd recalled the story of a family friend who heard of her desire to study mathematics. "[This woman] was decades older and mentioned that she too had hoped to study mathematics," remembered Taussky-Todd. "That was more than I could take. In a flash, I saw myself decades older saying exactly the same words to a young woman. It seemed unbearable." By the fall of 1925, she enrolled in mathematics at the University of Vienna. and began studying under the famous German number theorist Philip Furtwanger.

At the University of Vienna, Taussky-Todd focused on number theory and received her Ph.D. in 1930. Soon afterward, she accepted an invitation from the prestigious Mathematisches Institut in Göttingen, Germany, to help with the publication of the first volume of the collected works of the German number theorist David Hilbert. On its completion, she returned to Vienna and worked with Karl Menger, a leading theorist of the Austrian school of economics. With a fellowship for the academic year 1934–1935, Taussky-Todd traveled to Pennsylvania's Bryn Mawr College, where she worked with the noted German mathematician Emmy Noether, whose recent work had marked her one of the most creative abstract algebraists of modern times. In Noether Taussky-Todd found a mentor and, although imperfect, she further fostered Taussky-Todd's love of mathematics and provided her with an acute awareness of the need for more talented women in the field.

From 1935 to 1937, Taussky-Todd held a Yarrow Research Fellowship at Girton College in Cambridge, England (part of Cambridge University), where she was awarded an honorary master's degree in 1937. She then taught at the University of London, where in 1938 she met her husband, fellow mathematician John Todd.

**1906** Taussky-Todd is born in Olmütz in the former Austro-Hungarian Empire.

**1930** Taussky-Todd receives her Ph.D. from the University of Vienna.

**1938** Taussky-Todd begins teaching at the University of London.

**1947** Taussky-Todd assumes a research post with the National Bureau of Standards.

**1957** Taussky-Todd accepts a position as a research associate at California Institute of Technology.

**1971** Taussky-Todd is named a professor at Caltech.

**1995** Taussky-Todd dies in Pasadena, California.

Although Taussky's main interest was initially number theory, she was to become what she later termed "a torchbearer" for the branch of mathematics known as matrix theory—a field that didn't exist in the 1930s. A matrix is a rectangular array of symbols, usually numbers, neatly arranged in columns and rows. Matrices play important roles in algebra, differential equations, probability and statistics, and many other fields, including engineering. "Still, matrix theory reached me only slowly," Taussky declared in a 1988 article in the *American Mathematical Monthly*. "Since my main subject was number theory, I did not look for matrix theory. It somehow looked for me."

That bonding arose during World War II, when Taussky was employed by the British Ministry of Aircraft Production at the National Physical Laboratory. From 1943 to 1946, she worked with a group investigating an aerodynamic phenomenon called flutter, and soon she was solving the differential equations necessary to obtain relevant information about an aircraft's vibrations. After her results were published in 1949, she was recognized by scholars as one who helped popularize the Gershgorin circle theorem.

The Todds moved to the United States in 1947, where they became researchers at the National Bureau of Standards; for her work there, Taussky-Todd has been described as a "computer pioneer." Taking advantage of the onrushing computer revolution, the Todds established the new matrix theory as an autonomous field. They remained at the NBS until 1957, when they accepted positions at the California Institute of Technology in Pasadena, California. Taussky-Todd was promoted to professorship in 1971, and recognized across the United States for her work in inertia theorems. With these accomplishments, she became the first woman to teach at Caltech under a formal appointment and the first woman named to full professor at that school.

Taussky-Todd was the recipient of the Ford Prize of the Mathematical Association of America, a member of the Austrian and Bavarian Academies of Science, and a Fellow of the American Association for the Advancement of Science. Additionally, she was a founding editor of the journal *Linear Algebra and Its Applications*, as well as one of its editors. In 1963, Taussky-Todd received the *Los Angeles Times* Woman of the Year Award. In 1965, she held a Fulbright Professorship at the University of Vienna. She was awarded an honorary doctorate of science by the University of Southern California in 1988. Taussky-Todd died in Pasadena in 1995. ◆

# Tereshkova, Valentina

MARCH 6, 1937– ● ASTRONAUT

Valentina Tereshkova was the first woman in space. On June 16, 1963, the 26-year-old Tereshkova was launched into orbit aboard Vostok 6 and in the next three days circled the Earth 48 times, more than the six American astronauts combined.

During her flight Tereshkova, using the call sign *Chaika* (Seagull), made television broadcasts to viewers in the Soviet Union, and also maintained regular radio contact with fellow cosmonaut Valery Bykovsky, whose Vostok 5 spacecraft was in orbit at the same time. The two spacecraft once passed within three miles of each other, and both returned to Earth on June 19, 1963.

Famed as a heroine of the women's movement in Soviet society, Tereshkova eventually went on to a career in politics. She married cosmonaut Andrian Nikolayev in a lavish state wedding in November 1963, in which Soviet leader Nikita Khrushchev gave away the bride. (Tereshkova and Nikolayev were divorced in 1982.)

Tereshkova was born March 6, 1937, in the village of Masslenikovo, Yaroslavl Region of Russia. At the age of 18 she joined her mother and sister, who had jobs at the Red Canal textile mill. While working at the mill Tereshkova took a correspondence course from an industrial school and, more significantly, joined a club for parachutists, eventually making over 120 jumps.

In September 1961, shortly after the flight of cosmonaut Gherman Titov, Tereshkova, like hundreds of other young Soviet men and women, wrote a letter to the space center asking to join the cosmonaut team. Unknown to her, cosmonaut training chief Nikolai Kamanin, had begun to consider the selection of a group of women parachutists for cosmonaut training.

Valentina Tereshkova

1937 Tereshkova is born in Maslenikovo, Russa.

1961 Tereshkova is selected for cosmonaut training.

1963 Tereshkova pilots *Vostok 6* and orbits the Earth 48 times.

1963 Tereshkova marries cosmonaut Andrian Nikolayev.

1969 Tereshkova graduates from the Zhukovsky Air Force Engineering Academy.

1976 Tereshkova earns a candidate of technical sciences degree.

1997 Tereshkova retires from the cosmonaut program.

Invited to Moscow for an interview and medical examinations in December 1961. Tereshkova passed, and in March reported with four other women to the training center. Valentina's mother and sister were told she had been selected for a special skydiving team.

Most cosmonaut memoirs claim that the women were welcomed "like brothers" by the pilots, but other sources state that some of the men were not pleased by the new recruits, who apparently had little or no flying experience. Years later Tereshkova confided to an American in the Apollo-Soyuz project that the other cosmonauts avoided her "because I have invaded their little playground and because I am a woman."

Nevertheless, Tereshkova and the others were subjected to the same centrifuge rides and zero-G flights as the male cosmonauts. Because the Soviet air force was still jealously guarding its role as sole provider of cosmonauts, the women were also enlisted as privates in the Soviet air force. (They were later commissioned as junior lieutenants.)

One of the women, Valentina Ponomareva, was a pilot, but Tereshkova and the others were not, so they were given basic flight training.

In the spring of 1963 Tereshkova, Ponomareva and Irina Solovyova were chosen to train specifically for the Vostok 6 flight.

Sergei Korolev's deputy, Vasily Mishin, claimed years later that the final choice concerning which of the women would fly in space was made by Krushchev himself, who glanced over their biographies and chose the one—Tereshkova—from a worker's family.

The flight itself seems to have disappointed Korolev, who felt that Tereshkova hadn't completed her schedule of experiments. She had further worried ground controllers by falling asleep so soundly she could not be wakened. Nevertheless, Vostok 6 was successful enough that its scheduled single-day duration was extended after launch.

In the years following Vostok 6, Tereshkova made many public appearances and trips to other countries. She and Nikolayev had a daugther, Yelena. Tereshkova and the other women cosmonauts attended the Zhukovsky Air Force Engineering Academy, graduating in 1969.

In 1965 and 1966 some of the women cosmonauts trained for a possible Voskhod and later a Soyuz flight, but neither plan received final approval. The group was disbanded in October 1969 and new women cosmonauts were not selected again until 1980. Tereshkova later earned a candidate of technical sciences degree (1976) and was eventually promoted to the rank of major-general, retiring in March 1997.

Tereshkova joined the Communist Party in 1962. She became a member of the Supreme Soviet in 1966 and, in 1974, a member of the Central Committee. She was elected to the Congress of People's Deputies in April 1989. Once the Soviet Union fell, Tereshkova lost her standing in the government, and is presumed to be retired and living in Moscow.

She has been the subject of two biographies, *This is "Seagull!"* by Mitchell Sharpe (1975) and *Valentina: First Woman in Space*, by Antonella Lothian (1993). ◆

# Thornton, Kathryn

AUGUST 17, 1952– ● PHYSICIST AND ASTRONAUT

Kathryn Thornton holds the record for space-walking by a woman astronaut. With fellow mission specialist Tom Akers, she made two seven-hour EVAs during the first Hubble Space Telescope repair mission in December 1993.

Earlier, in May 1992, she and Akers tested space station construction techniques and EVA rescue procedures aboard the orbiter Endeavour during STS-49. Thornton's seven-hour, 45-minute EVA was longer than the combined duration of the two previous woman space-walkers, Kathryn Sullivan and Svetlana Savitskaya. Earlier in the mission she took part in the successful retrieval and redeployment of the errant Intelsat VI communications satellite.

STS-49 was Thornton's second flight. In November and December 1989 she was a mission specialist aboard STS-33, a flight of the orbiter Discovery during which the National Security Agency electronic intelligence satellite Mentor was deployed into geosynchronous orbit. Thornton and fellow mission specialist Story Musgrave also conducted a number of experiments in space medicine during the five-day mission.

Thornton made her fourth flight as payload commander for STS-73. This October-November 1995 flight of the orbiter Columbia carried a crew of seven and the second U.S. Microgravity Laboratory.

Thornton was born Kathryn Cordell Ryan on August 17, 1952, in Montgomery, Alabama, where she grew up, graduating

Kathryn Thornton

from Sidney Lanier High School there in 1970. She attended Auburn University, receiving a B.S. in physics in 1974, and earned her M.S. (1977) and Ph.D. (1979) in physics from the University of Virginia.

While a graduate student at Virginia, Thornton took part in nuclear research programs at Oak Ridge National Laboratory, Brookhaven National Laboratory, the Indiana University Cyclotron Facility, and the Space Radiation Effects Laboratory. In 1979 she was awarded a NATO post-doctoral fellowship which enabled her to study at the Max Planck Institute for Nuclear Physics in Heidelberg, West Germany. Returning to the United States in 1980, she went to work at the Army Foreign Science and Technology Center in Charlottesville, Virginia.

Thornton was one of the 17 astronaut candidates selected by NASA in May 1984. In July 1985 she qualified as a Shuttle mission specialist. Among her technical assignments was serving on an escape test crew, working in SAIL, and serving as capcom for several 1990 Shuttle missions.

She resigned from NASA in May 1996 to return to her alma mater, the University of Virginia, as professor of mechanical and aerospace engineering. ◆

# Uhlenbeck, Karen

AUGUST 24, 1942– ● MATHEMATICIAN

"Whenever I get a free week and start doing mathematics, I can't believe how much fun it is. I'm like a 12-year-old boy with a new train set," Karen Uhlenbeck told *Alcalde Magazine*. Although she may have the excitement of a 12-year-old, the calling to mathematics did not come to Uhlenbeck until much later in life—which both scholars and students find hard to believe given Uhlenbeck's string of back-to-back accomplishments. Uhlenbeck is engaged in mathematical research that has applications in theoretical physics and has contributed to the study of instantons, models for the behavior of surfaces in four dimensions— fancy wording for a mathematician who has helped provide understanding of the fundamental properties of matter in the universe. As one of a handful of mathematicians who is considered an expert in theoretical physics, Uhlenbeck is sensitive to the low number of women in her field, and considers herself an advocate of women in mathematics.

Karen Keskulla Uhlenbeck was born in Cleveland, Ohio, in 1942. When Uhlenbeck was in third grade, her family moved to New Jersey. Lots of subjects interested her as a child, but she felt that girls were discouraged from exploring many activities. In high school, she read the American physicist George Gamow's books and the English astronomer Fred Hoyle's books on astrophysics. "I'd go to the library and then stay up all night reading. I used to read under the desk in school," Uhlenbeck recalled.

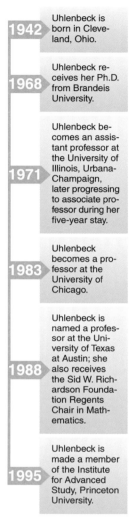

Her passion for physics ignited by Gamow, Uhlenbeck entered the University of Michigan with the intention of studying the subject, and only later changed her major to mathematics.

She received her bachelor's degree in mathematics in 1964. She then spent a year studying math at the prestigious Court Institute in New York. She married the biophysicist Olke Cornelis Uhlenbeck in 1965 and then pursued graduate study in mathematics at Brandeis University under a National Science Foundation fellowship. Uhlenbeck received her Ph.D. in mathematics from Brandeis in 1968, and then began her first teaching position at the Massachusetts Institute of Technology. The following year she moved to Berkeley, California, where she was a lecturer in mathematics at the University of California from 1969 to 1971. There she studied general relativity and the geometry of space-time.

Despite her track record, Uhlenbeck struggled to secure a permanent position. "I was told, when looking for jobs after my year at MIT and two years at Berkeley, that people did not hire women, that women were supposed to go home and have babies. So the places interested in my husband—MIT, Stanford, and Princeton—were not interested in hiring me," she revealed candidly in a 1996 interview. A 1992 *Science* magazine article concurs with Uhlenbeck's observation. At that time, there were 300 tenured men—and only two women—at the top 10 math departments in the United States. The article maintains that part of the problem clearly lies in the larger culture, where math is not considered feminine. It acknowledges Uhlenbeck, the only female mathematician in the National Academy of Sciences, who said she is "always aware that I was brought up to do something different than I'm doing now."

In 1971, Uhlenbeck became an assistant professor at the University of Illinois at Urbana-Champaign, where she and her husband were hired. In 1974, she was awarded a Sloan Fellowship that lasted until 1976, enough time to reassess her life and develop mentoring relationships, most notably with the gauge theory analyst Lesley Sibner. Recently divorced, Uhlenbeck moved to Chicago, where she enjoyed a brief stint at Northwestern University as a visiting associate professor. She then settled for a time at the University of Illinois at Chicago from 1977 to 1983, first as associate professor and then professor. In 1979 she returned to Berkeley—this time as a Chancellor's Distinguished Visiting Professor. She also enjoyed a brief fellowship at Princeton University during this time.

A breakthrough came for Uhlenbeck in 1983 when, fresh from a visiting professorship at Harvard, she received her professorship at Chicago and was awarded the prestigious MacArthur Fellowship, which supported her work for five years and allowed her to begin serious studies in physics. Although her research focused on differential equations, she was drawn to Maxwell's equations for electromagnetism. By clarifying the complex interrelationships of curved spaces in four dimensions (length, height, width , and time), with new equations that described the fundamental subatomic particles, Uhlenbeck was credited with expanding Albert Einstein's theory of relativity.

Although Uhlenbeck's work is difficult to describe (admitting herself that "mathematicians do exotic research"), her mathematical interests include a rich blend of differential geometry, gauge theory, the calculus of variations, integrable systems, and duality in physics (geometry generated by physical theories). She views her role as mathematician as one who abstracts complex ideas for simplified use in a variety of areas, including economics and physics. In recognition of her contributions, she was elected to the American Academy of Arts and Sciences in 1985 and to the National Academy of Sciences in 1986.

In 1987, Uhlenbeck went to the University of Texas at Austin as visiting professor, where she broadened her understanding of physics by studying with the American physicist Steven Weinberg. In 1988, she received the Alumni Achievement award from Brandeis University and an honorary doctor of science degree from Knox College. That same year, she was also made a professor at Texas and awarded a Sid W. Richardson Foundation Regents Chair in Mathematics.

Concerned that students were being discouraged because of their sex, Uhlenbeck joined a National Research Council planning group to investigate the representation of women in science. She also spearheaded a mentoring program for women in mathematics, and was one of the founders of the Institute for Advanced Study at Park City Mathematics Institute. "It's hard to be a role model, however, because what you really need to do is show students how imperfect people can be and still succeed," Uhlenbeck penned in a personal essay. She believes mathematics should be fun and challenging, and strives to communicate this to her students. Deemed by her colleagues as "the most eminent mathematician alive today," Uhlenbeck continues to teach at the University of Texas. ◆

"I sometimes feel the need to apologize for being a mathematician, but no apology is needed."
Karen Uhlenbeck, on her chosen profession, *Alcade* magazine, 1988

# Waelsch, Salome

OCTOBER 6, 1907– ● BIOLOGIST AND GENETICIST

If you spoke with Salome Waelsch, the 93-year-old **geneticist** would say that throughout her professional career, she has had to combat three prejudices: being Jewish, a woman, and a scientist—all in an era when women did not pursue such lofty ambitions as advanced degrees and university posts. For more than 50 years, Waelsch has studied the role of genes in the early stages of development and cellular differentiation, research that is important to the treatment of congenital diseases. In addition, she takes her place in history among women "firsts," having taught the first course in medical genetics in the United States.

Born Salome Gluecksohn in Danzig, Germany, in 1907, Waelsch spent her early years being educated in public schools. The death of her father to the flu epidemic of 1918 and the loss of the family's estate following World War I forever left impressions on Waelsch. Despite her success academically, Waelsch didn't grow up with the intention of being a scientist; instead she "just slipped into it" as a college student, then never looked back.

Determined to get a college education, Waelsch attended the universities of Königsberg, Berlin, and Freiburg, with a strong desire to major in classical languages. Her interest in biology arose as the result of a friend's offhanded suggestion that she take a course in it. "That was the beginning," she said in 1993. "I found my love." Eventually Waelsch entered a doctoral program in genetics at Freiburg, where she studied under the mentorship of the eminent German geneticist Hans Spemann,

**geneticist:** a scientist who studies genetics and the functions of genes in humans and animals.

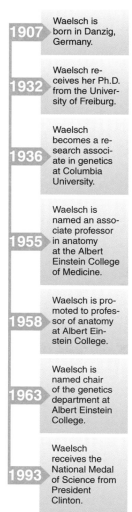

and received her Ph.D. in zoology in 1932. In retrospect, Waelsch counts her training with the 1935 Nobel Prize winner as a mixed blessing, as Spemann was philosophically opposed to the work of American geneticists, and thus restricted his students from investigating questions that combined both embryological and genetic techniques.

"The narrowness of mind expressed ... both on the intellectual and scientific level surprised me greatly," Waelsch said in a paper she gave at the Conference on Embryonic Origins in Yugoslavia in 1986. Waelsch would have to engage in later research before answering those questions herself.

Although she graduated with honors, Waelsch's job opportunities were slim. As mentioned in the introduction of the book, *The Outer Circle: Women in the Scientific Community*, although women scientists in the early part of the 20th century managed to break through many of the barriers excluding them from graduate education in science, they did not succeed in gaining access to the research and faculty positions that were almost entirely granted to men. In that same book, Waelsch remembered that in 1932, one prospective employer said to her: "You, a woman and a Jew, forget it." However, that same year she obtained an appointment as a research assistant in cell biology at the University of Berlin.

Perhaps the most important event that occurred during her one-year tenure at Berlin was her marriage to the biochemist Rudolf Schoenheimer. Together, they emigrated to the United States in 1933 after the Nazi dictator Adolf Hitler ordered universities to fire Jews. Schoenheimer was offered a position at Columbia University's College of Physicians and Surgeons in New York City. His equally qualified wife received no similar offer, however, although she was granted permission three years later to work in the lab of the famous geneticist Leslie Dunn, without pay. "Imagine, I felt grateful to work for nothing," she said. As a research associate in 1936, she began her lifetime pursuit of studying how specific genes in an organism affect the development and differentiation of various body parts within the embryo.

Rudolf Schoenheimer died in 1941, and a little more than a year later, in 1943, Salome married a second time, to the biochemist Heinrich B. Waelsch. The couple had two children; Waelsch was widowed again in 1966. Balancing her personal and professional life made Waelsch one of the first women scientists in the United States to have both a career and a family.

In 1953, after working with Dunn for 17 years and "deprived ... of any chance of a career," Waelsch decided that it was time to move on. "I simply did not see why I couldn't get an assistant professorship when I was doing everything an assistant professor did, but when I asked the chairman for such an appointment, he just said, 'What? You, a woman,'" she told the *New York Times* in 1993. Despite such overt prejudice and limited prospects, Waelsch began to look for a job. On the recommendation of a colleague, Waelsch landed a research associate position in Obstetrics and Gynecology at the College of Physicians and Surgeons at Columbia University, a job she would hold for two years. Although this was a worthy career move, Waelsch's major professional break came in 1955 with the founding of the Albert Einstein College of Medicine in New York City, where she was offered the post of associate professor of anatomy, a position she held until 1958, when she was promoted to full professor. During this period Waelsch taught new courses in medical genetics. In 1963 her title was changed to professor of genetics and she was made chair of the department of genetics. In 1988 she was named professor emerita, and continued her research into the early 1990s.

Waelsch commented on the future of women in science. "There are more opportunities," she said in 1993, "but it is still harder for women than for men.... After all, the burden of balancing career and family life always is greater for women." Since 1979, Waelsch has been a member of the National Academy of Sciences, and a fellow of the American Academy of Arts and Sciences since 1980. She has been bestowed the prestigious National Medal of Science, which President William Clinton awarded Waelsch in 1993, and the Genetics Society of America's Thomas Hunt Morgan Medal, which she received in 1999. Despite many obstacles, Waelsch emerged as a model of perseverance and success. ◆

> Waelsch's major professional break came in 1955 with the founding of the Albert Einstein College of Medicine in New York City.

# Walker, Mary Edwards

### November 16, 1832–February 21, 1919 ● Physician

A physician and women's rights advocate, Mary Edwards Walker was born on November 16, 1832 in Oswego, New York. She was the youngest of the five daughters of Alvah Walker, a physician, educator, and farmer, and Vesta

Mary Edwards Walker

Whitcomb, a teacher and cousin of agnostic lecturer Robert Ingersoll. Alvah and Vesta were among a small minority who believed that women should receive a full education and enter a profession. Alvah also believed that tobacco, liquor, and tight clothing were major health hazards and did not require his daughters to wear corsets at home.

Walker received her early education in a school run by her parents and sisters on the family farm in Oswego. Walker next attended the Falley Seminary in Fulton, New York. She left in 1852 to return to the vicinity of Oswego, where she taught in a village school. Encouraged by her father, she chose to enter the medical profession in defiance of social convention, which held that teaching was the only profession fit for a woman. In 1853 Walker overcame the many barriers placed in her way and entered Syracuse Medical College. She graduated with a physician's certificate in 1855, only six years after another woman became the first to receive a medical degree in the United Stares. Women physicians were still extremely uncommon, and Walker was the only woman in her class.

After graduating, she practiced in Columbus, Ohio, for a few months before establishing a practice in Rome, New York. In 1855 Walker married Albert Miller, a medical student, in an unorthodox Unitarian ceremony in which she did not wear a wedding dress and omitted the promise to obey from her vows. She kept her maiden name. They separated in 1859 after he admitted to being unfaithful, and she won a New York divorce in 1869 on grounds of adultery.

Meanwhile, during the 1850s Walker became an outspoken advocate of dress reform. Like her father, she believed that tight-fitting clothes were a very dangerous health hazard because they restricted the body's physical processes. She advocated Amelia Bloomer's recommended dress for women as soon as Bloomer's costume appeared in 1850; it consisted of a short skirt over wide pantaloons. In 1857 she became a writer for the newspaper *Sibyl,* a dress reform publication edited by Lydia Sayer Hasbrouck, and attended a dress-reform convention that year. She also began advocating other women's causes, denouncing anti-abortion laws and backing equal pay for men and women.

Walker faced many obstacles in the practice of medicine. Women were considered too frail and naive to learn about the workings of the human body and too prone to hysteria to cope with the unpleasant aspects of a physician's work. Therefore, Walker had only a few patients, and they expected her to set lower fees than male physicians. Therefore, when the outbreak of the Civil War in 1861 created a demand for physicians for the Union Army, Walker immediately journeyed to Washington, D.C., to apply for a commission as an army surgeon. She was turned down then and several additional times; no woman had ever served as an army officer, and the surgeon general was reluctant to break that tradition.

Walker served as a nurse first in the Patent Office in Washington in 1862. In the fall of 1862 she became an unofficial doctor in Virginia field hospitals. In September 1863 Walker moved on to Tennessee, where, despite objections, she became assistant surgeon to the 52nd Ohio infantry. Walker not only treated Union soldiers, but sometimes crossed Confederate lines to help civilians. In April 1864 she took a wrong turn and was arrested by the Confederates. Walker spent four months in jail and then was traded "man for man," as she later expressed it.

In October 1864 Walker was finally was granted a commission as an assistant U.S. Army surgeon, the first woman to

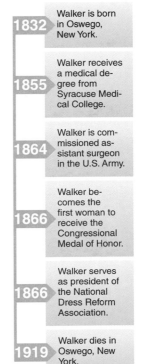

1832 — Walker is born in Oswego, New York.

1855 — Walker receives a medical degree from Syracuse Medical College.

1864 — Walker is commissioned assistant surgeon in the U.S. Army.

1866 — Walker becomes the first woman to receive the Congressional Medal of Honor.

1866 — Walker serves as president of the National Dress Reform Association.

1919 — Walker dies in Oswego, New York.

receive one (although she was not given an officer's commission). She was assigned to take charge of the women's prison hospital in Louisville, Kentucky, and next headed an orphanage in Clarksville, Tennessee. Walker left army service early in 1865. In January 1866 she received from President Andrew Johnson the Congressional Medal of Honor upon the recommendation of Generals George H. Thomas and William T. Sherman. Walker was the first woman to be given the medal.

Immediately after the war, Walker worked for a short time as a journalist in New York City and then attempted to establish a medical practice in Washington. Not much later, she virtually abandoned medicine and devoted most of her time to social reform. Arrested in New York City for dressing like a man, Walker won a court case that put an end to arrests of women in the city for that reason.

In 1866 Walker served as president of the National Dress Reform Association. Soon afterward she teamed up with Washington lawyer Belva Ann Lockwood to fight for women's rights, and especially women's suffrage. Walker became very influential in the suffrage movement, sharing platforms with leading advocates like Susan B. Anthony and Lucy Stone. However, she divided the movement by arguing that the Constitution already granted women the ballot, and that therefore constitutional amendments to give them the vote should be opposed. In addition, her pursuit of dress reform for women, which she considered even more important that obtaining the vote, alienated many suffragists. In the last decades of the 19th century, Walker's influence declined sharply. She wrote two books: *Hit* (1871), which is partly autobiographical, and *Unmasked, or the Science of Immortality* (1878), which reflects her belief in spiritualism, or psychic phenomena.

In 1917 Walker suffered a heavy personal blow when the army's Adverse Action of Honor Board took away her Medal of Honor on the grounds that her relationship with the army was unclear. She continued wearing the medal, although she was informed that it was a crime to do so. During one of her visits to Washington to have the medal restored, Walker fell on the Capitol steps and injured herself seriously. Without ever fully recuperating, she died in Oswego, New York, on February 21, 1919. In 1977 Walker's Medal of Honor was posthumously restored by the Army Board for the Correction of Military Records. ◆

# Wheeler, Anna Pell

MAY 5, 1883–MARCH 26, 1966 ● ALGEBRAIST

Anna Pell Wheeler, who was the daughter of Swedish immigrants who came to the United States about 10 years before she was born, was one of history's best-known 20th-century research mathematicians; her specialty was linear algebra of infinitely many variables, a branch of mathematics now called functional analysis. Despite her many achievements as a researcher, teacher, and administrator, perhaps the greatest distinction she received was becoming the first woman to give the Colloquium Lectures at the American Mathematical Society meetings in 1927—the only woman who would do so until 1980.

Born Anna Johnson in Hawarden, Iowa, in 1883, the shy Midwesterner grew up in Akron, Iowa, where her family moved when she was nine. Little is known of her early childhood, except that she attended public school in Akron. In 1899, she enrolled in the University of South Dakota, where she showed great promise in mathematics. The professor of mathematics, Alexander Pell, recognized her talents and encouraged her to continue in her studies. She received her bachelor's degree in 1903 and went on to earn two master's degrees: one from the University of Iowa in 1904, and another from Radcliffe College in 1905, where she studied under the mathematician Maxime Bôcher.

Pell Wheeler then won a Wellesley Fellowship to study at the respected University of Göttingen, in Germany, in 1906 and 1907. There she attended the lectures of some of the greatest mathematical minds in Europe, including the renowned German number theorist David Hilbert, and Hermann Minkowski, who is credited with laying the mathematical foundation for the theory of relativity. Under Hilbert's mentorship, Pell Wheeler's research turned toward integral equations while studying infinite dimensional linear spaces. Her former professor, Alexander Pell, met Pell Wheeler in Germany in 1907, and the two were married.

When Pell Wheeler received her Ph.D. in mathematics from the University of Chicago in 1910, she was the second woman in the history of the school to claim such an accomplishment. However, finding a full-time teaching position was

> **"Don't believe anything unless you have thought it through for yourself."**
>
> Anna Pell Wheeler's admonition to her students

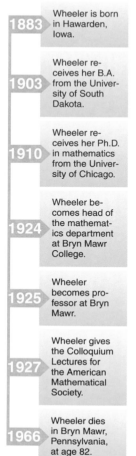

**1883** Wheeler is born in Hawarden, Iowa.

**1903** Wheeler receives her B.A. from the University of South Dakota.

**1910** Wheeler receives her Ph.D. in mathematics from the University of Chicago.

**1924** Wheeler becomes head of the mathematics department at Bryn Mawr College.

**1925** Wheeler becomes professor at Bryn Mawr.

**1927** Wheeler gives the Colloquium Lectures for the American Mathematical Society.

**1966** Wheeler dies in Bryn Mawr, Pennsylvania, at age 82.

another task entirely. As she said to a friend, "There is such an objection to women that they [the universities] prefer a man even if he is inferior both in training and research." Her breakthrough came when she substituted for her husband, who had suffered from a stroke, at the Armour Institute of Technology in Chicago, where she proved her competency. Although she wasn't offered a position at Armour, she was hired as an instructor in mathematics at Mount Holyoke College in Hadley, Massachusetts, in 1911. She was promoted to associate professor in 1914, and remained at the school until 1918.

Her next move was to the small women's college, Bryn Mawr, in Pennsylvania, where she took a position as an associate professor in 1918. Her husband, who was 25 years her senior, died in 1920. In 1924, Pell Wheeler became chair of the mathematics department, becoming a full professor in 1925. That same year she married Arthur Leslie Wheeler, a classics scholar who had just become professor of Latin at Princeton University in New Jersey. She moved to Princeton to be with him, while teaching part-time at Bryn Mawr until his death in 1932. She then returned to Bryn Mawr full-time until her retirement in 1948.

A maverick in the field of mathematics, Pell Wheeler urged her students to persevere toward their doctorates, even though women still weren't recognized as equal to their male counterparts in academia. During her tenure at Bryn Mawr College, seven of her graduate students received doctorates in mathematics. And it's no accident that, in 1940, she received recognition from the Women's Centennial Congress as one of the 100 women who had succeeded in nontraditional careers. Pell Wheeler was also instrumental to mathematician Emmy Noether's relocation to Bryn Mawr as a visiting professor in 1933 after she fled Nazi Germany. The two women became great friends, as Pell Wheeler was sympathetic toward Noether's struggle to establish a career in mathematics as a woman in Germany, and the rejection she experienced after being uprooted from her homeland.

Pell Wheeler's work at Bryn Mawr took her beyond mentoring her students. Recognizing the need to strengthen the reputation of the school's mathematics department, Pell Wheeler suggested reducing teaching loads so that more research could be carried out by the faculty and also encouraged professional exchanges with other Philadelphia schools. During this time of increasing administrative responsibilities, Pell Wheeler remained active in publishing the results of her research in integral equations and functional analysis. However, her Colloquium Lectures were never published. Ever active, Pell Wheeler served on the council and the board of the American Mathematical Society and was also a member of the Mathematical Association of America and the American Association for the Advancement of Science. She died in Bryn Mawr in 1966 after suffering a stroke. ◆

# Wong-Staal, Flossie

AUGUST 27, 1946– ● GENETICIST AND AIDS RESEARCHER

The word HIV (human immunodeficiency virus) and its final stage of infection, AIDS, cannot be mentioned apart from one of its leading researchers, the celebrated geneticist Flossie Wong-Staal. In 1984, she became the first scientist to clone the HIV virus and work out its molecular structure. As a result, Wong-Staal is an internationally recognized leader in virology and professor at the University of California at San Diego (UCSD), where she heads her own lab and holds the Florence Riford Chair in AIDS Research. In 1990, Wong-Staal was hailed as one of the top woman scientists of the 1980s and the fourth-ranking scientist under age 45 by the Institute for Scientific Information.

Flossie Wong-Staal was born Yee-ching Wong in mainland China in 1946. The Wong family moved to Hong Kong in 1952, shortly after the Chinese government fell under communist rule. At the request of the nuns who taught at Wong's elementary school, her father renamed her Flossie after the typhoon that had just swept the city.

"I never planned on becoming a scientist when I was young," Wong-Staal revealed. In fact, no woman in her family had ever worked outside the home or been interested in science. "I did not really have a role model in my family when I was growing up.... However, my parents did take pride in me when I did well in school and encouraged me to pursue an academic career. Surprisingly my being female was not an issue

> "If I had to advise young people going into science, I think that would be my major selling point, the excitement it generates."
>
> Flossie Wong-Staal, in the UCSD School of Medicine *Catalog*

**1946** Wong-Staal is born in Canton, China.

**1965** Wong-Staal immigrates to the United States and begins her studies at UCLA.

**1972** Wong-Staal receives her Ph.D. in molecular biology from UCLA.

**1973** Wong-Staal begins work at the National Cancer Institute in Bethesda, Maryland.

**1984** Wong-Staal clones HIV genes.

**1990** Wong-Staal moves to the University of California at San Diego to hold the Florence Riford Chair in AIDS Research.

**1994** Wong-Staal is named director of the Center for AIDS Research at UCSD.

with them," Wong-Stall told an interviewer. Indeed, the Hong Kong school system recognized young Wong's talents and steered her toward science. Although the subject was "chosen" for her, in high school Wong's interests turned toward biology.

To attend college, she immigrated to the United States in 1965 and majored in molecular biology (the structure and function of the chemicals in living organisms) at the University of California at Los Angeles (UCLA). She graduated in 1969 and continued on to graduate studies, during which she became a research assistant in bacteriology (the study of bacteria). While working toward her Ph.D., she married Steven Staal, a medical student at UCLA. Wong-Staal earned her Ph.D. in 1972, and then held a fellowship at UCSD Medical Center from 1972 to 1973. Although she and her husband were later divorced, Wong-Staal kept her married name.

In 1973, Wong-Staal and her husband accepted research positions at the National Institutes of Health, a group of research facilities in Bethesda, Maryland. It was during her tenure at the National Cancer Institute that Wong-Staal established a name for herself and accomplished an historical milestone. Working in the laboratory of Robert Gallo, one of the few researchers investigating the possibility that viruses could cause cancer in humans, she was a part of the team that discovered the T-cell (a type of immune system cell) leukemia virus. These studies were among the first to analyze the biochemical aspects of human retroviruses, the mysterious family of viruses that in 1983 would turn out to include HIV.

In 1994, after Gallo's laboratory was credited with the co-discovery of HIV (which they shared with scientists in France's Pasteur Institute) Wong-Staal cloned the virus's genes and worked out the chemical sequence of each gene and its function. "I think it's exciting to be part of a discovery, to know you're finding out things that have never been known before," she said in the 1999–2000 UCSD School of Medicine Catalog.

In 1990, Wong-Staal left the National Cancer Institute for UCSD to become a professor of medicine and biology and hold the Florence Riford Chair in AIDS Research. With a grant from the National Institutes of Health, the Center for AIDS Research was established in 1994 with Dr. Wong-Staal as its director. Wong-Staal was elected to the Institute of Medicine that same year.

Her current efforts include finding a vaccine and a cure for HIV infection. Because of the urgency of the AIDS epidemic

**Advancement of Women in Science, Engineering, and Technology Act**

In 1998 the Science Committee of the House of Representatives gave unanimous approval to H.R. 3007, a bill calling for the creation of a Commission on the Advancement of Women in Science, Engineering, and Technology. Supporters of this commission pointed to the fact that women continued to be underrepresented in these fields (22 percent of the total science workforce and just 10 percent of engineers), and hoped that the commission could look at the barriers women face and at programs that could be (and have been) effective in bringing more women into these traditionally male-dominated fields. The bill was sponsored by Congresswoman Connie Morella (R–MD). Representatives of several prominent scientific groups testified or wrote in favor of the bill, including Monica Moman-Saunders of the American Society of Mechanical Engineers and Catherine Jay Didion of the Association for Women in Science. Such supporters noted that in a time of low unemployment, the need for qualified scientists was great, and would only increase in the coming years with the explosion of the Internet and information technology. Women, who make up over half of the overall workforce, would have to be trained in science in greater numbers to meet this high demand for skilled labor. In addition to gathering data and receiving input from researchers, this committee would work with the National Science Foundation to issue a policy recommendation to Congress on how best to address the gender gap in the sciences. The committee would be terminated after this reporting was completing.

At the time of its passage, the bill had acquired a somewhat broader mission, and was titled the Advancement of Women, Minorities, and the Disabled in Science, Engineering, and Technology Development Act. The U.S. Senate passed the bill without objection in October, 1998, and President William Clinton signed it into law immediately.

and the elusive nature of the virus, her approach is multifaceted. In the early 1990s, Wong-Staal took the charge of leading her research team in gene therapy as a way to combat AIDS. Confident of this new therapy, she said in 1996, "It's no longer whether something will happen or not—it's more a matter of how long it will take." She and collaborators at the University of Northern Illinois have developed a therapeutic gene called a ribozyme, which produces an enzyme that recognizes HIV's genetic material and destroys it. Her team began to introduce the ribozyme into the patient's bone marrow cells and trigger long-term resistance to HIV infection. This approach is one of the most promising weapons developed to fight HIV, and the second treatment the U.S. government has approved for testing in AIDS patients. With such determination, it's clear that Wong-Staal will brand the 21st century with her reputation as a leading fighter of HIV and AIDS. ◆

# Wright, Jane Cooke

NOVEMBER 20, 1919– ● PHYSICIAN AND CANCER RESEARCHER

Jane Cooke Wright is a descendent of an American medical legacy that includes the first African American graduate of Yale Medical School, the first black president of Meharry Medical College, and, in her father, Louis Wright, one of the first black graduates of Harvard Medical School and the first African American physician to be appointed on staff at a New York City hospital.

Wright was born in New York City on November 20, 1919. She was educated in private schools and earned a full academic scholarship to Smith College. Upon her graduation in 1942, Wright enrolled in New York Medical College and received her medical degree in 1945. This accomplishment was followed by an internship and residency at the Bellevue Hospital in New York City, then a two-year residency at Harlem Hospital, where Wright specialized in internal medicine. In 1947, Wright married David Jones, Jr., and the couple have two daughters. She stayed on at Harlem Hospital as a school and visiting physician, and later became a clinician at the hospital's cancer foundation. Wright focused her research on tumor response and growth to the application of chemotherapy and other drugs. Her outstanding work in her research led to her succeeding her father as the foundation's director upon his death in 1952.

Three years later, Wright was named director of the cancer chemotherapy research department at the New York University Medical Center, where she also taught research surgery. Wright continued to explore the effects of chemotherapy on animals and humans. In 1961, Wright was named an adjunct professor at the Medical Center and was named vice president of the African Research Foundation, a position whose duties took her on a

Jane Cooke Wright

mission to East Africa. President Lyndon Johnson appointed Wright to a national commission on heart disease, cancer, and stroke; the commission's findings resulted in a new national network of treatment centers for the diseases.

Wright's academic career continued to flourish, as she was named associate dean and professor of surgery at New York Medical College in 1967. Wright has won numerous awards and honors over the years which have recognized the importance and significance of her research. Wright continues her academic work and research as emerita professor of surgery at New York Medical College, a post she has held since 1987. ◆

# Wu, Chien-Shiung

MAY 29, 1912–FEBRUARY 16, 1997 ● PHYSICIST

The nuclear fission pioneer Chien-Shiung Wu "turned physics on its head," when, in 1956, she conducted an experiment that disproved the theory that movement in nature is always symmetrical, forever changing the way people think about the universe. But that was only the beginning for this accomplished professor and research scientist, whose achievements make up a long list of woman "firsts." Already recognized as the first woman instructor in Princeton University's physics department (1943), Wu was the first to receive an honorary doctorate of science from Princeton (1958), the first to head the American Physical Society (1975), and the first to receive the Wolf Prize from the State of Israel (1978). In 1990, she became the first living scientist to have an asteroid named after her. Hailed by *Newsweek* as the "Queen of Physics," Wu en-

Chien-Shiung Wu

**1912** Wu is born in Liu Ho, China.

**1940** Wu earns her Ph.D. in physics from the University of California at Berkeley.

**1943** Wu becomes the first female instructor in physics at Princeton University.

**1944** Wu joins the Division of War Research (part of the famous Manhattan Project) at Columbia University.

**1946** Wu begins a 35-year association with Columbia University, becoming a full professor in 1958.

**1957** Wu announces the results of her parity experiment, which receives worldwide acclaim.

**1997** Wu dies from a stroke in Manhattan, New York.

joyed a three-decade-long career at Columbia, where she redefined women's roles in science.

Wu, whose first name means "strong hero" in Chinese, was born in Liu Ho, China, near Shanghai, in 1912, shortly after the overthrow of the Qing dynasty. Her father, Wu Zhong-Yi, opened the first school for girls in China. His wife, Fan Fuhua, became a tutor, and the couple became known as strong advocates for education. "I want every girl to have a school to go to," he told his daughter. They encouraged young Wu to strive toward academic excellence, and when Wu began her scientific career, her father said, "Ignore the obstacles … just put your head down and keep walking forward."

Wu attended her father's elementary school until she was nine, then enrolled in a teacher training program at the Suzhou Girls School, a boarding school about 50 miles from home. Frustrated at the lack of science instruction there, she taught herself physics, chemistry, and mathematics using the books and notes of other students. Upon graduation as valedictorian, Wu enrolled in the National Central University in Nanjing as a mathematics major but soon switched to physics. "If it hadn't been for my father's encouragement, I would be teaching grade school somewhere in China now," Wu said years later. She earned a bachelor's degree in 1934, and for two years taught physics at the university level.

Because China did not offer a graduate program for physics, in 1936 Wu left China and enrolled at the University of California at Berkeley, where she earned her Ph.D. in 1940. Although her achievements at Berkeley merited a faculty appointment, Wu was not offered a job. From 1940 to 1942 she stayed at Berkeley as a lecturer and research assistant, and her postdoctoral work established her as an expert in nuclear fission. The year 1942 was a time of great turmoil in China, already in the throes of World War II. That same year, Wu married the physicist "Luke" Chia Liu Yuan, and the couple decided to make the United States their home. They moved to the East Coast and Wu began a teaching position at Smith College in Northampton, Massachusetts.

During the war, physicists were in demand at universities, opening the door for Wu to take a job at Princeton University as the school's first female instructor. In 1944, Wu was recruited to join Columbia University's Division of War Research, where her meticulous testing methods and knowledge of nuclear fission were pivotal to the Manhattan Project, a secret government program that produced the first atomic bombs. While working on the project, Wu helped develop radiation detectors and helped create an ultra-low-temperature device that was used to study symmetry in relation to nuclear structure.

Despite her remarkable achievement and brilliant problem-solving skills, Wu was passed over for many faculty positions at Columbia until she became an associate professor in 1952; she was finally named a full professor in 1958. During her time at Columbia, Wu gained a reputation for spending long days in the lab. She is reported to have said, "There is only one thing worse than coming home from the lab to a sink full of dirty dishes, and that is not going to the lab at all." Wu enjoyed a long career at Columbia, where she was appointed as the first Pupin Professor of Physics in 1972.

Wu was a senior research scientist at Columbia when she performed the historic experiment that disproved one of the then widely accepted "laws" of physics, known as the conservation of parity. She based her research on the theoretical work of two Chinese American physicists, Chen Ning Yang and Tsung-Dao Lee. Their principle stated that, on a nuclear level, an object and its mirror image will behave the same way. Wu challenged this principle by studying the beta particles given off by the radioactive substance, cobalt-60. By disproving this theory, Wu allowed new and more correct views about neutrinos to emerge, and also brought herself worldwide acclaim when she announced her results in 1957. She also brought attention to Yang and Lee, who won the 1957 Nobel Peace Prize for their work in physics. Indeed, Wu recognized this as perhaps her most intriguing work. "I have always felt that in physics, and probably in other endeavors, too, you must have a total commitment. It is not just a job. It is a way of life."

Although Wu was not included in the Nobel Prize, she was awarded many prestigious honors. In 1958, Wu became a member of the National Academy of Sciences. That same year, she was granted an honorary doctorate of science from Princeton University, the first of many honorary degrees that would come from schools like Rutgers University (1961), Yale University (1967), Russell Sage College (1971), and Harvard University (1974). In 1964, she became the first woman to receive the Comstock Prize from the National Academy of Sciences. In 1975, Wu received the National Medal of Science.

"**Chien-Shiung Wu was one of the giants of physics. In the field of beta decay, she had no equal.**"
Tsung-Dao Lee, Columbia University professor and Nobel Prize winner, on Chien-Shiung Wu, 1997

Later in her career, Wu conducted research into molecular changes in hemoglobin associated with sickle-cell anemia. She retired from Columbia in 1981 as professor *emerita*, but remained active into her 70s, lecturing widely and speaking on behalf of women in the sciences. In 1997, Wu died of a stroke in Manhattan, New York. ◆

# Yalow, Rosalyn Sussman

JULY 19, 1921– ● PHYSICIST

"The first telescopes opened the heavens; the first microscope opened the world of microbes," the biochemistry pioneer Rosalyn Yalow said in 1977 when she became the second woman in history to accept the Nobel Prize in Medicine. Early in her career, Yalow believed that the use of radioactive materials, which was the focus of her life's research, would open the world of medicine. She was right. She earned the prestigious award for co-developing radioimmunoassay (RIA), a technique that uses radioactive isotopes to measure small amounts of biological substances in human blood. In fact, it can measure such minute amounts that the Nobel Prize committee compared it to detecting a half cube of sugar dissolved in a 3,600-square-mile lake one foot deep. Yalow's discovery ushered in a new era in medicine, making it possible for doctors to diagnose conditions caused by the slightest changes in hormone levels.

Rosalyn Yalow

**1921** Yalow is born in the Bronx, New York.

**1945** Yalow receives a Ph.D. in physics from the University of Illinois.

**1950** Yalow begins a 20-year run as a physicist and assistant chief of the radioisotope unit at the Veterans Administration Hospital in New York.

**1970** Yalow is promoted to chief of the Nuclear Medicine Service at the VA Hospital.

**1973** Yalow becomes director of the Solomon A. Berson Research Laboratory.

**1977** Yalow becomes the second woman in history to receive the Nobel Prize for Medicine.

**1991** Yalow retires from the VA Hospital.

Yalow was born Rosalyn Sussman in Bronx, New York, in 1921. Even though her parents were not schooled past the eighth grade, they believed in the importance of an education. Encouraged by her parents who maintained "girls were as important as boys," Yalow began to read before kindergarten, despite the fact that her family owned no books. "Stubborn and determined," she became interested in mathematics as a child, but then quickly turned her interest to science, specifically chemistry, in high school. After graduation from Walton High School, Yalow enrolled in Hunter College, a women's school in New York City, where she graduated with honors in 1941 as the first student to receive a degree in the school's new physics department.

Yalow wanted to go to medical school, but being Jewish and a woman, she realized she had a slim chance of being admitted. She opted for her second choice: physics. However, anti-semitism still existed; in fact, Purdue University made the following response to her application: "She is from New York. She is Jewish. She is a woman. If you can guarantee her a job afterward, we'll give her an assistanceship." Yalow entered secretarial school instead, but because the United States was on the brink of entering World War II, graduate schools needed students and were willing to look beyond gender. Later in 1941, Yalow received a teaching assistanceship in physics at the University of Illinois at Urbana-Champaign, the first woman accepted by that school's College of Engineering since 1917. "I tore up my stenography books," Yalow said later. It wasn't until her first meeting that she realized she was the only woman among the college's faculty of 400. In 1943, she married A. Aaron Yalow, a fellow physics student, and in 1945 received her Ph.D. in nuclear physics.

That year, Yalow returned to New York and worked briefly as an assistant engineer at the Federal Telecommunications Laboratory where—again—she was the only woman engineer. In 1946 she took a position at Hunter College as a lecturer and temporary assistant professor in physics, where she would teach until 1950. In 1947, Yalow became a consultant in nuclear physics at the Veterans Administration Hospital in the Bronx, New York, where they were conducting research on the medical applications of radioactive materials. Yalow turned a janitor's closet into the first radioisotope laboratory there, and forever called the hospital home. She soon partnered with Solomon A. Berson, a resident in internal medicine at the hospital, and the two scientists collaborated together on their research for more than 20 years, until Berson's death in 1972 (making him ineligible to share the Nobel Prize).

Their first research involved using isotopes to study blood volume and diagnose thyroid diseases by measuring iodine metabolism. Yalow and Berson then adapted the same method to hormones, including insulin. They showed that adult diabetics did not always suffer from an insufficiency of insulin in their blood, as scientists then thought, but that an unknown factor was blocking the action of insulin. They also showed that the injected insulin obtained from animals was being inactivated by human immune systems. By 1959, the team had perfected their method, called radioimmunoassay. RIA was then used by other medical professionals to screen blood banks for deadly diseases, to test newborns for underactive thyroids, to determine the correct dosage levels of antibiotics, to seek out foreign substances in the blood, to check fetuses for deformities; and to test and correct hormone levels in infertile couples. Thanks to RIA, the field of endocrinology (the study of ductless glands and hormones) was revolutionized. Their work also generated a new science: neuroendocrinology, the study of the way the brain controls the body's hormone systems.

In 1970, Yalow was promoted to chief of the Nuclear Medicine Service at the VA Hospital and in 1972 Yalow was named the senior medical investigator at the VA hospital. In 1973 she became director of the Solomon A. Berson Research Laboratory. Yalow has received a number of prestigious awards in recognition of her role in the development of RIA, including the Albert Lasker Basic Medical Research Award, which she was the first woman to receive in 1976. Besides the Nobel Prize, Yalow has enjoyed more than 30 honors, including a membership in the National Academy of Sciences (1975) and the American Academy of Arts and Sciences (1979). She has also held professorships at the Albert Einstein College of Medicine in Yeshiva University, Montefiore Hospital and Medical Center, and Mount Sinai School of Medicine, all in New York City.

An outspoken advocate of women in science, Yalow believes that woman must fight for opportunities. "When I got my degree at the University of Illinois in 1945, the number of women Ph.D.s in physics was 2 percent. Now it's up to 3 percent," she told the *Chicago Tribune* in a 1981 interview. However, she believes with equal fervor that the gender issue

**"Women, even now, must exert more effort than men do for the same degree of success."**
Rosalyn Sussman Yalow, on how a woman should approach a career in science, quoted in *Nobel Prize Women in Science*, 1998

shouldn't be factored into one's accomplishments. She refused the *Ladies Home Journal* Woman of the Year prize in 1978 because her inclusion would have implied that her work was extraordinary for a *woman*, rather than simply being acknowledged as extraordinary for a *scientist*. In 1988, Yalow received the nation's top award in science, the National Medal of Science. Although she retired from the VA Hospital in 1991, she is an active speaker on behalf of science education. ◆

# Young, Roger Arliner

1899–NOVEMBER 9, 1964 ● ZOOLOGIST

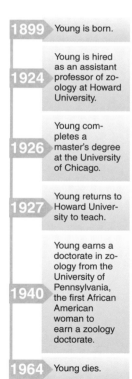

1899 Young is born.

1924 Young is hired as an assistant professor of zoology at Howard University.

1926 Young completes a master's degree at the University of Chicago.

1927 Young returns to Howard University to teach.

1940 Young earns a doctorate in zoology from the University of Pennsylvania, the first African American woman to earn a zoology doctorate.

1964 Young dies.

Roger Arliner Young was the first African American woman to earn a doctoral degree in zoology, which she received from the University of Pennsylvania in 1940. In an era when few black scientists had the opportunity to conduct scientific research, Young published a number of papers on marine eggs based on experiments she had conducted at the Marine Biological Laboratory in Woods Hole, Massachusetts, the premier biological research institute in the country. She was the first black woman to do experimental biology at this institution.

Young was born in Clifton Forge, Virginia. She entered Howard University in 1916 and studied zoology under the eminent black scientist Ernest Everett Just, one of the leading zoologists in the United States. When she completed her undergraduate work at Howard, she was hired as an assistant professor of zoology in 1924. During that same year she published the results of her observations on the morphology of the contractile vacuole and feeding canals in the microorganism in *Paramecium caudatum*.

Young received a master's degree in zoology in 1926 from the University of Chicago, where she was elected to Sigma Xi, the national science honors society. From 1927 until 1939 she taught at Howard, serving as acting head of the zoology department in Just's absence in 1929. She spent her summers doing research at Woods Hole.

Young's research, both alone and under Just, the leading biologist of his time in the study of normal marine eggs, was noteworthy. Her work on the paramecium challenged the prevailing theory on the role of the contractile vacuole and received favorable comments from scientists in both the United States and Europe. Burdened by a heavy teaching load and few financial resources, Young saw her career begin to flounder in the 1930s. After losing her position at Howard in 1936, she rallied to continue her research, publishing three papers between 1936 and 1938 and completing her doctoral work at the University of Pennsylvania under L. V. Heilbrunn in 1940.

Much of Young's research during this time continued the work she had begun with Just consisting of studies of the effects of ultraviolet radiation on sea-urchin eggs. From 1940 until her death she taught at a number of black colleges in the South, including the North Carolina College for Negroes, Shaw University (where she served as chair of the biology department), and Southern University in Louisiana. ◆

# Time Line of Events Involving Women in Science

## c. 160 B.C.

First record is made of a woman practicing medicine in China.

## 400

Fabiola (St. Fabiola), a Christian noblewoman, founds the first *nosocomium*, or hospital, in Western Europe. After establishing this hospital in Rome, she founds a hospice for pilgrims in Porto, Italy.

Hypatia of Alexandria is one of the first female mathematicians and certainly the most important. Her work with conic sections still held significance nearly 1,400 years after her death in 415, and it took until the 18th century for another female mathematician of her significance to appear.

## 1484

The first printing press owned and operated by a woman is that of Anna Rugerin of Germany who takes over her late husband's business.

## 1774

The first female astronomer of note, German–English Caroline Herschel builds the best reflector telescope (using a mirror) to this time with her brother, William Herschel, also an astronomer. Together they grind the best lenses in Europe and use them to search the skies. Caroline Herschel later discovers eight comets by herself.

## 1808

Sophie Germain describes the theorem that is later named after her in a letter to Carl Gauss. Her theorem, which was in the field of number theory and involves the mathematical puzzle called Fermat's last theorem, comes to be known as Germain's theorem and turns out to be the most important work on Fermat's theorem in a period spanning more than 100 years.

## 1822

Mary Ann Mantell and her husband Gideon discover the first fossil to be recognized as that of a dinosaur in Sussex, England.

## 1826

Mathematician Mary Somerville publishes *The Magnetic Properties of the Violet Rays of the Solar Spectrum*, only the second paper by a woman to be read in the proceedings of the Royal Society in London.

## 1828

Amateur paleontologist Mary Anning makes an important Jurassic discovery, finding pieces of the skeleton of a *pterodactyl* in the cliffs near the seaside town of Lyme Regis in England.

## 1847

On October 1, Maria Mitchell, an American astronomer, discovers a comet. Her discovery brings her to the attention of the scientific world and earns her a gold medal from the King of Denmark, making her the first woman to win such a medal. In 1848 she is elected the first female member of the American Academy of the Arts and Sciences.

## 1849

The first woman to receive a medical degree in the United States is Elizabeth Blackwell. She graduates with highest honors this year from Geneva Medical College (now a part of Syracuse University) in New York.

## 1854

The modern nursing practice is founded by the work of English nurse Florence Nightingale, who organizes care for the sick and wounded during the Crimean War.

**1855**

The first female dentist in the United States is Emmeline R. Jones.

**1857**

Joining her sister, Elizabeth, Dr. Emily Blackwell opens a hospital in New York City called the New York Infirmary for Women and Children. Emily took sole charge of the hospital in 1858 and then, again with her sister, opened the Women's Medical College of the New York Infirmary in 1868.

**1866**

Physician Mary Edwards Walker becomes the first woman to receive the Congressional Medal of Honor for her work as an assistant U.S. Army surgeon in the Civil War.

**1875**

Dr. Emeline Horton Cleveland apparently becomes the first woman ever in recorded history to perform a major surgery when she successfully removes ovarian tumors.

**1884**

Zoologist Rosa Smith Eigenmann is appointed curator of ichthyology—the first known woman curator of an ichthyological collection—at the San Diego–based California Academy of Sciences, an organization of which she was a life member.

**1888**

Antonia C. Maury aids in the discovery of Mizar, the first binary star in the Big Dipper, and discovers the second binary star, Beta Aurigae, on her own.

**1889**

Susan LaFlesche Picotte graduates from the Women's Medical College in Philadelphia and becomes the first Native American female physician in the United States.

**1893**

Geologist Florence Bascom becomes the first woman to receive a Ph.D. from Johns Hopkins University in Baltimore.

## 1895

Grace Emily Chisholm, an English mathematician, becomes the first woman to receive a German doctorate through the regular examination process. She attends Göttingen University in Germany because females are not admitted into English graduate schools.

## 1898

The Curies discover polonium and radium. Marie and Pierre Curie discover two new radioactive substances. The first, which they name polonium in remembrance of Marie's native country, is brought to the attention of the Academy of Sciences on July 18, 1898; the second is called radium and is brought forward on December 26, 1898, in note to the Academy of Sciences.

## 1903

Marie and Pierre share the Nobel Prize in Physics with Henri Becquerel for the discovery of radioactivity.

## 1905

Biologist Nettie Maria Stevens publishes a paper on X-Y chromosomes and receives the Ellen Richards Research Prize. The X-Y theory later proves very important to geneticists in understanding gender determination.

## 1906

Marie Curie (1867-1934), Polish-French chemist, assumes her husband Pierre's professorship at the Sorbonne after he is killed in a traffic accident. She becomes the first woman ever to teach there.

## 1909

Mary Eliza Mahoney gives the opening address to the National Association of Colored Graduate Nurses' (NACGN) first annual meeting in Boston, where she is elected national chaplain. As chaplain, she is responsible for the induction of new officers.

## 1910

The first woman to become a qualified pilot is the Baroness de Laroche who receives her *brevet de pilote d'aéroplane,* or pilot's license, in France. She dies in 1919 in an airplane accident. On September 2, 1910, Blanche Scott becomes the first American woman to fly an aircraft solo.

## 1911

Marie Curie is awarded the Nobel Prize in Chemistry for her work on radium. She is the first scientist to obtain the Nobel Prize twice.

## 1912

Ida Henrietta Hyde becomes the first woman member of the American Physiological Society. She is best known for inventing the microelectrode, a tiny probe that enables researchers to electrically or chemically stimulate a cell and record the activity the stimulation causes.

## 1913

The International Committee on Photographic Magnitudes decides to adopt Henrietta Leavitt's standard for determining the magnitude of stars. This standard was known as the Harvard Standard and was utilized until 1940.

## 1918

Astronomer Annie Jump Cannon begins publishing the *Henry Draper Catalog,* a nine-volume set that categorizes photographs of stars. Cannon invented the classification system by which the stars were organized, identifying several major classes of stars and dividing each class into subclasses, using a system of letters and numbers to name them. This system was later adopted by the International Astronomical Union and is still in use today.

Chemist Emma Perry Carr publishes her first paper on spectroscopy (the analysis of the dispersion of emissions, such as particles or radiation, according to a property such as mass or energy) entitled "The Absorption Spectra of Some Derivatives of Cyclopropane." Her paper is one of the first American contributions to the field of spectroscopy.

## 1919

Chemist Katherine Burr Blodgett becomes the first female scientist hired by General Electric Research Laboratory in Schenectady, where 20 years later she discovers "invisible," or nonreflecting, glass. Blodgett achieved another first in 1926 when she became the first woman to earn a Ph.D. in physics from Cambridge University in England.

Alice Hamilton, a physician best-known for the important strides she made in the new field of industrial medicine, becomes the first woman faculty member at Harvard University.

**1924**

Helen Rosenbach Deutsch garners broad recognition after delivering her first essay on female psychology. That same year she is asked to head the newly established Vienna Training Institute.

Anna Pell Wheeler becomes head of the mathematics department at Bryn Mawr College and continued to encourage female students to earn doctorates throughout her career as an educator.

**1925**

Florence Rena Sabin (1871-1953), American anatomist and biologist, becomes the first woman member of the U.S. National Academy of Sciences.

Botanist Ynes Mexia travels to western Mexico and returns with 33,000 plant specimens, including 50 new species and one, *Mexiathmus mexicanus*, named in her honor.

Dr. Florence Rena Sabin is elected to the National Academy of Sciences and also joins the Rockefeller Institute for Medical Research, becoming the first woman to be a full member of the institute.

**1928**

Anthropologist Margaret Mead publishes *Coming of Age in Samoa* (1928), the first and best known of her 32 books. The book covers adolescence and social roles in Samoan teenagers.

**1930**

Lillian Moller Gilbreth wins the first Gilbreth Medal (named after her husband, Frank) granted by the Society of Industrial Engineers for her work in time and motion studies. The Gilbreths life was later featured in the movie *Cheaper by the Dozen*.

**1932**

The first solo flight by a woman across the Atlantic Ocean is made by American aviator Amelia Earhart. She flies from Newfoundland, Canada, to Northern Ireland in a Lockheed Vega monoplane in 13 hours, 30 minutes.

**1934**

Neuropsychiatrist Lauretta Bender develops the Bender-Gestalt Visual Motor Test to diagnose learning and emotional problems in children.

## 1936

Anna Freud authors *The Ego and the Mechanisms of Defence*, a seminal work on ego psychology that moved the emphasis of psychology from conflicts in the unconscious toward a study of the mechanisms by which the ego protects itself from anxiety.

Inge Lehmann discovers the Earth's inner solid core for the first time, one of the most important advances in our knowledge of Earth's interior in the 20th century.

## 1938

Lise Meitner leads a team that discovers nuclear fission after four years of studying the products formed when uranium is bombarded with neutrons. Forced to flee Nazi Germany just as she is making her groundbreaking discovery, Meitner never receives proper credit for her breakthrough.

## 1940

Roger Arliner Young becomes the first African American woman to earn a doctoral degree in zoology, which she receives from the University of Pennsylvania.

Chemist Mary Engle Pennington is awarded the Garvan Medal by the American Chemical Society, which specifically honors women for their achievements in chemistry. Pennington is honored for her work in the evolution of frozen foods and shipping refrigerated food.

## 1942

Leona Wood Marshall Libby is the only woman present for the first nuclear chain reaction, which takes place under the football stands at the University of Chicago on December 2, 1942. The discovery was made by the primary team working on the Manhattan Project, which discovered the atomic bomb; Libby was the only woman on the primary team.

## 1943

Working at Harlem Hospital in New York City, Myra Adele Logan becomes the first woman to perform open heart surgery, the ninth operation of its kind anywhere in the world.

Chien-Shiung Wu becomes the first female instructor in physics at Princeton University.

### 1947

Margaret Cornelia Morgan Lawrence, one of the first black women psychiatrists in the nation, becomes the first African American trainee at the Columbia Psychoanalytic Clinic for Training and Research, from which she receives a Certificate in Psychoanalysis in 1951.

Biochemist Gerty Radnitz Cori, her husband Carl, and one other scientist win the Nobel Prize in Medicine for their "discovery of how glycogen is catalytically converted." The conversion, which occurs when, during periods of physical activity, glycogen in the muscles is broken down into glucose, a source of energy. Lactic acid left behind after the conversion is sent from the muscles to the liver, where it is converted back into a sugar and returned to the muscles, where it is converted to glycogen and the cycle begins all over again. The process is still known as the "Cori cycle."

### 1948

Anthropologist Ruth Fulton Benedict becomes the first woman to achieve the status of full professor on the faculty of the political science department at Columbia University.

### 1949

Maria Goeppert-Mayer publishes a paper describing "spin-orbit coupling," a new theory on nucleons creating energy. This new nuclear shell model accounts for many values of nuclear spin and magnetic momentum.

Grace Hopper joins the Eckert-Mauchly Computer Corporation in Philadelphia as a senior mathematician. There, she creates FLOMATIC, the first English-language data processing language, which is used as the starting point for the creation of the Common Business Oriented Language (COBOL) programming language.

Marjorie Lee Browne receives her Ph.D. in mathematics from the University of Michigan, one of the first two African American women to receive such a degree at any university in the United States.

### 1950

The first human to survive a kidney transplantation is Ruth Tucker, a 49-year-old American woman dying from chronic uremia. American surgeon Richard Lawler of Chicago transplants a kidney from a cadaver (dead body) into his patient who survives for a short time.

Helen Octavia Dickens becomes the first African American woman to be named as a fellow of the American College of Surgeons.

Rachel Fuller Brown and Elizabeth Lee Hazen present their discovery of the drug nystatin to the National Academy of Sciences. Nystatin is the first antibiotic created to fight fungus infections and is still used today to fight infections of the skin, mucous membranes, and intestinal tract.

## 1951

Geneticist Rosalind Elsie Franklin begins her groundbreaking work that would unlock the mysteries of DNA. Her March 1953 paper announcing the discovery of the double-helixed DNA is too late–American scientists James Watson and Francis Crick announce the same discovery two weeks before Franklin and are credited with the enormously important breakthrough, even though it is now widely believed that Watson may have stolen an important photograph from Franklin's research to reach his conclusion.

## 1952

Pediatrician Virginia Apgar invents the Apgar Score System to judge the health of newborns. The system is designed to rate an infant on a scale of 0 to 2 on five infant signs, one minute and five minutes after birth. The five functions are heart rate, respiration, reflex irritability, muscle tone, and color.

## 1953

The "shark lady," zoologist Eugenie Clark, publishes her book *Lady With a Spear* that recounts her adventures conducting underwater research on sharks and other marine life.

R. Louise McManus founds the Institute for Nursing Research in Nursing Education at Teachers College, which is part of Columbia University in New York. This institute is the first university center for research and training in nursing in the United States.

## 1954

Anne Anastasi's most famous book, *Psychological Testing*, is published. In addition to providing a thorough overview of the principles of psychological testing, it covers intelligence, aptitude, and personality tests in detail. In each of the book's six updates, Anastasi addressed new trends in testing.

Mamie Phipps Clark's work on racial identity and self-esteem play an important part in the landmark Supreme Court case, *Brown v. Board of Education of Topeka*, which ends desegregation in the schools.

## 1955

Ruth Lloyd Smith is named associate professor at the Howard University college of medicine, a position she holds until her retirement in 1977.

Jewel Plummer Cobb establishes the Tissue Culture Research Laboratory at the New York University Bellevue Hospital Medical Center.

## 1956

Eight years of data collection and analysis by a group of scientists led by Dorothy Hodgkin yields the structure of vitamin $B_{12}$. In 1964, Hodgkin is recognized for her accomplishment when she is awarded the Nobel Prize in chemistry.

Cecilia Helena Payne-Gaposchkin is the first woman to obtain the rank of full professor at Harvard through regular faculty promotions when she is named professor of astronomy; she later chairs the astronomy department for 10 years.

## 1957

Astrophysicist Margaret Burbidge, together with her husband and two other scientists, publishes a major scientific paper that shows how the heavy chemical elements are produced by nuclear reactions inside stars. The theory is important because it shows that the elements that make up our everyday world—even our bodies—once came from stars.

## 1962

Charlotte Friend receives the prestigious Alfred F. Sloan Award for Cancer Research for her groundbreaking work proving that viruses can cause some forms of cancer.

Pediatrician Mary Ellen Avery publishes her findings in a 1962 issue of the medical journal *Pediatrics* showing that premature babies who die from respiratory distress syndrome (RDS) suffer from a lack of a substance known as pulmonary surfactant, which leads to their death. The article pointed the way to successful therapies for RDS.

Environmentalist Rachel Carson publishes her most famous book, *Silent Spring,* which details the effect pesticides have on the environment.

## 1963

The first woman in space is the Soviet Union's Valentina Tereshkova, who flies in *Vostok* 6. As a cotton mill worker and amateur parachutist, she is essentially a passenger in the ground-controlled spacecraft.

Neuroendocrinologist Berta Scharrer publishes *Neuroendocrinology*, which becomes a leading text in the field.

## 1964

Helen Taussig is awarded the Medal of Freedom by President Lyndon Johnson for her lifelong achievements in pediatric medicine, including her discovery that the drug thalidomide caused severe birth defects.

Helen Sawyer Hogg, a brilliant astronomer who had a gift for making science understandable to the lay person, is the first woman elected president of the Royal Canadian Institute.

Stephanie Kwolek develops KEVLAR, a high-strength fabric that is five times stronger than steel and is used in the bulletproof vests used by police officers. It is also used in radial tires, skis, sails, tennis rackets, fiber optic cables, brake pads, suits for firefighters, helmets, parts of space vehicles and airplanes, and cut-resistant gloves used by butchers and surgeons.

## 1966

Physician Dorothy Brown is the first African American woman elected to the Tennessee State Legislature.

## 1970

Julia Bowman Robinson's work and research leads to the solution of David Hilbert's "Tenth Problem", a complicated mathematical equation Six years later, she becomes the first female president of the American Mathematical Society.

## 1971

Jeanne Spurlock wins the Edward A. Strecker M.D. Award from the Institute of the Pennsylvania Hospital for outstanding contributions to psychiatric care and treatment. She is the first African American and the first woman to receive the award.

Mathematician Mina Rees becomes first female president of the American Association for the Advancement of Science.

## 1972

Meave Leakey leads a team in Kenya that discovers parts of a human skull that is labeled Skull 1470, from the genus *Homo* ( Skull 1470 is the object's catalog number in the Kenya Natural History Museum). The skull provides crucial evidence supporting the view that *Homo* emerged at least two million years ago.

Pharmacologist Candace B. Pert helps discover opiate receptors in nerve cells, the chemical lock on nerve cells that binds with natural opiates in the human body and determines a human being's behavior, mood, and health.

Physician Janet Rowley discovers the first recurring "translocation" of a chromosome to be identified for a disease in any species. The important discovery demonstrates that specific types of cancer are caused by particular changes in chromosomes.

## 1973

Astrophysicist Jocelyn Burnell wins the Michelson Award for the discovery of pulsars, which are a special type of neutron star that "pulse," beams of radiation at regular intervals. Burnell had the distinction of discovering the first four pulsars, and her discovery opened up a whole new field of astrophysics.

## 1974

Microbiologist Lynn Margulis teams with James Lovelock to advocate the Gaia hypothesis, which states that the earth as a whole is a living being that forms one interdependent, self-regulating symbiotic system.

## 1976

Dixy Lee Ray becomes the first female governor of Washington State after a distinguished career in zoology, academic life, and public service.

## 1977

Zoologist Jane Goodall, who is famous for her work with chimpanzees, founds the Jane Goodall Institute, which raises funds to support conservation.

Physicist Rosalyn Sussman Yalow becomes the second woman in history to receive the Nobel Prize for Medicine for co-developing radiommunoassay, a technique that uses radioactive isotopes to measure tiny amounts of biological substances in human blood.

## 1978

Mary Douglas Leakey discovers the footprints of human ancestors, which she believes to be 3.7 million years old, on the Serengeti Plain of Tanzania.

## 1980

Elaine Crosby is awarded the National Medal of Science for her lifetime contributions to the study of the nervous system of vertebrates.

## 1981

Vandana Shiva starts the Research Foundation for Science, Technology, and Ecology, which is dedicated to the grassroots movement fighting logging and supporting other environmental issues.

## 1983

The first American woman astronaut, Sally Ride, is launched into space aboard the space shuttle *Challenger* on mission STS-7. She is accompanied by four male astronauts who, with her, comprise the first five-person crew to be launched into space. During their six-day mission, they deploy three satellites and demonstrate the shuttle's remote manipulator system by retrieving one satellite from orbit. This is the first time a satellite is retrieved by a manned spacecraft.

Zoologist Dian Fossey publishes *Gorillas in the Mist,* her famous book about her life among the mountain gorillas that lived in the African country of Rwanda.

Geneticist Barbara McClintock wins the Nobel Prize for Medicine for her research on genetics and the self-regulation of cells, an area she had worked on for the 30 years leading up to the award.

## 1984

Kathryn Sullivan becomes the first American woman to walk in space when she spends 3.5 hours outside the orbiter *Challenger* on October 11.

## 1986

Zoologist Biruté Galdikas founds Orangutan Foundation International.

Physician Rita Levi-Montalcini is named corecipient of Nobel Prize for her work and research in the discovery of nerve growth factor (NGF) and its precise makeup. NGF has been used in the treatment of such diseases such as Alzheimer's and Parkinson's, as well as aiding burn patients.

Biochemist Joan Argetsinger Steitz receives the National Science Medal for her outstanding work and career in molecular biology.

## 1988

Biochemist Gertrude Bell Elion (along with two corecipients) wins the Nobel Prize for her outstanding career contributions to drug research, including her discovery of 6-mercaptopurine, or 6-MP, a drug still used against leukemia today. In 1974, she also discovered a drug called acyclovir, used against shingles, the Epstein-Barr virus, and herpes encephalitis, and later played a role in the development of the AIDS drug AZT.

## 1989

Katherine Esau receives the National Medal of Science for her career achievements in the field of botany, which included publishing five textbooks that were recognized as the best in her field.

Joanne Simpson becomes the first female president of the American Meteorological Society.

## 1990

Mary-Claire King identifies a gene that can cause breast cancer, which is called BRCA1. Four years later, she further discovered that the gene was located on chromosome 17. Her work led to important advancements in the study of breast cancer.

## 1991

Dr. Bernadine Healy caps a long career of public service when President George Bush names her director of the National Institutes of Health. She would later be named president of the American Red Cross in 1999.

## 1992

Mae C. Jemison, who five years earlier had become the first African American female astronaut, becomes the first African American woman to actually go into space on September 12 when the space shuttle *Endeavor* is launched.

Geneticist Maxine Singer receives the National Medal of Science for "her outstanding scientific accomplishments and her deep concern for the societal responsibility of the scientist."

## 1993

Kathryn Thornton sets the record for the longest space walk by a woman when she makes two seven-hour walks during the first Hubble Space Telescope repair mission in December. Her walks are longer than the previous two longest walks by a woman combined.

Astronomer Sandra Faber takes over as the leader of the Deep Image Multi-project Spectrograph (DEIMOS) team at the Keck Observatory. Her work makes possible large surveys of the distant universe for the first time by increasing spectrographic power trained on distant galaxies by a factor of 10.

Chemist Darleane Christian Hoffman is part of a team of researchers that confirms the existence of seaborgium (element 106), the heaviest element found so far.

Chemist Isabella L. Karle becomes the first woman to win the Franklin Institute's Bower Award and Prize in Science, which she receives in honor of her career achievements in the field of crystallography. Crystallography is a science that tries to determine which atoms are connected to which, and how they are arranged in respect to each other in a crystal lattice. Her work made it easier for scientists to understand the structure of substances.

Ellen Ochoa becomes the first Hispanic-American woman to fly in space during a mission of the space shuttle *Discovery*.

Biologist Salome Waelsch receives the National Medal of Science for her work in zoology and her advocacy of women's equality in the world of science.

## 1994

Adriana C. Ocampo is part of a joint U.S.-Russian team that creates a new hypothesis on why dinosaurs became extinct millions of years ago, finding more definitive proof that a huge asteroid hit the Earth 65 million years ago, causing the atmosphere to fill with life-killing sulphur dioxide.

Biologist Elizabeth F. Neufeld is awarded the National Medal of Science for her work in biochemistry and molecular biology.

Vera Cooper Rubin receives the National Medal of Science award for her work in astronomy.

Geneticist Flossie Wong-Staal is named director of the Center for AIDS Research at the University of California at San Diego, where she continues her research into AIDS and HIV issues.

## 1995

The first woman to pilot a U.S. space shuttle is American astronaut Eileen Collins. She conducts a successful STS-63 shuttle mission.

Bonnie Jean Dunbar is aboard mission STS-71 on the *Atlantis* when it becomes the first American space shuttle to dock with the Russian spacecraft *Mir*.

Shirley Ann Jackson is the first woman appointed head of the U.S. Nuclear Regulatory Commission. Her entire career is filled with firsts—first African American woman to earn a Ph.D. at the Massachusett's Institute of Technology, first African American to serve as a commissioner for the Nuclear Regulatory Commission, and the first African American woman to lead a major research university (Rensselaer Polytechnic University).

Biochemist Christiane Nüsslein-Volhard is named a corecipient of Nobel Prize in Medicine for her research and work on the genetic makeup of fruit flies that determines body shape and arrangement. Her work was an important contribution to the worldwide effort to discover the genetic plan in all life forms, including humans, for many of the genes that control development of fruit fly embryos are the same in humans

## 1996

The first American woman to board the orbiting Russian space station, *Mir*, is astronaut Shannon Lucid. She transfers from a U.S. space shuttle that is docked with *Mir*. Three days later, two Americans, Linda Godwin and Michael Clifford, make the first space walk from the shuttle to *Mir*.

## 1998

Mathematician Cathleen Morawetz becomes the first female mathematician to win the National Medal of Science, the nation's most important scientific award.

## 2000

Chemist Susan Solomon wins the highest award given by the American Meteorological Society, the Carl-Gustaf Rossby Research Medal, for her work contributing to the understanding of the chemistry of the stratosphere.

# Article
# Sources

The following authors contributed the new articles for **Macmillan Profiles:** *Women in Science:*

Mary Carvlin
Michael Levine
Gina Misiroglu
Mike O'Neal

The following articles were adapted from the *Encyclopedia of Physics*, published by Macmillan Library Reference:

| ARTICLE | AUTHOR |
|---|---|
| Curie, Marie | Jules Six |
| Meitner, Lise | Ruth Lewin Sime |

The following article was adapted from the *Encyclopedia of Computers*, published by Macmillan Library Reference:

| ARTICLE | AUTHOR |
|---|---|
| Hopper, Grace Brewster Murray | Donald D. Spencer |

The following articles were adapted from the *Encyclopedia of African-American Culture and History*, published by Macmillan Library Reference:

| ARTICLE | AUTHOR |
|---|---|
| Brown, Dorothy | Susan McIntosh and Robyn Spencer |
| Browne, Marjorie Lee | William T. Fletcher |
| Cobb, Jewel Plummer | Gerard Fergerson |
| Dickens, Helen Octavia | Vanessa Northington Gamble |
| Elders, Joycelyn | Greg Robinson |

Granville, Evelyn Boyd          Sylvia Trimble Bozeman
Kittrell, Flemmie Pansy         Sasha Thomas
Lawrence, Margaret Morgan       Sabrina Fuchs and Lydia McNeill
Lloyd, Ruth Smith               Kenneth R. Manning
Logan, Myra Adele               Lydia McNeill
Mahoney, Mary Eliza             Thaddeus Russell
Spurlock, Jeanne                Margaret J. Jerrido
Wright, Jane C.                 Robert C. Hayden
Young, Roger Arliner            Evelynn M. Hammonds

The following articles were adapted from the *Dictionary of American Biography*, published by Charles Scribner's Sons:

| ARTICLE | AUTHOR |
| --- | --- |
| Apgar, Virginia | M. Virginia Wyly |
| Gilbreth, Lillian Moller | Frederick S. Voss |
| Goeppert-Mayer, Maria | Karen E. Johnson |
| Mead, Margaret | Jane Howard |
| Payne-Gaposchkin, Cecilia | Barbara B. Jackson |

The following articles were adapted from the *Encyclopedia of Earth Sciences*, published by Macmillan Library Reference:

| ARTICLE | AUTHOR |
| --- | --- |
| Carson, Rachel Louise | Patricia Dasch |
| Lehmann, Inge | Erik Hjortenberg |
| Mitchell, Maria | Dorit Hoffleit |

The following articles were adapted from the *Who's Who in Space*, published by Macmillan Library Reference:

| ARTICLE | AUTHOR |
| --- | --- |
| Bondar, Roberta | Michael Cassutt |
| Dunbar, Bonnie Jean | Michael Cassutt |
| Godwin, Linda | Michael Cassutt |
| Lucid, Shannon | Michael Cassutt |
| Ride, Sally Kristen | Michael Cassutt |
| Sullivan, Kathryn | Michael Cassutt |
| Tereshkova, Valentina | Michael Cassutt |
| Thornton, Kathryn | Michael Cassutt |

The following articles were adapted from the *Scribner Encyclopedia of American Lives*, published by Charles Scribner's Sons:

| ARTICLE | AUTHOR |
| --- | --- |
| Bender, Lauretta | Karen M. Venturella |
| Clark, Mamie Phipps | Jack Meacham |

Deutsch, Helene Rosenbach
Friend, Charlotte
Libby, Leona Wood Marshall
Robinson, Julia Bowman
Taussig, Helen

Gillian Silverman
Marilyn Elizabeth Perry
Marilyn Elizabeth Perry
Betty B. Vinson
Marilyn Elizabeth Perry

The following articles were adapted from the *Encyclopedia of Chemistry*, published by Macmillan Library Reference:

| **ARTICLE** | **AUTHOR** |
|---|---|
| Hodgkin, Dorothy Crowfoot | Kathleen Holley |
| Joliot-Curie, Irène | Claire A. Baker |

The following article was adapted from **Macmillan Profiles:** *Latino Americans* published by Macmillan Library Reference:

| **ARTICLE** | **AUTHOR** |
|---|---|
| Novello, Antonia | Mary Carvlin |

The following article was adapted from the *Encyclopedia of the American West* published by Macmillan Library Reference:

| **ARTICLE** | **AUTHOR** |
|---|---|
| Picotte, Susan LaFlesche | Janet R. Fireman |

# Photo Credits

Photographs appearing in *Women in Science* are from the following sources:

Apgar, Virginia (page 6): AP/Wide World
Benedict, Ruth Fulton (page 18): Library of Congress
Blackwell, Elizabeth (page 21): Library of Congress
Bondar, Roberta (page 30): The Gamma Liaison Network
Brown, Dorothy (page 32): Meharry Medical College Archives
Brown, Rachel Fuller (page 33): Library of Congress
Browne, Marjorie Lee (page 36): Kenschaft, Patricia
Burnell, Jocelyn Bell (page 41): Corbis
Cannon, Annie Jump (page 46): Corbis-Bettmann
Carson, Rachel (page 51): AP/Wide World
Cobb, Jewel Plummer (page 68): AP/Wide World
Cori, Gerty Radnitz (page 71): AP/Wide World
Curie, Marie (page 76): Corbis
Dresselhaus, Mildred S. (page 88): Archive Photos
Elders, Joycelyn (page 99): AP/Wide World
Elion, Gertrude Belle (page 100): Corbis
Fossey, Dian (page 110): Gamma Liaison Network
Freud, Anna (page 116): AP/Wide World
Friend, Charlotte (page 118): Library of Congress
Gilbreth, Lillian Moller (page 127): AP/Wide World
Godwin, Linda (page 130): Gamma Liaison Network
Goeppert-Mayer, Maria (page 132): Library of Congress
Goodall, Jane (page 135): Library of Congress
Granville, Evelyn Boyd (page 138): University of Texas at Tyler
Hamilton, Alice (page 139): Library of Congress
Healy, Bernadine (page 145): Gamma Liaison Network

Herschel, Caroline Lucretia (page 149): Library of Congress
Hodgkin, Dorothy Crowfoot (page 151): AP/Wide World
Hopper, Grace (page 158): Corbis
Hypatia (page 162): Corbis
Jackson, Shirley Ann (page 165): AP/Wide World
Jemison, Mae C. (page 168): AP/Wide World
Joliot-Curie, Irène (page 170): Library of Congress
Karle, Isabella L. (page 173): AP/Wide World
Kovalevskaya, Sofia (page 180): Library of Congress
Leakey, Meave (page 187): Gamma Liaison Network
Levi-Montalcini, Rita (page 198): AP/Wide World
Lucid, Shannon (page 207): Archive Photos
McClintock, Barbara (page 216): AP/Wide World
Mead, Margaret (page 223): AP/Wide World
Meitner, Lise (page 226): Library of Congress
Mitchell, Maria (page 230): Library of Congress
Neufeld, Elizabeth F. (page 237): AP/Wide World
Nightingale, Florence (page 240): Public Domain
Noether, Emmy (page 243): Archive Photo
Novello, Antonia (page 247): Gamma Liaison Network
Nusslein-Volhard, Christine (page 250): AP/Wide World
Ochoa, Ellen (page 255): Public Domain
Patrick, Ruth (page 260): AP/Wide World
Pennington, Mary Engle (page 265): Corbis
Pert, Candace B. (page 269): Gamma Liaison Network
Rees, Mina (page 276): Library of Congress
Ride, Sally Kristen (page 279): Public Domain
Sabin, Florence Rena (page 289): Library of Congress
Singer, Maxine (page 302): Corbis
Solomon, Susuan (page 307): AP/Wide World
Somerville, Mary (page 310): Corbis
Sullivan, Kathryn (page 321): Gamma Liaison Network
Taussig, Helen (page 323): Library of Congress
Tereshkova, Valentina (page 329): Library of Congress
Thornton, Kathryn (page 332): Gamma Liaison Network
Walker, Mary Edwards (page 340): Corbis-Bettmann
Wright, Jane Cooke (page 348): AP/Wide World
Wu, Chien-Shiung (page 349): AP/Wide World
Yalow, Rosalyn Sussman (page 353): Library of Congress

# Additional Resources

## GENERAL SOURCES

### BOOKS

Ambrose, Susan A. *Journeys of Women in Science and Engineering: No Universal Constants*. Temple University Press, 1997.

Bailey, Martha J. *American Women in Science 1950 to the Present: A Biographical Dictionary*. ABC-Clio, 1998.

Bailey, Martha J. *American Women in Science: A Biographical Dictionary*. ABC-Clio, 1994.

De Angelis, Gina. *Science & Medicine (Female Firsts in Their Fields)*. Chelsea House Pub., 1999.

Fort, Deborah C. *A Hand Up: Women Mentoring Women in Science*. Association for Women in Science, 1995.

Glover, Judith. *Women and Scientific Employment*. St. Martin's Press, 2000.

Hunter, Shaun. *Leaders in Medicine (Women in Profile)*. Crabtree Pub., 1999.

McClure, Judy. *Healers and Researchers: Physicians, Biologists, Social Scientists (Remarkable Women, Past and Present)*. Raintree/Steck Vaughn, 2000.

Morse, Mary. *Women Changing Science: Voices from a Field in Transition*. Perseus Press, 1995.

Nies, Kevin Allison. *From Priestess to Physician: Biographies of Women Life Scientists*. California Video Inst., 1996.

Nies, Kevin Allison. *From Sorceress to Scientist: Biographies of Women Physical Scientists*. California Video Inst., 1991.

Ogilvie, Marilyn Bailey and Joy Dorothy Harvey, eds. *The Biographical Dictionary of Women in Science: Pioneering Lives From Ancient Times to the Mid-20th Century*. Routledge, 2000.

Ogilvie, Marilyn B. *Women in Science: Antiquity Through the Nineteenth Century: A Biographical Dictionary With Annotated Bibliography.* MIT Press, 1990.

Ottaviani, Jim. *Dignifying Science.* G.T. Labs, 1999.

Proffitt, Pamela, ed. *Notable Women Scientists.* The Gale Group, 2000.

Rayner-Canham, Marelene F., et al. *A Devotion to Their Science: Pioneer Women of Radioactivity.* Chemical Heritage Foundation, 1998.

Rosser, Sue Vilhauer. *Women, Science, and Society: The Crucial Union.* Teachers College Press, 2000.

Shearer, Benjamin F. and Barbara Smith Shearer, eds. *Notable Women in the Physical Sciences.* Greenwood Publishing Group, 1997.

Stanley, Autumn. *Mothers and Daughters of Invention: Notes for a Revised History of Technology.* Scarecrow Press, 1993.

Stille, Darlene R. *Extraordinary Women of Medicine.* Children's Press, 1997.

Warren, Wini. *Black Women Scientists in the United States.* Indiana University Press, 2000.

Wasserman, Elga. *The Door in the Dream: Conversations with Eminent Women in Science.* National Academy Press, 2000.

Yount, Lisa. *A to Z of Women in Science and Math.* Facts on File, Inc., 1999.

Yount, Lisa. *Contemporary Women Scientists.* Facts on File, Inc., 1994.

Yount, Lisa. *Twentieth-Century Women Scientists.* Facts on File, Inc., 1995.

Zierdt-Warshaw, Linda, et al. *American Women in Technology: An Encyclopedia.* ABC-Clio, 2000.

## WEBSITES

Agnes Scott College: Biographies of Women Mathematicians, http://www.agnesscott.edu/lriddle/women/women.htm

Archives of Women in Science and Engineering, http://www.lib.iastate.edu/spcl/wise/wise.html

Association for Women in Mathematics, http://www.awm-math.org/

Black Women in Mathematics, http://www.math.buffalo.edu/mad/wmad0.html

Celebration of Women Anthropologists, http://www.cas.usf.edu/anthropology/women/index.html

Data Banks of Scientists, http://www.ceemast.csupomona.edu/nova/scientist.html

Distinguished Women of Past and Present, http://www.distinguishedwomen.com/index.html

*Encyclopedia Astronautica,* http://www.friends-partners.org/~mwade/spaceflt.htm

Faces of Science, http://www.princeton.edu/~mcbrown/display/faces.html

The MacTutor History of Mathematics Archive, http://www-groups.dcs.st-and.ac.uk/~history/index.html

Museum of Women in Science and Technology, http://www.amazoncity.com/technology/museum/

NASA Astronaut Biographies, http://www.jsc.nasa.gov/Bios/

National Women's Hall of Fame, http://www.greatwomen.org/index.html

Past Notable Women of Computing, http://www.cs.yale.edu/homes/tap/past-women-cs.html

San Diego Supercomputing Center: Women in Science, http://www.sdsc.edu/ScienceWomen/index.html

Women in American History, http://www.women.eb.com/women/index.html

Women in Science, http://library.thinkquest.org/20117/intro.shtml

Women in Science, http://www.humboldt.edu/~jlm12/fem-science.html

Women in Technology International, http://www.witi.com/index-c.shtml

## INDIVIDUALS

### ANASTASI, ANNE

Anastasi, Anne. *Psychological Testing.* Prentice Hall, 1997.

### ANNING, MARY

Anholt, Laurence. *Stone Girl, Bone Girl: The Story of Mary Anning.* Orchard Books, 1999.

Brighton, Catherine. *The Fossil Girl: Mary Anning's Dinosaur Discovery.* Millbrook Press, 1999.

Brown, Don. *Rare Treasure: Mary Anning and Her Remarkable Discoveries.* Houghton Mifflin, 1999.

Fradin, Dennis. *Mary Anning, the Fossil Hunter.* Silver Press, 1997.

SDSC: Women in Science: Mary Anning, http://www.sdsc.edu/ScienceWomen/anning.html

### APGAR, VIRGINIA

National Women's Hall of Fame: Virginia Apgar, http://www.greatwomen.org/apgar.htm

Women in American History: Virginia Apgar, http://www.women.eb.com/women/articles/Apgar_Virginia.html

### BASCOM, FLORENCE

GSA History of Geology: Florence Bascom, http://geoclio.st.usm.edu/fbascom.html

Women in Science: Florence Bascom, http://library.thinkquest.org/20117/bascom.html

## BENDER, LAURETTA

Psychological Testing and Assessment: Lauretta Bender, http://www.mayfieldpub.com/psychtesting/profiles/bender.htm

## BENEDICT, RUTH FULTON

Benedict, Ruth. *An Anthropologist at Work: Writings of Ruth Benedict.* Greenwood Press, 1977.

Caffrey, Margaret M. *Ruth Benedict: Stranger in This Land.* University of Texas Press, 1989.

Mead, Margaret. *Ruth Benedict.* Columbia University Press, 1974.

Modell, Judith Schachter. *Ruth Benedict, Patterns of a Life.* University of Pennsylvania Press, 1983.

Celebration of Women Anthropologists: Ruth Benedict, http://www.cas.usf.edu /anthropology/women/ruthb/ruthbenedict.htm

## BLACKWELL, ELIZABETH

Blackwell, Elizabeth. *Pioneer Work in Opening the Medical Profession to Women: Autobiographical Sketches.* Schocken Books, 1977.

Chambers, Peggy. *A Doctor Alone; a Biography of Elizabeth Blackwell: The First Woman Doctor, 1821-1910.* Abelard-Schuman, 1958.

Peck, Ira. *Elizabeth Blackwell: The First Woman Doctor.* Millbrook Press, 2000.

Schleichert, Elizabeth. *The Life of Elizabeth Blackwell.* Twenty-First Century Books, 1992.

National Women's Hall of Fame: Elizabeth Blackwell, http://www.greatwomen.org/blkwele.htm

Women in Science: Elizabeth Blackwell, http://library.thinkquest.org/20117 /blackwell.html

## BLACKWELL, EMILY

Distinguished Women of Past and Present: Emily Blackwell, http://www .distinguishedwomen.com/biographies/black-em.html

National Women's Hall of Fame: Emily Blackwell, http://www.greatwomen.org/blkwelem.htm

Women in American History: Emily Blackwell, http://www.women.eb.com/women/articles/Blackwell_Emily.html

## BLODGETT, KATHERINE BURR

Inventor of the Week: Katherine Blodgett, http://web.mit.edu/invent/www /inventorsA-H/blodgett.html

## BONDAR, ROBERTA

Bondar, Roberta. *Touching the Earth.* Key Porter Books, 1994.

The Astronaut Connection: Roberta Bondar, http://www.nauts.com/bios/csa /bondar.html;20000516235105533

Encyclopedia Astronautica: Roberta Bondar, http://www.friends-partners.org /~mwade/astros/bondar.htm

## BROWN, DOROTHY

Data Bank of Scientists: Dorothy Lavinia Brown, http://www.ceemast.csupomona.edu/nova/brown1.html

## BROWN, RACHEL FULLER

Baldwin, Richard S. *The Fungus Fighters: Two Women Scientists and Their Discovery.* Cornell University Press, 1981.

Inventor of the Week: Rachel Fuller Brown, http://web.mit.edu/invent/www /inventorsA-H/HazenBrown.html

## BROWNE, MARJORIE LEE

Agnes Scott College: Marjorie Lee Browne, http://www.agnesscott.edu/lriddle/women/browne.htm

Black Women in the Mathematical Sciences: Marjorie Browne, http://www.math.buffalo.edu/mad/PEEPS/browne_marjorie_lee.html

## BURBIDGE, MARGARET E.

Biography – Margaret Burbidge,

http://www.physics.gmu.edu/classinfo/astr103/burbidge.html

## BURNELL, JOCELYN BELL

Data Bank of Scientists: Jocelyn Bell Burnell, http://www.ceemast.csupomona.edu/nova/burn.html

A Science Odyssey: Jocelyn Bell, http://www.pbs.org/wgbh/aso/databank/entries /babell.html

## CANNON, ANNIE JUMP

Distinguished Women of Past and Present: Annie Jump Cannon, http://www .distinguishedwomen.com/biographies/cannon.html

National Women's Hall of Fame: Annie Jump Cannon, http://www.greatwomen.org/cannon.htm

SDSC: Women in Science: Annie Jump Cannon, http://www.sdsc.edu /ScienceWomen/cannon.html

## CARR, EMMA PERRY

Data Bank of Scientists: Emma Perry Carr, http://www.ceemast.csupomona.edu/nova/carr.html

## CARSON, RACHEL

Gartner, Carol B. *Rachel Carson.* Ungar Pub. Co., 1983.

Hynes, H. Patricia. *The Recurring Silent Spring.* Pergamon Press, 1989.

Lear, Linda. *Rachel Carson: Witness for Nature.* H. Holt, 1997.

National Women's Hall of Fame: Rachel Carson, http://www.greatwomen.org
/carson.htm

Rachel Carson Homestead, http://www.rachelcarson.org/

## CHÂTELET, MARQUISE DU

Agnes Scott College: Émilie du Châtelet,
http://www.agnesscott.edu/lriddle/women/chatelet.htm

Oregon State Philosophy Department: Émilie, Marquise du Châtelet-Laumont,
http://www.orst.edu/instruct/phl302/philosophers/chatelet.html

## CLARK, EUGENIE

Butts, Ellen R. and Joyce R. Schwartz. *Eugenie Clark: Adventures of a Shark Scientist.*
Linnet Books, 2000.

Clark, Eugenie. *The Lady and the Sharks.* Harper & Row, 1969.

Clark, Eugenie. *Lady with a Spear.* Ballantine Books, 1974.

Dr. Eugenie Clark, http://www.uimage.com/people/ec/

## CLARK, MAMIE PHIPPS

Markowitz, Gerald and David Rosner. *Children, Race, and Power: Kenneth and Mamie
Clark's Northside Center.* University Press of Virginia, 1996.

Webster University: Mamie Phipps Clark, http://www.webster.edu/~woolflm
/mamieclark.html

## CLARKE, EDITH

Distinguished Women of Past and Present: Edith Clarke, http://www
.distinguishedwomen.com/biographies/clarke.html

## CLEVELAND, EMELINE HORTON

Women in American History: Emeline Horton Cleveland,
http://www.women.eb.com/women/articles/Cleveland_Emeline_Horton.html

## COBB, JEWELL PLUMMER

Faces of Science: Jewel Plummer Cobb, http://www.princeton.edu/~mcbrown
/display/cobb.html

Jewel Plummer Cobb, http://www.accessctr.org/jpchmpg.html

## CORI, GERTY RADNITZ

Jewish Student Online Research Center: Gerty Theresa Radnitz Cori, http://www.us-israel.org/jsource/biography/cori.html

National Women's Hall of Fame: Gerty Theresa Radnitz Cori, http://www.greatwomen.org/cori.htm

Women in American History: Gerty Theresa Radnitz Cori, http://www.women.eb.com/women/articles/Cori_Gerty_Theresa_Radnitz.html

## CROSBY, ELIZABETH CAROLINE

Alabama Women's Hall of Fame: Elizabeth Caroline Crosby, http://home.judson.edu/extra/fame/crosby.html

## CURIE, MARIE

Curie, Eve. *Madame Curie: A Biography*. Da Capo Press, 1986.

Giroud, Françoise. *Marie Curie, a Life*. Holmes & Meier, 1986.

Pflaum, Rosalynd. *Grand Obsession: Marie Curie and Her World*. Doubleday, 1989.

Quinn, Susan. *Marie Curie: A Life*. Addison-Wesley, 1996.

Reid, Robert. *Marie Curie*. Collins, 1974.

Raynal, Florence. "Marie Curie: A Nobel Prize Pioneer at the Pantheon," http://www.france.diplomatie.fr/label_france/ENGLISH/SCIENCES/CURIE/marie.html

Marie Sklodowska-Curie, http://hum.amu.edu.pl/~zbzw/ph/sci/msc.htm

## DEUTSCH, HELENE ROSENBACH

Deutsch, Helene. *Confrontations with Myself: An Epilogue*. Norton, 1973.

Roazen, Paul. *Helene Deutsch: A Psychoanalyst's Life*. Transaction Publishers, 1992.

Sayers, Janet. *Mothers of Psychoanalysis: Helene Deutsch, Karen Horney, Anna Freud, Melanie Klein*. W.W. Norton, 1991.

## DICKENS, HELEN OCTAVIA

Albion College: African American Scientists: Helen Octavia Dickens, http://educate.albion.edu/art/aframsci/elizabeth.htm

## DRESSELHAUS, MILDRED S.

Women in Technology International: Mildred Dresselhaus, http://www.witi.com/center/witimuseum/halloffame/1998/mdresselhau.shtml

## DUNBAR, BONNIE JEAN

Encyclopedia Astronautica: Bonnie J. Dunbar, http://www.friends-partners.org/~mwade/astros/dunbar.htm

NASA Astronaut Biographies: Bonnie J. Dunbar, http://www.jsc.nasa.gov/Bios/htmlbios/dunbar.html

## EASTWOOD, ALICE

Ross, Michael Elsohn. *Flower Watching with Alice.* Carolrhoda Books, 1997.

Wilson, Carol. *Alice Eastwood's Wonderland; the Adventures of a Botanist.* California Academy of Sciences, 1955.

## EIGENMANN, ROSA SMITH

SDSC: Women in Science: Rosa Smith Eigenmann, http://www.sdsc.edu /ScienceWomen/eigenmann.html

## ELDERS, JOYCELYN

Elders, Joycelyn and David Chanoff. *Joycelyn Elders, M.D.: From Sharecropper's Daughter to Surgeon General of the United States of America.* Thorndike Press, 1997.

Jones, Chester R. *Dancing with the Bear and the Other Facts of Life: The Story of Dr. M. Joycelyn Elders, Former U.S. Surgeon General.* Delta Press, 1995.

Encarta Online: Joycelyn Elders, http://www.encarta.msn.com/events/black_history _month/encarta/06DC9000.asp

Women in American History: Joycelyn Elders, http://women.eb.com/women /articles/Elders_Joycelyn.html

## ELION, GERTRUDE BELLE

National Inventors Hall of Fame: Gertrude Belle Elion, http://www.invent.org/book/book-text/39.html

National Women's Hall of Fame: Gertrude Belle Elion, http://www.greatwomen.org/elion.htm

Women in American History: Gertrude Belle Elion, http://www.women.eb.com/women/articles/Elion_Gertrude_Belle.html

## ESAU, KATHERINE

Women in American History: Katherine Esau, http://www.women.eb.com/women/articles/Esau_Katherine.html

## FABER, SANDRA

Professor Sandra Faber homepage,

http://www.ucolick.edu/~board/faculty/faber.html

## FOSSEY, DIAN

Freedman, Suzanne. *Dian Fossey: Befriending the Gorillas.* Raintree Steck-Vaughn Publishers, 1997.

Hayes, Harold T.P. *The Dark Romance of Dian Fossey.* Simon and Schuster, 1990.

Kevles, Bettyann. *Watching the Wild Apes: The Primate Studies of Goodall, Fossey, and Galdikas.* Dutton, 1976.

Montgomery, Sy. *Walking with the Great Apes: Jane Goodall, Dian Fossey, Biruté Galdikas*. Houghton Mifflin Co., 1991.

Mowat, Farley. *Woman in the Mists: The Story of Dian Fossey and the Mountain Gorillas of Africa*. Warner Books, 1987.

Shoumatoff, Alex. *African Madness*. Vintage Books, 1990.

Fagerqvist, Malin. "Dian Fossey," http://home.swipnet.se/~w-46558/fossey/

## FRANKLIN, ROSALIND ELSIE

Sayre, Anne. *Rosalind Franklin and DNA*. Norton, 1975.

SDSC: Women in Science: Rosalind Franklin,
http://www.sdsc.edu/Publications/ScienceWomen/franklin.html

Women in Science: Rosalind Franklin, http://library.thinkquest.org/20117
/franklin.html

## FREUD, ANNA

Coles, Robert. *Anna Freud: The Dream of Psychoanalysis*. Addison-Wesley, 1992.

Dyer, Raymond. *Her Father's Daughter: The Work of Anna Freud*. J. Aronson, 1983.

Heller, Peter. *A Child Analysis with Anna Freud*. International Universities Press, 1990.

Malcolm, Janet. *In the Freud Archives*. Vintage Books, 1985.

Sayers, Janet. *Mothers of Psychoanalysis: Helene Deutsch, Karen Horney, Anna Freud, Melanie Klein*. W.W. Norton, 1991.

Young-Bruehl, Elisabeth. *Anna Freud: A Biography*. Summit Books, 1988.

The Anna Freud Centre, http://www.annafreudcentre.org/

## FRIEND, CHARLOTTE

Diamond, Leila and Sandra R. Wolman, eds. *Viral Oncogenesis and Cell Differentiation: The Contributions of Charlotte Friend*. New York Academy of Sciences, 1989.

Distinguished Women of Past and Present: Charlotte Friend, http://www
.distinguishedwomen.com/biographies/friend-charlotte.html

## GALDIKAS, BIRUTÉ

Galdikas, Biruté M.F. *Reflections of Eden: My Years with the Orangutans of Borneo*. Little, Brown, 1995.

Gallardo, Evelyn. *Among the Orangutans: The Biruté Galdikas Story*. Chronicle Books, 1993.

Kevles, Bettyann. *Watching the Wild Apes: The Primate Studies of Goodall, Fossey, and Galdikas*. Dutton, 1976.

Montgomery, Sy. *Walking with the Great Apes: Jane Goodall, Dian Fossey, Biruté Galdikas*. Houghton Mifflin Co., 1991.

Spalding, Linda. *A Dark Place in the Jungle*. Algonquin Books of Chapel Hill, 1999.

Great Canadian Scientists: Biruté Galdikas, http://www.science.ca/scientists /Galdikas/

## GERMAIN, SOPHIE

Bucciarelli, Louis L. and Nancy Dworsky. *Sophie Germain: An Essay in the History of the Theory of Elasticity*. Kluwer Boston, 1980.

Nova Online: Math's Hidden Woman, http://www.pbs.org/wgbh/nova/proof /germain.html

O'Connor, J.J. and E.F. Robertson. "Marie-Sophie Germain," http://www-groups .dcs.st-and.ac.uk/~history/Mathematicians/Germain.html

SDSC: Women in Science: Sophie Germain, http://www.sdsc.edu/Publications/ScienceWomen/germain.html

## GILBRETH, LILLIAN MOLLER

Gilbreth, Lillian Moller. *As I Remember: An Autobiography*. Inst. of Industrial Engineers, 1998.

Graham, Laurel. *Managing on Her Own: Dr. Lillian Gilbreth and Women's Work in the Interwar Era*. Inst. of Industrial Engineers, 1998.

The Gilbreth Network, http://gilbrethnetwork.tripod.com/

National Women's Hall of Fame: Lillian Gilbreth, http://www.greatwomen.org/glbrth.htm

SDSC: Women in Science: Lillian Moller Gilbreth, http://www.sdsc.edu /Publications/ScienceWomen/gilbreth.html

## GODWIN, LINDA

Encyclopedia Astronautica: Linda Maxine Godwin, http://www.friends-partners.org/~mwade/astros/godwin.htm

NASA Astronaut Biographies: Linda M. Godwin, http://www.jsc.nasa.gov/Bios/htmlbios/godwin.html

## GOEPPERT-MAYER, MARIA

Dash, Joan. *A Life of One's Own; Three Gifted Women and the Men They Married*. Harper & Row, 1973.

Argonne National Laboratory: Maria Goeppert Mayer, http://www.ipd.anl.gov /library/internet/mgm.html

National Women's Hall of Fame: Maria Goeppert Mayer, http://www.greatwomen.org/mayer.htm

SDSC: Women in Science: Maria Goeppert Mayer, http://www.sdsc.edu /Publications/ScienceWomen/mayer.html

## GOODALL, JANE

Goodall, Jane and Philip Berman. *Reason for Hope: A Spiritual Journey*. Thorndike Press, 2000.

Goodall, Jane. *Through a Window: My Thirty Years with the Chimpanzees of Gombe.* Houghton Mifflin, 1990.

Kevles, Bettyann. *Watching the Wild Apes: The Primate Studies of Goodall, Fossey, and Galdikas.* Dutton, 1976.

Montgomery, Sy. *Walking with the Great Apes: Jane Goodall, Dian Fossey, Biruté Galdikas.* Houghton Mifflin Co., 1991.

The Jane Goodall Institute, http://www.janegoodall.org/

## GRANVILLE, EVELYN BOYD

Faces of Science: Evelyn Boyd Granville, http://www.princeton.edu/~mcbrown /display/granville.html

Granville, Evelyn Boyd. "My Life as a Mathematician," http://www.agnesscott.edu/lriddle/women/granvill.htm

## HAMILTON, ALICE

Women's History on the Web: Alice Hamilton

http://women.eb.com/women/articles/Hamilton_Alice.html

## HAZEN, ELIZABETH LEE

Baldwin, Richard S. *The Fungus Fighters: Two Women Scientists and Their Discovery.* Cornell University Press, 1981.

Inventor of the Week: Elizabeth Lee Hazen, http://web.mit.edu/invent/www /inventorsA-H/HazenBrown.html

## HEALY, BERNADINE

American Red Cross: Bernadine Healy, http://www.redcross.org/healybio.html

*DISCovering Biography* on GaleNet: Bernadine Healy, http://www.gale.com /freresrc/womenhst/healyb.htm

## HERSCHEL, CAROLINE LUCRETIA

Ashton, Helen and Katharine Davies. *I Had a Sister: A Study of Mary Lamb, Dorothy Wordsworth, Caroline Herschel, Cassandra Austen.* R. West, 1977.

Clerke, Agnes M. *The Herschels and Modern Astronomy.* Cassell and Co., Ltd., 1901.

O'Connor, J.J. and E.F. Robertson. "Caroline Lucretia Herschel," http://www-groups .dcs.st-and.ac.uk/~history/Mathematicians/Herschel_Caroline.html

## HODGKIN, DOROTHY CROWFOOT

Dodson, Guy, Jenny P. Glusker, and David Sayre, eds. *Structural Studies on Molecules of Biological Interest: A Volume in Honour of Professor Dorothy Hodgkin.* Oxford University Press, 1981.

Ferry, Georgina. *Dorothy Hodgkin: A Life.* Cold Spring Harbor Laboratory Press, 2000.

Glusker, Jenny P. and Margaret J. Adams. "Dorothy Crowfoot Hodgkin (1910-1994)," http://curie.che.virginia.edu/scientist/hodgkin.html

SDSC: Women in Science: Dorothy Crowfoot Hodgkin, http://www.sdsc.edu/Publications/ScienceWomen/hodgkin.html

## HOFFMAN, DARLEANE CHRISTIAN

Women in Technology International: Dr. Darleane C. Hoffman, http://www.witi.com/center/witimuseum/halloffame/2000/dhoffman.shtml

## HOGG, HELEN SAWYER

Webb, Michael. *Helen Sawyer Hogg*. Copp Clark Pitman, 1991.

SDSC: Women in Science: Helen Sawyer Hogg, http://www.sdsc.edu/Publications/ScienceWomen/hogg.html

University of Toronto Astronomy: Helen Sawyer Hogg, http://www.astro.utoronto.ca/hsh.html

## HOPPER, GRACE

Billings, Charlene W. *Grace Hopper: Navy Admiral and Computer Pioneer*. Enslow Publishers, 1989.

Schneider, Carl J. and Dorothy Schneider. *Grace Murray Hopper: Working to Create the Future*. Sofwest Press, 1998.

Whitelaw, Nancy. *Grace Hopper: Programming Pioneer*. Scientific American Books for Young Readers, 1995.

Grace Murray Hopper Profile, http://www.ruku.com/hopper.html

Maisel, Merry. "Tribute to Grace Murry Hopper," http://www.sdsc.edu/Hopper/GHC_INFO/hopper.html

## HYDE, IDA HENRIETTA

Grinstein, Louise S., Bierman, Carol A., Rose, Rose K, ed., *Women in the Sciences*. Greenwood Press, 1997.

## HYPATIA

Dzielska, Maria. *Hypatia of Alexandria*. Harvard University Press, 1995.

Hypatia of Alexandria, http://www.polyamory.org/~howard/Hypatia/index.html

O'Connor, J.J. and E.F. Robertson. "Hypatia of Alexandria," http://www-groups.dcs.st-and.ac.uk/~history/Mathematicians/Hypatia.html

## JACKSON, SHIRLEY ANN

Faces of Science: Shirley Ann Jackson, http://www.princeton.edu/~mcbrown/display/jackson.html

National Women's Hall of Fame: Shirley Ann Jackson, http://www.greatwomen.org/jackson.htm

Women in Technology International: Shirley Ann Jackson, http://www.witi.com/center/witimuseum/halloffame/2000/sjackson.shtml

## JEMISON, MAE C.

AppleMasters: Mae Jemison, http://www.apple.com/applemasters/maejemison/

Encyclopedia Astronautica: Mae C. Jemison, http://www.friends-partners.org/~mwade/astros/jemison.htm

Faces of Science: Mae C. Jemison, http://www.princeton.edu/~mcbrown/display/jemison.html

## JOLIOT-CURIE, IRÈNE

McKown, Robin. *She Lived for Science: Irene Joliot-Curie*. J. Messner, 1961.

Forum Polonia: Irene Joliot-Curie, http://www.forum-polonia-houston.com/f-irene.htm

## KARLE, ISABELLA L.

Karle, Isabella Helen,

http://w1.xrefer.com/entry/172829

## KING, MARY-CLAIRE

Anixt, Julie. "Mary-Claire King: Geneticist and Political Activist," http://students.haverford.edu/wmbweb/medbios/jaking.html

## KITTRELL, FLEMMIE

*Notable Women Scientists*. Gale Group, 2000.

## KOVALEVSKAYA, SOFIA

Cooke, Roger. *The Mathematics of Sonya Kovalevskaya*. Springer-Verlag, 1984.

Kennedy, Don H. *Little Sparrow: A Portrait of Sophia Kovalevsky*. Ohio University Press, 1983.

Koblitz, Ann Hibner. *A Convergence of Lives: Sofia Kovalevskaia, Scientist, Writer, Revolutionary*. Rutgers University Press, 1993.

Kochina, P. IA. *Sophia Vasilyevna Kovalevskaya, Her Life and Work*. Foreign Languages Pub. House, 1957.

Agnes Scott College: Sofia Kovalevskaya, http://www.agnesscott.edu/lriddle/women/kova.htm

O'Connor, J.J. and E.F. Robertson. "Sofia Vasilyevna Kovalevskaya," http://www-groups.dcs.st-and.ac.uk/~history/Mathematicians/Kovalevskaya.html

## KWOLEK, STEPHANIE L.

The Chemical Heritage Foundation: Stephanie L. Kwolek, http://www.chemheritage.org/EducationalServices/chemach/pop/slk.html

Inventor of the Week: Stephanie Kwolek, http://web.mit.edu/invent/www/inventorsI-Q/kwolek.html

Women in Technology International: Stephanie Kwolek, http://www.witi.com/center/witimuseum/halloffame/1996/skwolek.shtml

## LAWRENCE, MARGARET MORGAN

Lightfoot, Sara Lawrence. *Balm in Gilead: Journey of a Healer*. Addison-Wesley Pub. Co., 1988.

## LEAKEY, MARY DOUGLAS

Leakey, Mary. *Disclosing the Past*. McGraw-Hill, 1986.

Leakey, Mary. *Olduvai Gorge: My Search for Early Man*. Collins, 1979.

Morell, Virginia. *Ancestral Passions: The Leakey Family and the Quest for Humankind's Beginnings*. Simon & Schuster, 1995.

Dente, Jenny. "Mary Douglas Nicol Leakey 1913–1996," http://uts.cc.utexas.edu/~dente/mleakey.htm

## LEAKEY, MEAVE

The Latest Leakey Searches for Our Earliest Ancestors, http://www.calacademy.org/calwild/archives/sum99/leakey.html

## LEAVITT, HENRIETTA SWAN

Distinguished Women of Past and Present: Henrietta Swan Leavitt, http://www.distinguishedwomen.com/biographies/leavitt.html

SJSU Virtual Museum: Henrietta Swan Leavitt, http://www.sjsu.edu/depts/Museum/lea.html

Women in American History: Henrietta Swan Leavitt, http://women.eb.com/women/articles/Leavitt_Henrietta_Swan.html

## LEHMANN, INGE

American Geophysical Union: Inge Lehmann, http://www.agu.org/inside/awards/lehmann2.html

## LEVI-MONTALCINI, RITA

Dash, Joan. *The Triumph of Discovery: Women Scientists Who Won the Nobel Prize*. Julian Messner, 1991.

Levi-Montalcini, Rita. *In Praise of Imperfection: My Life and Work*. Basic Books, 1988.

Nobel e-Museum: Rita Levi-Montalcini, http://www.nobel.se/medicine/laureates/1986/levi-montalcini-autobio.html

## LIBBY, LEONA WOOD MARSHALL

Libby, Leona Marshall. *The Uranium People*. Scribner's, 1979.

## LLOYD, RUTH SMITH

*Notable Women Scientists*. Gale Group, 2000.

## LOGAN, MYRA ADELE

Women in Science: Myra Adele Logan,
http://library.thinkquest.org/20117/logan.html

## LUCID, SHANNON

Encyclopedia Astronautica: Shannon Lucid, http://www.friends-partners.org/~mwade/astros/lucid.htm

NASA Astronaut Biographies: Shannon Lucid,
http://www.jsc.nasa.gov/Bios/htmlbios/lucid.html

Women of NASA: Shannon Lucid, http://quest.arc.nasa.gov/women/bios/sl.html

## MAHONEY, MARY ELIZA

Distinguished Women of Past and Present: Mary Eliza Mahoney, http://www
.distinguishedwomen.com/biographies/mahoney-me.html

Hall of Black Achievement: Mary Eliza Mahoney,
http://www.bridgew.edu/HOBA/mahoney.htm

## MARGULIS, LYNN

Lynn Margulis, http://www.geo.umass.edu/faculty/margulis.html

## MCCLINTOCK, BARBARA

Craig, Patricia Parratt. *Jumping Genes: Barbara McClintock's Scientific Legacy: An Essay about Basic Research from the Carnegie Institution of Washington*. Carnegie Institution, 1994.

Fedoroff, Nina and David Botstein, eds. *The Dynamic Genome: Barbara McClintock's Ideas in the Century of Genetics*. Cold Spring Harbor Laboratory Press, 1992.

Keller, Evelyn Fox. *A Feeling for the Organism: The Life and Work of Barbara McClintock*. W.H. Freeman, 1983.

Cold Spring Harbor Laboratory: Barbara McClintock,
http://www.cshl.org/public/mcclintock.html

Nobel Prize Internet Archive: Barbara McClintock,
http://www.almaz.com/nobel/medicine/1983a.html

## MCMANUS, R. LOUISE

National Women's Hall of Fame: Louise McManus,
http://www.greatwomen.org/mcmns.htm

## MEAD, MARGARET

Bateson, Mary Catherine. *With a Daughter's Eye: A Memoir of Margaret Mead and Gregory Bateson*. HarperPerennial, 1994.

Freeman, Derek. *The Fateful Hoaxing of Margaret Mead: A Historical Analysis of Her Samoan Research.* Westview Press, 1999.

Grosskurth, Phyllis. *Margaret Mead.* Penguin Books, 1988.

Lapsley, Hilary. *Margaret Mead and Ruth Benedict: The Kinship of Women.* University of Massachusetts Press, 1999.

Mead, Margaret. *Blackberry Winter: My Earlier Years.* Kodansha International, 1995.

Mead, Margaret. *Margaret Mead, Some Personal Views.* Walker, 1979.

Orans, Martin. *Not Even Wrong: Margaret Mead, Derek Freeman, and the Samoans.* Chandler & Sharp Publishers, 1996.

## MEITNER, LISE

Crawford, Deborah. *Lise Meitner, Atomic Pioneer.* Crown Publishers, 1969.

Rife, Patricia. *Lise Meitner and the Dawn of the Nuclear Age.* Birkhäuser, 1999.

Sime, Ruth Lewin. *Lise Meitner: A Life in Physics.* University of California Press, 1996.

Bartusiak, Marcia. "The Woman Behind the Atomic Bomb," http://www.ocgy.ubc.ca/~monahan/meitner.html

Lise Meitner Online, http://www.users.bigpond.com/Sinclair/fission/LiseMeitner.html

SDSC: Women in Science: Lise Meitner, http://www.sdsc.edu/Publications /ScienceWomen/meitner.html

## MEXIA, YNES

The Handbook of Texas Online: Ynes Mexia de Reygades, http://www.tsha.utexas.edu/handbook/online/articles/view/MM/fme54.html

## MITCHELL, MARIA

Gormley, Beatrice. *Maria Mitchell: The Soul of an Astronomer.* W.B. Eerdmans Pub. Co., 1995.

Mitchell, Maria. *Maria Mitchell: Life, Letters & Journals.* Reprint Services Corp., 1991.

Wright, Helen. *Sweeper in the Sky: The Life of Maria Mitchell.* College Avenue Press, 1997.

Distinguished Women of Past and Present: Maria Mitchell, http://www.netsrq.com/~dbois/mitchell.html

National Women's Hall of Fame: Maria Mitchell, http://www.greatwomen.org/mtchl.htm

## MORAWETZ, CATHLEEN SYNGE

Agnes Scott College: Cathleen Morawetz, http://www.agnesscott.edu/lriddle/women/morawetz.htm

Association for Women in Mathematics: Cathleen S. Morawetz, http://www
.awm-math.org/noetherbrochure/Morawetz83.html

O'Connor, J.J. and E.F. Robertson. "Cathleen Synge Morawetz," http://www-groups
.dcs.st-and.ac.uk/~history/Mathematicians/Morawetz.html

## NEUFELD, ELIZABETH

*Notable Women Scientists*. Gale Group, 2000.

## NIGHTINGALE, FLORENCE

Baly, Monica E. *Florence Nightingale and the Nursing Legacy: Building the Foundations of Modern Nursing & Midwifery*. BainBridgeBooks, 1998.

Dossey, Barbara Montgomery. *Florence Nightingale: Mystic, Visionary, Healer*. Springhouse Corp., 2000.

Nightingale, Florence. *Florence Nightingale: Her Wit and Wisdom*. Peter Pauper Press, 1975.

Small, Hugh. *Florence Nightingale: Avenging Angel*. St. Martin's Press, 1999.

Wellman, Sam. *Florence Nightingale: Lady with the Lamp*. Barbour, 1999.

Florence Nightingale Museum, http://www.florence-nightingale.co.uk/

Florence Nightingale Tribute, http://www.dnai.com/~borneo/nightingale/

## NOETHER, EMMY

Brewer, James W. and Martha K. Smith, eds. *Emmy Noether: A Tribute to Her Life and Work*. M. Dekker, 1981.

Dick, Auguste. *Emmy Noether, 1882-1935*. Birkhäuser, 1981.

Agnes Scott College: Emmy Noether,
http://www.agnesscott.edu/lriddle/women/noether.htm

O'Connor, J.J. and E.F. Robertson. "Emmy Amalie Noether," http://www-groups
.dcs.st-and.ac.uk/~history/Mathematicians/Noether_Emmy.html

SDSC: Women in Science: Emmy Noether,
http://www.sdsc.edu/ScienceWomen/noether.html

## NOVELLO, ANTONIA

Hawxhurst, Joan C. *Antonia Novello: U.S. Surgeon General*. Millbrook Press, 1993.

The Glass Ceiling: Antonia Novello,
http://www.theglassceiling.com/biographies/bio23.htm

National Women's Hall of Fame: Antonia Novello,
http://www.greatwomen.org/nvllo.htm

## NUSSLEIN-VOLHARD, CHRISTIANE

Nobel e-Museum: Christiane Nüsslein-Volhard, http://www.nobel.se/medicine
/laureates/1995/nusslein-volhard-autobio.html

### OCHOA, ELLEN

Encyclopedia Astronautica: Ellen Ochoa, http://www.friends-partners.org/~mwade/astros/ochoa.htm

NASA Astronaut Biographies: Ellen Ochoa, http://www.jsc.nasa.gov/Bios/htmlbios/ochoa.html

### PATRICK, RUTH

Women Environmental Leaders: Ruth Patrick, http://www.mtholyoke.edu/proj/cel/patrick.htm

### PAYNE-GAPOSCHKIN, CECILIA

Payne-Gaposchkin, Cecilia. *Cecilia Payne-Gaposchkin: An Autobiography and Other Recollections*, 2nd ed. Cambridge University Press, 1996.

Ceclia Payne-Gaposchkin, http://watt.physics.carleton.edu/Astro/pages/marga_michele/Cecilia_Payne.html

### PENNINGTON, MARY ENGLE

Grinstein, Louis, Rose, Rose K., Rafailovich, Miriam, ed. *Women in Chemistry and Physics*. Greenwood Press, 1993.

### PICOTTE, SUSAN LaFLESCHE

Tong, Benson. *Susan La Flesche Picotte, M.D.: Omaha Indian Leader and Reformer*. University of Oklahoma Press, 1999.

Wilkerson, J.L. *A Doctor to Her People: Dr. Susan La Flesche Picotte*. Acorn Books, 1999.

National Library of Medicine: Susan La Flesche Picotte, http://www.nlm.nih.gov/exhibition/if_you_knew/if_you_knew_12.html

### RAY, DIXY LEE

Guzzo, Louis R. *Is It True What They Say about Dixy?: A Biography of Dixy Lee Ray*. Writing Works, 1980.

### REES, MINA

Agnes Scott College: Mina Rees, http://www.agnesscott.edu/lriddle/women/rees.htm

O'Connor, J.J. and E.F. Robertson. "Mina Spiegel Rees," http://www-groups.dcs.st-and.ac.uk/history/Mathematicians/Rees.html

### RICHARDS, ELLEN HENRIETTA SWALLOW

Hunt, Caroline Louisa. *The Life of Ellen H. Richards, 1842-1911*, Anniversary ed. American Home Economics Association, 1958.

Distinguished Women of Past and Present: Ellen Henrietta Swallow Richards, http://www.netsrq.com/~dbois/richards-es.html

Women in American History: Ellen Henrietta Swallow Richards,
http://women.eb.com/women/articles/Richards_Ellen_Henrietta_Swallow.html

## RIDE, SALLY KRISTEN

Camp, Carole Ann. *Sally Ride: First American Woman in Space*. Enslow Publishers, 1997.

Hopping, Lorraine Jean. *Sally Ride: Space Pioneer*. McGraw-Hill, 2000.

Encyclopedia Astronautica: Sally Ride, http://www.friends-partners.org/~mwade/astros/ride.htm

NASA Astronaut Biographies: Sally Ride, http://www.jsc.nasa.gov/Bios/htmlbios/ride-sk.html

Women of NASA: Sally Ride, http://quest.arc.nasa.gov/women/bios/sr.html

## ROBINSON, JULIA BOWMAN

Reid, Constance. *Julia, a Life in Mathematics*. Mathematical Association of America, 1996.

Agnes Scott College: Julia Bowman Robinson, http://www.agnesscott.edu/lriddle/women/robinson.htm

Association for Women in Mathematics: Julia Robinson, http://www.awm-math.org/noetherbrochure/Robinson82.html

O'Connor, J.J. and E.F. Robertson. "Julia Bowman Robinson," http://www-groups.dcs.st-and.ac.uk/~history/Mathematicians/Robinson_Julia.html

## ROWLEY, JANET DAVISON

Albert and Mary Lasker Foundation Living Library: http://www.laskerfoundation.org/library/rowley/bib-all-rowley.html

Janet Rowley's Home Page: http://ben-may.bsd.uchicago.edu/CCB/faculty/rowley.html

## RUBIN, VERA COOPER

SJSU Virtual Museum: Vera Cooper Rubin, http://www.sjsu.edu/depts/Museum/rubinv.html

Thompson, Katrina. "Vera Rubin's Dark Universe," http://web.physics.twsu.edu/lapo/vr.htm

## SABIN, FLORENCE RENA

Bluemel, Elinor. *Florence Sabin; Colorado Woman of the Century*. University of Colorado Press, 1959.

Downing, Sybil and Jane Valentine Baker. *Florence Rena Sabin, Pioneer Scientist*. Pruett Pub. Co., 1981.

Kaye, Judith. *The Life of Florence Sabin*. Twenty-First Century Books, 1993.

Phelan, Mary Kay. *Probing the Unknown; the Story of Dr. Florence Sabin*. Crowell, 1969.

Women in American History: Florence Rena Sabin,
http://women.eb.com/women/articles/Sabin_Florence_Rena.html

**SCHARRER, BERTA**

American Association of Anatomists: Berta Scharrer, http://www.anatomy.org
/anatomy/dberta.htm

**SHIVA, VANDANA**

Profile of Vandana Shiva

http://iisd1.iisd.ca/pcdf/1996/shiva.html

**SIMPSON, JOANNE**

Earth Sciences Directorate: Joanne Simpson,
http://webserv.gsfc.nasa.gov/ESD/jsimpson.html

Keesey, Lori. "Joanne Simpson's Meteoric Climb to the Top," http://www.grandtimes
.com/simpson.html

**SINGER, MAXINE**

Carnegie Institute of Washington: Maxine Singer, http://www.ciw.edu
/CIW-president.html

**SOLOMON, SUSAN**

Susan Solomon, http://www.cbacareers.com/careermags/ceng/solomon.html

**SOMERVILLE, MARY**

Patterson, Elizabeth Chambers. *Mary Somerville and the Cultivation of Science,
1815–1840.* Kluwer Boston, 1983.

Somerville, Mary. *Personal Recollections, from Early Life to Old Age, of Mary Somerville.* AMS Press, 1975.

Agnes Scott College: Mary Fairfax Somerville,
http://www.agnesscott.edu/lriddle/women/somer.htm

O'Connor, J.J. and E.F. Robertson. "Mary Fairfax Greig Somerville,"
http://www-groups.dcs.st-and.ac.uk/history/Mathematicians/Somerville.html

**SPURLOCK, JEANNE**

National Medical Fellowships: Jeanne Spurlock, http://www.nmf-online.org
/scholars_hall_fame_spurlock.htm

**STEITZ, JOAN ARGETSINGER**

*The Herald-Sun* Online: http://www.herald-sun.com/cityomed/com/steitz.html

**STEVENS, NETTIE MARIA**

Women in American History: Nettie Maria Stevens,
http://women.eb.com/women/articles/Stevens_Nettie_Maria.html

## SULLIVAN, KATHRYN

Encyclopedia Astronautica: Kathryn Dwyer Sullivan, http://www.friends-partners
.org/~mwade/astros/sullivan.htm

NASA Astronaut Biographies: Kathryn D. Sullivan,
http://www.jsc.nasa.gov/Bios/htmlbios/sullivan-kd.html

## TAUSSIG, HELEN

Baldwin, Joyce. *To Heal the Heart of a Child: Helen Taussig, M.D.* Walker, 1992.

CoolPeople.com: Helen Brooke Taussig, http://www.coolpeople.com/legends/hbt.asp

Distinguished Women of Past and Present: Helen Brooke Taussig, http://www
distinguishedwomen.com/biographies/taussig.html

National Women's Hall of Fame: Helen Brooke Taussig,
http://www.greatwomen.org/taussig.htm

## TAUSSKY-TODD, OLGA

Zassenhaus, Hans. *Number Theory and Algebra: Collected Papers Dedicated to Henry
B. Mann, Arnold E. Ross, and Olga Taussky-Todd.* Academic Press, 1977.

Agnes Scott College: Olga Taussky-Todd,
http://www.agnesscott.edu/lriddle/women/todd.htm

Association for Women in Mathematics: Olga Taussky-Todd, http://www
.awm-math.org/noetherbrochure/Taussky-Todd81.html

O'Connor, J.J. and E.F. Robertson. "Olga Taussky-Todd," http://www-groups
.dcs.st-and.ac.uk/~history/Mathematicians/Taussky-Todd.html

## TERESHKOVA, VALENTINA

Sharpe, Mitchell R. *"It is I, Sea Gull;" Valentina Tereshkova, First Woman in Space.*
Crowell, 1975.

Distinguished Women of Past and Present: Valentina Vladimirovna Nikolayeva Tereshkova, http://www.distinguishedwomen.com/biographies/tereshko.html

Encyclopedia Astronautica: Valentina Vladimirovna Tereshkova,
http://www.friends-partners.org/~mwade/astros/terhkova.htm

## THORNTON, KATHRYN

Encyclopedia Astronautica: Kathryn Cordell Ryan Thornton, http://www
.friends-partners.org/~mwade/astros/thornton.htm

NASA Astronaut Biographies: Kathryn C. Thornton,
http://www.jsc.nasa.gov/Bios/htmlbios/thornt-k.html

## UHLENBECK, KAREN

Association for Women in Mathematics: Karen Keskulla Uhlenbeck,
http://www.awm-math.org/noetherbrochure/Uhlenbeck88.html

Michigan Greats: Karen K. Uhlenbeck,
http://www.research.umich.edu/research/news/michigangreats/uhlenbeck.html

O'Connor, J.J. and E.F. Robertson. "Karen Keskulla Uhlenbeck," http://www-groups
.dcs.st-and.ac.uk/~history/Mathematicians/Uhlenbeck_Karen.html

## WAELSCH, SALOME

"Salome Waelsch," http://web.mit.edu/afs/athena.mit.edu/org/w/womens-studies
/www/dev-bio/waelsch3.html

## WALKER, MARY EDWARDS

Leonard, Elizabeth D. *Yankee Women: Gender Battles in the Civil War.* W.W. Norton,
1994.

Snyder, Charles McCool. *Dr. Mary Walker: The Little Lady in Pants.* Arno Press,
1974.

"Mary Edwards Walker," http://www.tulgey.org/~snark/mary-edwards-walker.html

"Mary Edwards Walker: Civil War Doctor," http://www.northnet.org
/stlawrenceaauw/walker.htm

## WHEELER, ANNA JOHNSON PELL

Agnes Scott College: Anna Pell Wheeler,
http://www.agnesscott.edu/lriddle/women/wheeler.htm

O'Connor, J.J. and E.F. Robertson. "Anna Johnson Pell Wheeler,"
http://www-groups.dcs.st-and.ac.uk:80/~history/Mathematicians/Wheeler.html

## WONG-STAAL, FLOSSIE

"Flossie Wong-Staal, Ph.D.,"
http://hsrd.ucsd.edu/Cfar/FWS_Homepage/FWS.HTML

U·X·L Biographies. "Flossie Wong-Staal,"
http://www.gale.com/freresrc/womenhst/wongsta.htm

## WRIGHT, JANE COOKE

*Notable Women Scientists.* Gale Group, 2000.

## WU, CHIEN-SHIUNG

Contributions of Women to Physics: Chien-Shiung Wu,
http://www.physics.ucla.edu/~moszkows/earlynp/wu2.htm

National Women's Hall of Fame: Chien-Shiung Wu,
http://www.greatwomen.org/wu.htm

## YALOW, ROSALYN SUSSMAN

Straus, Eugene. *Rosalyn Yalow, Nobel Laureate: Her Life and Work in Medicine.* Ple-
num Trade, 1998.

Distinguished Women of Past and Present: Rosalyn Sussman Yalow, http://www.distinguishedwomen.com/biographies/yalow.html

Jewish Student Online Research Center: Rosalyn S. Yalow, http://www.us-israel.org/jsource/biography/Yalow.html

National Women's Hall of Fame: Rosalyn Yalow, http://www.greatwomen .org/yalow.htm

## YOUNG, ROGER ARLINER

Faces of Science: Roger Arliner Young, http://www.princeton.edu/~mcbrown /display/young.html

SDSC: Women in Science: Roger Arliner Young, http://www.sdsc.edu/Publications /ScienceWomen/young.html

# Glossary

**absolute temperature scale** A temperature scale that has the lowest possible temperature—at which all molecular motion ceases—set at zero.

**absolute zero** The temperature at which all atomic and molecular motion ceases. Absolute zero is about 0 K, -273&Epsi;C, or -459&Epsi;F.

**AC (alternating current)** Electric current in which the direction of flow changes back and forth rapidly and at a regular rate.

**acidity** The quality, state, or degree of being acid. Acidity is usually measured as the concentration of hydrogen ions in a solution using the pH scale. A greater concentration of hydrogen ions means a more acidic solution and a lower corresponding pH number. Strictly speaking, an acidic solution has a pH less than 7.0.

**acquired immunodeficiency syndrome (AIDS)** A disease of the immune system believed to be caused by the human immunodeficiency virus (HIV). It is characterized by the destruction of a particular type of white blood cell and susceptibility to infection and other diseases.

**actinomycetes** Rod-shaped bacteria found in the soil which produce antibiotics.

**adenine** A purine base which codes hereditary information in DNA and RNA.

**adenosine triphosphate (ATP)** High-energy molecule that cells use to store energy; ATP drives energy-requiring processes such as biosynthesis (the production of chemical compounds), growth, and movement.

**aerodynamics** The study of the motion of gases (particularly air) and the motion and control of objects in the air.

**alternating current (AC)** Electric current in which the direction of flow changes back and forth rapidly and at a regular rate.

**alternation of generations** A general feature of the life cycle of many plants, characterized by the occurrence of different reproductive forms that often have very different overall body patterns.

**alternator** An electric generator that produces an alternating current (as opposed to direct current).

**altimeter** An aneroid barometer used to measure altitude.

**anabolism** The process by which energy is used to build up complex molecules.

**anesthesiology** The branch of medical science relating to substances used in surgical procedures to render the patient temporarily unconscious.

**anthrax** A disease in warm-blooded animals which can be passed along to humans by handling infected products; characterized by lung lesions and external ulcerating nodules.

**antidiuretic hormone** Chemical secreted by the pituitary gland that regulates the amount of water excreted by the kidneys.

**antigen** Any substance that the body considers foreign, such as a bacterial cell, that stimulates the body's immune system to produce antibodies against it.

**archaeoastronomy** The study of the astronomy of ancient people.

**astrophysicist** An astronomer who studies the solar system and the universe utilizing the principles of physics and astronomy.

**athlete's foot** A ringworm of the foot.

**atom** The smallest particle of which an element can exist.

**bacteria** Single-celled microorganisms that live in soil, water, plants, and animals that play a key role in the decay of organic matter and the cycling of nutrients. Some are agents of disease.

**bacteriology** The study of bacteria, a single-celled organism which is too small to be seen with the naked human eye

**barium** A metallic element of the alkaline-earth group; occurs only in a combination with other elements.

**benzene** A colorless, flammable toxic used as a solvent.

**beta amyloid protein** A protein that accumulates in the brains of Alzheimer's disease victims.

**biopsy** The surgical removal of tissue from a person's body that is then studied under a microscope to determine whether it is benign or malignant. (Pronounced BY-op-see.)

**bismuth** A heavy, brittle metallic element that resembles arsenic chemically; used in pharmaceuticals and alloys.

**blueshift** The Doppler shift observed when a celestial object is moving closer to Earth.

**Bolshevik** An individual allied with the extreme Russian Social Democratic Party that came to power in Russia through armed insurrection in November, 1917; a Communist.

**bone marrow** The spongy tissue found in the center of most large bones that produces the cellular components of blood white cells, red cells, and platelet

**capillaries** Microscopic vessels in the tissues that carry fluids such as blood and lymph and that join veins to arteries.

**cartography** Map making.

**cast** Fossil formed when a mold is later filled in by mud or mineral matter.

**cast iron** A term used to describe various forms of iron that also contain anywhere from 0.5 to 4.2 percent carbon and 0.2 to 3.5 percent silicon.

**celestial navigation** Moving on the earth by observing the positions of celestial bodies.

**CFCs (chlorofluorocarbons)** A family of chemical compounds consisting of carbon, fluorine, and chlorine that were once used widely as propellants in commercial sprays but regulated in the United States since 1987 because of their harmful environmental effects.

**chemical thermodynamics** That part of chemistry dealing with heat changes accompanying chemical reactions.

**chronic myocarditis** Repeated inflammation of the heart, especially the middle layer of the heart wall.

**chronometry** The science of measuring time.

**CMB (core-mantle boundary)** Also known as the Gutenberg discontinuity; the seismic transition zone separating Earth's mantle from the underlying outer core.

**computed tomography (CT)** An X-ray technique in which a three-dimensional image of a body part is put together by computer using a series of X-ray pictures taken from different angles along a straight line; often called CAT scan (computerized axial tomography).

**congenital** Existing at the time of birth.

**copernican system** Theory proposing that the Sun is at the center of the solar system and all planets, including Earth, revolve around it.

**critical temperature** The temperature at or above which no amount of pressure, however great, will cause a gas to liquefy.

**cryobiology** The study of the effects of extremely low temperature conditions on living organisms.

**crystallography** The study of crystal formations and their structure.

**cytoplasm** The protoplasm of a cell apart from its nucleus; is the site of most of a cell's chemical activities.

**czarist** Description of a nation or state under the rule of a czar, an autocratic leader or ruler.

**deciduous** Plants that lose their leaves at some season of the year, and then grow them back at another season.

**deoxyribonucleic acid (DNA)** Large, complex molecules found in the nuclei of cells that carries genetic information for an organism's development.

**diatomaceous earth** A finely divided rocklike material obtained from the decay of tiny marine organisms known as diatoms.

**dopamine** A chemical in the brain that is associated with feelings of pleasure or reward.

**dosimetry** Measurement of a dosage of radiation.

**dwarf galaxies** An unusually small, faint galaxy.

**dyslexia** An inability to sometimes properly see letters as they appear in sequence.

**electrocardiograph** A machine which produces graphic records of the variation in electrical potential caused by the electrical activity of the heart muscle and detected at the body surface.

**electroconvulsive Therapy** Treatment of mental disorders through the use of an electric current which induces a coma on the patient.

**electromagnetism** A form of magnetic energy produced by the flow of an electric current through a metal core. Also, the study of electric and magnetic fields and their interaction with electric charges and currents.

**ellipses** A plane section of a right circular cone, which is a closed curve.

**embryology** The study of the embryo and its development from a single-celled zygote to the establishment of form and shape.

**emerita** A female professor retired from professional work yet continuing to hold this rank as an honorary title.

**eminent** Supremely gifted and competent at a craft or profession.

**endoplasmic reticulum** The network of membranes that extends throughout the cell and is involved in protein synthesis and lipid metabolism.

**endorphins** Large opioid peptides.

**enzymes** Numerous complex proteins produced by living cells which catalyze biochemical reactions at certain body temperatures.

**ether** Also spelled aether; the medium that was once believed to fill space and to be responsible for carrying light and other electromagnetic waves.

**ethnology** A science which classifies mankind into origin and race, relations, and characteristics.

**eukaryotic cells** Cells of higher organisms containing a true nucleus bonded with a chemical membrane

**Fluorescence** Luminescence (glowing) that stops within 10 nanoseconds after an energy source has been removed.

**fluoroscope** An imaging device which utilizes X-rays to view internal body structures on a screen.

**fungicidin** An antifungal medicine designed by Elizabeth Lee Hazen which could be used on humans.

**gamma ray** Short-wavelength, high-energy radiation formed either by the decay of radioactive elements or by nuclear reactions.

**general theory of relativity** A theory of gravity put forth by Albert Einstein in 1916 that describes gravity as a distortion or curvature of space-time caused by the presence of matter.

**geneticist** A scientist who studies genetics and the functions of genes in humans and animals.

**geodesy** A branch of mathematics which determines the areas and figures of large portions of the earth's surface; also measures the curvature of the earth.

**gerontology** A scientific branch dedicated to the study of aging and the problems of elderly people.

**glucose** A sugar which is the usual form in which carbohydrates are assimilated by animals.

**glycogen** A tasteless amorphous white polysaccharide that is the principal form in which animal tissues store carbohydrates.

**guanine** A purine base containing genetic information in DNA and RNA.

**Gutenberg discontinuity** Also known as core-mantle boundary (CMB); the seismic transition zone separating Earth's mantle from the underlying outer core.

**Gutenberg low velocity zone** Seismic transition zone between the lithosphere and the underlying asthenosphere.

**heliocentric** A heliocentric model of the solar system places the Sun at the center with the planets and Earth orbiting around it.

**hematology** The study of the configuration of the blood and blood forming tissues.

**hemoglobin** The protein pigment in red blood cells that transports oxygen to the tissues and carbon dioxide from them.

**herbarium** A collection housing dried plant specimens which are arranged and mounted in a systematic fashion.

**histamine** A compound in cells that is released in allergic and inflammatory responses and causes small blood vessels to widen, decreases blood pressure, increases gastric secretions, and constricts smooth muscles.

**Hodgkin's disease** A type of cancer characterized by enlargement of the lymph nodes, spleen, and liver and with accompanied weight loss, heavy sweating, and itching of the skin.

**hyaline membrane disease** A respiratory disease suffered by some newborn babies, characterized by the inability of the baby's pulmonary air sacs to properly collapse.

**hydrology** Science dealing with the distribution, properties, and circulation of water on the earth's surface and atmosphere.

**hyperbola** Curve formed by the intersection of a double-right circular cone with a plane cutting both halves of the cone.

**ichthyologist** A zoologist specializing in studying fish of all kinds.

**immunosuppressant** Something used to reduce the immune system's ability to function, like certain drugs or radiation.

**inert gases** Also known as rare or noble gases; the elements argon, helium, krypton, neon, radon, and xenon, which are unreactive gases and form few compounds with other elements.

**infrared** Wavelengths slightly longer than visible light, often used in astronomy to study cool objects.

**infrared detector** An electronic device for detecting.

**intrinsic** An essential internal part of an object or being.

**invertebrate** Animal lacking a spinal column (backbone).

**ionization** The process by which atoms or molecules lose electrons and become positively charged particles.

**isomer** A compound that has the same number and type of atoms in its molecules as another compound.

**Jurassic Period** A period identified by paleontologists which began roughly 205 million years ago; the period of the Mesozoic era between the Cretaceous and the Triassic periods, and distinguished by the presence of dinosaurs and the first appearance of birds.

**kwashiorkor** A protein-deficiency disorder found among children characterized by wasting, loss of hair and skin pigmentation, anemia, blindness, and other symptoms.

**kaparoscope** A device consisting of a long flexible tube that contains a light source that allows a physician to look into the abdominal cavity without making a large incision in the abdominal wall.

**leukocyte** A white blood cell that is an important part of the body's defense mechanism.

**lithography** The process of writing or putting designs on stone with a greasy material and of making printed impressions from it.

**LOX** An abbreviation for liquid oxygen.

**luminosity** The relative quantity of light an image or body gives off.

**lysogenic cycle** A viral replication cycle in which the virus does not destroy the host cell but coexists within it.

**lymphoma** A condition called by a tumor of the lymphoid tissue.

**lytic cycle** A viral replication cycle in which the virus destroys the host cell.

**lysosomal enzymes** A range of degradative enzymes, most of which operate best at acid pH.

**magna cum laude** Graduating from an educational institution "with great distinction."

**marasmus** A protein- and calorie-deficiency disorder characterized by the wasting away of muscle and skin in children.

**meiosis** Process of cell division by which a diploid cell produces four haploid cells. (Pronounced mie-OE-sus.)

**melanin** Dark brown or black pigmentation in animals and/or plants.

**metamorphism** The physical constitutional change in rocks effected by pressure, heat, and water; a rock which changes condition into a more crystalline form.

**metastasis** Spreading of a cancerous growth by shedding cells that grow in other locations. (Pronounced me-TAS-ta-sis.)

**meteorology** The science of the atmosphere and its phenomena, particularly focusing on variations of heat and moisture, winds and storms.

**microbiology** The study of organisms- such as bacteria, yeasts, and viruses too small for viewing with the naked human eye.

**mineralogy** The study of the crystallography, physical, and chemical properties of minerals; the classification of minerals and methods of distinguishing them.

**mitochondrial sequencing** Ordering of studying energy reproduction and cellular respiration in organisms.

**mitochondrion** The power-house of the cell that contains the enzymes necessary for turning food into energy.

**mitosis** Process of cell division resulting in the formation of two daughter cells genetically identical to the parent cell.

**morphogenesis** The process of cell formation and produce the complex shapes of adults from the simple ball of cells deriving from the division of the fertilized egg

**mucopolysaccharidoses** An inherited disease in humans resulting from the body's inability to break down glycosaminoglycans.

**mucous membranes** Membranes rich in mucous glands; membranes which line the body passages and cavities which communicate with the exterior both directly and indirectly.

**mutagen** Any substance or any form of energy that can bring about a mutation (change) in DNA (deoxyribonucleic acid).

**nascent oxygen** Oxygen that consists of molecules made of a single oxygen atom, O.

**neap tides** Period of minimum tidal range that occurs about every two weeks when the Moon and Sun are at 90-degree angles to each other (the first and third quarter moons).

**nebula** Bright or dark cloud, often composed of gases and dust, hovering in the space between the stars. (Plural nebulae.)

**neuroanatomy** Study of the makeup of the human brain.

**neuroendocrinology** The study of functional and anatomical relationships between the nervous system and the endocrine system.

**neurology** The study of the nervous system.

**neuropathology** Pathology of the nervous system.

**noble gases** Also known as inert or rare gases; the elements argon, helium, krypton, neon, radon, and xenon, which are unreactive gases and form few compounds with other elements.

**nucleic acids** Various acids made up of a sugar or derivative, phosphoric acid, and a base found in cell nuclei.

**nutation** The small, slow variation or nodding of Earth's axis due to the influence of the Moon.

**nystatin** An antibiotic which is used in the treatment of vaginal yeast infections, and other fungal diseases of the skin, mouth, throat, and intestinal tract.

**obstinate** Stubborn, not easily dissuaded.

**oceanographer** A scientist who studies the history, lifeforms, and characteristics of the earth's oceans.

**oligotrophic** An unproductive aquatic region with a relatively modest nutrient supply.

**omnivore** Plant- and meat-eating organism.

**opiates** Any drug that enduces sleep.

**organelle** A membrane-bounded cellular organ that performs a specific set of functions within a eukaryotic cell.

**oxidation** A chemical reaction in which oxygen reacts with some other substance and in which ions, atoms, or molecules lose electrons.

**paleontologist** A scientist who studies fossils and rocks to help determine the earth's physical history and the geological time periods in which dinosaurs and other animals roamed the earth.

**parabola** A plane curve generated by a moving point; its distance from a fixed point equals the distance from a fixed line.

**parallax** The difference in direction or change of position of an object in the sky when it is viewed from two different points on Earth.

**paramecium** Free-swimming organism commonly found in freshwater ponds which feeds on bacteria and other particles; reproduces asexually by binary fission.

**partial differential equations** A differential equation which contains at least one partial derivative.

**peripheral nervous system** The portion of the nervous system in an organism that consists of all the neurons outside the central nervous system.

**peristalsis** Wavelike motion of the digestive system that moves food through the system.

**pesticides** Chemical agents used to destroy plants.

**petrography** The system of describing and classifying rocks.

**pH** A measure of acidity or alkalinity of a solution referring to the concentration of hydrogen ions present in a liter of a given fluid. The pH scale ranges from 0 (greatest concentration of hydrogen ions and therefore most acidic) to 14 (least concentration of hydrogen ions and therefore most alkaline), with 7 representing a neutral solution, such as pure water.

**phagocytosis** The process by which certain cells engulf and digest microorganisms and consume debris and foreign bodies in the blood.

**pharmacology** A medical science dealing with the discovery, chemistry, manufacturing, effects, and uses of drugs.

**piezoelectric** Referring to a material that becomes electrically charged when compressed, generating an electric current.

**piezoelectricity** Electricity produced when a crystal is squeezed or made to vibrate.

**pneumococcus** The bacteria which is the cause of pneumonia..

**polonium** Radioactive metallic element, emitting a helium nucleus to form an isotope of lead.

**polymerization** A chemical process in which molecules of the same compound combine to form a long chain of large molecules called a polymer (like a plastic).

**positron** A positively charged particle.

**primatology** The study of primates.

**prostaglandins** Hormone-like substances produced by body tissue that regulate important bodily functions, such as blood pressure.

**psychometrics** A field of mental testing of intelligence, aptitude, and interest.

**pulmonary stenosis** A defect of heart valves which can either be acquired or congenital.

**reactant** A compound present at the beginning of a chemical reaction.

**recessive gene** The state or genetic trait that can express itself only when two genes, one from both parents, are present and act as a kind of code for creating the trait, but will not express itself when paired with a dominant gene.

**refractor telescope** Telescope that directs light through a glass lens, which bends the light waves and brings them to a focus at an eyepiece that acts as a magnifying glass.

**rheumatic fever** A disease involving the inflammation of the joints and damage to heart valves preceded by a streptococcal infection.

**ribonucleic acid (RNA)** A nucleic acid found in all living cells which plays a role in transferring information from DNA to the protein-forming system of the cell.

**ringworm** A disease of the skin, hair, or nails in man or domesticated animals caused by fungi and seen as ring-shaped discolorations on the skin.

**schizophrenia** A mental disorder characterized by a identifiable decrease in an individual's ability to function in everyday life; the presence of differing qualities or antagonistic parts.

**seismology** The study of earthquakes.

**serotonin** A naturally occurring chemical that affects nerve transmissions in the brain and influences a person's moods, among other emotions.

**slag** A by-product of the reactions by which iron is produced, consisting primarily of calcium silicate.

**somatic nervous system** A collection of nerve cells that carries messages from the central nervous system to muscle cells.

**spectroscopy** A branch of physics related to the theories and interpretations of interactions between matter and radiation.

**spherical trigonometry** Trigonometry as applied to the principles and functions of spherical triangles and polygons.

**subduction** Tectonic process that involves one plate being forced down into the mantle at an oceanic trench, where it eventually undergoes partial melting.

**suffragist** An individual in support of the full enjoyment of the right to vote, usually associated with the struggle for a woman's right to vote.

**summa cum laude** Graduating from an educational institution "with highest distinction."

**superconductivity** The ability of a material to conduct electricity without resistance. An electrical current in a superconductive ring will flow indefinitely if a low temperature (about -260&Epsi;C) is maintained.

**syphilis** A contagious venereal disease which can continue over many years if left untreated.

**tilth** The physical structure of soil.

**transcutaneous electrical nerve stimulation (TENS)** The use of electric currents passed through the skin to relieve pain in a specific area of the body.

**trajectory** The curve that a body or object negotiates in space; a progression.

**transuranic elements** Elements which are heavier than uranium and decay to lighter elements in a matter of milliseconds.

**tuberculosis** A disease highly communicable in man and other vertebrates which is characterized by toxic symptoms or allergic reactions primarily impacting the lungs.

**ultracentrifuge** A machine that spins at an extremely high rate of speed and that is used to separate tiny particles out of solution, especially to determine their size.

**vacuole** A space-filling organelle of plant cells.

**villi** Fingerlike projections found in the small intestine that increase the absorption area of the intestine.

**volumetric analysis** A classical quantitative technique in which a solution of known concentration is reacted exactly with an unknown and a calculation is performed to find the amount of the unknown present.

**wave propagation** An increase in the amount of wave lengths in the movements of objects

**wernicke's area** An area in the cerebrum that processes information from written and spoken language.

**X-ray crystallography** Procedure enabling researchers to look within the structure of crystals and their formations.

**xylem** Plant tissue consisting of elongated, thick-walled cells that transport water and mineral nutrients. (Pronounced ZEYE-lem.)

**yaw** Tendency of an aircraft to rotate in a horizontal motion, with the left wing forward and the right wing backward, or vice versa.

**zygote** A fertilized egg; a diploid cell formed by the union of two haploid gametes.

# Index

**415**